D0772896

Tocqueville and the French

Françoise Mélonio

Translated by Beth G. Raps

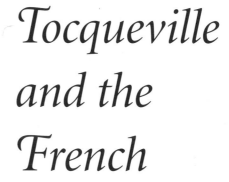

Tocqueville and the French

University Press of Virginia

Charlottesville and London

Originally published as *Tocqueville et les Français,*
© 1993 Aubier, Paris

The University Press of Virginia
© 1998 by the Rector and Visitors of the University of Virginia
All rights reserved
Printed in the United States of America

First published 1998

The paper used in this publication meets the minimum requirements
of the American National Standard for Information Sciences—
Permanence of Paper for Printed Library Materials, ANSI Z39.48-1984.

Library of Congress Cataloging-in-Publication Data

Mélonio, Françoise.
    [Tocqueville et les Français. English]
    Tocqueville and the French / Françoise Mélonio : translated by Beth G. Raps.
        p.   cm.
    Includes bibliographical references and index.
    ISBN 0-8139-1778-6 (cloth : alk. paper)
    1. Tocqueville, Alexis de, 1805–1859—Influence. 2. Historians—France—
Biography. 3. Democracy—France—Public opinion. 4. Public opinion—France.
5. Political culture—France.
    I. Title.
    DC36.98.T63M4513 1998
    944'.007202—dc21   97-33328
                                                                        CIP

Contents

Foreword

ALEXIS DE TOCQUEVILLE is the most widely shared icon of Franco-American political culture. Evocations of his vision of America add authority and gravitas to our most solemn political occasions. President Clinton drew upon Tocqueville's observations in his State of the Union Address in January 1995, adding his own citation to half a century of presidential precedents. Newt Gingrich, the Speaker of the House of Representatives, had anticipated Clinton in this regard when he opened the 104th Congress a few weeks earlier. Tocqueville's words also are routinely incorporated into Supreme Court decisions, presidential election campaigns, and across the political spectrum from Pat Buchanan to Progressives attempting to renew the American left.

Although more diverse in their use and evaluation of Tocqueville's writings, American scholars pay homage to his impact upon our culture. Academics usually pounce upon opportunities to use anniversaries as occasions for commemoration. In 1985 at least four major conferences celebrated the 150th anniversary of *Democracy in America*'s publication in 1835. They were sponsored by the Claremont Institute in California, the American Sociological Association, the Library of Congress, and the City University of New York. In one respect, however, the commemoration of *Democracy* in America went further than most. Another sesquicentennial conference was held at Yale University five years later, in 1990, in honor of the publication of the second half of *Democracy* in 1840. This uniquely extended anniversary is emblematic of a vast scholarly enterprise regularly dispersed through books, articles, papers, and the visual media. Tocqueville's inspiration has been institutionally enshrined in a major international organization, the Tocqueville Society. Its bilingual journal, *The Tocqueville Review/La Revue Tocqueville*, is devoted to the systematic comparison of social thought and institutions in Europe and America.[1]

Tocqueville resonates with similar intensity in French political culture. The decade of the 1980s marked an apotheosis of Tocquevillean consensus. The late president François Mitterrand and the French government discussed the fine points of Tocqueville's views on prison systems (the ostensible purpose of his journey to the United States in 1831). The château de Tocqueville in Normandy became an object of pilgrimage for French politicians. Tocqueville was invoked in French discussions of political decentralization of power and the proper constitutional limits of legislative or executive power. Tocqueville's prestige reached a high point during the commemoration of the bicentennial of the French Revolution. His *Old Regime and the Revolution* (1856) was the point of departure for a major reorientation in French historiography. Scholars simultaneously debated the Revolution's status as the foundation of modern world history and hypothesized the ending of French exceptionalism. The debate reverberated through a decade-long explosion of scholarship on the French Revolution. The entire corpus of Tocqueville's publications, letters, notes, and conversations has acquired the status of a national cultural treasure. A state-sponsored academic national commission has long presided over the publication of his complete works. Whether or not, as one French writer put it, "the whole of France has become Tocquevillean,"[2] his standing has never seemed more secure.

For most Americans, Tocqueville is *Democracy in America* and the experiences that led to its creation. Tocqueville and his traveling companion, Gustave de Beaumont, left us a detailed report on preindustrial America in the midst of its great transcontinental expansion.[3] Their notes are a means of glimpsing a world we have lost. *Democracy* itself has become the repository of essential, if often threatened, truths about America in the century and a half since its publication. Tocqueville provided us with the most important single text with which to see our virtues and defects.

Democracy in America also has a history in America. Nineteenth-century writers generally gave it a distinguished place in the development of political thought. It was widely used as a classic textbook on the functioning of United States institutions. At the turn of the century, however, his influence seemed to wane. The rural and small-town America that he had described had been transformed by industrialization, urbanization, and class conflict. The necessity for expanded state-sponsored institutions made his praise of a decentralized voluntarist society seem less relevant for an economy undreamed of in his *Democracy*.

The great surge of Tocqueville's reputation in America as a social thinker, rather than only as an acute observer of the early Republic, came during two decades following the Second World War. Liberal assumptions concerning modern social evolution had been deeply threatened. Their future seemed problematic. America emerged from the war powerful and prosperous, but challenged by an expanding Soviet Communism. In this context Tocqueville's writings began to be reexamined.[4] Social scientists and historians reacted against the Progressive perspective that had framed American history within a dialectic of left/right class conflict. They developed a counterconstruct that drew upon two of Tocqueville's strongest images of America. Born free, America had become the most egalitarian society on earth. Its political and social conditions offered vital lessons for modern peoples, all equally fated to approach a similar equality of conditions. Second, America had avoided passing through the cycles of dictatorship and class hatred that plagued continental Europe in its transition to modern equality.[5] Tocqueville's perspective implied that the United States had escaped and might continue to avoid the dual curse of many Old World societies, despotism and social revolution.

This vision of American exceptionalism was immeasurably reinforced by the balance of world power that emerged from the Second World War. The closing prophecy of the *Democracy* of 1835 starkly juxtaposed Russia and America as the two nations each of which is to be "called by some secret design of Providence one day to hold in its hands the destinies of half the world." As the United States and the Soviet Union drifted into the polarization of the Cold War, Tocqueville's brief nineteenth-century contrast between Russia and America, between egalitarian liberty and despotism, between "the plow and the sword," was transformed into a contemporary ideological confrontation between Western liberal capitalism and Eastern Marxian socialism. At its crudest, Tocqueville became the adopted champion of the free world against Marx in the ideological equivalent of a Western showdown. In 1962 the editor of *The Happy Republic: A Reader in Tocqueville's America* put it succinctly: "To those who ask, 'What is the importance of Tocqueville in world politics?' it is enough to reply that he is the answer to Marx."[6]

Had this been the whole story of the Tocqueville's resurgence, his reputation and thought probably would not have continued their ascent when the Cold War stabilized and the "Happy Republic" became a distinctly unhappy Republic in the late 1960s. In the 1970s and 1980s the attraction of Tocqueville's *Democracy* continued unabated. It proved to be richer and more varied in appeal than had been anticipated by the postwar generation of scholars. Among the new generation, who dramatically rejected the conformism implicit in the consensus vision of American history, some were attracted by the civic Tocqueville who so eloquently described voluntary association as the lifeblood of liberty. Others were drawn to the somber prophet who "saw through the promise of material prosperity and egalitarian ideals to the invisible oppression that Herbert Marcuse was laying bare in books like *One Dimensional Man*."[7] In the closing decades of the twentieth century Tocqueville's thought clearly provided more than a suggestive alternative to the powerful Marxian prognosis of modern industrial society. *Democracy* offered a point of departure for confronting the dangers of bureaucratization, atomization, and secularization. Scholars sought to analyze the role of "habits of the heart" and religious values in the maintenance of a free society. Tocqueville continues to enjoy popularity across a broad range of the American ideological spectrum—conservatives, liberals, and communitarians.[8]

However varied the motifs drawn from *Democracy*, for most Americans Tocqueville remains embodied in a single seamless book produced at a privileged moment in our history.[9] Except for Tocquevillean scholars, it suffices that *Democracy* was received in France with almost universal enthusiasm and took its rightful place among the classics. Royer-Collard, a doyen of French liberalism, delivered the verdict on the morrow of its publication: "Since Montesquieu there has been nothing like it." This was "the unanimous verdict" in France, echoed George Wilson Pierson in his classic *Tocqueville and Beaumont in America* a century later.[10] And so it has remained. So pervasive is this image of instant and enduring success that American scholars can infer that Tocqueville's work was less well appreciated in the United States than in his own country. After all, how could the work of a Catholic aristocrat, based upon only nine months of observations, ranging over an impossibly ambitious series of themes, and addressed to a French audience, really find "a comfortable home in the American mind"?[11]

Françoise Mélonio's *Tocqueville and the French* quickly demolishes such a perspective. Whatever discomfort Americans may have expressed about Tocqueville during the past century and a half is as nothing compared with the reactions of many of his own countrymen. First there was the matter of national pride. Americans needed to read no further than the Introduction to the *Democracy* of 1835 to discover that their young Republic had provided Tocqueville with both the inspiration and the materials to discern "the whole future." If the whole future could be glimpsed in America, where was France? Twenty years later Tocqueville compounded the narcissistic wound. His *Old Regime and the French Revolution* (1856) depicted a rather enviable alternative past drawn from English history. Each of Tocqueville's major works premised that France's polity was deeply, if not fatally, flawed. One must not underestimate the impact of such counternarratives on French self-esteem. French history had already designated France as the heartland of medieval Western civilization, the pacesetter of early modern culture, the pioneer nation of the worldwide democratic revolution. For a generation the battle standards of the French army moved triumphantly across Europe from Madrid to Moscow. Each of Tocqueville's major works had to compete with the memory of extraordinary France, of history's chosen people. That vision still shimmered in the *Memoirs* of Charles de Gaulle: "Old France burdened by history, bruised by wars and revolutions, relentlessly going back and forth from grandeur to decline, but straightened, century after century, by the genius of renovation . . . a great people, made for example, enterprise, combat, always the star of History.[12]

Tocqueville shared deeply with his countrymen all the glories and all the prides of France. They constituted a psychological hurdle for many readers on all parts of the French political spectrum. It is no wonder that Tocqueville's books seemed less jarring to English-speaking readers on both sides of the Atlantic than they did to his compatriots. Did one really need to go, even imaginatively, to the land of the Philistines (or Puritans, or slaveholders) in search of redemption? For royalists, clericals, and imperialists, for revolutionaries, socialists and republicans, was Paris so bereft of prophets? In every generation there were a host of Frenchmen who denied or denounced any beneficent futurity to the Americans.

Readers of *Tocqueville and the French* will discover that in France he was far more than an austere meditator. Françoise Mélonio illuminates a profoundly discordant history. To most of his immediate contemporaries Tocqueville was neither a philosopher nor a historian, but a political combatant. Every one of his adult readers was living under a different regime than the one into which they had been born. In his own brief fifty-four years Tocqueville lived under five constitutions and seven regimes. France witnessed not only a succession of unstable political systems but a succession of Tocquevilles—a writer of two *Democracy*s, a member of two academies, a representative of two parliamentary regimes sandwiched between two antiparliamentary regimes. He died as he had been born, under a Bonaparte at the pinnacle of his autocratic power.

Tocqueville confronted French contemporaries as the embodiment of paradoxes. The descendant of an ancient noble family, he proclaimed in his first major work the providentiality of his order's decline and fall. Born a Catholic, he made a prescription for the survival of that faith that was denounced by many coreligionists as a cure worse than the disease. At one point or another, he clashed with the standard-bearers of all of the political regimes under which he lived. Even knowledgeable readers may be surprised to discover that the peak of Tocqueville's nineteenth-century status as a French culture hero came only in the 1860s, when he was safely dead, and every reader will be fascinated by the analysis of Tocqueville's subsequent descent into trivialization, derision, and oblivion.

Mélonio's closing section deals with the return of Tocqueville after the Second World War. The "Tocqueville renaissance," when it came, was a phenomenon astonishing even to those who witnessed and helped to create it. It now requires an exercise of the historical imagination to recapture the Tocqueville on whom I began to do research forty years ago as a Fulbright scholar in Paris. At that moment only one French book had been published on Tocqueville in almost half a century. That was a biography by Antoine Rédier of the right-wing Action française. For Rédier *Democracy in America* was a youthful folly, repented of in maturity by an indelible aristocrat who returned to, and died in, the traditions of his fathers.

Mélonio's book marks the beginning of the serious history of Tocqueville's international revival. From a comparative perspective, I need only note that the French recovery of Tocqueville came later than its counterpart in the United States. One might hypothesize that his triumph had to await the emergence of a truly postrevolutionary France. The breakthrough occurred in a society that "was almost unrecognizable to those," like Eric Hobsbawm, "who knew it before the Second World War." Behind this observation, shared by François Furet, is the hypothesis that France has converged with America to a greater extent in the last forty years than at any point in their mutual histories. Raymond Aron began to invoke Tocqueville to challenge the alternative sociological traditions of Durkheim and Marx in the 1950s and early 1960s. But François Furet could mobilize the Tocquevillization of France only with "the end of the era of *marxisant* intellectual hegemony."[13]

Mélonio's closing chapter is also an invitation to historians and social scientists to rethink Tocqueville's relation to our contemporary world. Ironies abound. In 1840 Tocqueville considered one chapter of his "second" *Democracy* particularly worthy of independent dissemination: "Why Great Revolutions Will Be-

come Rare." Eight years later that prophecy was quietly buried in the debris of
the revolutions of 1848 and remained dormant for more than a century. Tocqueville's premier postrevolutionary prognosis seems to have regained some of its
allure in the late twentieth century. On the other hand, who today would accept
Tocqueville's casual peripheralization of his discussion of race relations in the
Democracy, where it is described as tangential to democracy and irrelevant to
Europeans? The European is no longer "man par excellence" in America, and
racially, European exceptionalism is gone with the wind.[14]

Tocqueville and the French is a pioneering investigation of the turbulent dialogue between Tocqueville and the French during their long march toward
democracy. Mélonio brings to her study a unique combination of qualifications.
As a leading member of the Tocqueville national commission, her intimacy with
the Tocquevillean archive is profound. Better than any previous scholar living or
dead, she integrates an unparalleled range of French reactions to Tocqueville into
her study. Nothing less comprehensive would have enabled her to speak with
such authority upon this extraordinarily volatile relationship between a political culture and one of its most brilliant products.

Seymour Drescher
Professor, History Department
University of Pittsburgh

Notes

1. See, inter alia, Jesse R. Pitts and Olivier Zunz, "Celebrating Tocqueville's *Democracy in America*, 1835–1985," a special edition of the *Tocqueville Review* 7 (1985/86), containing papers from conferences at Washington, in August and October 1985, and at Paris,
in June 1985; Abraham S. Eisenstadt, ed., *Reconsidering Tocqueville's Democracy in America* (New Brunswick: Rutgers Univ. Press, 1988), stemming from a twin conference at City
University of New York in October 1985; and Eduardo Nolla, ed., *Liberty, Equality, Democracy* (New York: New York Univ. Press, 1992), containing papers from a conference at Yale
University in April 1990. C-SPAN has formed an Alexis de Tocqueville Advisory Committee, of scholars and educators, to develop television programming on Tocqueville's
journey to America.

2. J. C. Casanova, "Tocqueville dans ses oeuvres," *L'Express*, Feb. 20–26, 1987, 102.

3. See, above all, George W. Pierson, *Tocqueville and Beaumont in America* (New York:

Oxford Univ. Press, 1938); James T. Schleifer, *The Making of Tocqueville's Democracy in America* (Chapel Hill: Univ. of North Carolina Press, 1980); and the repetition of Tocqueville's journey by Richard Reeves, *American Journey: Traveling with Tocqueville in Search of Democracy in America* (New York: Simon and Schuster, 1982).

4. See, inter alia, Robert Nisbet, "Many Tocquevilles," *American Scholar* 46 (1976): 59–75; Lynn Marshall and Seymour Drescher, "American Historians and Tocqueville's *Democracy*," *Journal of American History* 55 (1968): 512–32; and Sean Wilentz, "Many Democracies: On Tocqueville and Jacksonian America," in Eisenstadt, *Reconsidering*, 207–28.

5. See, inter alia, Louis Hartz, *The Liberal Tradition in America: An Interpretation of American Political Thought since the Revolution* (New York: Harcourt Brace, 1955); David Riesman, with Nathan Glazer and Reuel Denney, *The Lonely Crowd: A Study of the Changing American Character* (New Haven: Yale University Press, 1961), Seymour Martin Lipset, *The First New Nation: The United States in Historical Perspective* (New York: Basic Books, 1963); Marvin Meyers, *The Jacksonian Persuasion: Politics and Belief* (Stanford: Stanford Univ. Press, 1955); and Olivier Zunz, "Tocqueville and the Writing of American History in the Twentieth Century: A Comment," *Tocqueville Review* 7(1985/86): 131–35.

6. George E. Probst, ed., *The Happy Republic: A Reader in Tocqueville's America* (New York: Harper Torchbooks, 1962), xiii; see also Seymour Drescher, ed., *Tocqueville and Beaumont on Social Reform* (New York: Harper and Row, 1968), ix-xvii.

7. On the breadth of Tocqueville's appeal, see James T. Kloppenberg, "Life Everlasting: Tocqueville in America," *Tocqueville Review* 17:2 (1996): 19–36. For a description of "left" and "right" Tocquevilleans, see Peter Berkowitz, "The Art of Association," *New Republic*, June 24, 1996, 44–49.

8. See, inter alia, Robert Bellah, et al., *Habits of the Heart: Individualism and Commitment in American Life* (Berkeley: Univ. of California Press, 1985); Robert D. Putnam, "Bowling Alone: America's Declining Social Capital," *Journal of Democracy* 6:1 (1995): 65–78; "Bowling Alone: Revisited," *Responsive Community* 5 (1995): 18–33; Joshua Mitchell, *The Fragility of Freedom: Tocqueville on Religion, Democracy and the American Future* (Chicago: Univ. of Chicago Press, 1996); Ronald William Dworkin, *The Rise of the Imperial Self: America's Culture Wars in Augustinian Perspective* (Lanham, Md.: Rawan and Littlefield, 1996); and Sanford Kessler, *Tocqueville's Civil Religion: American Christianity and the Prospects for Freedom* (Albany: State Univ. of New York Press, 1944). I omit a plethora of scholarly studies by American scholars focusing upon various aspects of Tocqueville's life, writings, and relationships in the context of European thought and social conditions.

9. On the mix of French and American experiences in the composition of the *Democracy in America*, see, inter alia, Seymour Drescher, "Tocqueville's Two *Démocraties*," *Journal of the History of Ideas* 25 (April–June 1964): 201–16; Drescher, "More than America: Comparison and Synthesis in *Democracy in America*," in Eisenstadt, *Reconsidering*, 77–93; Jean-Claude Lamberti, *Tocqueville and the Two "Democracies*," trans. Arthur Goldham-

mer (Cambridge: Harvard Univ. Press, 1989); and James T. Schleifer, "How Many Democracies?" in Nolla, *Liberty*, 193–205.

10. Pierson, *Tocqueville and Beaumont*, 4.

11. Berkowitz, "The Art of Association," 44–45.

12. Quoted by Stanley Hoffman, *Decline or Renewal? France since the 1930s* (New York: Viking Press, 1974), 231, from de Gaulle's *Mémoires de Guerre* (Paris, 1954), 1: 1, and *La France et son armée* (Paris, 1938), 277.

13. Both quotes are from E. J. Hobsbawm, *Echoes of the Marseillaise: Two Centuries Look Back on the French Revolution* (New Brunswick: Rutgers Univ. Press, 1990), 100–110. For a similar perspective, see François Furet and Mona Ozouf, eds., *A Critical Dictionary of the French Revolution*, trans. Arthur Goldhammer (Cambridge: Harvard Univ. Press, 1989), xx. As late as 1960 Raymond Aron was quite cognizant of the disparity between Tocqueville's stature in France and in the United States (conversations with Raymond Aron, at Harvard University, fall 1960).

14. For an incisive reassessment of Tocqueville's influence on the historiography of "separate spheres" in the United States, see Linda K. Kerber, "Separate Spheres, Female Worlds, Woman's Place: The Rhetoric of Woman's History," *Journal of American History* 75:1 (1988): 9–39.

*Tocqueville
and the
French*

Introduction: The Transition to Democracy

Our modern democracies were born in two revolutions: the American in 1776 and the French of 1789. Each claims to be a model. Yet what astonishes us is that while both revolutions resulted from the Enlightenment, they gave rise to political traditions so different that we can only measure the extent of their differences. In the United States, Christianity and democracy, tradition and Enlightenment philosophy, private interest and public good, cohabit—while French attempts to build a new society from the bottom up have been blocked for over a century by the arduous task of combining liberalism and democracy.

Why such disparity? How can we explain France's unique political history? Haunted by their origins, the French of the nineteenth century sought the answer in the Revolution, as if such a starting point contained the genetic code of their history. They found within it that array of political forms among which the nineteenth century incessantly vacillated: constitutional monarchy, republic, empire. Sometimes it seemed to presage failure and sometimes the Republic triumphant. Historians often have followed suit, turning the history of France's democratic transition into the history of a revolution, and always the same one, whether considered enduring or ended.

The aim of this book is to loosen the grip of this tyrannical fascination with France's origins. The nineteenth century was no meaningless interval between a founding moment and the Republic's ultimate maturation into wisdom, regardless of what date one assigns the latter event—1880 or 1945 or later still. The French required a long transition before being able to invent democracy from their twin legacy of absolutism and revolution, on the one hand, and the mixed fascination and incomprehension they felt for the rival American experiment with democracy, on the other. Turbulence and rapid shifts in direction have been part of France's exploration at a theoretical level of the possibilities offered by a system still new enough not to be taken for granted.

Within the French invention of democracy, one body of work towers over all the others, that of Alexis de Tocqueville. Using his works, the French have given shape to their fears and hopes. If we follow their quarrelsome dialogue with Tocqueville, we will follow the rocky path of French democratic transition.[1]

Tocqueville's mind was profound but narrow. He tirelessly examined just one question over and over again—the relation between freedom and equality in modern societies. His one search was for the way to accommodate democracy. Too great a distinction has been made between Tocqueville the sociologist and American observer of *Democracy in America* and Tocqueville the French historian and writer of *The Old Regime and the French Revolution* and the posthumous *Recollections* or, in French, his *Souvenirs*. Such disciplinary divisions were foreign to the nineteenth century. Tocqueville's works comprise a single theoretical cycle, a democratic tragedy like Balzac's human comedy. His genius lay less in his breadth of perception than in his acuity in observing what was unprecedented in modern society.

This acuity owed much to a chance circumstance of birth. Early on, Tocqueville perceived the gap between hierarchical society and the modern era. The revolutionary fault line that ran through French history also ran through his family's own history. He loved to recall that his maternal great-grandfather, the illustrious Malesherbes, "after having defended the people before King Louis XVI, defended King Louis XVI before the people ... twin examples."[2] Tocqueville's father, Hervé, was imprisoned during the Terror and saved by Thermidor. Hervé was a devoted servant of the Restoration monarchy, being made first prefect and then peer of France. He had Ultramontanist leanings but allied himself with Enlightenment traditions. Thus he supported Martignac's experiment with decentralization in 1828. In the spirit of Montesquieu, he also published studies in 1847 and 1850 on the causes of the French Revolution.[3] He criticized the kings' deafness to the spirit of the moment and the nobles' tight grasp on privilege. His son agreed.

Sorely tried by the Terror, Tocqueville's family, however, did not all side with the Enlightenment. In the jail cells of the Revolution, his mother had contracted the penitential piety and morbid attachment to a mostly imaginary ancien régime that define lachrymose Restoration legitimism. She sang sadly about Louis XVI's death to the young Alexis. From his own family, therefore, Tocqueville inherited both belief in the Enlightenment and the anxiety about a modernity to which scholars have all too often reduced his beliefs.

Family memory was not the only means by which the ancien régime and the Revolution pressed in on Tocqueville. In 1828–30 the monarchy again immured itself in a reactive stance, which only resulted again in the king's fall. As in 1789, a choice was forced between the Revolution and the ancien régime. Tocqueville's family chose the latter. Joylessly, Tocqueville himself opted for modernity, pledging allegiance to the new regime. It was "a disagreeable time," he wrote. Because Tocqueville was an aristocrat who supported democracy, the French Revolution did not completely belong to others, but neither was it entirely his, although he did not reject it. Tocqueville remained attached to the ancien régime yet sought to assent to the modern era—a delicate position. His importance lies in having turned family misfortune into the starting point for his systematic thinking, forging theoretical innovation from aristocratic archaism. He saw—more clearly than anyone else—that aristocratic values were crumbling, that going backward in time was impossible, and that the French feeling for equality was passionate. Thus in a single movement, he made sovereignty's exalted status understandable in the uniqueness it conferred on French political culture, terrorized by the fear of return to a regime based on privilege.

Heir to the contradictory legacies of the ancien régime and the Revolution, Tocqueville did not find the French experience exemplary. In 1830, as he was sadly coming to a truce with modernity, he decided to travel to the United States to study democracy in the making. There he discovered the obverse of French democracy: equality joined to freedom, faith to reason, sovereignty to self-government, public welfare to private interest. As an heir of English wisdom, America offered France a moderate example of democratic transition. No doubt the model could not be copied, because the history of the two nations was too dissimilar, but something could be learned from it nonetheless.

Tocqueville, along with Montesquieu, is the only thinker common to both American and French cultural heritages and the one who explored the disparity between American and French democracy most profoundly. Aristocratic, he is also the most famous of democracy's *ralliés*. A man at the margins of several worlds, both the ancien régime and the Revolution, France and America, he owes the originality of his thought to this unusual position. For the French, his work is a site of transition and exchange between heterogeneous intellectual universes—in other words, a conceptual Atlantic Ocean.

As Braudel taught us, sites of transit—seas and oceans—are historians' preferred arenas, for here they can most clearly see borrowing and conflict among societies. The French were called to make democracy their own by appropriating Tocqueville's works and by harvesting the dual fruit of aristocratic values and the American model. Nothing shows better how hard this was than the shifts in French fellow-traveling with Tocqueville over the past 150 years: interpretations of Tocqueville are part of France's own "fashion system," as Barthes termed that semiotic system of cultural codes.

In the United States, *Democracy in America* was a dignified classic by 1835, published for use by students and recommended by self-improvement societies. Despite an eclipse in the late nineteenth century, the book has always served as a mirror in which Americans enjoyed contemplating their own virtue. Nothing of the sort happened in France. First, various factions passionately claimed Tocqueville for their own, drawing from his works to fuel polemical arguments as successive emergencies demanded. Next, Tocqueville was, if not forgotten, at least abandoned from 1880 to 1950. As early as the Second Empire, he was saddened at being viewed as an old fogy by the young. Still worse, after 1880 he was not part of France's pantheon of republican heroes but was thought of "as a kind of solemn ancestor, weighted down by his false collar, wrapped in a triple length of white batiste, majestic in his spectacles, redoubtable in his judgments, inexhaustible in his dissertations."[4] In other words, dullness personified. Stripped of their political virulence, his works lost even their scholarly pertinence. History, sociology, and political studies all become sciences at the end of the nineteenth century, diligently inventorying Tocqueville's mistakes, the better to relegate him to the prehistory of knowledge. Thus until about 1950, there remained no more of Tocqueville than the faint imprint of a distant authority. In 1942, when *Souvenirs* was reprinted, nothing foreshadowed Tocqueville's grand return.

And how enigmatic was that post-1950 return: constant references to Tocqueville as a prophet, though fraught with anachronism, reveal a new political complicity between him and today's readers. By calling him a prophet, they make Tocqueville contemporary, giving him new descriptive pertinence and instant prescriptive power. Tocqueville was a prophet of democracy in the nineteenth century, a prophet of revolution in 1848, a prophet of the German threat before 1870 and 1914. Today, Tocqueville is the prophet of totalitarianism and the era of the masses, of Vatican II, of the danger of nationalization and rampant socialism, of modern individualism. More than anyone else, he is a prophet within the very rich French prophetic line that began with Rousseau. At one time his works were found to be scientifically outdated by the French. Today, their renewed pertinence is affirmed, without wondering how this renewal has come about. As a rationale, most merely repeat Sainte-Beuve, that Tocqueville thought first before he learned anything and that the universality of his thought rose above the changes which affect the societies we live in. This is just another way of saying that Tocqueville's thought prospers from its failings and that authors' methods escape obsolescence to the extent of their blindness to the world around them.

The very disparity in the response to Tocqueville's works is thus an enigma inviting us to reevaluate both their meaning and our own history. Tocqueville's thought cannot be interpreted outside the democratic tradition from which it emerged and to which we are heirs. Every work is doubtless born of its own era, but political works most of all. Since politics became a matter of public opinion in the eighteenth century, the writer as public commentator has been held responsible for the community's collective destiny. Tocqueville was sufficiently aware of this to want to achieve success[5] and to shape his words in order to attain it. "A serious act, meaningful, irrevocable,"[6] his works would gain their full impact only when echoed by common opinion. Hence their tragic grandeur, in which the salvation of France is played out.

Yet the relation of his works to their time does not tell the whole story any more than their meaning can be fully grasped by studying each interpretation of them in turn. There is a mystery in their survival. By what metamorphosis did Tocqueville the old fogy become a dignified, classic political writer?

The disparity of response to Tocqueville's works also invites us to break with interpretation of the nineteenth century as a linear transition to the present. It asks us to view the French nineteenth century (which lasted until the 1950s) as a historical cycle in which the same questions recur, the same aporia confront thinkers. For although Tocqueville's works have been illuminated by commentaries, they have also served to evaluate and measure such commentaries and have been the center around which critical dialogue turned. Examining Tocqueville's uncomfortable introduction into French thought means depicting French societal opposition to ancien régime resurgences through 1875 or 1880 and delineating the French invention of an indigenous democratic model that owed little to Tocqueville or America. Does the renewal of interest in Tocqueville that began in 1950 mean that his model is now obsolete, even though for so long it seemed to the French the end of democratic transition?

1

The New Political Science, 1820s–1830s

T OCQUEVILLE is often perceived as a great recluse, foreign to his century and class. Nothing predisposed the sickly young man from a conservative aristocratic family, by career an unremarkable magistrate, to become more than a minor notable who turned his back on his era. In Tocqueville's milieu the army and diplomacy were honorable careers—but literature? Tocqueville suffered from the scorn that greeted his early works. "I was seen as a strange man," he recalled, "deprived of a career, who wrote to kill time, on the whole a distinguished occupation, considering that it was at least better to write badly than to chase girls."[1]

The extraordinary success from 1835 on of Tocqueville's call for a "new political science" would remain inexplicable were Tocqueville not articulating the concerns of his era in that call. His contribution was one of unusual solutions to inherited questions. To Tocqueville, developing a political science did not mean solitary prospecting but a practical politics of forging a path amid the passions and prejudices of the era, even exposing oneself to ostracism and misunderstanding. Tocqueville's political science can only be understood by examining the questions to which it responded and the twist it gave the commonplaces of his age.

Tocqueville's Heritage

Transitional Generations: Liberal and Doctrinaire Legacies

Tocqueville's works emerged from his sense that the constitutional monarchy's compromise between egalitarian claims and its ancien régime legacy was precariously forged. He owed this sense to family misfortunes but in his works

7

gave it the well-argued form he derived from reading the writings of his elders. Starting in 1828, he distanced himself from his parents' extremely conservative monarchism, rejecting the illusion of a return to the past. He accepted 1789 as a definitive point of rupture within French history. By the same token he accepted, along with his liberal or Doctrinaire predecessors, the sense that he too belonged to an obscure transitional generation. Like those predecessors, he watched democracy "overflowing all banks,"[2] and like them, he believed in the inexorable course of history: "Rivers do not flow backward toward their source. Past events do not return to nothingness."[3] Tocqueville's writing draws over and over on the river metaphor introduced by the Doctrinaires.

Accepting the liberal diagnosis, Tocqueville also adopted liberal objectives. Since everything has been destroyed, we must rebuild—a difficult task. The passion for destruction that continued after the Revolution kept society in a state of civil war. Since 1820 the Restoration had endured plot after conspiratorial plot which demonstrated the impossibility of a consensus on institutions.

Hence the need to end the Revolution, which had been an aim even of the people of 1789. During the Restoration it became the high stakes of politicians and the intellectual enterprise of historians, who were invested with great spiritual authority by a nation seeking its identity. Thus, through his lectures at the Sorbonne in 1820–22 and again in 1828–30, political leader and historian Guizot attempted to inculcate respect for the past in the young, in order to reestablish the unity of the nation through the ages.

The enterprise undertaken by historians fulfilled "a real and profound, though dimly sensed, need among thinkers in France"[4] and was the key to their success among youth. Tocqueville taught himself through reading their works. As a very young man, he read Augustin Thierry and kept several of his works in his library. He also perused Thiers, whose servile fatalism[5] he detested, and went to hear Guizot's lectures on French history in 1829 and 1830. A studious auditor, he took notes in which we can read a disciple's admiration. Yet from them emerges a dissent that foreshadows political and theoretical confrontations to come. His family's misfortunes made Tocqueville more attentive than the bourgeois-born Guizot to the difficulty of attaining stability in a regime based on opinion, "claiming both liberty and power, the seed of progress, discovery, and effort, principle of instability and revolution."[6]

Tocqueville had received his curiosity about history and the desire to end the Revolution from his elders. Experience reinforced his intellectual inheritance.

Under the Restoration the ancien régime and the Revolution had not yet been eradicated politically, socially, or judicially. At a modest level Tocqueville could see the persistent virulence of the combat between the old society and the new. At the tribunal of Versailles, where he served from 1827 to 1832 as a *juge auditeur,* a judge new to the bench who was unremunerated, he associated with magistrates who had been on the job since the ancien régime. Longevity at the time signaled competence: in their lawmaking judges might freely resort to old royal custom, revolutionary legislation, the Napoleonic code, or the laws of the Restoration—demonstrating the discontinuity of French history. Tocqueville could easily see how futile were Restoration efforts to restore links with the past. In April 1825 the government deemed it necessary to rehabilitate the losers by indemnifying those whose lands had been confiscated by the Revolution. In 1824 these had been inventoried in a vast prefecture-by-prefecture survey, the better to ensure satisfaction of complaints. In the numerous lawsuits that followed this imprudent refreshing of memories, Tocqueville was twice called upon to deliver sentences, once in 1828 and again in 1829. This experience allowed him to witness how utterly the Revolution had reversed fortunes, but even more the virulent hatred between émigrés who had become strangers in their own nation and a people attached to their newfound possessions. Thus Tocqueville perceived the difficulty of completing the Revolution, not in books but in practice; he saw the runaway enclosures that followed successive spoils taking and simmering hatreds among the groups of claimants. "What is done is done," he concluded. "We must finish with the past; it is time that the bloody book of our Revolution be closed for ever. If liberty is a priceless good, then stability is another, perhaps valued too little in our day."[7]

To achieve stability, there had to be agreement on the basis of sovereignty. Thinking about sovereignty was stimulated by the very experience of the Restoration, which was not reducible to a return to the ancien régime. By defining the legitimate use of liberty, the charter had opened a public arena for the exchange of ideas wherein the French could tumultuously teach themselves democracy. In 1814 the Restoration inaugurated the practice of budgetary discussions, and France entered the modern era of parliamentary procedure. It was an ambivalent entrance, however, more tactical than concerted, with factions opportunistically fighting for their hidden agendas. The Ultras massed behind Chateaubriand called for representative institutions to limit the monarch's slight inclination to reforms; Doctrinaires defended Louis XVIII's prerogatives in order to speed reforms; both moves were cynical. Everyone felt the charter was merely a transaction between the two parties of opinion that divided France, at best a peace treaty, at worst a ceasefire giving combatants the time to rearm in the dark. The solution to the uneasy situation had yet to be invented.

Such a solution was sought in restructuring sovereignty by creating intermediary institutions that diffused power and made its abuses more difficult. The nature of these institutions varied. They might be the municipal councils studied by Prosper de Barante in 1821 in his *Des communes et de l'aristocratie* or the associations promoted by Alexandre de Laborde. It might be a new aristocracy, one based on ability (so dear to the Doctrinaires), one of producers (as called for by Saint-Simon), or even the old nobility whose flattering portrait was sketched by Montlosier. Together these aspirations explain the positive response of the young generation of liberals, neo-Catholics, Ultras, and Saint-Simonians to the king's brief support for Minister Martignac's liberal, although quite timid, experiment with decentralization (January 1828–8 August 1829).

Tocqueville shared their youthful enthusiasm for the Martignac experiment. He had good family reasons for doing so. His father, Hervé de Tocqueville, had been a member of the commission charged by Martignac with studying the replacement of royal nomination by election to municipal and general councils.[8] Hervé was in favor of restricted reforms, provided they did not usurp the king's power. But Alexis was much more of an innovator than his father, and much more aware of the crisis of legitimacy faced by the regime. In early 1830 he allied himself with young liberals and republicans of the group Aide-Toi, le Ciel T'Aidera, whose name was inspired by Guizot's well-known liberal dictum, "Heaven helps those who help themselves." Tocqueville often went to the electoral meetings, which had begun increasing in number. Two texts written before the July Revolution of 1830[9] show us the direction of his thinking. Tocqueville clearly grasped the tactical nature of belonging to the charter. As the legitimacy of the monarchy crumbled, he discovered with the emphatic exaltation of disappointed youth that people always choose reason as a means and never an end. "Everyone is trying to fool everyone else."[10] Modern politics was no longer an art of truth but the art of producing an unstable consensus by verbal trickery. Sophistry had replaced Christian political theology and Enlightenment philosophical politics. It is true that few eras had said so much about fidelity and practiced it so little. It is also true that in the rapid flow of events, as Chateaubriand said, "changing one's mind was to do as everyone else had done."

At a very early point, therefore, Tocqueville had the same questions his elders had regarding decentralization, creating a new aristocracy, how to teach democracy, and the instability of opinion. They preceded his American experience and were only driven home by the July Revolution of 1830, which made it even more obvious to Tocqueville that a return to the old order was impossible.

The Revolution shook spiritual consensus no less than it had shaken the country's foundations. Doctrinaires, liberals, and Saint-Simonians now all deemed it necessary to reestablish a religion or at least some spiritualist philosophy. But absolutism seemed also to have brought about the downfall of Catholicism. The Restoration church, with scant theological intelligence and near-crazed desire for revenge, once again linked its destiny to the monarchy, though the monarchy was perceived as fragile. At best, the Enlightenment was accused merely of having failed to avert the Terror; at worst, of having caused it. Theodore Jouffroy brilliantly expressed this spiritual disarray in his article "Comment les dogmes finissent" published in *Le Globe* of 24 May 1825: faith was dead, the Enlightenment led only to disenchantment, and not until the new generation of predestined apostles appeared would a new ontology emerge.

> Superior to everything around them, they allow themselves to be dominated neither by renewed fanaticism nor by the atheistic egoism that had become so widespread in society. They try the past and despise the incredulousness of the present; they abhor its corruption. They also have a sense of their mission and the knowledge of their era. They understand what their forefathers did not at all, and what the corrupt tyrants over them refuse to hear. They know what a revolution is, and they know it because they have come at the right time.[11]

Tocqueville shared Jouffroy's unease and also hoped for a providential meeting of the course of history and humanity's salvation. His education had given him experience with both traditions of the ancien régime church, Ultramontane and Gallican. Faithful to the Restoration's many efforts to expiate the crimes of the Revolution, his mother was an admirer of the Jesuits. Tocqueville's Gallican father placed him in the care of Father Lesueur, a Jansenist who, hardly a liberal, raised young Alexis in austere piety, and who had been Hervé's own preceptor. But from adolescence on, Tocqueville distanced himself from these religious forms with their legitimist ties. Heir to the Enlightenment, he distrusted ecclesiastical institutions that tended to conflate political power with spiritual mission. In addition, his readings of the eighteenth-century philosophers, especially Voltaire and Rousseau, and his attendance at the high school of Metz infused him with a skepticism which probably never left him.[12]

Tocqueville thus knew the difficulty of belief yet continued to deem philosophy an insufficient basis for social order. We find in him very early on an uneasiness with the results of dogma, inspired by Jouffroy and by Lamennais's *Essai sur l'indifférence en matière de religion* and developed in *Democracy*. "The centuries of enlightenment," he wrote in 1830,

> are centuries of doubt and discussion. There is no fanaticism, but there is little belief and thus little of the kind of action which would be sublime if life eternal existed, yet absurd under the contrary hypothesis. Here, enthusiasm is like a kind of sudden fever; it does not draw its inspiration from the usual state of the soul. A taste for the positive grows as doubts increase. Finally, the entire world becomes an insoluble problem for the person who hangs on to the most readily sensed objects and finally ends flat on his belly against the earth, for fear that the very ground will not provide solid footing.
>
> Yet we cannot deny that there are many feelings which become purer. Thus, love of country becomes more reasonable, more carefully considered, religion better understood by those who still believe in it, love of justice more enlightened, and the common good better understood, but all these feelings lose in strength what they gain in perfection. They more greatly satisfy the mind but affect life the less.[13]

Tocqueville thus shared his predecessors' painful concern with France's ability to reconcile liberalism with democracy. His legitimist roots have been much emphasized; he was as much a son of his time as of his family. He had the ability to upset popular beliefs only because he was so concerned with the common problems of his time.

A Son of His Century

Yet Tocqueville was no Doctrinaire disciple. First, he belonged to a different social class than most Doctrinaires. The July Revolution is often thought of as merely a leg up provided to office seekers, replacing the aristocracy with the bourgeoisie. Liberals like Thiers and Guizot were in the winners' camp; aristocratic Tocqueville was in the losers'. After three years of abortive attempts to be promoted to the rank of unpaid *juge substitut*, in June 1830 he achieved his goal. But by depriving him of support, the July Revolution ensured he would maintain his previous position. Tocqueville could have sullenly gone off to sulk, as did most legitimists. Instead, he pledged allegiance to the new regime—in vain, for he resigned on 21 May 1832, having attained only unremunerated positions in the magistracy. He had been eliminated before starting his career.

In addition to his difference in social class from the Doctrinaires, there was his gap in age. Tocqueville was too young to be among the Restoration public commentators born during the final years of the eighteenth century. The July Revolution coincided with the Doctrinaires' political maturity and allowed them to hold center stage, to the detriment of those younger who had been unable to prove themselves. Tocqueville all his life remained a politician upon whom hopes ride but nothing more—as leader of the "young Left" under the July Monarchy and as still-inexperienced minister during the Second Republic before he was swept aside by the empire. Tocqueville was of Musset's generation, a child of his century who had come too late, after the great battles.

Tocqueville had developed sharp eyes during his youth. To him 1830 was not merely the year when the king's legitimacy had to some degree slipped into the quasi-legitimacy of the Orleans line, "kings of the French." He also saw in it the sign of a change in modernity which disqualified legitimists' retrogressive efforts while emptying the Doctrinaire program of its progressive content.

Tocqueville had distanced himself from the legitimists since the end of the Restoration. After the July Revolution, this grew worse. Toward the unseated monarchy he retained "a remnant of hereditary affection"[14] which in his eyes it did not deserve, yet without thinking it could revive.[15]

He was hardly kinder toward liberals or Doctrinaires. Like Chateaubriand, he was too much the aristocrat to believe that any government could endure founded on the bourgeoisie's lively egotism. What was irresistible for Tocqueville about democracy was its distributive justice. The social cataclysm that had destroyed the aristocracy's grandeur should not leave the bourgeoisie's sordid mediocrity untouched. The Doctrinaires' role had been brilliant, but that had changed once they had beaten the aristocracy. Now, all that remained of their program was defense of the position they had won. The filial affection Tocqueville showed Royer-Collard after 1835 was that shown venerable debris from the past who allow us to relive history vicariously. Whatever the extent of his intellectual debt to the Doctrinaires, beginning with the Restoration's final spasms Tocqueville had chosen not to fight "the irresistible momentum of his century." Thus in 1830 he assumed the Doctrinaires' old role of intellectual critic which they had played under the Restoration.

A man of the Enlightenment as much as the Doctrinaires were, a child of his time in his sharp sense of the direction of that era, nothing limns Tocqueville's ambiguity more sharply than the portraits of him left by his contemporaries. Having seen him at Mme Recamier's, Custine wrote his friend Varnhagen von Ense on 22 February 1841: "He is puny, skinny, small, and still young: he looks like an old man and a child. He is the most naive of ambitious men, his gaze is charming, but he lacks frankness; his mouth is old and badly shaped, his color is bilious."[16] Setting aside Custine's jealousy of a fellow author, the image of a wizened child is nonetheless revealing in an era when romanticism held up the ideal of youth. The image does not refer merely to Tocqueville's sickly physique, rather starchy politeness, and ever so slightly moralizing conversation. It also marks his place within the culture of his era. Late antiquity and the Middle Ages had celebrated the eternal nature of holy wisdom spared by change in the *puer senex*. The "young-old" writer of the nineteenth century was instead the incarnation of an era galloping ahead, one in which the ruin of the fathers' world prematurely aged those who still held onto it. "Young-old" Tocqueville embodied youth obsessed by the crumbling away of the past. Some praised his hasty maturity, others deemed him old-fashioned.[17] Such dissent indeed reveals the originality of his thought, halfway between the ancien régime and the Revolution.

Departure for America

Choosing to travel to America to seek the remedy for the French illness also shows the distance Tocqueville took from his family and the Restoration's commentators. As an obedient son or a faithful disciple, Tocqueville should have gone to England. Since Montesquieu, English institutions were deemed to be admirable, and political tourists enthusiastically made trips across the Channel.[18] England seemed somehow to prefigure the great French revolutionary experience. The era's diffuse providentialism read into the English Revolution of the seventeenth century the foreshadowing of the next century's French Revolution.

Tocqueville had initially shared Doctrinaire interest in England. After planning a London excursion in 1824, he began studying English history in 1825 and explored in turn the parallel between the English Revolution of 1640 and the

French Revolution of 1789.[19] In his eyes the events of 1830 put an end to the political importance of the English experience. English government, a mix of aristocracy and democracy, became for France merely a conservative ideal. Tocqueville had to look elsewhere to find a model to understand the democratic evolution he sensed was inevitable.

But why America? America had almost no political prestige. True, since 1820 that country was no longer dreamed of as primitive and exotic, and there was a vague understanding that it was the proving ground for some great political, liberal, democratic experiment.[20] But public opinion, united in its ignorance, remained divided in judgment. America's only ardent defenders were the little band of republicans whose passion had been stimulated by Lafayette's triumphant trip to the United States from 13 July 1824 to 4 October 1825. Tocqueville's traveling companion Beaumont was related to Lafayette, whose granddaughter he later married. They solicited a note of introduction from the great man, but the malicious joy with which Tocqueville noted Americans' small esteem for Lafayette tells us that he only deemed Lafayette great by reason of the events where chance had positioned him, and that Lafayette did not inspire his desire to travel to America.[21]

Though Tocqueville was by birth a stranger to the republican tradition, his royalist origins may have given him some slight interest in America. Joseph de Maistre himself had praised American political prudence in his *Considérations sur la France.* Among those close to Tocqueville, some had been grateful to America for providing them refuge, purpose, or adventure. This was true of Hyde de Neuville, exiled under Bonaparte and then ambassador to Washington. It was also true of Monsignor de Cheverus, former bishop of Boston, and it was especially true of Tocqueville's cousin Chateaubriand. But such occasional fondness became scarcer after Andrew Jackson was elected president of the Union in 1828. From the woods of Tennessee, as redoubtable with the sword as he was wretched at the podium, Jackson was the perfect representative of a nation of hicks. He could only repulse the civilized French. In Tocqueville's milieu America remained "a babe in swaddling clothes," to quote de Maistre. True, it had a growing population, feverish activity, and unequaled commercial prosperity, but it also had low morals, scant government, and no culture at all.

Tocqueville was steeped in these prejudices. At twenty, enthusiastic about English history, he had not read much of Chateaubriand's praise for the American republic in the *Journal des Débats* of 24 October 1825 on the occasion of Lafayette's return from the United States. "Of all the spectacles which show us human inconsequence and weakness," he wrote, "the most deplorable is that of genius which has taken a false path and causes the great reason which heaven gave it for another end to serve the ruin of its compatriots and nation. . . . In America I recognize only one Republic, that of the United States. The only task worthy of genius should be to show us the difference which exists between this Republic and us, not to abuse us with lying resemblances."[22] When he suddenly decided to leave for America in August 1830, it was therefore not out of allegiance to familial tradition or to progressive thought but due to three things: biographical necessity, a recent shift in public opinion, and a new theoretical project.

The biographical necessity: America was far away. What better destination for a young aristocrat hoping to loosen his ties to legitimists? "I go to America," wrote Tocqueville, and "fifteen months go by. Lines between the political parties grow sharper in France. One clearly sees which party is compatible with the grandeur and tranquillity of one's country. One thus returns with a clear and pronounced opinion, free of partisan engagement toward anyone at all. This trip all by itself has removed you from the most popular class. The acquaintances you have made among such a celebrated people put the finishing touch on your being set apart from the crowd." What remained was to publish in order to "let the public know of your existence and bring yourself to the attention of the parties." What he also had to do to get a mission was to invent a "pretext not political but which makes us appear particularly deserving of the attention of the government, whichever government it may be, and ensures us its benevolence upon our return."[23]

Tocqueville found the pretext with his friend Beaumont, who was a *juge substitut* on the Versailles tribunal. It was a study of American prisons, the subject of a 31 October 1830 proposal they made to the Interior Ministry. This clever choice was based on a new public concern. Prison reform had attracted the attention of enlightened people. Even before 1830, the inquiries of the Royal Society of Prisons, founded by Decazes, had begun to increase. A few exemplary studies had been made in nearer countries like Switzerland or England. But America was seen as the birthplace of penal reform. As early as 1796, La Rochefoucauld-Liancourt had studied Philadelphia's prisons. Under the Restoration, Taillandier had translated Louisiana's penal code, and in 1828 Charles Lucas had published his *Système pénitentiaire en Europe et aux Etats-Unis,* which won the Montyon Prize. Renewed interest in penal system reform after 1830 allowed Tocqueville and Beaumont to receive the precious authorization for their absence and official patronage, although without financial support.

Public interest in American prisons was merely an indication of a more general fascination with the American republic. In the early months of the July Monarchy, when the future still seemed uncertain, everyone sought lessons from the United States. The expression "model republic" spread, with no corresponding increase in knowledge of America. Tocqueville was sharp enough to perceive public expectations. "We are leaving," he wrote, "with the aim of examining in detail and as scientifically as possible all the inner workings of this vast American society which everyone talks about and no one knows. And if events permit us the time, we plan to bring back the elements of a fine work, or at least of a new one; for there is nothing on this subject."[24]

In fact, the Americans had no Montesquieu to offer. "No great writers there have hitherto inquired into the general principles of legislation. The Americans have lawyers and commentators, but no jurists; and they furnish examples rather than lessons to the world" (*DA* 1:315). Thus Tocqueville's strength was his response to public concern for accommodating democracy—positioning himself in the new terrain of America, whose importance was already felt. He satisfied vague expectations by means of the fortunate match of a question of great currency with an almost unknown subject.

From the Plan to the Book: In Search of Moral Leadership

Conversion to Democracy

Thus Tocqueville went to the United States to find out how to think about democracy. The length of his stay did not seem equal to this ambition: nine months, from 11 May 1831 to 20 February 1832. An impatient minister and cholera raging in France hastened his return. Despite his rigorous survey methods, the period of observation was only a prelude to a second trip, one made in his mind. Yet the first was irreplaceable. The trip made a happy political man of a skeptical magistrate.

We can date the phases of this conversion. In New York, where he sojourned from 11 May to 2 July, Tocqueville was initially quite hesitant. This market society whose government was still in its infancy had nothing to entice a young aristocrat. "Everything I see fails to excite my enthusiasm," he noted at that time, "because I attribute more to the nature of things than to human will." But he could not keep from envying the patriotism of the American people and the ease with which they "kept themselves in order by the simple sentiment that there is no safeguard against oneself other than in oneself."[25] His conversion took place in Boston (7 September–3 October) where Tocqueville, discovering what well-ordered equality might mean, joined the side of democracy. In fact, democracy triumphed irresistibly. It was only at the end of September that he decided to write a book about American institutions to bear witness to the French that contented democracy could exist, for he had seen it. On 12 January 1832 he articulated his plan for the first time, beginning with his intention

> to describe very precisely what we can hope and fear from liberty. In France we have had anarchy and despotism in all their forms for a hundred years, but never anything which resembled a republic. If royalists could see the internal functioning of a well-ordered republic, the deep respect its people profess for their acquired rights, the power of those rights over crowds, the religion of law, the real and effective liberty people enjoy, the true rule of the majority, the easy and natural way things proceed, they would realize that they apply a single name to diverse forms of government which have nothing in common. Our republicans would feel that what we have called the Republic was never more than an unclassifiable monster . . . covered in blood and mud, clothed in the rags of antiquity's quarrels.[26]

Tocqueville thus returned from America invested with the duty to bear witness. The first volume of *Democracy,* which he published in 1835, bears the imprint of Tocqueville's vindicatory mission which makes it the handbook of modern democracy. *Democracy* is a work intended to assist a people in danger. "I believe," Tocqueville wrote, "that a person should have to account to society for one's thoughts as much as one's abilities. When one sees one's peers in peril, the obligation of every person is to come to their aid."[27]

And that was urgent. In Europe "the time was coming" when democracy would triumph. Tocqueville took on the stance of a John the Baptist of democracy, clamoring in the desert, Wake up before it is too late. The movement toward democracy "is not yet so fast that it cannot be guided. Their fate [of the European nations] is still in their own hands; but very soon they may lose control." He added, "And let it not be said that it is too late to try."[28] Opposing the resignation of the doomsayers, Tocqueville called on the French to take destiny in hand without delay—on the American model. Like prophets and sermonizers, Tocqueville argued that there were risks associated with "delayed conversion."

The meaning of Tocqueville's divine promulgation of democracy has been much debated. It is unclear. Tocqueville had no theology, and his invocation of Providence did not come from any evidence of divine presence. He also had no explicit teleology. As early as adolescence, he had been convinced that theory was useless or, even worse, a profitless burden. He wrote to his friend Charles Stöffels on 22 October 1831: "On the immense majority of things it is important for us to know, we have only probabilities, almosts. To despair that this is so is to despair of being a man, for that is one of the most inflexible laws of our nature. . . . I have always considered metaphysics and all the purely theoretical sciences, which serve no purpose in life's reality, to be voluntary torment that man has agreed to inflict on himself."[29] In 1858 he explained to the philosopher Bouchitté that the subtlest metaphysics gave no clearer information than the grossest common sense about why the world was as it was or about "the reason for the destiny of that singular being we call man, to whom just enough light has been given to show him the miseries of his condition and not enough to change them."[30] What a poor thing man is. Tocqueville brought Pascal's critique of the limitations of reason up to date to use against all those who postulated that rational discourse was identical to the real. Tocqueville's later hostility toward Hegel[31] would have no other origin than his rejection of secular providentialism and the disgust often felt by fine minds for speculation beyond common practice.

Thus recourse to Providence appeared in part as a rhetorical amplification of the defeat of the aristocracy, or as a consoling myth. Democracy's irresistible advance was essentially a historical fact on a wide scale, and Providence gave Tocqueville's intuition about the tendencies of social bodies the appeal of an objective law. Providence is the word for what was in fact perceived merely by intuition—what we feel, what is right in front of everyone but cannot be proved; what is based more on judgment than on savvy reason.

Invoking Providence thus meant being able to explain what was not scientifically demonstrable, and even more than that, choosing what was to be explained. If one was clever, one might discern the truth of Christian revelation—at last unveiled—within the show put on by the democratic world being born. In this democratic world Tocqueville perceived humanity's true picture, drawn with the simplicity of nature in which all are fellows.[32] Invoking Providence thus meant choosing to see the whole of human activity through the lens of Christian universalism, taking the side of working for a resolution to the duality between history and the end of history in the equal freedom of all God's children.

Thus conceived, recourse to Providence gives history no sense of necessity. "It is true that around every man a fatal circle is traced beyond which he cannot pass; but within the wide verge of that circle he is powerful and free; as it is with man, so with communities" (*DA* 2:334). Human equality and power are "irresistible," but human history, open to the possibility of freedom, is the fruit of cooperation between God and human beings. The affirmation of the irresistible nature of historical progression is thus continually eroded by the introduction of degrees and delays to such a level that Tocqueville, that famous "prophet," mainly used the language of prediction only to remind us of his rejection of absolute determinism.

A New Political Science

Recourse to Providence does not imply that for Tocqueville political science was some form of theology, phenomenology of mind, or natural history. Having affirmed both Providence and liberty in the same breath, Tocqueville could circumscribe his political field and thus seek within it some specific rationality. The first *Democracy* presents itself as an inquiry into democratic rule.

Tocqueville's approach was not without precedent: social inquiries began in the eighteenth century and had entered their golden age in the first half of the nineteenth century. Their primary focus was on social ills. Society was considered a living organism, its sickness betraying systemic dysfunction. Taking an interest in pauperization, criminality, and prostitution allowed one to diagnose society systematically in order to develop a remedy. Tocqueville's voyage was part of this great current within statistical and qualitative social inquiry, if only in its choice of focus on prisons, the subject more likely than any other to obtain an academic prize and public recognition. Regarding American society, in 1835 the French still had only the bitter and superficial tales of English travelers such as Basil Hall, Mrs. Trollope, or Hamilton and specialized studies by missionaries or civil engineers; Tocqueville's uniqueness lay in extending his investigation to American society as a whole.

Democracy retains little of this methodical style of inquiry.[33] Tocqueville always preferred the expository mode to narrative or description and stressed deductive clarity and a general approach. Although the frontispiece of the first *Democracy* reminds one of his *Penitentiary System*, there is nothing in the text itself that recalls Tocqueville's prison study or the book he wrote about it.[34] The book tells us almost nothing of his trip;[35] its author's self appears almost exclusively to pronounce moral judgments universal in application. Tocqueville was sufficiently wary of offending the tastes of the era to explain away his silences with polite reasons—one must be brief so as not to wear out one's audience of fine readers; discretion is obligatory in the observer who gathers confidences. Yet it is hard to imagine what his American interlocutors would have lost of their patriotic pride by having it divulged. Rejecting the picturesque and the singular is more a matter of style than discretion. Tocqueville preferred expository clarity to the illusion of reality created by abundant documentation. "I am more and more persuaded," he wrote, "that general effect is the first among a book's merits and that one must have the heart to make what sacrifices are necessary to attain it."[36] It is not the absence of facts in the classical writing style, ruled by preference for the general, which should surprise us—it is their presence. Every tale stands as a rhetorical figure, and Tocqueville introduces into his works only what he calls "general facts," exempla in the sermonic tradition.

As an example, let us examine the way he studies the survival of the aristocracy in the United States.

> Mark, for instance, that opulent citizen, who is as anxious as a Jew of the Middle Ages to conceal his wealth. His dress is plain, his demeanor unassuming; but the interior of his dwelling glitters with luxury, and none but a few chosen guests, whom he haughtily styles his equals, are allowed to penetrate into this sanctuary. No European noble is more exclusive in his pleasures or more jealous of the smallest advantages that a privileged position confers. But the same individual crosses the city to reach a dark countinghouse in the center of traffic, where everyone may accost him who pleases. If he meets his cobbler on the way, they stop and converse; the two citizens discuss affairs of the state and shake hands before they part. (*DA* 1:180)

This tale, drawn from life using travel notes, has an illustrative role and is not meant as evidence. Generalities are dominant: of the main character, we know only his opulence, luxury, and insolence. Description is replaced by appeal to common experience, for example, the conventional comparison between the European nobleman and the Jew of the Middle Ages also found in Michel Chevalier's writing. Even the choice of the antagonistic figures of rich man and shoemaker recalls La Fontaine and emphasizes type over individual. There is nothing unexpected about the actors' conduct: the prophetic future tense of the original makes certain that they will not part before discussing affairs of state and, gives the example all the impact of an object lesson. This is less a description than an attempt to convince by including the reader in the tale through resorting to the demonstrative, "Mark, for instance, that opulent citizen." The very construction of this little play, in which inequality at the last moment turns to equality, shows how conventional the equality proclaimed is and denounces political democracy as a mystifying universe.

Thus political science for Tocqueville consisted much more of knowing how to judge and string ideas together than in knowing the details of institutions and customs. "One must not be concerned with uttering the most complete truth, but with the most readily grasped and the most useful truths";[37] the only aim of his study of the American republic was to develop the art of accommodating democracies. "My aim," wrote Tocqueville, "has been to show, by the example of America, that laws, and especially customs, may allow a democratic people to remain free" (*DA* 1:329).

In America, Tocqueville first of all found affirmation of his rejection of government by notables. In 1830 Guizot and the Doctrinaires had turned the vote into a function reserved for the Enlightenment's aristocracy. According to Tocqueville, the Doctrinaires' cult of reason and Enlightenment served to mask a conflict of interest. Social divisions constituted societies: rich and poor were "two rival nations which have existed since the beginning of the world."[38] There is thus no wise legislator able to utter the Good, no government for all, and in fact no mixed government that keeps the scales balanced between contradictory interests. Property-owning voters could claim as much as as they liked to be repositories of the public good: the truth about the notables' system was that it meant bourgeois domination, just as the truth about democratic rule meant domination by the majority. All regimes were class regimes.[39]

Middle-class rule was established in France in 1830, an unstable and illegitimate compromise between divine-right sovereignty and popular sovereignty. Its main effect was to ruin the prosperity it claimed to ensure. By keeping the majority of citizens out of power, it inculcated indifference to the res publica. The competence of experts in state matters allowed them to drain the nation of its strength by maintaining "a drowsy regularity in the conduct of affairs which the heads of administration are wont to call good order and public tranquillity" (*DA* 1:90). Tocqueville sided with what an American had told him, and it was hardly democratic: "The people often lack common sense, but still the machine functions and the state prospers."[40]

Setting aside popular controversies for and against the republic, because democracy was irresistible whether one went toward it willingly or reluctantly and the system based on ability would never achieve "anything great or durable,"[41] Tocqueville sought the "key to the great social enigma" that is the existence of a happy republic. The difficulty obviously lay in setting aside the memories of the Terror that haunted the French.[42] In 1835 Tocqueville was obsessed by Rousseau and terrified of the all-powerful nature of popular sovereignty. All his efforts thus were devoted to presenting an anti-Rousseauian notion of popular sovereignty, by showing how such sovereignty was compatible with liberty, provided power was highly decentralized and popularly debated in the press.

Decentralized: to the French notion of a unified, indivisible sovereignty, Tocqueville contrasted the American concept of a mass of communities. He also rejected the Rousseauian cult of general will and the Thermidorians' individualistic liberalism.

But self-government was only one aspect of society's self-regulation. Tocqueville turned all of social life into a great school for responsibility—the legal system, for example, with citizen participation on juries, and public opinion, with discussions of parties and newspapers, both of which he referred to by the generic term *association*. As a polemic, Tocqueville's argument was directed against the conservative wave of liberal and Doctrinaire public commentators who so early on showed themselves unfaithful to the liberty they had called for under the Restoration with passage of the law of 16 February 1834 against town-crying and the sale of newspapers, that of 10 April 1834 on associations, and the one of September 1835 against republican newspapers. Tocqueville's entire strategy consisted of showing that the order so dear to conservatives could only be ensured by the very freedom of assembly they denied the French citizen—we have launched our ship, now we must take the risk. There was no middle ground between servitude and the other extreme of liberty. Any politics that attempted to stop history, any dream of an established order, belonged to "one of those illusions which commonly mislead nations in their times of sickness."[43] Democracy was not the site of any miraculous feeling of identity among people but a form of government caught in the relations between classes in conflict.

In 1835 this necessary dispersion of power was less important to Tocqueville than that the exercise of power be controlled. He sought less to revive democracy through popular participation than to temper it in order to furnish guarantees to minority populations. This is why he combined democratic liberalism with a defensive liberalism concerned with protecting individuals and tempering the power of the majority. "I am therefore of the opinion that social power superior to all others must always be placed somewhere; but I think that liberty is endangered when this power finds no obstacle which can retard its course and give it time to moderate its own vehemence" (*DA* 1:260). Tocqueville had retained the notion developed by thinkers about representative government—Sieyès, Constant, Guizot—that politics obeys the rules of social division of labor. The people are "incapable" of governing, even of choosing well, precisely because they are the people, stuck in the material necessities of their existence (*DA* 1:201–2). But Tocqueville's strength was in going beyond the received wisdom which pitted democracy against representation to show that the two-step election process was part of the very nature of democracies, in which the public good stems from competing opinions that are purified through the process of selecting representatives.

This is how we can explain the recognized importance of the second chamber, elected in two stages. For Tocqueville, the senate's function was not to be the conservatory of the nobility in some indulgent concession to the nation's past but to preserve a space for deliberation which he neatly called "the time to sit." Thanks to the two-step election process[44] and legislative debate between the two houses, the senate brought plurality to the expression of national will. Majority opinion, upon learning majority was not unanimity, learned to take the minority into account, thus braking majority power without doing away with it. That American invention of the two chambers, the serendipitous effect of a federated constitution, remained to be instituted in France in some artful way.

The powers of the judiciary and of religion were the other cornerstones of Tocqueville's liberal structure made of temperaments and balancings. Justice and religion, through their emphasis on rights, served to block democracy's excesses and introduced human and divine tribunals to which the oppressed might appeal.

Thus Tocqueville's book presented, both full-face and in profile, the idea he had conceived at the start of his project: to teach the French, deprived of political education, the secrets of gradually organizing a democracy. "Secrets," for though all the West might be growing just one crop—democracy—the analogy does not imply that every society was carrying out the work of equality in the same way, or that one could serve as model to the others. Democratic institutions were less important to a society's topography than where it began, that is, the circumstances and history which fashioned its customs.[45] Tocqueville was suggesting spiritual exercises for becoming democratic to his contemporaries—not importing an American model erected as the goal of history.

Tocqueville and Public Space: *Democracy*'s Readers

Tocqueville had sought to write the handbook of democratic transition. The work's aim determined its audience, who were not partisans. *Democracy* sets itself apart from the confused melee of political passions, and as a result its introduction recalls the prologue to Rousseau's *Confessions:* "This book is written to favor no particular views" (*DA* 1:16). In the same vein, Tocqueville wrote in 1840: "If the readers of my book find in it a single phrase intended to flatter either of the great parties that have agitated our country, or any one of the petty factions that in our day harass and weaken it, let them raise their voices and accuse me" (*DA* 2:vii).

Tocqueville taught the spirit of their religion to republicans who had become atheists because of their revolutionary memories. To those who blindly thought of return to the monarchy of Henry IV or Louis XIV, he taught equality. Yet he gave his two audiences unequal attention. While many democrats were not estimable,[46] ancien régime partisans believed in courage, patriotism, generosity, and the Enlightenment (*DA* 1:13). All these conservatives would tend toward democracy of their own accord if the republicans' muddleheaded fanaticism did not dissuade them. Are these hints in Tocqueville of an inherited preference? On this count, aristocratic prejudice matters less than historic vision. Tocqueville did not believe measured evolution toward democracy possible except under the direction of the enlightened classes. The "public," coextensive in theory with the community of French people, in fact was limited to the elites. If a new political science was needed for a brand-new world, it was for use by "the most powerful, the most intelligent, and the most moral classes of the nation," by "those virtuous and peaceful individuals whose pure morality, quiet habits, opulence, and talents fit them to be the leaders of their fellow men"[47] and who constituted "public opinion," formed by the collective use of critical reasoning.

No doubt Tocqueville did imagine his audience would grow larger as democracy progressed, as people's knowledge grew and suffrage expanded correspondingly. But for all that, he did not believe that political elites would disappear nor, as Michelet did, fool himself that he was writing for the people. The need for elites was a result of the functional division of labor in any society, even the most democratic.[48] The audience he targeted was the two social halves of the era's elites: jurists, an aristocracy of specialists, and "men of the world," the repositories of common sense.

Such an image of the public determined the work's character, which sought both weight and brevity. Weightiness alone was worthy of notables; brevity was a gesture of politeness toward the man of the world, who was easily wearied. It is also Tocqueville's rejection of specialization and insistence on the universality of political eloquence, translated stylistically. Thus nothing is farther from erudite affectation than Tocqueville's works, to such a degree that precision in them suffers as a result, in the author's own opinion: "Yet how can I be clear and at the same time brief? I can scarcely hope to escape these different evils. Ordinary readers will complain that I am tedious, lawyers that I am too concise" (*DA* 1:141). The philosophical and legal imprecision of Tocqueville's language and the insufficiency of his analyses have been criticized since the end of the nineteenth century. This criticism ignores Tocqueville's desire to be read by all members of the political class.

This concern with provoking collective decisions rather than arousing learned controversies is clear from the way the book was published. Tocqueville affectedly claimed to be above the passions and tastes of his day in his speculation about his likely lack of success. But there was nothing of the naive writer in exile about him. The connection between the masterful writer and his participation in public life is the driving force of his biography. Seeking to forge a meeting of the minds, he worked just as hard to ensure the distribution of his work as to write in the common language of right-thinking people.

Tocqueville first had his manuscript copied in 1834 so he could submit it to his father and brothers whose corrections are preserved in the Beinecke Library. As he wrote, he read the work to Kergorlay, a legitimist and a childhood friend, and to Beaumont. Bouchitté, a Versailles professor, endured four successive readings. The fascination the work holds over readers derives in part from this plural writing practice, which took others' objections into account and remained open to uncertainty. From his publisher Tocqueville sought only technical assistance in production and commercial help with distribution. Let us follow the negotiations which led to publication of the work on 21 January 1835. They will illuminate the author's intentions as much as they will the reception of his work.

Tocqueville did not want a publisher who specialized. Thus Fournier, who had published *Penitentiary System,* was no longer suitable. In 1834 Tocqueville signed a contract with Charles Gosselin, who had published Sir Walter Scott, Lamartine, James Fenimore Cooper, Hugo, and Balzac and had a solid relationship with the press.[49] The agreement was marked by great mutual wariness:

Tocqueville committed to just one edition, for France alone; Gosselin printed only a trial run, to gain a sense of the market. This was common practice. In fact, the self-educated Gosselin was not an authority on a work's quality and rarely read his authors. He was "the least intellectual man in the world," Tocqueville wrote; "he saw in ideas only a means of making money."[50] And indeed Tocqueville's self-esteem was ruffled:

> If the aforementioned Gosselin had read my manuscript, the result of [my trip] would not have been flattering for me, for to the degree to which I answered his questions about the book's subject, I saw fear begin to run rampant in him. And he finally said he would only print 500 copies. I seemed astonished by this latter resolution, and thus he explained his motives to me: it is not *much* more expensive, true, to print 1,000 rather than 500. But if the work does not sell, one *loses* all that surplus. When, on the contrary, one must print a second edition, it costs more than if one had first printed the necessary number, but one is on a more certain path. In the first way of doing things, one is less likely to *lose*; in the other, one is likely to *earn less*. Given the state of bookselling, one must resolve to target small, secure profits. I found this fairly reasonable, but the result is still that he is quite afraid either of losing or of earning little with me.[51]

Gosselin was well able to side with success, however. Three months after the first edition, he welcomed Tocqueville "with the most radiant face in the world: 'Well then! it seems you have written a masterpiece!'"[52] Yet successive editions of the first *Democracy* brought about no change in his initial contract. Gosselin never made more than cautious print runs in answer to obvious demand; Tocqueville never saw him as anything other than an "enemy," "fat cheeks," or "the factory man."

True, the work's success was doubtful. The public disliked political literature, hurt by the competition among newspapers. Pamphlets and brochures alone attracted interest, and their number swelled during crisis periods, only to drop thereafter. This emphasis placed on current events gave a cyclic character to all intellectual production in political economy, politics, and administration. High points marked changes in government (1815, 1830–31) and, to a lesser degree, changes in reign (1820) or periods of disturbance (1827–29). Beyond these times of crisis, only an author's notoriety might snatch a work from anonymity.[53] The popularity of works on America grew steadily from the Restoration until 1848, but this curve had two peaks, 1830–31 and 1848, a sign that America was interesting mainly as a controversial model of the republic. Tocqueville's book was published in a downward phase of the cycle for general political literature and political periodicals, and for books on the United States in particular. In 1835 it responded to the questions current during 1830–31.

In such a difficult market and in a country where politics was rarely the object of serious scholarship, how could *Democracy* have become a bestseller? Tocqueville's strategy hardly seems innovative, at least at first glance. He drew on his network of familial and professional relations, and the only unusual thing he did was to refuse to publish galleys or even chapter headings in advance to tempt readers. "I am convinced," he wrote, "that I will only show myself to my own disadvantage by revealing myself in so detailed a fashion and that favorable impressions, if they are to exist, can come only from the whole of the book."[54] There was no anticipated reading at the Academy or in any of those places where opinions were formed. Tocqueville was aware of the nature of his talent, which was more likely to seduce by ruminating on a few key ideas than by seeking an effect, formula, or paradox that would make a success of the galleys.

Thus nothing[55] seemed to predestine the work of this young author, known only as a specialist on prisons, to brilliant success. The profusion of reviews and public interest surprised everyone, starting with Gosselin, who had been content to run a few noisy notices and beg public subscriptions.[56] But three print runs (in January, June, and late 1835) reached about 2,000 copies. Editions four through seven, from 1836 to 1839, put about 4,000 more copies into circulation. Outside France, at least four Belgian editions, Spanish, German, and Greek editions, plus a limited Danish edition attest to the work's success. *Democracy* enjoyed lively success in England, which surprised Tocqueville most of all, "clever people . . . having predicted that it would not sell, and that the publisher would lose his money. But in this century of democratic revolution, everything about democracy sells, in any language."[57]

It is hard for us to assess how unusual it was to print about 6,000 copies in five years. Lack of systematic record keeping and the many smaller runs made possible by the printing technology of the era make any quantitative evaluation uncertain. However, if we take 500 to 1,000 copies as an average figure for political titles, we can estimate that *Democracy* went beyond ordinary bounds for its genre.

So Tocqueville had glory—without the popularity. More widely distributed abroad and better received in France than most political works, *Democracy* never reached the masses, who in any case did not participate in national political life. The book's reception was bounded by the narrow space of "public life" during the first half of the nineteenth century.

Letters and newspapers allow us to discern who Tocqueville's readers were. *Democracy*'s rapid success was helped by Tocqueville's reputation as an expert on prisons. *Penitentiary System*, published in 1833 by Tocqueville and Beaumont, is often disregarded today, because it seems written more out of opportunity than out of intellectual necessity. And even at that, Tocqueville left most of the work to his co-author, writing up little more than the statistical notes. Yet the work played an essential role in *Democracy*'s reception by the social network into which it integrated its author.

Under the July Monarchy philanthropic specialization was the fashionable public commentator's indispensable calling card, and the penitentiary question was assuredly the topic with the highest status.[58] By forging his public role as specialist quite deliberately, Tocqueville won a political role, academic status, and international renown all at the same time, to such degree that to discredit him, his adversaries shamelessly called him "Prison Reformer Tocqueville."[59] He served as rapporteur to the Chamber on plans for prison reform in June 1840 and July 1843 and in 1836 won the Montyon Prize of the Académie Française for *Democracy*, as he had for *Penitentiary System* three years earlier. Rapid publication of English and German translations ensured him pride of place among humanitarians in Europe and the United States.[60]

Penitentiary System was important not only for the useful connections it brought Tocqueville. Philanthropy and political thinking were inseparable under the July Monarchy. To the regime's partisans, who were convinced they had finally ended the Revolution, crime seemed the tail end of the political upheavals that had ceased. On the other hand, for republicans and legitimists, criminality was proof of the regime's perversity, a symptom of present evil, not the residue of old dysfunction. This is how the reception of *Penitentiary System* could prefigure that of *Democracy*.

On the one side, the legitimists dominated in their appreciation of Tocqueville as scion of a great family, humanitarian and intellectual critic of the regime.[61] On the other, republicans[62] and the Protestants[63] were favorable to America on principle. The praises in 1833 for *Penitentiary System* were the same as those proffered in 1835. The "impartiality," moral sense, concern for the possible, and attention to political cultures in their diversity won approval.

Democracy, less specialized, found a wider audience. It received about thirty reviews in the French press, plus sporadic mentions and articles in the foreign press. Three books were written about it by United States experts, the American Eugene A. Vail, the Frenchman Poussin, and the German Duden.[64] In criticizing Tocqueville's superficial brilliance, their aim was to capture for themselves the interest *Democracy* incited. In Guillaume Tell Poussin's work, this actually became malevolent plagiarism. Poussin's *Considérations sur le principe démocratique qui régit l'union américaine et de la possibilité de son application à d'autres états* plagiarized the first *Democracy*.[65] His *De la puissance américaine* plagiarized the second. Poussin was no neophyte. He had emigrated to the United States in 1815 as an expert in railroads and public works and had begun a fertile if not a glorious literary career on his return to France in 1832. Public works, political institutions—anything would serve to praise America. He thought he had found the path to success with his "critical examination" of *Democracy*. "My goal," he stated with hypocritical modesty, "is to have the work I examine better appreciated through those facts and conclusions which it seems to me go most directly to satisfying the author's aim, by rectifying those which my experience makes me feel are less correct and by removing entirely those which are foreign to it" (9). He then either inserted mountains of quotations , often not presented as such, or accumulations of statistical data on the country's geography, school system, and treatment of its civil servants. The distance he took from Tocqueville is only the result of a wish to praise the United States at all costs. Tocqueville was wrong to believe that the wealthy had retreated from politics and that the press had committed excesses; he had been misled by abolitionist propaganda—and so on. Poussin never rose to any typological reflection on political societies. Plagiarism is homage the mediocre give the talented and shows both *Democracy*'s success and the originality of its approach to commonplaces.

There are other signs of its success. There were plays on its title, so much had the book become an obligatory reference point: *De la démocratie dans les sociétés modernes* (Guizot, 1837), *De la démocratie nouvelle* (Alletz, 1837), *De la démocratie en France* (Guizot, 1849), *L'aristocratie en Amérique* (Gaillardet, 1883). The author was presented at the most exclusive salons: at the duchesse de Dino's, where old Talleyrand, Royer-Collard, Berryer, and the duc de Noailles were often seen; at Mme d'Aguesseau's, Mme Ancelot's, and Mme Récamier's at the Abbaye-au-Bois. Tocqueville was so weighted down by praise that he was "always tempted to do as those new nobles in Bonaparte's court who, not recognizing their names, move aside to make way for themselves upon entering a salon the first time they are announced by their titles."[66]

Yet Tocqueville's audience remained quite limited. People of letters hardly read him at all.[67] As early as 1835 the separation between literature and what was later called the human sciences had begun. On one hand, there were the new forms of fiction—the realism of Balzac-style novels, the great popular novels of Alexandre Dumas and Eugène Sue—on the other, the belles lettres, the Academy's and the *Journal des Débats*'s bastions of traditionalism. Among literary critics, only Sainte-Beuve and Villemain took an interest in Tocqueville.[68] But then, Villemain was an Academy man charged with awarding the Montyon Prize, and Sainte-Beuve was the Academy's spirit incarnate even before he was elected to it.

To understand the antagonism between these two notions, we would do well to listen to Balzac in 1842 describing the "unibible author," his words cleverly, nastily illustrated by a caricature of Tocqueville dashing toward the Institut de France, that institution for good behavior invented for serious and literary thinkers of conviction. The extraordinary author had managed

> to make a book that is moral, governmental, philosophic, philanthropic all at the same time, from which one can excerpt a few more or less fine-sounding pages for any occasion. . . . His name can never again be spoken except accompanied by this long epithet: "Mister Marphurius who did Germany and the Germans." It becomes a title, a fiefdom. And what a fief! It produces a swarm of decorations sent from every court and entitles one to some section or another at the Institut.

Tocqueville's success? Balzac attributed it to snobbery of the potbellied bourgeoisie who run to buy some Tocqueville, pursuing the intelligence that escapes them. It looked good socially, displayed nicely on bookshelves—but reading that dead weight! "They excuse themselves from reading it while claiming that they have."[69] This satire, turned acid by the literati's envious hatred toward overly well-to-do political writers, pulls together all the defining qualities of political writers, of which Tocqueville was the exemplar with his gravity of tone, concern for public recognition, and dual career in letters and statesmanship.

No references to Tocqueville were made in periodicals for young people, women, or the masses like *La Mosaïque*, Charton's *Le Magasin Pittoresque*, or Emile de Girardin's *Le Musée des Familles*. Here, James Fenimore Cooper's image of America won out, of the Indians' and pioneers' primitive El Dorado. Tocqueville would have no place in *Le Musée des Familles* or *Le Magasin Pittoresque* until later, when *The Old Regime and the French Revolution* and especially his letters were published. By that time Tocqueville seemed less America's political commentator and more a moralist whose basis was solid principles useful to youth: submission to duty, the taste for work well done, love of France.

Tocqueville's work, useless to women, the masses, and the literati, all people of passion more than of reason, found an exclusive spot within the public political arena[70] whose precise outlines it mirrors. Newspapers pillaged *Democracy* freely.[71] The academies used Tocqueville to guide their thinking. And early on Tocqueville sought from them social recognition of his intellectual authority. As early as 1835 or 1836, he was a member—albeit not a very active one—of the learned societies of Cherbourg and Versailles, the better to support his electoral maneuvers. A two-time winner of the Académie Française's Montyon Prize, he was evermore in the Institut de France's good graces and on 6 January 1838 was elected to the Academy of Moral Sciences. In its haste to capture the young lion, the Institut created a vacant spot in its Academy of Moral and Political Sciences by transferring Jouffroy into philosophy. Tocqueville had won a seat in the parliament of ideas.[72] For the rest of the nineteenth century, the Academy of Moral Sciences would be the privileged harbor of his thought.

But for Tocqueville, academies were merely an entrée into the world of politics. *Democracy* served as his electoral platform,[73] or rather as a pledge of progressive leanings quite useful to the son of a Carlist family. It mattered little in fact whether the austere book was read. "When a voter," wrote a friend of Tocqueville's, "asks me 'What in reality are M. de Tocqueville's opinions?' I say to him, 'Have you read his *Democracy*?' 'Of course' the voter answers me, who certainly has not read it. 'Well, isn't that enough for you?' And the voter is satisfied."[74] After 1835 Tocqueville's name almost always appeared with "celebrated author of *Democracy*" trailing after it.[75]

Yet Tocqueville did not enter the Chamber easily. Political commentators were hardly rare within its walls. The regime was proud to have a few very able men among those elected, and solid knowledge of the American system was welcome in parliamentary debate. Tocqueville was ill served by the noble origins used against him successfully in the 1837 elections. Yet by 1835 he had gained the esteem of senior politicians of all stripes. His work was cited at the podium—not without a certain bad faith.[76] But even the most abusive appropriation had its importance: "You must be a considerable public commentator for an orator to invoke your name in one of the chambers."[77] Throughout the nineteenth century Tocqueville's work lent itself to polemical purposes—according to some, because of its vagueness, and according to others, because of its subtlety. Subtle or vague, the work in any case owed its success to this indeterminacy. "I please many people of conflicting opinions," wrote Tocqueville, "not because they understand me, but because they find in my work, by considering it only from a single side, arguments favorable to their passion of the moment."[78]

If Tocqueville was pulled in so many directions, it was because he was deemed impartial due to his contradictory roots in the ancien régime and the new society. As Malesherbes's great-grandson and an admirer of Jefferson, it was hard for him to take sides. Praise of his "touching probity"[79] led him to decide against himself and his class. He immediately seemed the man desperately needed in the Chamber who would by his free spirit reveal Reason within conflicts of interest. Legitimists, those in the ministries, and dynastic opposition agreed that "as remarkable talent arises, the duty and interest of the government is to bring it into the sphere where the various powers created by the constitution are in motion." The problem was that "the very grandeur of [Tocqueville's] talent was prejudicial to him."[80] His political failures, the oblique reading his work received, and the polite indifference given his parliamentary perorations pointed to the failure of the ideal of Reason promoted by the July regime.

Despite the praises given this new Montesquieu, Tocqueville's work was immediately caught up in the conflicts of interest. Well received by legitimists and the opposition, including republicans and socialists, it was hardly to the taste of the partisans of power.

For legitimists, Tocqueville held two assets, his family and his philanthropic speciality. Very early on legitimists favorable to representative government wrote long, and often severe, analyses of his work.[81] But those who remained faithful to absolute monarchy were silent about it, to such degree that having read Tocqueville marked the division within the legitimist current.[82]

On the other side, the constitutional Left, republicans, and even socialists were much kinder. A center-left newspaper, *Le Courrier Français,* was chosen to launch the book's prepublication press campaign on 24 December 1834. On 25 February and 4 March 1835, the liberal Protestant paper *Le Semeur* devoted a long analysis to *Democracy* which particularly satisfied Tocqueville. In June, Corcelle, a former Carbonaro who had conspired against despotism in Italy, wrote a well-researched article for the *Revue des Deux Mondes* which began an enduring friendship between the two men.

Tocqueville met with an especially resounding welcome among republicans. *Le National* made him their spokesman against the *Débats* throughout 1835. *Le Bon Sens* ran two articles about him in early February. Louis Blanc in the *Revue Républicaine* (April and May 1835) and Cerisé in Buchez's paper *L'Européen* (November and December 1835) used the opportunity to discuss their political doctrines at length. Neither Beaumont nor Chevalier were similarly honored. The private papers of Cabet and Proudhon show the sympathy of the theoreticians of socialism themselves.[83] Though Tocqueville gained no points with republicans or socialists because of family, profession, or ties of friendship, he gave them food for thought just when the American model had lost its attraction and they had begun tearing each other apart over the meaning of the Republic. In reading Tocqueville, republicans were called to choose between pluralist democracy and absolute republic, between civil society divided by conflicts of interest and affirming national sovereignty.[84]

Early legitimist and republican commentary contrasts sharply with the reserve toward the book shown by partisans of power. The latter's delayed commentary accompanied Tocqueville's success rather than creating it.[85] And even at that, their main objective was to reject any potential application of the American model to France—to deny any practical import to Tocqueville's work. Even worse, in 1837 Tocqueville became for this group the symbol of the egalitarian frenzy sweeping France. The attack was launched in April 1837 by Edouard Alletz's book *De la démocratie nouvelle,* whose title echoed Tocqueville's. The *Journal des Débats, Le Moniteur,* the *Revue des Deux Mondes,*[86] and ultimately Guizot himself in an anonymous article in the *Revue Française* in October 1837 all quickly gave Alletz's work a reception as triumphant as it was undeserved. On the other hand, *Le Siècle,* an enthusiastic supporter of Tocqueville's October–November electoral campaign, ran two very critical reviews of Alletz's book and Guizot's praises of it on 26 November and 26 December. This political antagonism signified radical opposition in doctrine. For Alletz, the Doctrinaires' pale champion, democracy's march was nothing more than a societal return to childhood. The future lay in the preponderance of the middle classes whose importance Tocqueville had underestimated.

The opposition between Tocqueville and Guizot had started before Tocqueville's departure for America. Now it burst forth in 1837, and political life made it much nastier until 1848.[87] Alletz against Tocqueville was, at a philosophical level, Guizot's war against the rest of France. The combatants' mismatch shows how tightly the Doctrinaires were clinging to a conservative status quo, while public opinion was turning toward democracy. Aristocrat Tocqueville on the side of democracy symbolized the tactical alliance of legitimists, the Left opposition, and republicans[88] against the now-conservative Doctrinaires whose infidelity to the cause of liberty he revealed.

Thus Tocqueville's thought did not go over well in the regime's camp. It mainly attracted those whose political views were changing—legitimists coming around to democracy, republicans recently disappointed with America. Tocqueville himself as a thinker was tormented, uncertain what shape the future would take. His most important contribution was a culture of opposition, rather than one of a regime, and the sketch of a dream, not a painting of reality. *Democracy* was an event because it gave shape to fears about the July regime's stability. "Those very people who have condemned innovative attempts when they turn into the turbulence of demonstrations cannot mistake this voice which whispers in the bowels of Europe, growing and rising little by little, awakening every human creature, rousing and disturbing them with its unknown, powerful words."[89] All opponents agreed on the poor education French democracy had provided, "dreamy, uncertain, and revolutionary."[90]

This is why Tocqueville can be viewed as part of the lineage of writers who joined fidelity to the past with sullen allegiance to democracy, like Chateaubriand and Stendhal. Their common denominator is an aristocratic sensibility nostalgic for intellectual distinction even more than social distinction, combined with a democratic call for civil equality and freedom of conscience. The family resemblance lies more in this common sensibility that causes them to act in concert than in mutual influences.

Tocqueville is the theoretical match of the Romanesque world created by Stendhal in *Lucien Leuwen,* the novel about Orleanist power that Stendhal abandoned in November 1835 several months after *Democracy* came out. *Lucien Leuwen* depicts the fall of the July regime. Its hero Lucien is another Tocqueville, torn between a past he rejects and an uncertain future, sensitive to social instability and as infatuated with honor as Don Quixote. For Stendhal, as for Tocqueville, America may prefigure France's future. But if they admire its political regime, they detest what Stendhal called its "abominable vulgarity." Although there is convergence between them, *Democracy* was only important to Stendhal as confirmation of an earlier image of the United States. Stendhal's admiration for American institutions was in fact quite precocious. As early as 1805 he planned to move to Louisiana. The idea of less government and his admiration for representative government came from reading Destutt's *Commentaire sur l'esprit des lois* in 1817 and from spending more time with Lafayette after 1821. Stendhal's scant taste for American customs only increased as he read Tocqueville. He shared the distaste of his friend Victor Jacquemont, who in 1828 had returned from the United States very critical of it.[91]

With Tocqueville and Chateaubriand, the family resemblance in sensibility is more obvious. Chateaubriand was already an old man during the era of *Democracy,* and he did not need his young nephew to learn about democracy's advances. Yet he read the younger man's work attentively and complimented him with the affected modesty that was common to him: "People were already talking about me a little when I saw you as a child at Verneuil. In your turn, you will see me in infancy: people will talk of you and I will be forgotten" (unpublished letter of 11 January 1835). In *Democracy,* Chateaubriand found a companion to his final reflections and confirmation of the rightness of his intellectual journey.[92]

Could Tocqueville's work—aided by the fears of its era—influence common sense in things political the way Stendhal and Chateaubriand were able to do in the realm of imagination?

The New Political Science

Handbook for the New Era

In 1835 its opening axiom made *Democracy* successful: the rise of equality is irresistible and providential. Literary histories and bibliographic entries reduce the book to this premise, as if Tocqueville had been satisfied with spinning out the metaphor of the overflowing river of democracy sweeping away the past in its course.

The emphasis given to the introduction's radical rhetoric can be explained by its polemical character. Tocqueville was trying to speak forcefully. Accepting democracy was what separated the Left from every partisan of the status quo, represented in the government by the Doctrinaires. Dissent was not about the existence of Providence at work in history—there was no doubt about this in the historicist nineteenth century. Rather there was disagreement about the nature of Providence's design. For some, Providence tended to maintain natural inequalities. For others, it prescribed equality in civil rights combined with real inequalities considered collectively useful. And for still others, on the Left, there was defense of the idea of irresistible progress toward material equality for all. Thus debate on Tocqueville's providentialism underscores the ambiguity in the notion of equality of condition.

Counterrevolutionaries criticized Tocqueville for resigning himself to universal social leveling by proclaiming its inevitable triumph. As early as 1835 they called Tocqueville a criminal or, even worse, an idolator for having denounced the vulgarity of democracies so thoroughly without fighting them. For Custine, there was nothing worse than Tocqueville's "providential politics." Christ did not come to found a party of Christian democrats;[93] the spiritual was not the same as the temporal. In fact, if God had to choose, he would, according to Custine, lean toward the aristocracy, for

> there is no equality in any of the Creator's immediate works, neither material ones nor spiritual ones. That is the work of human pride, the product of popular jealousy. . . . Rule of the earth must belong to certain men of great character who sacrifice things to ideas or to the masses, which prefer and will always prefer the pleasure of riches to the pleasure of thought! There is a choice to be made between the reign of the spirit of goodwill and the reign of necessary material things.[94]

As a Christian democrat, Tocqueville was thus an inconsequential Christian. What of his talent, honesty, faith? His greater lucidity than Lamennais? Those were even worse. By pushing the infinite into politics, exploiting Providence to promote democracy, he was guilty of a new Gallican-style impiety making the church serve the throne. He was cheating others and himself as well, "an error no less fatal than a crime, in a world where evildoers so cleverly use the weapons given them by the good."[95]

The Doctrinaires did not go so far in their critique. They did not reject Providence's predilection for equality, but this predilection only applied to equality of civil rights. While they indeed shared Tocqueville's vision of the democratic river, all their efforts consisted in staunching its destructive power. Whence Guizot's virulence toward Tocqueville:

> Some have said that we could meditate and pontificate as much as we like regarding current society, but all our meditations and all our words would be in vain, and that there was, fortunately or unfortunately, a fait accompli, a parti pris, and we could do nothing about it, we would do nothing about it. Yes, there is a fait accompli, we certainly hope so. But is it perfect and fixed as well as accomplished? Is there nothing to be said about it, nothing to do? I cannot have such utter disregard for the human spirit in general, or especially for the wisdom of my own time.[96]

For Guizot, Tocqueville's proclamation of the autonomy of individual will to the detriment of the rights of Truth, as Truth shows itself to enlightened minds, destroyed morality. Guizot is no philosopher of liberty. For him, liberty in human beings is only the power to obey Truth. The notion of ability, which betrays his social narrow-mindedness, is also related to a theory of reason and a theology positing an economics of salvation which invests seekers after Right with the mission to guide humanity.

This argument of Guizot's was found among all writers concerned with preserving the elites. Tocqueville had mistaken bourgeois domination as a brief transition when in fact it was the future of humanity. He had not grasped "the genius of the class to whom Providence had given the destinies of the political world." He would have found it "the subject of a great and fine book" to study how in France the bourgeoisie "came to possess power in such plenitude and security as to permit a principle to develop its consequences so broadly."[97]

To defend their inegalitarian "providential politics," legitimists and ministry officials found in *Democracy* weighty ammunition: material equality in 1835 came more from intuition about the future than empirical evidence. American history opportunely showed this. Tocqueville had made slavery an accident of history, foreign to the democratic character of American society. New York's race riots from the summer of 1834 to the summer of 1835 showed how untenable that position was. On 2 February 1835 the legitimist *Gazette de France* accused Tocqueville of asking Europe to admire "a country of tricolored humanity, where the red men who are indigenous watch themselves being exterminated by white men who usurp their places, where black men are sold pell-mell along with beasts of burden in the public squares. A touching example of equality, admirable proof of independence." Ministerial officials[98] and legitimists used this tension between egalitarian principles and real inequalities to show that democracy was an incomprehensible monster. From the existence of racism, they deduced the lie of democracy. Equality was merely "fictive" in the land of the "self-proclaimed republicans." In the South blacks were slaves; in the North they had only the "nominal liberty" that whites had given them out of self-interest.[99] Thus democracy merely had its own shameful hierarchy, proof that there was no social form possible other than a hierarchical one. The truth of democracy was aristocracy, an aristocracy more cruel for being masked.

On the other hand, republicans made Tocqueville the prophet of alliance with the Republic. They approved his demonstration that the movement from civil to political rights was irresistible. *Le Bon Sens* cited long passages from his introduction; *Le National* did so as well but replaced his resort to Providence with the affirmation of progress, which clearly shows Tocqueville's distance from the lay republican tradition. Doubtless, *Democracy* was not read outside the limited circle of cultivated republicans. Within the considerable mass of workers' pamphlets of the 1830s, only the typographer Adolphe Boyer, like Tocqueville, called on men of goodwill to convert to democracy before it was too late.[100] Tocqueville's authority, because he was a convert, was the best weapon against "men who do not believe in the future of society and who remain impassive before the pains of the people, or against others who coldly say 'the time has not yet come.'" Or against all those who, following England's example, take "a false and dangerous path." And so it was that under Boyer's pen, the Tocquevillean tragedy took on all the social agitation of the era: "Please, let us go forward, let us move. For the status quo is death for all, poverty and hunger for the worker." Yet republicans deplored Tocqueville's lack of audacity and fearful stammerings; he lacked belief in progress.[101] Such a reproach would be made over and over again by later republicans and Bonapartists who shared the same historicism.[102]

Although Tocqueville was able to paint the march of equality, albeit tremblingly at times, the Left had a hard time seeing what telos he assigned its march. Republicans scarcely took note of this ambivalence, being mainly concerned with the regime's form and with political rights. But socialists wondered about the meaning of political rights combined with social inequality that destroyed any enjoyment of them. Cabet, who found his double curiosity about political philosophy and the United States[103] satisfied in *Democracy*, concluded from Tocqueville's work that the movement toward equality of fortune was irresistible. He liked this providentialism, in which he read the future success of his utopian society, Tocqueville's praise for popular sovereignty, and especially his acerbic criticism of the domination of the middle classes. If America was imperfect, as Tocqueville had shown, for Cabet this was because it had failed to achieve economic emancipation. "Without inequality of fortune, there would be neither corrupted nor corrupters."[104] "Economically, one must start by abolishing the quasi-slavery of what is called the white populace, make poverty disappear, establish equality of fortune and community. It is the same thing for the mass of the poor who are veritable white slaves or quasi-slaves. It is a question of equality of fortune. It is a question of community."[105] Thus Georges Sorel was correct to claim that the socialists had transferred Tocqueville's providentialism to the economy.[106] But Tocqueville, who in fact hated the socialists, could only have had passing authority for them. Real equality for Tocqueville meant only unending calls for an unattainable objective.

This controversy over Tocqueville's "providential politics" shows clearly how much historicism, even in the nineteenth century, owed Christian rhetoric. Some criticized the idolatry that led to worshiping history's course without resisting it, then invoked God's name in calling for a change in direction; others emphasized the dangers of delayed conversion. In both cases the argument owed less to any embryonic material equality than to the shake-up in sensibilities produced by the Revolution, to which the old categories of Christian rhetoric gave form. In 1835 Tocqueville's glory came from utilizing rhetoric that gave democracy's coming the grandeur of Destiny.

A Constitutional Data Bank

Conscientious readers who get beyond the preface notice the pedagogical position Tocqueville took in the body of the work. That America was exemplary, that it was a "legislative paradise," was a commonplace. Readers fail to separate the descriptive from the normative in *Democracy,* and so the work is one of "philosophy,"[107] rather than political science or what we would call sociology. It was a "plea" (*Moniteur du Commerce*) whose "generous sentiments" (Rossi) were praised. It had a "parliamentary gravity" (Salvandy), even a kind of "aridity" (*Le Semeur*). The loftily moral activity of reading Tocqueville was scarcely entertaining—which is why women were excused from it. To all readers, its obvious predecessor in both subject and style was Montesquieu.[108] Today's political writers readily compare *Democracy* to *The Spirit of Laws.* Those of 1835 were less sophisticated. Reference to Montesquieu was often mere laudatory hyperbole, but it also meant some political evaluation and notion of method. Montesquieu was politically revered as an authority by every partisan of representative government from the *Gazette de France*'s legitimists to the *National*'s moderate republicans.[109] In terms of method, Montesquieu was felt to have founded a school, to which Thiers and Mignet also belonged, "a school content to report faithfully on things, whose goal is to be instructive, whose obligation is to be exact, whose tales have all the simplicity about them of witnesses giving testimony, whose sincere pen, more concerned with telling the truth than with being admired, articulates all facts arranged in the order in which they took place and accompanied by their true circumstances."[110] Tocqueville's art of revealing effects and impacts was inherited from Montesquieu (Lutteroth), as were his understanding the present to illuminate the future (Salvandy) and avoiding the sentimental effusion so prized by the romantics (Sainte-Beuve): "M. de Tocqueville is severe in his forms, didactic and rational in his conclusions, as a man who believes that logic governs the world. His book is the rigorous development of a central idea, and one feels that imitating Montesquieu combined with the desire for a sober tone impedes the flight of a happy nature, taking from it perhaps more than it gives."[111] Tocqueville was thus the one who put *The Spirit of Laws* into practice by studying the machinery of a great republic whose soaring flight Montesquieu could not predict.[112]

But Tocqueville's philosophy was less appreciated than his erudition. *Democracy*'s virtue lay in its being a data bank from which bits of knowledge could be drawn. From 1835 on, it made the tales of English travelers and the rare constitutional works translated from their American originals pale into insignificance.[113] In addition to the introduction, all commentators emphasized the constitutional studies of book 1 where Tocqueville's descriptive prejudice is the most marked. Chapters 5 and 8 especially deal with current events: the community and decentralization; the regime's nature (republic or monarchy); unitary or bicameral organization of legislative power; the expansion of suffrage; the risk of tyranny of the majority. *Democracy* was used by the French as a good manual to American legislation[114] which allowed reflection on the relationships between the state and civil society in modern societies.

On this count, Proudhon[115] was Tocqueville's most attentive reader. His reading proceeded from a philosophical interest in the question of sovereignty and its limits. He was not blind to Tocqueville's hesitation about the advance of democracy, and he concluded that Tocqueville "knows nothing of morals or politics" although Tocqueville defended the cause of liberty and equality with "a religious sentiment that pleases and uplifts." But he was grateful to Tocqueville for allying himself with popular sovereignty while rejecting the ideal of a mixed regime based on domination by leading citizens. "As we read M. Tocqueville," he wrote, "we see that everything good in American government comes directly from the principle of the sovereignty of the people." According to Proudhon, we must understand what sovereignty is, without simply giving it lip service, and Tocqueville did not escape this tendency.[116] But Tocqueville at least perceived the dangers of political and intellectual tyranny by the majority. After citing Tocqueville at length, Proudhon concluded, "This is what proves indeed that the method of majority voting is a child's game, or rather a barbarian's. In every question about which there can be a difference of opinion, it is through a casuistic operation that they should be decided, and not by votes." Proudhon's essay "What Is Property?" affirmed anew that democracy was not exhausted by suffrage. *Democracy* inspired him to comment:

> What is monarchy? The sovereignty of one man. What is democracy? The sovereignty of the people or, to put it better, of the national majority. But it is still the sovereignty of one man in the place of sovereignty of the law, sovereignty of will in place of sovereignty of reason, in a word—of passions in the place of right. Without a doubt, when a people go from monarchic to democratic government, there is progress, because by increasing the number of sovereigns, there is greater likelihood that reason will be substituted for will. But ultimately this is no revolution in government, because the principle has remained the same. And so today we have the proof that with the most perfect democracy, one can be unfree.[117]

Thus Proudhon's use of Tocqueville was primarily critical. He used Tocqueville to reflect on illegitimacy and usurpation, and in slipping from self-government to federalism, he radicalized Tocqueville's appeal to civic participation by shifting its emphasis from self-government to federalism.

Whatever has been said about it, the partial similarity in their thinking implies no intellectual servility toward Tocqueville on the part of Proudhon. It is true that both works show common themes: the providential development of equality of material conditions, the possible tyranny of the majority, refusal to limit democracy to suffrage, wariness toward sovereignty, and concern that there be a societal contract.

But Proudhon mainly used Tocqueville as a weapon of war. He rejected all of Tocqueville's constructive side. Where Tocqueville believed in balance of power, Proudhon commented, "That is the Directory and the July Monarchy." Through his wariness toward constitutional checks and balances, Proudhon condemns all such cautious policy making to prefer a "legal-scientific" government. The legislative abstinence and moderation Tocqueville preferred were not virtues to Proudhon.[118] Proudhon might have criticized Tocqueville in the same terms in which he criticized Montesquieu:

> Moderation in everything is certainly a very fine thing, but can it serve as principle and guide in lawmaking? Just as the magistrate does not make the decision to apply or not to apply the law when the action called for is sufficiently clear and manifestly planned for by law, so the legislator is not master of lawmaking as he sees fit, using conveniences of rigor, moderation, temperament, opportunity, climate, or passions, etc., upon which to base himself. The princi-

ples of all laws exist; we have only to apply and extend them: to achieve this we must not think about the people's advantage or convenience, we must think about logic. Laws are not police rulings. Recommending moderation to the legislator is like telling geometry to shorten the radius within the circumference, to slant his perpendiculars a bit, and curve his angles.[119]

Although Proudhon read the second *Democracy,* which he cited in 1846 in *Philosophy of Poverty,* politics increased opposition between the two men. Tocqueville showed only contempt for Proudhon in 1848.[120] Under the Second Empire, Proudhon had only contempt for Tocqueville's spiritual sons the liberals, who were too respectful of national unity in his eyes.[121] Yet Proudhon remains an exception. Most often, reflection on the tyranny of the majority was limited to a few frightened stammerings at remembering the Terror.[122]

How to Accommodate Democracies

Although 1835 readers sometimes found legislative recipes in Tocqueville's book, to be applied with discernment, the absence of doctrine in it was nonetheless deplored. This is because American customs, the ultimate foundation of a good government, seemed too narrowly constrained by geography and history to be easily exported. "Every society is identical with itself."[123] One might certainly admire America from time to time. The legitimists appreciated its moral order; ministry officials, its English aristocratic heritage;[124] the republicans, its form of government. But all that remained secondary, for the American experience seemed so utterly aboriginal in both the priority it accorded to the autonomy of its citizens and the role it gave religion.

Tocqueville found the secret of a well-tempered democracy in a kind of civic humanism. Self-government also explains the vitality of communal life and the flowering of associations. In 1835 his apology for communal life was appealing but only equivocally so, for the notion of community seemed tied to both nature and the social contract. It was an extension of the family as well as a voluntary association and was praised by both legitimists and republicans. It is better to examine what readers said of the then-new notion of association in order to grasp the true trail left by Tocqueville's political science.

In 1835–36 both the government and the opposition sought to emphasize the pacific side of American associations, the better to point the finger at disorderly French ones.[125] The Protestant paper *Le Semeur* had an easy time attributing American associative virtues to Protestantism. All of this induced no deep reflection because it made associations an exclusively American phenomenon. Louis de Carné spoke for many when he wrote: "My temperament makes me, I confess, sorry not to be American, English, or Belgian on this score. But one nationality cannot be decanted into another, and peoples may change their institutions without changing their nature."[126]

Thus readers remembered only Tocqueville's reservations in *Democracy,* outdoing themselves noting that Tocqueville did "not himself have a very clear idea of the specifics" he recommended. Associations were close to anarchy, the press was naturally an enemy of order, political parties attracted the mediocre: the 1835–40 debate defined positions in terms that hardly changed throughout the nineteenth century. Both Right and Left were reluctant to admit the legitimacy of factions, which meant admitting plurality in interests and opinions.

The Jacobins feared that associations would disturb the transparency and immediacy of the relationship between citizen and popular sovereign. In this notion they showed their inheritance of the Catholic idea of unity, often without knowing or intending it.[127] The Left's repugnance for the associative principle is most clearly seen in the commentaries published by Buchez's disciples in their journal *L'Européen.* His socialist group took the singular position of reclaiming Catholic tradition, imbued with loathing for individualism and utopian communitarianism, while attempting its laborious synthesis with science and the Revolution. Buchez himself was not a thinker of the highest order, but he consolidated the Left's contradictory aspirations. He had begun a Carbonaro, become a Saint-Simonian and then a Catholic, and his theory of history mixed archaism and modernity in a way that made France the avant-garde of the universal and providential march toward socialist progress. It is not surprising that his disciples felt only mitigated admiration for Tocqueville. In the two articles of 25 November and 25 December 1835 that he devoted to *Democracy,* Dr. Cerisé found facts and sententious formulas in Tocqueville's work, but "no absolute moral doctrine."[128] The United States was the land of "socially organized selfishness," with "individualism in religion and in morals exemplified by the Protestant spirit; individualism in politics and social economy, manifesting in federalism." The American republic was "one of those fortuitous associations which happen on earth without recognizing any spiritual laws, without accomplishing any function, without leaving a trace of their voluntary cooperation with Christian works."[129] The United States was on the margin in the providential history of progress. The fate of men of color became the sign of irresistible slippage from individualism into brutal, ferocious, and stupid despotism. And the roots of the evil that would do away with the United States were precisely those things which Tocqueville admired: balance of power, self-government, many voluntary associations, and the principle of autonomy deployed by Protestantism.

The Doctrinaires, the butt of sarcasm from the Buchez school for their explicit or hidden Protestantism, were less hesitant about social divisions. Like the American Federalists, they were fearful of the people abusing their power.[130] But they were not resigned to the American-style bipartisan system. Plurality of interests seemed a symptom of unruliness which presaged tyranny or anarchy. For them, the virtues of rule by the propertied classes were the solution to the conflict between "aristocrats" and democrats. This they thought abolished class antagonism by making the upper classes representatives for the true interests of the lower.[131] Among the Doctrinaires true acknowledgment of individual autonomy and social diversity did not mean going so far as giving up the dream of a social flock calmed by the shepherd's crook of the notables.

Scorn for American individualism thus was widespread across the political spectrum, rooted in the conviction that private interests necessarily corrupt. Recognizing the fertile divergence of interests was an American idea, not a French one. The pluralist conception of developing national consensus that Tocqueville suggested was contrary to his readers' obsession for unity. This disparity reflects two divergent concepts of public good. For Tocqueville, the public good emerged from the collective exercise of judgment; there could be no immediacy in the popular will nor transparency in representation. National will was to be built in layers through institutions and social structures that set opinions in competition with each other by relating them to the notion of law inscribed within each person's conscience. On the other hand, French tradition was built upon the notion of a Good which transcended individual claims. This is why Tocqueville's allowances for temperaments and mediations seems directly contrary to the prerogatives of sovereignty.

Tocqueville seemed closer to French opinion in his search for a spiritual consensus. In 1835 *Democracy* benefited from the ephemeral renewal of interest in things religious, exemplified by the success of Lacordaire's preaching at Notre Dame. In Tocqueville, Catholics of the *Ami de la Religion et du Roi* and the *Revue Européenne* and *Le Semeur*'s Protestants found the reflection of their usual conversations on the necessity of religion in every modern society, as well as a few new arguments to use in discussing the relative merits of Protestantism and Catholicism.

More importantly, Tocqueville offered new ways to think about the difficult relationship between politics and religion, and in this, his book had an impact across Europe. In Europe there was no pleading for spiritual renewal without wondering about interference between religion and political society. Everywhere the churches had been connected with absolutism; everywhere, liberalism had been linked to freethinking. It was the case in France, and it was so in Germany, where the prince was both the political ruler and the religious head, and where deism was a weapon of the democrats.[132] It was especially true on the Italian peninsula, where reconciling democratic aspirations with a Catholic heritage was more difficult than elsewhere.

One Italian example is theologian Antonio Rosmini, the celebrated reformer and friend of Manzoni and Cavour. In his effort to promote liberalism in Italy, Father Rosmini encountered *Democracy*, which he discussed in his *La società ed il suo fine* (1837).[133] From French conservatives and Doctrinaires Rosmini had already learned fear of democracy's universal mediocrity and oppression of minorities. Reading Tocqueville inspired him not to be satisfied with detesting modernity. He learned both that democracy was not essentially irreligious and that satisfaction of needs was not necessarily immoral.[134] The task of moralists was to develop a theory of justice under democracy.

Rosmini took up Tocqueville's critique of majority rule. If we combine legitimacy and legality, what guarantee remains to the oppressed individual? Though he took up the same question, he rejected Tocqueville's answer. To guarantee justice, Tocqueville countered majority tyranny with the wisdom of assemblies, waiting periods, and deliberation; society might find within itself a rational basis, however little enlightened individuals were in their heart of hearts. Rosmini was dissatisfied with this resort to prudence and individual moral conscience. He preferred, to Tocqueville's vague spirituality, Catholicism's natural law: eternal truth emanates directly from the bosom of the Lord, and it alone can raise human rights above fluctuations in opinion. The difficulty with this lies in avoiding a perilous confusion between theology and politics.[135] How can religion and politics be separated while preserving the submission of every citizen to the precepts of an established religion? Rosmini arrived at no clearer solution than Tocqueville had. In 1848 his failure to influence papal politics in a liberal direction showed how difficult it was to reconcile an established church with representative democracy, even a bourgeois democracy based on property as Rosmini hoped for.

Tocqueville's works were not themselves innocent of the aporia to which they lead their readers. His thought is made singularly opaque by the choice of the exceptional experience of America. In effect Protestantism, as practiced by the Americans, offered a mix of old and new which was difficult to think about clearly. On one hand, it exalted individual autonomy; each is his or her own priest. In this, there is nothing more democratic or more opposed, it seems, to the Catholic idea of a hierarchical community of believers. This was the source, in 1835, of the anti-Protestant furor of Buchez's band of Catholic-leaning socialists and, on the other hand, the democratic pride of the Protestants of *Le Semeur*. But in fact, this Protestantism, insofar as it is universally practiced, at least in lip service, imposes a morally uniform behavior. The Puritanical model in its original purity required a resurgence of the biblical mind-set. Among early Puritan preachers incessant recourse to the images, symbols, and prescriptions of the Old Testament led to a more ponderous moral and social legislation. The American people, the new Israel, were the people of God organized as political society. According to Mosaic tradition, faith will be judged by conformity to meticulously rigid law more than by the interiorization of Grace. This model, where political and religious societies coincide in a universal allegiance to law, is not without its analogy to the experience of medieval *christianitas,* which Protestants denounced for its archaism,[136] while most Catholics eagerly tried to position themselves in the familiar terrain of moral order. Those who feared democracy unfailingly cited Tocqueville's adage that for a people to be free, they must believe—an adage they twisted to make it serve the preservation of acquired rights and the prevention of revolution.[137] The American model seduced some by the rights it accorded individual moral conscience and others by the moral order it ensured. Tocqueville never dispelled the ambiguity; the second *Democracy* was to examine the religious question from a new point of departure.

Tocqueville's readers criticized him for being too American, whether the subject was the nature of equality, the concept of sovereignty, or the role of religion. What bothered them was not so much a particular aspect of custom but his renunciation of the central role played by French nationality. His conflation of the two histories repelled them, intensifying their efforts to cast doubt on the durability of the American experiment, as though its ephemeral nature would disqualify its principles. In their campaign of denigration, material was to be found in Tocqueville's very last chapter, devoted to the Union's future. They made prophecies out of Tocqueville's pessimistic conjectures ventured in conclusion, foreseeing the decline of the American empire the better to condemn the Union's democratic model, as though the course of a nation's history were its government's ordeals.

The wealth of the American Union was so patent that even its most zealous detractors had to recognize at least its existence. But must one assume the excellence of its institutions from this prosperity? Tocqueville showed himself cautious on this count, connecting liberty and prosperity only in a long-term sense.[138] By making liberty a means to wealth or power, one ran the risk of endangering the very principle of morality. In 1835 such caution ran counter to public opinion's diffuse conflation of right and action. Nothing shows this more clearly than the intensity with which monarchists and republicans debated the political significance of economic superiority, by finding an argument in Tocqueville which he did not develop.

Of course, monarchists tried to show that one could not argue from American prosperity to the excellence of republican government[139] and that the American future was monarchy, as Tocqueville himself had thought in 1831. Pellegrino Rossi, law professor and friend of Guizot, saw in the European model the ultimate accomplishment of history: civil equality without political equality, monarchy rather than republic. America was a merely ephemeral democracy; it was a

> new country, with no antecedents, no history, placed in quite particular economic circumstances. America offers civil equality and actual equality so close together in a way that belongs only to it, which does not exist and will never exist in our older societies, and which will cease to exist in America as the country ages. . . . Mature men do not return to infancy; it is infancy which strides into maturity. It is America which, in its own way, strides toward Europe; Europe cannot make itself American.[140]

Democrats and republicans adopted the opposite approach, deducing the excellence of America's republic from its prosperity—but not without a certain discomfort. Convinced that only France incarnated the universal, they judged American predominance transitory, whence their irritation at Tocqueville's prediction of Russian and American superiority. The popular modern parallel drew attention only as it seemed to imply condemnation of French nationality.[141] In

1839 Louis-Napoléon shared republican hesitance about Tocqueville's prophecies, foreshadowing the way Second Empire Bonapartists would appropriate the heritage of republican providentialism.[142]

In 1835, therefore, Doctrinaires and republicans shared the same prophetic rationalism which would guarantee all peoples access to the French ideal. The Right as well as the Left took exception to *Democracy*'s decentering of French history. "Never will [France] cease to march at the head of human societies, like the luminous cloud which guided Israel in the desert," cried Molé.[143] A clever argument, given that America was declaring itself the New Israel.

Thus in the 1830s Tocqueville found his most attentive readers within the legitimist and republican camps, often united in "Carlo-Republican" electoral alliances against the regime. They were delighted with Tocqueville's rejection of the notion that realization of history meant bourgeois triumph and his concern for the consequences of equality where it destroys solidarity between classes. They held onto the critical view and few constitutional recipes in his work, but no doctrine. They could only take Tocqueville's "new political science" in small doses.

Tocqueville Prescribes through His Work: The Second Republic and the American Constitutional Model

Tocqueville's political science found an audience only after Guizot's fall. Guizot had made the longevity of his rule the guarantor of his own legitimacy. When he fell, he demonstrated the correctness of Tocqueville's prophecy that had denounced the instability of a mixed aristocratic-democratic system. The preface to the tenth edition of the first *Democracy*, published in mid-March 1848 and widely reprinted in the press, cleverly recalled the author's clairvoyance while conferring the mantle of republicanism on him. Confined to the opposition under the July Monarchy, Tocqueville had his time of glory during this period.

He benefited from the many attempts at decentralization and local renewal. In 1835 *Democracy* had seduced its readers with its apology for communal life. It found a fresh audience in 1848 when attempts were made to reform the state's constitution and when Tocqueville was a deputy, as were his friends: Barrot, among those allied with the Republic; Louis de Kergorlay and Arthur de Gobineau, who ran the legitimist *Revue Provinciale,* leading the reformers. The Tocquevillean distinction between political and administrative centralization, also found among legitimists, became a commonplace whose origin was forgotten.[144] Promoting the twin principles of political centralization and administrative decentralization became the order of the day for the central committee for administrative decentralization, formed by the Assembly with Cordier as president and Béchard as secretary. But contrary to received opinion, the legitimist Right had no monopoly on calls for decentralization. A new Carlo-Republican alliance developed on 18 October 1848 during debates on the constitution in which the subject was internal administration. Tocqueville was quiet, careful not to seem to ally himself to a legitimist party he knew had no future[145] or with the democrats, compromised by their collusion with the radical Left of La Montagne. But as it had been in 1835, *Democracy* was cited at length at the podium by both sides of the new alliance.[146]

With this renewal of public favor came increased interest in the American model. To many, 1848 seemed a return to 1830. While demonstrations of friendship increased between the American big sister and the younger French republic, public interest in the American Constitution grew passionate. Curiosity about the American republic had never entirely disappeared, but 1848 brought new practical interest in constitutional studies. Seven French editions of the American Constitution were published between April and September 1848, in 1,000 or 1,500 copies per run. It was commented on tirelessly by the press and in high-minded circles,[147] and Tocqueville suddenly became what he had been in 1835: an emulator of Montesquieu, the authority one calls on or combats, the young intellectuals' bedside author.[148] Conservatives used their '30s strategy once more. Some brought up Tocqueville's reservations about America.[149] Others criticized what they saw as Tocqueville's blindness, like Félix de Courmont, in *L'Opinion Publique*: "By the pomp of its style and the charm of its theories, [*Democracy*] has seduced our minds, spread the most erroneous beliefs, and highlighted a system which, because of the prestige of principles that disappoint, engenders only corruption and political bad faith. . . . Why not have shown us that Americans do not bow to the symbol of liberty but instead kneel to receive paternal benediction before the golden calf?"[150] On 29 July in an article in which he imagined addressing Tocqueville, Courmont thought he had found the answer: "Perhaps you wanted us to find every possible opinion in your book—perhaps you sought, like the Apocalypse, to make *Democracy in America* a gigantic, mysterious book, with no possible conclusions?"

Tocqueville the criminal, hazy in his thinking, defender of a mercantile democracy—such were the themes heard among reactionary thinkers, from Custine to Maurras. But in 1848 the traditional hostility of conservatives toward

America and thus toward Tocqueville deflated rapidly as the American model shifted from moderate republicanism to conservatism. In November, *L'Opinion Publique,* referring to the "excellent book" by M. de Tocqueville, praised the American spirit of independence, respect for religion, regional diversity, and even differences of fortune. It praised the bicameral system, the power of the judiciary, and the strong executive branch elected by universal suffrage.[151] In a complete reversal the next month, *L'Opinion Publique* suggested that socialists examine in America "what nonintervention by the state produces in matters which do not need it—both for the individual, whose value increases with everything he can do for himself, and for the society, which with minimal energies and expenditure obtains prodigious results." Thus, while the American model slid toward conservatism, Tocqueville gained the equivocal sympathy of the party representing order, who liked the Republic as long as it was authoritarian, decentralized, and not too egalitarian.

Tocqueville was not just an "authority." He helped implement his own doctrines in the development of the 1848 constitution, and we have the rare good fortune to be able to follow his dialogue with his contemporaries. On 17 and 18 May, the Assembly elected a constitutional committee comprised of a veritable constellation of great minds: Cormenin, one of the fathers of French administrative law; Marrast, who had been a writer for *Le National;* the jurist Vivien; Lamennais, who had just published a plan for the constitution; Tocqueville, Dufaure, and Beaumont. The committee held twenty-four meetings from 19 May to 17 June; we know its content and tenor from the fairly mediocre transcription of the proceedings by Woirhaye.[152]

In comments about it three years later, Tocqueville was to find the committee's work sterile. Institutions have their own logic, and doctrines have theirs; discussion on principles was often sacrificed to opportunism and the sharp sense of popular trends that drew all things along behind them. France "desired, with a kind of frenzy, that the work of the constitution be accomplished, and that power be seated if not solidly, at least permanently and regularly. France needed less a good constitution than some constitution."[153] Here, we are far from America's prudent development of its Constitution, even from the philosophical heights of revolutionary debates.

Yet Tocqueville's severity was excessive. True, he felt it important to refuse to father any constitution which would lead directly to a coup d'état. But reading the debates contributes much to understanding how his thought was received. On the commission he represented the "American school." The debates especially illustrate how inconsistent this school was and Tocqueville's gradual marginal-ization. The constitution makers argued over two points: the bicameral system and how the executive branch was to be organized. The commission, committees of deputies, and Assembly paid no attention to judiciary power or to control of constitutionality—a sign that they were unanimous in their refusal to question the limits of sovereignty.

In his defense of the bicameral system, Tocqueville was careful to disallow the threat of aristocratic resurgence. The second chamber must, as in the United States, have a democratic basis. Its mission was to provide the nation's repre-sentatives with time for reflection and to avoid a face-off between the Chamber and the president. Tocqueville was beaten on this fourteen to three. Debate then returned to the committees of deputies and went from there to the Assembly. After heated discussion on 25–27 September 1848, the Assembly followed the ma-jority of the commissioners by voting for a single chamber. For both Right and Left, a second chamber was conceivable only as a kind of retreat for the privi-leged. Tocqueville's thought owed much to the American experience, which was so little known in France,[154] and faced the same hostile lines of argument from 1835 through the end of the century. Notables recommended a second chamber as a means to preserve their supremacy. Republicans feared that a senate would become a source of factious division[155] or the refuge of the aristocracy.[156] This demonstrates how difficult it was in this period to conceive of a pluralist form of representation not based on social inequality.

The second point of discord was the strength of the executive. The constitu-tional commission debated the executive's power on 27, 30, and 31 May and 14 and 15 June. Tocqueville defended the commission's plan to the Assembly on 5 October 1848. On this score again, he was the man of democratic transition. He believed that monarchy's legitimacy would crumble. In 1848 the Orleanists were attached to their king only the way "pigs are attached to the memory of their sty," ever ready to wallow in another.[157] There was no other basis for the executive branch than universal suffrage. The difficulty lay in joining respect for popular sovereignty with preserving liberty and governmental efficacy. The United States offered no recipe. In the United States sovereignty divided between the states and the Union limited the president's powers. In France the great centralizing force of the state in constituting the nation gave the executive the power to distribute a great many seats, as Tocqueville explained during the commission's 27 May meeting; the preeminence of the executive became both necessary and dangerous, so imposing did the monarchic imagination remain. At this point Tocqueville juxtaposed theoretical reflection on the need for a strong executive with historical reflection on French idolatry of power, whence the inconsistency of the solution he then proposed.

To prevent the reincarnation of monarchy in the executive, he recommended limiting the length of the presidency, a two-step process of election by universal suffrage, and limiting powers. But to avoid the neglect implicit in government by the Assembly, he wanted to leave the president the wide powers of a constitutional monarch yet without a monarch's lengthy stay, inviolability, and irresponsibility. Beaten on his two-step electoral process, Tocqueville believed he could reconcile efficiency and liberty in an "unheard-of" arrangement that imposed responsibility upon both president and ministers. This allowed him to reconcile parliamentarianism with the French need for authority, neatly adapting the American model to French history. It was a clever move, but it led directly to the conflict between the president and the Assembly and the coup d'etat that Tocqueville in vain tried to avoid in 1851 by pleading for the possible reelection of Louis-Napoléon Bonaparte.[158]

Legitimists and conservatives did not share Tocqueville's anguished struggles. They had no trouble thinking about the executive: for them, the presidency was simply a time between kings. Bonapartists were quite unafraid of trampling liberty and hated the division of interests on which parliamentarianism was founded. They had a good time criticizing Tocqueville's incoherence, which had produced "a series of contradictory opinions, with no other link between them than the studied pallor of languishing prose." Listening to Tocqueville, Fortoul said he thought he could hear Rabelais's Pantagruel advising Panurge to marry and not to marry, for Tocqueville both advised the French to give power to their executive and advised them not to.[159]

Tocqueville's thought thus won over only republicans and their allies, who were torn between respect for the principle of universal suffrage and the fear of bringing absolutism back to life or making a bed for caesars to lie in. On the commission the widest gap was between two republicans from the *National.* Editor in chief Marrast feared a return of the royalty and was for the executive being named by the Assembly and given restricted powers.[160] Martin de Strasbourg, who liked to call himself a "republican from birth," was for election by universal suffrage of a president with broad powers including the right to dissolve the Assembly.[161] At the Assembly in October, the same division appeared, with most republicans, including Félix Pyat and Jules Grévy, fearing a division in national representation. A minority surrounding Tocqueville and Lamartine refused "a republic without republicans, a democracy minus the people,"[162] and pleaded for election of the president by universal suffrage. They promptly found themselves confused with the party supporting the existing order, which sought suffrage only to elect a master.

Paradoxically, Tocqueville's work was thus used by the party supporting the existing order and mostly rejected by the republicans who had liked it so well in 1835. Tocqueville, who sought to ensure the effective exercise of universal suffrage, was scorned by the very people who claimed to defend the Republic. Yet he differed from them only in his choice of method. Like them, he saw himself above all as part of a transition toward full recognition of popular sovereignty.[163] Like them, he noted the people's immaturity and persistent imaginal attachment to royalty. But republicans concluded from this that delay in implementing suffrage was needed. According to Victor Considérant, "The education of the people has not been achieved. Before we allow them to exercise all their rights, we must wait for them to appreciate them better."[164] Fear of return to the military dictatorship of Caesarism resurged with every crisis (16 May 1877, the Boulangist crisis, the Dreyfus affair), again reinforcing republican tendency to increase the representatives' power to the detriment of the executive's and to privilege republican forms over democratic politics. For Tocqueville, too, it was a question of waiting to allow the taste for liberty time to spread and the shades of Louis XIV and Bonaparte to slip away. A little while longer, and "the people will be used to republican forms," delivering themselves from the charm of the pretenders.[165] But deliverance can only come through practicing self-government. Only democratic politics could correct still-monarchic mores. In 1835 Tocqueville had believed that though in America moral freedom led to free institutions, in France free institutions might create moral freedom. The readers' lack of understanding in 1835 and the failure of a conservative republic in 1848 clearly show he was wrong, and that political culture was more a moral than a legal matter. From political science we must now turn to the philosophy of politics or history. This was precisely the ambition of the second volume of *Democracy*, published in 1840, and of *Old Regime*.

2

Moralist for Modern Times, 1840s

THE FIRST *Democracy* was a success. At thirty, its author was famous and resolved to strike again. But what to write? His readers did not see the need for a
sequel to *Democracy;* they thought him occupied with a great work on England,
as a good disciple of Montesquieu. Yet Tocqueville had planned a second work
on America, which he prudently announced as early as 1835. "My goal," he wrote,
"is to paint in the second book the influence which equality of conditions and
democratic government exert on civil society, habits, ideas and customs. But I
begin to feel less ardor for the accomplishment of this design" (*DA* 1:12). A clever
way of keeping the door open. His letters were more explicit. From England,
Tocqueville wrote his cousin Molé, "I will tell you that my only plan right now
is to give my work on democracy the final development which I had always intended to give it if the book succeeded, and which I was careful, in a sense, to seed
in advance at the end of the introduction."[1]

But nothing happened as planned. The "final development" did not enjoy the
success of the first volume, although today it is held to be a masterpiece. Readers' disappointment resulted from the design of the work itself. Through his incessant rewritings from 1835 to 1839, Tocqueville had drifted far from his original
plans. The story of his turning from a study of America to the tableau of democratic societies, from political science to moralizing, is what we must tell first.

The Work

It had all seemed so simple at the start. In late 1835 Tocqueville established a
plan according to which he eliminated issues that seemed to him too thorny, such

as education and the development of the moral sciences.[2] There was a time pressure: Tocqueville was old enough to be a deputy. Thus his early sketches show only rather conventional section headings. He first imagined two sections: the influence of democracy on ideas and the influence of democracy on feelings. But this structure would not allow him to deal with manners and customs. By the end of the year, he set this initial structure aside in favor of a tripartite one: the effects of democracy on thought, on the heart, and on customs. It all presaged a quick finish. But events, deaths, illnesses, and trips intervened. Editor, translators, and readers grew impatient. The writing took more than four years, during which Tocqueville struggled against his rebellious words. "You see," an exhausted Tocqueville wrote to Beaumont in 1839, "I must at all costs finish this book. It and I have a duel to the death—I must kill it, or it must kill me."[3] How to explain this change?

From America to the Democratic Type

Tocqueville had initially thought of studying American society by bringing Cuvier's paleontology into the human sciences. Cuvier said: "There exists a necessary relation among all the parts of any organized body, such that a man who encounters a part of one of them can reconstruct the whole. The same analytical tool can serve to explain most of the general laws that rule all things."[4] Society was like one enormous person with formal correlation between laws and customs. This organicism was not without precedent; Guizot had compared factual research with anatomy and lawmaking with physiology.

So it was to study the English seeds of American customs that Tocqueville went to England for the second time in the summer of 1835. He dashed over as if he were about to miss a play in order to watch the death convulsions of England's aristocracy. He came back convinced that England was walking peacefully toward democracy along the path the Continent had cleared. "The previous revolutions that the English have undergone were essentially English in substance and in form. . . . It is no longer so today: today it is the European revolution that is being continued among the English."[5] In the first *Democracy*, England was the past incarnate, and a specifically insular past. Now, its status had changed, and Tocqueville discovered in England two universal traits of modern democracy that had escaped him: the threat of impoverishment and a tendency toward centralization.

In America, Tocqueville had had neither the leisure nor the desire to visit factories. In England he went to many radical meetings and toured Birmingham's factories and Manchester's shantytowns. He left us his horrified stories, but sinister tales of Manchester, by authors from Montalembert to Engels, abound. What was important were the conclusions he drew. In contrast to Montalembert and the social legitimists, Tocqueville was not satisfied to praise traditional forms of patronage. In contrast to Engels, he refused to grant working-class impoverishment the status of a law of history. Without failing to recognize workers' poverty or the threat of the emergence of a capitalist aristocracy, he believed them less enduring than the democratic instinct of equality and gave them only a minor place in his book.

Revealing the social was thus less important an issue than the inevitable growth of the state. In the first *Democracy*, Tocqueville had thought centralization, specific to France, to be an accident of the power grabbing of kings. By studying the English poor laws promulgated in February 1834, he discovered how universal centralization was, and that America had only escaped it by accident. In his travel notes of 11 May 1835, he wrote: "Why is centralization rather a part of the habits of democracy? A great question to dig into ... a capital question."[6]

Tocqueville's observations in England were confirmed by philosophical reflection that he undertook at Royer-Collard's urging, also during 1835. Correspondence began between the old man of seventy-two and the young man of thirty in which the elder became a kind of spiritual director in whom the younger confided his intellectual uncertainties. With Royer-Collard, Tocqueville affirmed his taste for philosophical speculation applied to politics, in discussions on Plato, Plutarch, and Machiavelli. He could especially see the American model's limits more clearly and the difficulty of discerning what was truly democratic. "The great difficulty in studying democracy," wrote Tocqueville, "is to distinguish what is democratic from what is only revolutionary. . . . This is very difficult because we lack examples. There is no European people among whom democracy is well seated, and America is in an exceptional situation."[7]

In 1835 and 1836 then, Tocqueville came up against the impossibility of finding an empiric example of pure democratic type. America was exceptional; England was a mix of aristocracy and democracy; France was revolutionary. And yet these three societies were all raising the same democratic crop. With a sharper awareness than in 1835 of the difference between the object as constructed and the object found, Tocqueville transposed the notion of necessary correlation of forms to the level of type. Actual societies might be inconsistent but reinforced the coherence of their parts in always and increasingly conforming to type. "To conceive of men remaining forever unequal upon a single point, yet equal on all others, is impossible; they must come in the end to be equal upon all" (*DA* 1:53). Tocqueville returned to this circularity of cause and effect several times in his writings. Equality favored materialism, which in turn favored equality, the "fatal circle" (*DA* 2:145). Democracy tends to increase state power, which in return accentuates its leveling effect (*DA* 2:291).

The difficulty is that in his description of types, Tocqueville was no longer guided by the order of things as he was in his first *Democracy*. There, he had studied American institutions in the order in which they emerged. His initial outline of the second *Democracy* now survived only as an inadequate frame. "There are moments," wrote Tocqueville, "when I feel a kind of panicked terror. In the first part of my work, I confined myself to laws, which were fixed, visible points. Now it seems to me sometimes that I am in midair, and that I will inevitably crash into being common, absurd, or dull, without being able to stop myself."[8] Impelled to abandon his focus on the order of things and turn to the order of reason, Tocqueville forced himself to see patterns in a contingent universe, patterns which allowed him to affirm that "things are so far from combating each other that I can see how they agree" and are "less incoherent than they seem to be."[9] He did not avoid abusing the formulaic deductions that irritated readers increasingly as the century progressed. Boutmy[10] and d'Eichtal[11] also noted that for Tocqueville, things are not a certain way but that given their point of departure, they necessarily will be.[12]

Yet this determinism eroded quickly when Tocqueville introduced gradations which allowed for the idea that the same social status might have opposite, though unequally likely, consequences. Thus, equality might lead either to servitude or freedom, pantheism or mysticism. Tocqueville's language started with hyperbole only to end in limited terms. When the erosion was over, democratic variation was nothing more than the pattern of the variations which he observed. Type allowed him to elucidate the "penchants," "inclinations," "slopes" of a social state;[13] hidden tendencies and secret slopes[14] which Tocqueville most often referred to as "instinct,"[15] customs that had become second nature in spite of the actors and, for that reason, all the more irresistible.[16] Such a vocabulary recalls Pascal's calculus of probability, which Quételet's *Essai de physique sociale* applied to social events in 1835, and which Tocqueville thought the only certain path to knowledge.[17] Tocqueville offered a probability theory of democracy, though it was not formulated mathematically and did not always escape (self-)contradiction.[18] But his resort to the lexicon of tendencies also leads one to put him in the moralist lineage.[19] Witness the chaotic character of his reflections on human contrariness. Thus when Tocqueville tried to discern democracy's effects on ambition, he first thought—this is the common opinion—that democracy engenders the universal ambition for petty things; later, he became aware of the existence of "colossal" ambitions following the Revolution. How to reconcile a storm of petty ambitions with a few Rastignacs?[20]

Tocqueville's strategy was typical of the kind of thinking nourished by remorse and torment and draws Tocqueville closer to Pascal, not Pascal the calculator but the moralist. Like Pascal, Tocqueville incessantly inflicted upon himself and his readers the requirement to think throughout what was an unpredictable journey. "I do not take up the pen with the fixed intention of following a system," he wrote to John Stuart Mill. "I give myself to the natural movements of my idea, allowing myself to be led in good faith from one consequence to another. The result is that as long as the work is not finished, I do not know precisely where I am going, or if I will ever arrive."[21]

This is why the writing took such an erratic course, marked by missed opportunities. In the spring of 1836, Tocqueville realized part 2 would need two volumes. In November 1836 he admitted to his English translator Reeve, "I would never have imagined that a subject which I had already explored from so many angles could show me so many new faces."[22] Illness and then an initial electoral campaign in November 1837 delayed completion of the work until 1838. This was a sign of Tocqueville's difficulty in keeping control of his work as it slipped from a study of American customs into a tableau of democratic culture, a shift whose measure he did not take until he reread the entire work. "Now I can see more or less the whole book," he wrote Royer-Collard in 1838, "and I realize that it is much more about the general effects of equality on customs than about the particular effects it produces in America."[23]

From Fear of Anarchy to Fear of Inertia

Thus in 1838 there came a second shift, this time not in Tocqueville's method but in the political meaning of his work. Entering politics, Tocqueville suddenly distanced himself from the Doctrinaires.

Riots had marked the early years of the July Monarchy. In 1836 the permanent revolution, as it was already called then, seemed at a close. Tocqueville had hoped this improvement would allow liberalization. In 1838 this hope seemed dashed. Guizot continually shook the scarecrow of revolution to pursue his repressive politics; he muzzled the press and constrained electoral will through administrative pressuring. As a result, public spirits were sinking in the France of the July regime, and the ability to imagine great things was fading. Public life began to be seen as merely a way to get rich. The bourgeoisie, to use *Souvenirs*'s fine phrase, "had leased the state." The peasants of lower Normandy were no better than the Paris bourgeoisie. The Valognes electorate's "cud-chewing party"[24] preferred the darkness of their hearths and their cattle trading to Tocqueville's speeches. When Tocqueville complained about it, Royer-Collard pointed out its universality: "But your Normans! That is France, that is the world—that prudent, intelligent egotism, that is the honest folk of our time, in its finest details."[25]

The young, overly Parisian candidate's disillusionment caused him to rearrange his entire work. Through 1838 Tocqueville had accepted the liberals and Doctrinaires' distinction between democracy and revolution. Tocqueville had taken it even further at Royer-Collard's urging, thinking he would write a grand preface on this distinction. He did not completely abandon the concept after 1838, but he shifted his emphases. Fear of revolution faded before the horror induced by a nation of perpetual children, a herd of calves ambling to slaughter. Fear of inertia replaced fear of anarchy. In the spring of 1838, Tocqueville wrote a great chapter on the infrequency of revolutions under democracies, a chapter challenging Guizot, and he gave it in galley form to the *Revue des Deux Mondes*, which shows us how central it was to his thinking.

From July to October 1838, Tocqueville wrote his fourth section, on the political consequences of equality, which was truly a new treatment of questions touched on in 1835. It was in this unacknowledged rewriting that he noticed he had unconsciously changed the political meaning of the work,[26] so much so that from October 1838 to the end of 1839 he had to rewrite it all in a mass of fragments tirelessly recopied and modified in succession.

Democratic Corruption

This revision allowed Tocqueville to develop a dialectic of individualism and its obverse, voluntary servitude. The word *individualism*, used in 1835 by republican analysts of *Democracy*, had not been used by Tocqueville, who at that point was more fearful of the majority's ability to trample individual rights than the peaceful retreat of each person into a private sphere.

In writing the second *Democracy*, Tocqueville discovered how, in a mercantile society, the private pursuit of happiness can come to exclude concern for public life. He used the term *individualism* to mean that "mature and calm feeling, which disposes each member of the community to sever himself from the mass of his fellows" (*DA* 2:98). This individualism touched all arenas of social life. As universals, the Good, the True, and the Beautiful all crumbled away together; in the arts, egalitarian subjectivism replaced the principle of excellence. In morality, authority and faith disappeared, and only the fluctuating principle of utility remained. In science, Opinion was master. Everywhere, the singular and particular won out over the universal.

But what would become of the public good? The res publica was not so much abandoned as managed to the advantage of special interests. Political ideas entered the domestic economy, and "children were born to hold an opinion as they were born to their status."[27] The entire nation degenerated into a crowd of beggars. Socialists called for the right to work while the bourgeoisie grabbed for position.[28] In both cases the principle was the same—individuals prospering at the Treasury's expense.

Yet *Democracy* did not focus profoundly on political venality, nor was it better analyzed in Tocqueville's political speeches where he confined himself to a few "salutary rules of prudence" on parliamentary incompatibilities and on recruitment and advancement procedures in civil service.[29] Moreover, his practices showed him to be singularly changeable. "It is to my taste," he wrote, "as well as in my interest, to support in Paris every just demand which the communes and other public entities may formulate. It is also my intention and, I should add, my duty to assist to the best of my ability my compatriots who appear to me to deserve government favors and who are recommended by my friends."[30]

We can understand why his moral protestations were cause for laughter. Tocqueville was clearly concerned with maintaining his network of patronage. But the embryonic nature of his thinking on the mechanisms of corruption is much more the result of difficulty in thinking about the state. Like his readers, Tocqueville was quick to suspect the administration of putting up a smoke screen between the people and their representatives, and so he balked at establishing a rigid administration. Over the long term political venality was for him merely a circumstantial corruption, unstable and secondary, not deserving deep analysis.

In fact, Tocqueville's originality lies in his ability to show how individuals who promise themselves freedom are hampered by servitude. It is less anarchy that threatens us than the despotism it engenders. In 1835–36 Tocqueville believed in the gradual disappearance of the state with the march of democracy, as did Constant, Mme de Staël, and Jefferson. The second *Democracy* reverses this thesis by showing that as hierarchical connections dissolve and classes level, social power increases its grasp. State omnipotence and individual autonomy go together. Thus the rights of the child are only recognized because "in democracies, where the government picks out every individual singly from the mass to make him subservient to the general laws of the community . . . a father is there, in the eye of the law, only a member of the community, older and richer than his sons."[31] Power's increased prerogatives are not an accident but the rule.

This new mode of domination was not to be confused with violent usurpation and was not even incompatible with the compassion Rousseau had made the heart of his democratic theory. The entire fourth part of the second *Democracy* is devoted to the image, which Tocqueville knew was new, of the state "gradually taking over everything, everywhere substituting itself for the individual or placing the individual under its aegis, governing, regulating, *uniforming* everything and every person."[32] This is the state as economic regulator, "the first among the industrialists" of the nation, the welfare state making charity, forbearance, and mutual assistance unnecessary, "an immense and tutelary power" which is "absolute, minute, regular, provident and mild. It would be like the authority of a parent if, like that authority, its object was to prepare men for manhood; but it seeks, on the contrary, to keep them in perpetual childhood" (*DA* 2:318).

Looking at the notion of the welfare state or Providence, so long as power was not embodied in any one person, and life was lived in "this sort of compromise between administrative despotism and the sovereignty of the people" which characterized post-Napoleonic France, the reach of democratic corruption remained limited. Every citizen "may still imagine that, while he yields obedience, it is to himself he yields it" (*DA* 2:319–20). But this political form seemed to Tocqueville an "ephemeral monster," a transition either toward liberty or toward a new despotism which he depicts for us as "a sort of fusion . . . between the practices of civil officials and those of the military service. . . . the people would become the reflection of the army, and the community be regimented like a garrison" (*DA* 2:368).

Democratic Hygiene

Because the danger he foresaw had changed, Tocqueville had to modify the remedies he proposed. Of course the call to self-interest, to rational deliberation and religious sanction, was not absent from the first *Democracy*. But the function of these three principles was to ensure moral order in an anarchical society. Now Tocqueville had to conceive them as teaching the spirit of liberty to a dull-witted society.

In 1835 Tocqueville showed that in the United States, private interest was the "great principle . . . constantly to be met with in studying the laws" (*DA* 1:78). Government's primary objective was "to ensure the greatest wellbeing and to avoid the most misery to each of the individuals who compose it" (*DA* 1:252). In 1840 the second *Democracy* turned this American principle into a characteristic of democracy. The taste for well-being was "the prominent and indelible feature of democratic times."[33] Thus Tocqueville tried hard to construct a political philosophy starting with individual self-interest. That process, common to Anglo-Saxon philosophy, was hardly in line with French traditions.[34]

Tocqueville's attitude was above all pragmatic. Fighting the spirit of the times was useless. One must ally oneself with the philosophy of self-interest because it is "the best suited of all philosophical theories to the wants of the men of our time."[35] To which may be added a cautionary note: the "honest and lawful" (*DA* 2:144) quest for individual welfare should not be sacrificed to the "principle of public utility" or the "doctrine of political necessity" (*DA* 2:327), which often are no more than a mask for domination by the powerful.

But how to harmonize divergent individual interests and social groups? Tocqueville was not lured by the hope of conciliating private interests through the market's invisible hand. He instead introduced the notion of a pedagogy of interests. He saw individuals, and humanity as a whole, passing through "three successive stages": first, ignorance or instinctive devotion; second, the quasi-science of egotism; finally, complete enlightenment or thoughtful sacrifice.[36]

Those who seek to appear clever are satisfied with "little enjoyments" in the near term. But the truly clever can think long-term, reconciling utility and morality. The pedagogy of "enlightened self-interest" opens the long path to wisdom for those who do not possess the heart's gift of the taste for liberty: "enlightened self-interest is in no way contrary to the disinterested progress of Good. They are two different but not opposing things. Those great souls for whom this doctrine cannot suffice in a sense bypass self-interest and go beyond it, while ordinary souls stop there."[37]

The doctrine of enlightened self-interest is thus of only pedagogical interest. Tocqueville liked doctrines more for their moral effects than for their truth, this we know. If to win his point he set greed on the side of liberty, self-interest, however enlightened, was merely the means by which "the mind marshals its forces" to attain a taste for liberty. Tocqueville is too much a spiritualist to be tempted by the "rehabilitation of the flesh," which he denounced both in the Saint-Simonians' "materialism" and in the socialists' "politics of the belly."

In fact, *Old Regime* relied only marginally on the pedagogy of self-interest. Not that Tocqueville had ceased believing that prosperity and liberty coincided over the long term. But the experience of the Second Empire showed that the system of self-interest could combine with either despotism or liberty. "True," Tocqueville wrote at the time, "in the long run liberty always brings to those who know how to retain it comfort and well-being, and often great prosperity. Nevertheless, for the moment it sometimes tells against amenities of this nature, and there are times, indeed, when despotism can best ensure a brief enjoyment of them."[38] In Tocqueville's thinking, utility remained an uncertain means to teach Virtue. An appreciation for utility did not allow any final decisions about the validity of ends and did not exhaust discussion of the Right.

Parallel to his thinking about self-interest, Tocqueville was thus led to find a transcendental norm—the True, the Beautiful, and the Good, together without distinctions.[39] In this quest he joined in the modern process of the secularization of belief. Torn between doubt and the desire to believe, he felt he was an heir of the philosophes and held onto the two certainties that seemed to him to stem from reason: the existence of God and the soul's immortality, which were postulates of practical reason necessary to ensure retribution for actions. Tocqueville's God was like Pascal's, a hidden one—but Nature carries within herself the knowledge of Good and Evil. "If God did not give all people the gift to judge what is true, he accorded every one of us at least the power to sense what is good and honest, and that is enough to serve as a guiding thread in these shadows."[40] In fact, doctrinally speaking, Christianity and the Enlightenment were never opposed to one another except through misunderstanding. The American syncretism of reason and faith is the rule; their French antagonism, an accident.[41]

This transcendent norm was no less threatened in democratic societies even though it was rational. The dynamic of equality levels people and then looks to God, the ultimate sign of alterity. Democracy raises the norm to the status of a human-forged ideal. Tocqueville had seen this process of secularization at work in the America of 1830. There, Christianity was reduced to a civil religion. "People follow a religion the way our fathers took a certain medicine during the month of May," wrote Tocqueville. "If it does not do any good, people seem to say, at least it cannot do any harm, and, besides, it is proper to conform to the general rule."[42] In 1840 Tocqueville's analysis became more radical. Emerging from Catholicism, society was slipping relentlessly from Lutheranism to deism, then to pantheism, and finally to atheism. The American religion was a phase in this watering down which had already led Europeans from Catholicism to indifference.[43]

Yet this indifference imperiled the entire political order. Tocqueville was much less worried about a religion's truth than its political effects. He had no sympathy for mysticism or pietism. "A certain preoccupation with religious truths which does not go to the point of absorbing thought in the other world has therefore always seemed to me the state that conforms best to human morality in all its forms," he wrote to Kergorlay.[44] In the relationship to God, only distance from the All-Other and maintaining some space beyond society interested him. As soon as people's sense of transcendence deadened, they tended toward idolatry, whose purest example lay in what Tocqueville called "pantheism" which glued all people together, allowing them only to adore their own image and destroying their moral feeling. Like many of his contemporaries, Tocqueville was afraid of the spread of Spinoza's, Hegel's, or Saint-Simon's thought. In 1840 religion aimed less at fostering moral order than at challenging unjust orders. It sustained power less than it supported the infinite claim of law. The first *Democracy* had sought the institutional conditions for order; the second sought a religious pedagogy of the spirit of liberty.

The genesis of the work reveals the natural flow of Tocqueville's thought, which lurched ahead without preestablished plan or rigorous conceptual definition. Like Montaigne and Montesquieu, Tocqueville worried less about avoiding contradictions than about discovering the many sides to a question through interminable rewritings, oscillation between competing hypotheses, and advancing in his thinking without effacing prior problematics. This approach led to the unsettling quality of the work, which Tocqueville stubbornly insisted was a continuation of the first volume (*DA* 2:v).

Nothing in the 1840 volume reveals the gap between it and the 1835 book. Tocqueville originally had conceived a new title for it: *The Influence of Equality on Human Ideas and Sentiments.* He returned later to *Of Democracy in America.*[45] Was this the publisher's way of keeping a good thing going? Of course. But Tocqueville also feared he would appear too much a theoretician, a dangerous reputation for a deputy from an agricultural district. Thus the shift made in 1840 was willingly erased as though Tocqueville feared scaring his readers off by going from an object found to one constructed, from America to democracy.

A Failed Launch

Yet Tocqueville was still worried. He could not help knowing that he was working against the tastes of the public. He ran counter to some people's political prejudices by his alliance with democracy and to others' by his attachment to individual liberty, which had only a small place in democracies. "Men will not receive the truth from their enemies, and it is very seldom offered to them by their friends; on this very account I have frankly uttered it," Tocqueville argued (*DA* 2:vi).

The problem was that the second *Democracy* did not just displease—it ran the risk of wearying its readers. "I am already certain to be serious, and have an abominable fear of being boring," complained Tocqueville.[46] And readers in democratic times could not endure boredom. "As the time they can devote to letters is very short, they seek to make the best use of the whole of it. . . . They ask for beauties self-proffered and easily enjoyed; above all, they must have what is unexpected and new" (*DA* 2:59). The second *Democracy,* a work of wisdom more than knowledge, offers nothing unexpected but presents itself as an exhibition of the world we share together, whose only objective is "to restate completely, reasonably, and with some novelty a large number of things that have already been glimpsed or roughly portrayed by others."[47]

Explaining his failure in advance, Tocqueville tried to bend himself to the tastes of the day. He tried to be brief, then sadly resigned himself to publishing two volumes after so hopefully caressing the dream of concentrating his thoughts into one.[48]

Editor Gosselin[49] was unfazed by such fears. He felt at no great risk with an established author, a deputy and an academic to boot. So he printed 2,500 copies in an expensive in-octavo format, and 900 in-18, and brought out the book on 24 April, when all of the Paris elite were starting to think about their country homes. Gosselin had announced Tocqueville's new book regularly since 1837. He redoubled his efforts for the press launch now.[50] On 15 April 1840 Tocqueville published the book's essential chapter, "Des révolutions dans les sociétés nouvelles," in the *Revue des Deux Mondes.* More seductive advance proofs on American women or the degradation of culture went to publications with more frivolous audiences.[51]

The results of his efforts were meager. The second *Democracy* sold slowly until 1848, when Pagnerre, who had taken over Gosselin's stock, printed three new editions, responding to the increase of interest in the book due to the birth of the Republic. With the in-octavo edition sold out, the moderate republican Pagnerre, whose political sympathies were with Tocqueville, published the first popular edition of *Democracy* with 4,000 copies printed in two in-18 volumes. For the first time Tocqueville's work was accessible to a not-so-moneyed student public.[52] But these reprinted editions should not deceive us. A wider public increased the first *Democracy*'s renown, not the second's. In 1850 as in 1835, the French only paid attention to constitutional questions and only fought about whether it was urgent to ally oneself with the Republic.

The lukewarm temperature of public opinion was manifest in the low level of enthusiasm critics showed in presenting the book. The much-touted sequel to a famous book should naturally make some noise. America experts jumped on the occasion to remind the public of their existence with a few acerbic commentaries.[53] Tocqueville's friends diligently sang his praises, and ministry officials recalled the dangers of an untimely shift to democracy.[54]

All this meant little. *Democracy* was not in line with the era's current events, which the journals chewed over and over. Foreign politics interested the French only when conflict threatened. In 1840 the threat came from Egypt, not the United States. To which can be added the degradation of the image of America between 1835 and 1840 among all but the Protestants, who had a kind of sympathy on principle for their American coreligionists.[55] The United States was admired now only for its economic progress, which Tocqueville hardly cared about.[56]

As far as domestic politics was concerned, Tocqueville's book was no more timely. In 1840 the regime seemed well seated. Constitutional issues were no longer the order of the day. Instead, there was concern about riots, workers' coalitions, and socialist doctrines.[57] Tocqueville indeed handled social questions, but only by allusion. And the themes he dealt with—pantheism, individualism— were certainly in the air without being party or political questions. In France even an "impartial" writer was successful only insofar as he played the party game.

This is why most reviews were not published until the summer. And even then, Tocqueville had to remind his friends so that he could begin his local political tours preceded by flattering rumors from the Paris papers. Beaumont took it upon himself to write an article in *Le Siècle* of 26 August, pressured Sacy to write one for the *Journal des Débats,* and besieged the editorial board of *L'Univers.*[58] A whole series of articles came out from September to November: in September in *La Presse,* the *Revue des Deux Mondes,* and the *Revue de Paris;* in October in the *Journal des Débats, L'Univers Religieux,* and the *Gazette de France;* and in November in *L'Echo Français,* but this last account, an anonymous one, was written by the author's father! All of it gives one more the impression of a very energetic publicity campaign led by a lobby than spontaneous enthusiasm.

Disappointment was general, and worst among the republicans. In 1835 they had enjoyed the first *Democracy.* In 1840–41 they kept quiet, becoming openly hostile as the years went by. Doubtless this hostility was in part due to the Carlo-Republican alliance which had been tight in 1835 but had grown looser. In 1840 republicans had no more tactical reasons to flatter a legitimist offspring. But what distanced them from Tocqueville was above all doctrinal opposition.

The 1840s had been a very fertile time for them intellectually. In 1840 Louis Blanc's *L'organisation du travail,* Cabet's *Voyage en Icarie,* Pierre Leroux's *De l'humanité,* and Proudhon's *Qu'est-ce que la propriété?* were published. This was also the year *L'Atelier* was founded. In 1842 the republican party's attempt at doctrinal coherence found its expression in the *Dictionnaire politique* published by Pagnerre under Garnier-Pagès's direction.[59] How to explain Louis Blanc's silence, when he had been so prolific on *Democracy* in 1835? What of the silence by moderate republicans like Garnier-Pagès or Hauréau who later had friendly connections with Tocqueville, whose collaboration was planned for in the new 1848 edition of the *Dictionnaire politique?*[60]

The dictionary's authors, despite their concern for the respect of minorities, believed in the progress of democracy by extending the powers of a centralized, leveling state. They admired Rousseau, not Montesquieu. For them, the associative principle found its perfection in national association, and progress its motor in laws rather than customs. They thus rejected liberalism as soon as it identified with the rights of the individual.[61] This is why their hostility toward the United States grew, perceptible as early as 1835 and reaffirmed in the 1840s.[62]

Tocqueville was in no way an apologist for individualism. He favored the association, mother of democratic liberty. But he conceived of associations as the gatherings of individual wills, not their fusion into some single entity. Above all, he trusted reforms of customs more than of laws, and this was the cause of republican hesitancy toward him. We have proof in their critiques of him in 1842. Tocqueville took the floor twice to criticize the moral decline of Prime Minis-

ter Guizot in debate on 16 January 1842 and in his reception speech to the
Académie Française of 21 April 1842.[63] Along the same lines as the second *Democ-racy*, he analyzed individualism's misdeeds and the decline in civic feeling, con-cluding that a reform in mores was necessary. The legitimists were enchanted
by this denunciation of the "ministerial ruminants who get fat in the budget's
pastures."[64] Republicans and socialists found it overwrought: "This is no place to
moralize, to preach moderation and virtue; it is certainly not in that way that we
will manage to cure the passion for position—it is the very cause of this passion
that we must attack and fight. We must organize agricultural, manufacturing,
commercial, scientific, and artistic work so that all can find posts therein more
advantageous and more secure than ones with the state."[65]

Thus, despite their common opposition to the minister, Tocqueville set him-self apart from republicans and socialists by his preference for slow reform of
customs and his horror of legislative willfulness, a quality of political and doc-trinal sensibility that separates French liberal and Left traditions.

This growing hostility of the republicans was the sign of a general shift in in-terpretation of *Democracy* in a conservative direction. In 1840 Tocqueville seemed
much more somber than in 1835. No doubt he was, because he was distressed by
the July regime's development. But this increased pessimism owes much to
Tocqueville's own shift from studying laws to studying democratic culture.
Tocqueville joined, as many intellectuals do, an aristocratic aesthetic and a de-mocratic ethic. His cultural pessimism was often confused with political reticence
toward democracy. To conservatives, he seemed guilty of not pleading for reac-tionary politics; to the democrats he seemed to accept democracy only out of fa-talism: "He is like a traveler who courageously gets out on the stormy sea of the
future and only regretfully tears himself away from the tranquil majestic banks
of the past," wrote Sacy in the *Journal des Débats* of 9 October 1840.

Democracy was too distant from the intellectual habits of readers who sought
in it "what there was not . . . a true continuation in both form and content of
the first work,"[66] and they accused the title of having misled them.[67]

Anatomy of a Failure

Because they could not find their own thoughts in it, readers in chorus an-nounced their great weariness with the book. In 1835 *Democracy* had seemed to
address only serious men. In 1840 it was worse. "Reading M. de Tocqueville's book

is not something men of today are used to doing," wrote Rossi;[68] "it demands not merely eyes but also thought. It is no amusement, it is work." Tocqueville was aware that he had not reached the public he aimed for. "This book," he wrote, "by its nature will not impassion anyone. It leaves the spirit stunned and wounded."[69]

This wounding showed in two contradictory criticisms made of the book. On one hand, those who failed to grasp its structure[70] (which the author himself admitted was "somewhat obscure and problematic")[71] accused Tocqueville of theoretical timidity. But on the other hand, Tocqueville was accused of mitigating that lack of true synthesis by yoking facts together arbitrarily. The second *Democracy* seemed "a book of observation and practice elevated to the form of a rational hypothesis in order to be more impartial and persuasive."[72] Tocqueville's absorption in an idée fixe or monomaniacal attachment[73] to equality was criticized to the point that he was ridiculed as a salon dotard. Had Tocqueville noted the prosperity of Cincinnati? "You think that M. de Tocqueville will stop, examine the state, study it in detail, seek the causes for the effects which seem to him so marvelous—and you are wrong. It is so easy to put everything together, to attribute the results to motives seductive to the imagination or to readers' utopias, pleasing everyone and offering the opportunity for ringing phrases." Tocqueville "pulls out of his box a perfumed cigar, enjoys it, strikes his forehead with it. . . . a stream of light shoots out of his brain, and the knowing writer discovers that the prosperity of Cincinnati is due to the absence of slavery in the state of Ohio."[74]

The Obscure Clarity of the Idea of Equality

What irritated his readers was not so much the generality of Tocqueville's conclusions but the place where he applied those generalities. Tocqueville attributed to equality of conditions qualities and effects that since the eighteenth century had been attributed to the progress of civilization: utility, increased welfare, expansion of the middle classes. Nothing demonstrated the novelty of the substitution more clearly than Mill's reticence.[75] England, objected Mill, was not an egalitarian country but a middle-class country. Yet England received the qualities Tocqueville attributed to democracy strictly from its progress in commerce and industry: concern for individual welfare, preoccupation with utility to the point of intellectual numbness, the preeminence of wealth over privileges of birth. By reducing Tocqueville's analysis to a socioeconomic one and reinterpreting his work according to a linear progression toward an ever-increasing middle class and public welfare, Mill rejected as arbitrary all of Tocqueville's development of equality. For him, the importance Tocqueville gave equality was a characteristic of theoretical chauvinism. In France political equality had preceded the development of capitalist civilization. On the other hand, in England industrialization preceded democratization. By privileging equality, Tocqueville was merely reflecting the precocity of the egalitarian political experience in France.

Tocqueville himself had at first like Mill made the notion of civilization central to his thinking. In 1830 he described the state of a people who had "reached a high degree of civilization" in terms foreshadowing his 1840 description of servile democracies: "The social organism has planned for everything; the individual takes only the trouble to be born. For the rest, society takes him in his nurse's arms and holds him up as he walks, shoos danger away and he peacefully advances under the eye of this second Providence. The tutelary power that protected him during his life even watches over his ashes. . . . This is the reign of egotism."[76]

Thus Tocqueville substituted equality for civilization as the principle of history after due consideration. Not that he contested civilization's tendency toward greater well-being and middle-class expansion. He even makes this a condition of democracy, which can progress only to the degree to which inheritances are parceled out and wealth is distributed (*DA* 2:129). In contrast, poverty endangered civilization as well as democracy. In the wake of the social legitimists, the *Mémoire sur le paupérisme* of 1835[77] and the second *Democracy* show that an aristocracy can emerge from industry by "a twisted path" that creates a class of workers exposed without protection to periodic market crises. All of Tocqueville's efforts as a politician consisted in seeking new forms of property that had workers participating in industrial development or saving money so they could have greater well-being and middle-class independence. "I am very much of your opinion," he wrote Sophie Swetchine on 10 September 1856, "that a more equal distribution of goods and rights in this world is the greatest aim that those who conduct human affairs can have in view."[78]

Tocqueville therefore did not deny that the modern age was characterized by technical progress,[79] the rise of industry, and greater well-being. But for him, social dynamism resulted less from civilization's material progress than from the universal desire for equality. The idea of equality became the primary motor for change. A dynamic motor, because sharing wealth was never ultimately egalitarian, could never be, without doing violence to nature: "No communities have

ever yet existed in which social conditions have been so equal that there were neither rich nor poor" (*DA* 2:177). And if a people "unhappily attained that absolute
and complete equality of position, the inequality of minds would still remain,
which, coming directly from the hand of God, will forever escape the laws of
man" (*DA* 2:138).

That in democracies there is inherited money and intelligence, Tocqueville did
not doubt. What is astonishing is the indignation their existence incites in us.
Democracy advances through constant human effort to reduce the gap between
our insatiable desire for equality and an inegalitarian economy where well-being
does not become universal merely through the virtuosity of the market's hand.
As a result, the economy is only a limited structure compared with the decisive
importance of social representations. What held Tocqueville's interest was not so
much equality in action as equality as a norm of social existence: a new "faith,"
an "imaginary equality" that brought people together on a common level "in
spite of the real inequality of their conditions."[80]

This confused readers and led them to criticize Tocqueville for his unclear terminology. He was "always talking about equality as though it was a person who
ruled everything, did everything in a democracy."[81] Tocqueville himself in fact
recognized that what he meant by equality was multiple in meaning:

> I have frequently used the word "equality" in an absolute sense; nay, I have
> personified equality in several places; thus I have said that equality does such and
> such things or refrains from doing others. . . . These abstract terms which abound
> in democratic languages, and which are used on every occasion without attach-
> ing them to any particular fact, enlarge and obscure the thoughts they are in-
> tended to convey. . . . I do not know, indeed, whether this loose style has not some
> secret charm. . . . An abstract term is like a box with a false bottom; you may
> put in it what ideas you please, and take them out again without being observed.
> (*DA* 2:69–70)

Tocqueville's Blindness to National Differences

Tocqueville made himself harder to read by examining more than one society. That the comparisons were enlightening everyone agreed, but that a single
discourse could apply to several societies seemed impossible: "By thus sailing full
speed into the philosophy of history, M. de Tocqueville . . . could not avoid either
saying too much for such a specific subject as American democracy or saying too
little for a general subject which included, among others, France and the United

States, two ends of the democratic spectrum, the two opposing poles of liberty."[82] The result was that the work seemed more one of creative imagination than realistic analysis. Royer-Collard's reaction was representative on this score: "There is not a chapter which could not have been different in some ways than what you have written," he wrote to Tocqueville. "This is due, it is true, to the subject. You set yourself the task of imagining, of inventing rather than describing, and invention in some ways is arbitrary."[83]

Democracy in fact left little space for the principle of nationality, although Tocqueville had presaged its importance,[84] and omitting the nation could only rub French readers the wrong way,[85] as well as German and Slavic ones. Count Leo Thun, a Czech liberal, criticized Tocqueville for not having perceived that nationality's collective particularism was an essential explanatory principle of history:

> If we find, among the Americans, obstacles opposed to any sublime élan, I think I see the causes, and they have no necessary relationship to equality of conditions; for example, the spirit of commerce occasioned by the situation of the country they live in, and the lack of taste for the higher sciences which they inherited from their parents, and which we find even among their aristocratic cousins. Surely equality of conditions, when it reigns generally in Germany . . . will show a very different face. . . . I cannot keep from believing that knowledge of the state and the intellectual movement of the Germans would have led you to change somewhat the point of view from which you see your subject.[86]

Tocqueville's blindness to the principle of nationality, which contributed to political disappointment in 1849, also explained later reluctance to accept the second *Democracy*. The great works of disciples of the dissident Le Play which were devoted to America, like Rousiers's or Demolins's,[87] no longer took Tocqueville as their model. Anglo-Saxon superiority seemed to them due less to any democratic character than to the uniqueness of Anglo-Saxon experience. At the close of the century, national differences were felt by writers from Taine to Boutmy to be so important as to endanger the very idea of democratic universalism. His readers' uneasiness points to the blind spot in Tocqueville's 1840 method. By confining himself to a study of democratic universalism, he excised all that could not be compared, that was unique, in consequence, all that was historic. He emphasized the permanent to the detriment of change. According to Tocqueville, one could say about democracies what could be said then about primitive societies, that they have no history, either upstream or downstream. Democracies still bear the stigmata of ancient inequality, but this is merely residual; they are vulnerable to accidents—commercial crises, wars, or revolution, all destined to become increasingly rare. They even risk falling into the catastrophe of barbarism. But neither these accidents nor this catastrophe make a history, that is to say, a temporal continuity within which events take place, engendering a new meaning. As stagnant societies, democracies mark the end of history.

Discourse on Customs

Disturbed by the primacy of equality and Tocqueville's blindness to the idea of the nation, readers were even more disconcerted by his unusual project of typological discourse on customs. Under the July Monarchy the study of institutions had already developed clear outlines and its own canonized terminology. The study of customs seemed an immense field with vague outlines, more appropriate to the kind of picturesque description for which Tocqueville had little talent.[88] Readers who might have wished for "more motion, livelier colors"[89] were determined to feed their taste for exoticism with his chapters on religion but especially those on Americans' lack of culture and the emancipated appearance of American women. Several later undertook to rewrite Tocqueville's book as a travelogue, a perfect mix of seductive novelty and the demanded synthesis.[90]

The novelty of Tocqueville's project becomes most evident when we note how hard it was for his contemporaries to determine who his predecessors were. In 1835 he had been hailed as the new Montesquieu. In 1840 the comparison seemed pertinent only ironically. "M. de Tocqueville uses Montesquieu's style admirably well to make his superficial analyses," wrote *L'Univers*. "The difference between Montesquieu and M. de Tocqueville is that the former was gifted with historical feeling and poetical feeling to an eminent degree, whereas the second seems to be lacking in any. It is these two feelings that cause one to appreciate in the life of nations the enduring power of traditions and prior events, the influence of race, the land, the climate."[91]

By its generality Tocqueville's discourse was only interpretable when compared to the most ancient classical moralists' discourse, which sought to show human nature as identical across all nations of the world. Tocqueville retained the seventeenth-century moralists' chagrined severity toward human frailty, their disenchanted view of humanity's future. He can be compared to La Bruyère and especially to Pascal, whom he resembles in the direction of his thinking—always moving from effect to the reason for the effect.[92] From 1840 to today, it has been commonly agreed that his thinking proceeded forward by lurches and forced antitheses, as summed up epigrammatically by Sainte-Beuve: "No mind has ever placed so many prior objections in its own path and thought around itself so much before beginning: all the buts, ifs, and fors that might enter into a thoughtful mind he shook up beforehand and weighed carefully."[93] Tocqueville's discourse proceeded by rhetorical figures, like Pascal's. As the Old Testament for Pascal prefigured the New, America for Tocqueville prefigured France's future. And just as for Pascal God was hidden, for Tocqueville the providential promulgation of democracy remained obscure.

But Tocqueville was an unfaithful and a secular disciple. He did not seek after the City of God or talk about salvation, but only about improving the City of Man. In 1840 Villemain had noted this secularization in religious hermeneutics: Tocqueville approached the nature of democracy using empirical societies as "symbols" of that nature. "Of America he made the same use as the church had made of sacred history, when it sought in every tale of the past, a figure, an image of the present or the future."[94] Through descriptions of real American or French societies, a second meaning emerges, indecipherable except through the first. Today we often interpret Tocqueville's thought as an imperfect precursor of Weberian typology. But repositioned within its own time, his thought seems much more a hermeneutics which casts the course of history as the site where humanity gradually finds itself uniform, through the egalitarian imagination. Readers disagreed about what democracy really was, because Tocqueville refused to develop just one type.

Individualism and Servitude

But Tocqueville's membership in the classical lineage hardly allowed his contemporaries to understand the novelty of his analysis of how anarchy overturned can become servitude. The modern denunciation of individualism so popular today was more seductive in 1840 because it was familiar, not new. Criticism of individualism indeed predated Tocqueville. It ran through newspaper columns, infiltrated Chamber podiums, was breathed in preachers' sermons. It was common opinion that what defined modernity was fragmentation of faith, the end of dogma, the quest for the bizarre, the empire of fashion, and seeking after money as the sole universal means of exchange while all criteria for excellence crumbled. Tocqueville did not influence the common denunciation of modern individualism; that prospered through the end of the nineteenth century. In the 1890s we still find moralists like Brunetière and Gaston Deschamps denouncing the rule of the ephemeral and the cult of the ego;[95] we find writers and sociologists like Tarde and Bourget thinking about imitation, fashion, snobbery, and the democratic dialectic that leads from the exacerbation of individual particularities to universal insignificance. This aspect of Tocqueville's book is indiscernible within such an anonymous discourse of common opinion.

But Tocqueville's criticism of the invasion of political society by mercantile interests seemed sharper. Not that this was a first either: we find this in Bonald and among the legitimists. But the denunciation carried more weight coming from a democrat. Tocqueville seemed to be an intellectual critic who denounced Guizot's practices and those of his successors, for whom society's common ground and individuals' habitual horizons were shaped by material interests. Readers were delighted to find ammunition in Tocqueville to drive out July's engorged bourgeois, then Napoleon III's rascals, and the check-cashing deputies who had been bribed during the Panama crisis. But in all of it, nothing was stronger than the disapproval reserved for the rat race and the corrupt. Beyond opposition to the July regime, theoretical denunciation of individualism met with only sporadic attention from Tocqueville's readers. The empire's opponents no longer saw individualism as the perverse tendency of individuals to look out for themselves but as the defense of the individual against the state. When Lacordaire, succeeding Tocqueville at the Académie, criticized bourgeois individualism, he was called a "demagogue," a "socialist," and an "agitator."

In the nineteenth century the Tocquevillean critique of individualism was invisible within common discourse. Readers failed to perceive the reverse side, by which individuals who promise themselves liberty are hampered by servitude. The correlation between the advance of individualism and power's expansion is very much on the table today in discussions of democratic breakups. In Tocqueville's time the idea was new. In 1840, aside from Ampère who had had the benefit of the author's explanations face to face,[96] no one was interested in Tocqueville's tableau of tutelary despotism. Despotism still necessarily wore the face of the conventional republic of 1793.[97] State tutelage seemed beneficial at a time when individual human rights seemed still menaced by a counterrevolutionary reversal. More profoundly, the notion of voluntary submission by individuals ran counter to liberal optimism about free will. For Tocqueville's readers, voluntary servitude could never seduce democratic people, because "the democratic spirit is individual power and personal responsibility in their highest expression."[98]

Tocqueville—A Doctor without Patients?

Failing to agree with Tocqueville's diagnosis meant his readers balked at taking the recommended medicine. Tocqueville had promoted enlightened self-interest through a pedagogic concession to human weaknesses. He was deemed too moralizing by economists[99] and too "materialist" by the majority of French opinion, traditionally reluctant to recognize the merits of mercantile society.

Under the July Monarchy legitimists, Doctrinaires, and republicans in fact were mostly in agreement on the hierarchical opposition between body and soul that was the foundation of the truth of spiritualism and disqualified the materialism of self-interest. The very people who believed in the virtues of the market—American-style Protestants and ministry officials allied with Guizot—trusted more in religion to educate democracies than in any doctrine of enlightened self-interest.[100]

Their reticence toward utilitarianism, obvious as early as 1835–40, grew during the Second Empire out of opposition to the Bonapartists who legitimated the regime for the well-being it produced. Bonapartist Sainte-Beuve could denounce the outrageously aristocratic nature of Tocqueville's critique of "stomach politics" as loudly as he wanted, proclaiming, "There is nothing more respectable than the stomach, and no louder cry than that of poverty."[101] But enlightened opinion agreed more with Janet who deplored that Tocqueville "let his disdain for democratic societies show a bit too much, because he deemed them completely incapable of considering virtue dispassionately."[102] At the end of the nineteenth century, Renouvier's disciple Henry Michel reproached Tocqueville again for having been overly seduced by utilitarianism.[103] In all of these, we find the same thirst to dissociate the individual from the citizen, the same scorn for private interest, and thus the same reticence with regard to the American experience. This experience was judged impure because it combined the desire for autonomy, the dream of the promised land, a taste for public liberty, and freedom from want. For Tocqueville, the pedagogy of enlightened self-interest was a path explored and regretfully left behind; for most of his readers, it was a dead end.

By declaring utilitarianism insufficient to produce public well-being and by turning instead to religious feeling, Tocqueville should have pleased a mainly spiritualistic public. Yet his thinking seemed singularly opaque. The first *Democracy* had seduced because it had seemed to place established religion in the service of moral order and the prevention of revolutions. The second *Democracy* generally made religion a goad to the spirit of liberty, stumbling on the real obstacle of a dogmatic and authoritarian church. Concerned about "burning his fingers,"[104] Tocqueville confined himself to pleading for "any religion" (*DA* 2:145). He treated the role of ecclesiastical authorities so vaguely that the church seemed an imaginary principality. And in fact, his prudence in this case was no trickery. Tocqueville was certain of the unity of Christianity beyond divisions among Christians and of the flexibility of a doctrine which in every era "appeared, nevertheless, to lend itself . . . to the new tendencies."[105] In his eyes the only real enemy was the unbelief encouraged by denominational controversy.

But Tocqueville's readers were not in the least comfortable with these ambiguities. Protestants and Catholics were unanimous in denouncing in Tocqueville's apology for "any religion" the entrapment of religion within the bonds of mere reason.

For *L'Esperance*, the Protestant journal led by Monod,

> a vague and general notion that Christianity is true in some undefined sense is hardly anything other than belief in everything and nothing. . . . What is the result? Only passion and the dominant tendency of a century become one's guides, and whoever tries to counter them with an ideal or type of perfection is accused of attempting the impossible. This sort of fanaticism is the saddest symptom that has ever threatened humanity. We suffer to see such a high-minded intelligence as that of M. Tocqueville allow itself to be penetrated by it. Not only must his system of "any religion" produce such fatalism, but in his entire work, "the real future" completely destroys the ideal, and he finds to counter the ills he foresees in this future only the miserable expedients and powerless palliatives which his mind furnishes him after he has banished the ideal from his thought."[106]

More than twenty years later, reading *Old Regime*, Quinet in his turn grew indignant at "Tocqueville's weakness toward religion. Always the same Babel! Religion! But which? Is all of Tocqueville's life caught up in this Babel?"[107]

Conservative Catholics were no less disturbed by Tocqueville's method, which removed political society from the authority of Truth, and accused Tocqueville of inconsistency, because he claimed to juxtapose the democratic principle of autonomy in political society with the religious principle of authority in religious society. In 1856 legitimist Laurentie expressed regret that Tocqueville "seemed to feel that society had been created to govern itself; this would mean thinking that society had been given up by Providence to all the hazards of passion, fantasy, or human perversity."[108] Catholic reservations toward Tocqueville continued under the Third Republic among all those who opposed the Ralliement,[109] despite Rédier's efforts to save Tocqueville in spite of himself and to make of this "miscreant" contaminated by democratic miasmas a pillar of the Decalogue.

Liberals liked to denounce Tocqueville's unreality. Their wariness grew after 1848 when the church fell back into reaction. When Lacordaire called, as Tocqueville had, for the reconciliation of the church with modern society, Prévost-Paradol was quick to respond ironically:

> If the Catholic Church and liberty did not always agree in the Old World, should all the blame be placed on liberty? We are pleased to suggest to M. La-cordaire that he go to Rome and ask this question—if he has not already done so long ago and prudently withdrawn his question, knowing in advance what the answer would be. Why forget that it is religion, or even better, the claims to religious independence against an established church, that created the United States of America? Why would a religion of that kind, while departing for the New World in the company of liberty and blessing it and relying on it, have be-come hostile or suspicious toward its dear and inseparable companion? But is there any analogy between this history and our own, between this great good fortune, and our own glorious misfortunes?[110]

Thus the American experience, where the chance encounter of a multiplicity of faiths required the separation of church and state, had nothing to do with the "glorious misfortunes" of France, where the majority church clashed with de-mocracy.

While in private Tocqueville despaired,[111] he could try to show that the Catholic Church was egalitarian as hard as he liked by saying that it subjected all believers alike to the same authority. He convinced no one. For most readers, Catholic institutions had a natural affinity with monarchy and none at all with democracy.

The eccentricity of Tocqueville's thought within French culture explains his later political failures. As a young deputy, he had assigned himself the task of syn-thesizing the Enlightenment with religious belief and making the church and de-mocratic society able to cohabit by separating them.[112] The notion of separation might have seemed incongruous in an era of concordat. But Tocqueville favored a concordat that gave political power a hold on the church that was indispens-able to right order. He only envisioned separation of spheres of authority in order to avoid "that most detestable of all human institutions, a political religion, a re-ligion in the service of government which helps oppress people rather than prepare them for freedom."[113] Renewed war against the clergy in 1843–44, with the schools as the battlefield, marked the failure of this attempt.

Guizot's 1833 law had ensured teachers' freedom in primary schools. Secondary education, although in principle governed by state monopoly since Napoleon, was in fact given in both state schools and 113 small Catholic seminaries whose students were not all destined for the priesthood. The church hierarchy had used the pretext of this delicate situation to launch a violent campaign against the university system. Minister of Instruction Villemain riposted in 1844 with a highly illiberal bill. Tocqueville, who found this religious warfare archaic,[114] took the side of curricular freedom in the Chamber on 17 January 1844 and again in a series of unsigned articles which appeared in *Le Commerce*. *Democracy* had remained prudently silent on interference between politics and religion in the sphere of the schools. In his writings of 1843–44, Tocqueville filled in this gap in *Democracy*, seeking to position himself on "the terrain of *common rights*. Calling for liberty in teaching for everyone, by virtue of the principles of the constitution," he hoped this could take place without privileging anyone, and especially not the church.[115] But in reality, the distinction between common rights and exclusive rights for Catholics meant walking a thin line. The clergy saw in this recognition of common rights the first step toward domination that they only put off for better days.[116] In spite of himself, Tocqueville had given support to the Catholic party tactics. Suddenly, the man who had hated intransigent Catholics such as Veuillot had attracted the condescending goodwill of believers for his virtues, so unlikely in freethinkers.[117]

The university's defenders were also aware only of the tactical advantages the church might gain from its submission to common rights. From the *Journal des Débats* to the *National*, Tocqueville was asked to deign to come down from "abstractions to practical facts" and admit "that liberty in teaching proclaimed today would mean preserving a monopoly he does not want" (*Le National*, 9 December). At best, Tocqueville was accused of causing the Left to despair (*Le Constitutionnel*, 30 November), at worst of playing a reactionary game through hereditary collusion with legitimism (*Le Siècle*, 4 December). And on 7 December *Le National*, pastiching the cardinal of Retz and irked by Tocqueville's liberal tilting at windmills and his "old-young" leftist forty- or fifty-somethings party, wrote, "There were five or six melancholy men who seemed emptyheaded."

Liberals and republicans thus did not disagree with the utility of belief, none challenged the principle of liberty, but all deemed it prudent to stop there and accused Tocqueville of elaborating premature theories. As a fighting principle, laicity was not a liberal one. By 1843 or 1844 Tocqueville shed light on this discord between liberal principles and sectarian watchwords which had so long endured in French history: "Men who today call for liberty of teaching in the very name of liberty of the human spirit, in the name of the respect owed to conscience, and as one of the natural and necessary consequences of our new institutions now feel real oppression. . . . Every day, people pretend to confuse them with parties that have another goal than theirs, calling at the same time as they do, but out of different principles, for this same liberty."[118]

The same political misadventure, liberal politics interpreted as involuntary support for reaction, recurred in 1849. In the spring, France had sent an army against Rome to reestablish the papal seat before Austria took matters into its own hands.[119] On 2 June 1849, somewhat by chance, Tocqueville was named minister of foreign affairs in Barrot's cabinet and received as his portfolio the task of making guarantees to republicans in Paris and Rome, mediating between the pope and those who had been his subjects. Tocqueville had always deemed the pope's absolute temporal power poisonous to religion's true interests. He nonetheless felt he must break with his principles and aid the pope in recovering his throne while forbidding access to Rome for the reactionary troops of Naples, Austria, and Spain. He fell on 31 October, having taken on all the unpopularity of a restoration sought by others. To the republicans Tocqueville became the adversary of popular sovereignty and the idea of the nation.[120] To conservatives he became the prodigal son who turned out well late in life. Tocqueville's principles were those of the Revolution; their application seemed especially to benefit reaction.

Tocqueville's tribulations show what his thinking owed to the American experience, making it inaccessible to the French insofar as French history made conceiving of Christianity allied with the Enlightenment difficult. "The first truly liberal partisan of a complete separation between the temporal and the spiritual,"[121] Tocqueville was to remain a lonely partisan for a long time.[122]

Thus the second *Democracy* did not enjoy the success of the first. Tocqueville remained the American constitutional expert. His 1840 work influenced his image by overlaying the figure of a chagrined moralist on that of democracy's public commentator. Iconography, biographical dictionaries, satirical journals, and memoirs offer us some similarities in their portraits of him.

Tocqueville was never popular[123] among the caricaturists, who preferred extremists more readily reducible to a ridiculous trait. Proudhon delighted them.

Guizot and Thiers, the Chamber's heavyweights, never failed to catch their eye. But Tocqueville was both too obscure and too moderate to be mocked very well. Even when he was in power in 1849, he only appeared in engravings lost in the crowd of conservatives. His political coloration was undecided. Legitimist by blood, sent to the United States by the July government, then returned to sit among the Left opposition in 1848, he received the status of *republicain du lendemain*— became a republican only after the Republic was established. Restoring the pope made him appear to fall back among the partisans of order, however.[124] He disconcerted all "parliamentary statisticians" who denounced this "little congregational Restoration magistrate who went to America to be rebaptized a humanitarian liberal and brought us back a wandering massive book on the democracy to be found there."[125] His physical appearance symbolized this political vacillation: it seemed quite completely insignificant. Insignificant, his cold but regular features; insignificant, his sentimental pallor.[126] His eyes were half-veiled by melancholy, his bitter mouth twisted without his thin lips breaking into a smile. He had a severe and awkward air, rather outmoded. "Might it be just a touch of misanthropy that saddens his heart and colors his face?" people wondered.

Haughty, pale, and sickly, Tocqueville was the purest representative of the volatile race of intellectuals who float high over the heads of parties and realities. He wore a pince-nez. It became his emblem in Daumier's and Bertall's caricatures: Tocqueville was a man of distance; he was boring and moralizing when it was time for passionate pleas; he had the loftiness of his intelligence, true, but was "a bit dry in spirit and a bit absolutist in his ideas. . . . His language was studded with somewhat austere philosophical and moral maxims. He spoke slowly like a preacher, full of soft unctuousness, but a bit too monotonously."[127] And his "slightly treacly" eloquence, his "tea-taking style," and "fever for arguments worthy of young ladies' boardinghouses were unpopular."[128] When the legislative assembly deliberated, every deputy was imagined dawdling in his own particular fashion. Thiers was imagined having gone fishing in rough waters. Tocqueville was rereading his great book so he could finally remember it,[129] posing as usual "as [a] profound observer, methodical and reasoned."[130]

A solitary nature, awkwardness in action, and rigidity in thought—all these traits can be found in Rémusat's portrait of Tocqueville torn between a democratic mind-set and aristocratic customs. In 1835 Tocqueville's belonging to both the ancien régime and the Revolution seemed to confer the wisdom of a young old man upon him. After 1840 it doomed him to impotence:

> Tocqueville's great merit was having forged his opinions himself. Raised in royalism's counterrevolutionary lap, he shook off its yoke only by observing his own time. He thus became not only liberal but democratic, I mean convinced that the world was going to belong to democracy. That was a great show of force and independence of spirit for Malesherbes's great-grandson. But as he disdained legitimism without hating the legitimists, as he was exempt from any rancor against the Bourbons and their party, his liberalism, a pure work of his reasoning, was irreproachable, yet cold, and mediocrely persuasive. . . . He was a little man without style, of agreeable and regular features but sickly, overshadowed by a mass of brown curly hair which maintained his air of youth. His inanimate, sad face became more expressive when he talked. The livid pallor of his skin showed his ailing organs early in life, and people who did not wish him well suspected him of being bilious, envious, and all the rest. But he was not: he was just a little defiant, often ill, often discouraged with himself.[131]

The famous portrait[132] Chassériau painted of his friend in 1849 leaves us with the same feeling. Chassériau shows a man in power, confronted by the consequences of the European revolutions of 1848, yet his youthful aspect, his carefully tended hair, his forthright but distant gaze and pale face cause us to set Tocqueville far apart from a politics of compromise, of interests and balances. However ambitious he was, Tocqueville had nothing about him of the bourgeois man full of prideful success we are so burdened by in nineteenth-century academic painting. Chassériau gives Tocqueville "a face still dreaming of its own future,"[133] the face of a prince in exile. In fact, Tocqueville was only to find his place in French culture under the empire.

3

In Search of France's Identity, 1850s

TODAY we usually distinguish *Democracy* from *Old Regime*, the first a work of practical consequence, in the modern sciences of political science and sociology, the second a dispassionate work of history. The nineteenth century made no such distinctions. It constructed its political identity by examining its revolutionary origins. Like his contemporaries Tocqueville never studied anything other than the France of his day, whether traveling across miles to the United States or across years to the era of absolutism. Tocqueville had just published the first *Democracy* in 1835 when he quickly extrapolated the work historically to his own country in a brief essay in 1836, "Etat social et politique de la France avant et depuis 1789." In 1840 the second *Democracy* revealed how individualism could turn into voluntary servitude under democracies. Starting in 1842, Tocqueville studied this dialectic at work in the period from the Enlightenment to the empire. Thus if there is any gap between *Democracy* and *Old Regime*, it is not a topical one but a change in historical model. *Democracy* taught the French that modernity was inevitable, or rather that their break with the ancien régime was. *Old Regime* taught them about the continuity of French history and the crushing weight of the dead upon the living. In 1835 Tocqueville had sought to understand democracies synchronically with a systematic study of social forms. In 1856 he used a diachronic explanation of origins, looking more closely at the specificity of national political cultures.

Genesis of a Project

Tocqueville and Liberal Historiography

The break made by *Old Regime* is obvious when we compare it to Tocqueville's early historical texts of 1836 and 1842. When he wrote the 1836 essay,[1] Tocqueville had already broken with Guizot on one point. He did not believe that the end of history was middle-class domination and consequently preferred the American democratic model, not the English aristocratic one. Yet he did not reject the primacy Guizot attributed to social determinism. To both historians the political events of 1789 meant the end of any universal social evolution that led to equality. They therefore neglected the Revolution's story. The game had ended in 1789, the date history stopped. We could "close the history books for fifty years," wrote Tocqueville—the French will not change, or very little.

Such a social explanation is all too brief, and Tocqueville soon abandoned it. In the second *Democracy* political experience led him to examine the correlation between advancing development of state omnipotence and advancing social disintegration. What remained was to trace the phenomenon's historical origins. In April 1842 Tocqueville gave the eulogy for Cessac as his predecessor at the Académie Française.[2] The obscure Cessac's only literary claim to fame was having faithfully served both the Revolution and the empire. He was of that secondary race of people "who seem to desert themselves and to transport themselves entirely to the point of view of those who lead them." He was a fine pretext by which to depict the three successive stages of French history: the ancien régime, sinking under the weight of its vices; the fervor of 1789, a period of "highly imprudent generosity" when the French tried to construct a society both free and egalitarian; and last, social disintegration from which despotism seemed to arise spontaneously. It was said that Napoleon had genius but his art lay simply in playing on circumstance in order to dominate more easily.

Tocqueville dated the idea for *Old Regime,* written in 1856, to 1842.[3] Starting in 1842, he had had the idea that the ancien régime had left the French with a blank slate, and that their passion for equality had led them blindly to clear a path for military dictatorship. All that was lacking in his early essays was a systematic organization of their components by causality—the confirmation that absolute monarchy, the Revolution, and the empire did not merely succeed each other but gave rise one to the next—and that both revolutionary radicalism and Napoleonic bureaucracy were born of absolutism.

In the 1840s Tocqueville was still blind to the persistence of revolutionary passion in France.[4] He was much more concerned about the increasing development of administrative laws that codified practices inaugurated by the empire. Because he was more sensitive to the new rationality of the state apparatus than he was to the age of its origins, because he feared order more than revolutionary impulses, Tocqueville had construed the origins of modern France as Napoleonic more than absolutist or revolutionary.

However partial his change in perspective between 1836 and 1842, it nonetheless distanced Tocqueville from his contemporaries. His address to the Academy in 1842 was as coldly received as the second *Democracy.* In it Tocqueville unmasked the taste for servitude he saw hidden in France's complacency toward the Napoleonic legend. There was nothing more likely to rub the French—who in October 1840 had triumphantly celebrated the return of Napoleon's ashes—the wrong way. Molé's much-applauded response to Tocqueville shows how wide the gap was between Tocqueville and his contemporaries. Molé, who had faithfully served the emperor, attributed Tocqueville's severity to his youthful ignorance. In a nation that had come apart in the eighteenth century, Molé said, Napoleon had filled a "providential need" by restoring authority and "making France the most powerful country in the universe."[5]

Under the July Monarchy, Tocqueville was as marginal a historian as he was a deputy. He continued to struggle on two fronts: against the Jacobins who confused 1789 with 1793 in their veneration and against the order-mad conservatives. The two had in common an overt and latent reverence for state authority and the insidious penchant for throwing themselves into the arms of any providential dictator.

"And Here Is the Revolution Starting Up Again, For It's Always the Same."[6]

From being marginal under the July Monarchy, how did Tocqueville become the mirror of his time under the Second Empire?[7] The shift can only be explained by examining the events of 1848–51, when France revisited the Revolution—first the moderate Gironde version, then that of radical leftist La Montagne—only to end up again with a Bonaparte. Like all of his contemporaries, Tocqueville was tyrannized by memory. "It seemed we were always busier performing the French Revolution than continuing it."[8] Yet because the French already knew their roles, there was no need to rehearse. Once the troubles of June 1848 began, Tocqueville felt he was reliving the Terror. But it was a much gentler Terror, fearsome mostly because of the benumbed craving for law and order it inspired in well-meaning people, including Tocqueville himself briefly, in fact. Political hostility toward the Republic, diffuse in June 1848, became overt with the 1849 expedition to Rome and the electoral law of 31 May 1850, which in one stroke barred three million men from the electoral rolls. From that point on, Tocqueville deemed the rush toward servitude unstoppable. "I don't understand how this can last or how it will end," he wrote. "I see myself without a compass, without sails and oars on a sea whose shores I see nowhere, and tired of moving about in vain, I lie at the bottom of my craft and await the future."[9]

In Tocqueville the thinker benefited from the politician's misfortunes. The revolution of 1830 had hurried him to America; the coup d'état tossed him into history. It was the similarity he saw between the short revolutionary cycle of 1848–51 and the longer one of 1789–99 that gave him *Old Regime*'s structure. In parodic style his contemporaries had made a single event of the old and the new revolutions, of the First Empire and the Second. Thinking they were performing in the same play, they in fact did perform it again, with the fatalistic illusion of its inevitability. To escape the alienating rationale of repetition, Tocqueville tried to lay bare its mechanism by telling the story differently. Liberating and activist, the story as written by Tocqueville, which is often imagined to be sad, abstract, and arid, is above all a public and private conquest of happiness. "I am sure that I have never been so happy," wrote Tocqueville at the start of his study.[10]

Thus as early as 1850–51, Tocqueville used historical analogy to trace the numerous resemblances between the great Napoleon and his nephew Bonaparte, who was still only a prince-president. He was aware of trying to respond to the public's expectations: "At bottom, only the things of our time interest the public and interest me. The greatness and singularity of the spectacle the world of our time presents is too absorbing to allow much value to be attached to those historical curiosities that suffice for lazy, erudite societies."[11]

From July to September 1852, he developed this concordance between past and present in two allusive historical essays, "Comment la République était prête à recevoir un maître," and "Comment la nation en cessant d'être républicaine était restée révolutionnaire." In them, he depicted the Directoire as well as 1851 when despotism already reared its head, one of those "moments when the world resembles one of our theaters before the curtain rises. We know we will see a new show. We can already hear the preparations happening on stage."[12]

But Tocqueville did not allow himself to abuse the theatrical metaphor his contemporaries had so long adored. Repeated performances of the revolutionary play had changed its impact in his mind. It was one thing for grandeur to be found in a Robespierre or a Napoleon in talk of bygone eras, even to gild the guillotine, as did Louis Blanc and Lamartine, or give Napoleon a halo of heroism, like the wordy Thiers. But a Napoleon who cycled back to oppress the French, a degraded Napoleon the Small without the excuse of an ancien régime or an absolutist Europe to bring down, not even the excuse of genius—that was something else again. The prince-president Louis-Napoléon was too insignificant to be dignified as a historical cause. What had raised and borne this very ordinary pretender to power must be discovered. That was why, rather than following up his *Souvenirs* with a tale of the coup d'état,[13] Tocqueville began writing about the ancien régime, to explain French complacency toward Caesarism from that point of departure. *Democracy* of 1835 looked for the starting point of American liberal democracy in the first Puritans; *Old Regime* in the same way looked for Caesarism's starting point in absolutism.

The genesis of *Old Regime* recalls the adventurous writing of the second *Democracy,* its style marked by the author's successive lurches forward. In December 1852 Tocqueville turned his attention definitively to the ancien régime and Revolution, abandoning his study of the empire. From June 1853 until the middle of 1854, he worked in Tours on papers generally related to the eighteenth century, still thinking he was only developing the first part of his great work on the French Revolution. In March 1854 he realized that his study of the ancien régime, initially meant to be a brief introductory chapter, offered the stuff of an entire book. What remained was to discern absolutism's true physiognomy by contrasting the German old regime and administration of the French *pays d'état.* Tocqueville devoted the years 1854 and 1855 to this.

This gradual expansion of the length of the revolutionary event to the entire history of absolutism explains Tocqueville's constant process of rewriting. Begun on 1 December 1853 and interrupted with periods of research, the writing spread over two years, the initial design blurred by many crosscutting directions. One of his first readers, Kergorlay, bemoaned this way of writing via successive objections. "You must avoid fatiguing [readers] by tormenting them too much with overly great accumulation of nuances and points of view in the same passage. You must give in much more to the desire to please them completely by literary charm."[14] Tocqueville replied that "the first spurt is often very preferable in form to all that reflection upon it adds afterward. But the thought itself gains much from being deeply explored and kneaded, approached and approached again, turned over and over in my mind in all directions."[15]

A Philosophical and Activist History

Like *Democracy, Old Regime* calls the reader to a navigation of the high seas, in profound search for causes beyond circumstance and psychology. But this philosophical history was subordinate to a political conclusion.

The Historian's High-Seas Search

Unhappy in politics, Tocqueville knew that history was made only blindly. "The destiny of this world works by effect, but often contrarily to the desires of all those who produce it, like a kite which moves by the opposite action of the wind and the string."[16] *Old Regime* put this discovery of history's irony to work. Despotism is less a result of the will to power than gradual accrual of many small expedients intended to be temporary but which become permanent—for example, a fiscal measure passed by a king who, unnoticed, gradually increases his powers so as to line his own coffers. The entire work tries to show how "the principal and permanent cause" of people's isolation (123) was "the slow, persistent action of our institutions" (180). Tocqueville thus constructed a long policy history in which the rosary of successive revolutions was told: the overwhelming importance of Paris, "this first revolution" accomplished long before 1789, "progenitor of all the others" (77); the isolation of the nobility and the bourgeoisie, that other "revolution" (85)—so many phases in the "long period of gestation" (96) through which the revolutionary illness advanced, without its actors' knowledge.[17]

In the hierarchy of causes, sensibility and common practice thus counted more than laws. "I am quite convinced," wrote Tocqueville, "that political societies are not what their laws make them, but what they are prepared in advance to be by the sentiments, beliefs, ideas, habits of the heart, and human spirits composing them, what nature and education have made of them."[18] Tocqueville's new conception of historical causality was inseparable from his new method. Little was known of the ancien régime in 1850. Historians and the erudite, always "knowledgeable as far the knowledge they cultivated was useless,"[19] mainly studied ancient eras. The great historians of the nation seldom troubled themselves with archives, despite the encouragement given by Guizot and Augustin Thierry to France's great documentary collections. So Tocqueville could brag that he had reversed things by substituting a study of French political culture for tales of reigns. "Until now, it was the surface of the object that was shown," he wrote. "I have turned it over and shown the underside."[20]

As he had in America, he used a questionnaire. While he was in Bonn in June and July 1854, he interviewed university professors and a few administrators about the degeneration of the German nobility to a caste, changes in the legal status of peasant landholdings, the place of religion in society, and the spread of the Enlightenment.[21]

He added, as he had in America, administrative and legal literature searches. The work's preparatory notes differ little from the files Tocqueville set up for his parliamentary reports. The book owes its innovative character to the young magistrate's experience with the consequences of the 1825 law indemnifying émigrés and his later experiences as deputy and as a member of the Manche regional council. Tocqueville's research on periods before the eighteenth century was limited and secondhand. On the other hand, the choice of sources on the eighteenth century reflects the perspicacity of a man familiar with the terrain, capably penetrating administrative arcana by analogy of past with present.

Study of absolutist practices was not enough. Tocqueville also had to explain why the French were suddenly so hungry for radical change around 1750. Others had blamed Voltaire and Rousseau or, like Burke, the bloody madness of revolutionaries. For Tocqueville, there was but one subversive agent, one single guilty party in French history: it was absolutism that had deprived the French of political experience and condemned them to ignorant radicalism. *Old Regime*'s entire third book tries hard to follow the "quivering" of "the democratic spirit" in absolutism's final two decades. Tocqueville used few philosophical or economic works, perhaps no great loss in view of the fact that his unpublished sketches in the history of ideas read like hastily recopied textbooks.[22] The anonymous, common culture was more important to him than great books. The reception of ideas was more important than the ideas themselves, or rather they were only important transformed into passions.[23] Tocqueville was less interested in the intellectual origins of the notion of democracy than in the emergence of an egalitarian sensibility whose essential trait was envy. In *Democracy* Tocqueville had demonstrated that hatred of privilege grew as equality advanced. In *Old Regime* he depicted the peasant more impatient with domination as he became a landholder, and public opinion more irritable with privilege as the king made preliminary reforms. Envy was more the daughter of hope than of need.

Old Regime thus cleared the path for a new kind of history by explaining *mentalité*, practices, and passions with the notion of the *longue durée*. But Tocqueville sacrificed his accumulated documents to his desire to convince: "I might have cluttered up my pages with footnotes, but it seemed better to insert only a few and to relegate the rest to an appendix, with the page references indicated" (xv). Tocqueville shared with his contemporaries the conviction that knowledge was inseparable from its moral utility and that history's vocation was giving the present its political meaning.

History as an Allusive Politics

Like *Democracy*, *Old Regime* is above all a work of argumentation leading the reader from observations about Evil to hope of healing. But *Old Regime's* analysis of evils shines more brightly than its description of remedies. The entire book demonstrated French impotence at getting out of the old rut of despotism, seeming to agree with absolutism's eighteenth-century adversaries and later liberal historians about the contrast both had drawn between Roman slaves and free Teutons. Tocqueville took up Montesquieu's, Hume's, and Augustin Thierry's idea that Europe had had the same "Gothic" constitution throughout the Middle Ages. Destroyed on the Continent, it had survived in England and the United States.[24] Following Burke, he affirmed that European history was torn, but Burke had been off by four centuries—the tear in European history dated not from the French Revolution but from the fourteenth century.

In the fourteenth century feudal Europe was sufficiently uniform that the state of one country could be deduced from the others.[25] "Indeed at that time the political institutions in France and England were very similar. Subsequently, however, there was a parting of the ways, and as time went on, the two nations became ever more dissimilar" (98). On one hand, the regular, natural growth of liberty adjoined equality; this was the Anglo-Saxon axis which lead from feudalism to the English aristocracy and then to the United States, carrying to extremes "the republican element, which forms, so to say, the foundation of the English constitution and English habits" (254). Of this liberal tradition of self-government, the Continent retained only residual traces in the *pays d'état*.

For the Continent took a different path, in which equality grew sheltered by absolute government. France gave the most advanced demonstration of this Continental pathology; Germany and Russia, its archaic forms. Tocqueville declared that he was

> struck by the great analogy which existed between what happened in Würtemberg in 1836 and what happened in France in 1788, particularly concerning the position of the peasantry and landholding. On this point I am convinced that the best way to understand the state of these things in France in 1788 is not to study French documents which discuss this in old form with old ideas, and refer to institutions so destroyed that what we have before our eyes keeps us from understanding them—but to study German books . . . which are written today with today's ideas, even amidst old institutions, making the image of the past appear clearly to us, and making it understood.[26]

Russia was even more delayed. But for Tocqueville, Russia was "an America minus the Enlightenment and liberty," " a democratic society which causes fear,"[27] wherein, as under France's ancien régime, the notables' absenteeism facilitated bureaucratic oppression, as inefficient as it was ruinous. In 1856 Tocqueville redrew his famous 1835 parallel between the United States and Russia, this time to trace its historical roots. The destiny of the European nations was inscribed in their past: once-absolutist nations had revolution and socialism written all over them. The eighteenth century's tiny social groupings were an early sketch of socialist society: "Like those substances once thought indivisible in which modern scientists, the more closely they examine them, find more and more separate particles, the French bourgeoisie, while seemingly a uniform mass, was extremely composite" (94). "There was a vast gulf between the government and the private citizen; it was accepted as being the only source of energy for the maintenance of the social system, and as such, indispensable to the life of the nation" (68). Civil servants were the only aristocracy: the state tended to take charge of the economy, education, and even the organization of public benefits.

What is astonishing is that Tocqueville rejected the fatalism to which so many of his contemporaries succumbed. The Roman-German opposition did not reflect an ethnic determinism in Tocqueville but the process of political acculturation ensured by civil society among the "Germans" and by the state, which constituted the nation among the "Romans." In effect, the entire European continent had been "romanized" by adopting the Roman Empire's public law, which became the serfs' common law. Like France, Germany received from Rome both a repressive, public criminal code and the liberal civil code that came from Roman republican traditions. "There would doubtless be a grand canvas to be painted," Tocqueville wrote, "of the influence of Roman law from a political point of view on the modern world's destinies, and of the way Roman law functioned to introduce both democracy and servitude into the world. . . . What Roman law did in Germany it did a little bit everywhere, except in England. It perfected civil society everywhere, and everywhere has tended to degrade political society."[28] This schematic interpretation of European history was inseparable from the type of analysis Tocqueville preferred in his study. Trained as a jurist and a reader of Savigny, who in 1840 published his *Système de droit romain actuel*, Tocqueville had especially sought out professors of law in Bonn. Thanks to them, he had traced the gradual substitution of Roman law for German custom in matters of property and public organization.

In the ultimate reversal after having rejected ethnic determinism, Tocqueville went so far as to inscribe liberty in national temperament, which was the privileged site of determinism. The French seemed condemned to servitude by their political culture. But psychologically, they had only one constant trait—inconstancy. What a people! "Undisciplined by temperament, the Frenchman is always readier to put up with the arbitrary rule, however harsh, of an autocrat than with a free, well-ordered government by his fellow citizens, however worthy of respect they be. At one moment he is up in arms against authority and the next we find him serving the powers-that-be with a zeal such as the most servile races never display" (210–11).

Writers from Caesar to de Gaulle have drawn flattering portraits of a mythical France, evoking a nation created by Providence "for successes achieved or exemplary failures."[29] Prefacing a new edition of his *Histoire de la civilisation en Europe et en France* one year before *Old Regime,* Guizot consoled himself in this way for his aborted liberal hopes. The optimistic portrait Tocqueville drew of France was equally invented to the scale of his own need for hope. Yet it clearly shows that Tocqueville was no man for regrets, and even less one for scorn. History is only politics pursued by other means. And what would politics be without the desire for a tomorrow?

In fact, history offers a foretaste of sweet tomorrows. In Tocqueville there is a historical radicalism that shows American democratic liberty in embryo within medieval social bodies (102). It takes new reasons to invent the future from the myth of the past. It is an ambivalent radicalism. Tocqueville was not exempt from nostalgia for the aristocracy. But Tocqueville hardly stopped at aristocracy as a social state and turned the aristocracy into a tale of its family origins, a golden age, far distant and obscure. Tocqueville never joined the legal debate on France's old "aristocratic constitution." In 1861 Guizot must have seen what separated him from Tocqueville in this: "Democracy was the great and almost the only character in society and history on which he focused in his study."[30] As a social order, the aristocracy held Tocqueville's attention only by the mechanisms of its ineluctable corruption. As Barbey noted, Tocqueville took "the ancien régime in its final hour, in its most equivocal expression, when it was most without moorings."[31] Tocqueville sought to retain only aristocracy's principle of moral superiority, this "natural" preeminence "which flowed from the Enlightenment and from virtue" (*DA* 2:50) and impelled the generous heroes depicted by the playwright Corneille to grandeur and self-sacrifice by their desire for public respect. Tocqueville thus combined nostalgia for aristocratic excellence with hatred of caste privilege.

And in fact, no return to the aristocracy was possible. Absolutism had destroyed competing options, excluding any chance of the measured passage from aristocracy to democracy whose portrait Tocqueville had painted in his appendix on Languedoc. The history of Languedoc, the *pays d'état* where local life was flourishing, "could have" been the history of all of France if not for the despotic penchant of kings. The real history of Languedoc is thus also a fictional history, an imaginary history of France. It was a utopian history, but not lacking in virtue, for it gave flesh to the dreams of those who did not have the reality of liberty. The dream of Languedoc thus fulfilled the American dream and filled the same political function by giving the French reason for hope and the courage to try.

Tocqueville's history remained one written in complicity with readers who are asked to take an interest in their "fathers'" history, whose vices still worry them and whose virtues still serve them as examples.[32] As the nation's historian Tocqueville did not set himself apart from Guizot's inculcation of respect for France in his young students at the Sorbonne, from Michelet's or Jaurès's effusively communitarian attempt to return French history to the French people. For all of them, the history of France and especially the Revolution's history were a pedagogy of civic virtue.

Tocqueville in Search of an Audience

The Unlikely Reader

Yet Tocqueville did not stage any collective epiphany as Thierry, Guizot, Michelet, and later Jaurès did, the last-named making bourgeois revolution the indispensible prerequisite for proletarian revolution. Tocqueville was a "critical intellectual." He wrote the history of a failure, a penitential history with no innocent party except the people, the perpetually oppressed. He thus imagined he would have few readers. His letters abound in metaphors for his own fall from grace: "old beast," "old dotard," antediluvian animal, hermit.

Tocqueville assigned social causes to his marginality. Until 1848 the audience for political literature was the notables, dispossessed by the Second Empire. Tocqueville was in arms against Louis-Napoléon Bonaparte's immoderate taste for his buddies and for rogues. But the end of the notables also seemed an unavoidable consequence of the introduction of universal suffrage. "We have ceased entirely to be a literary nation," he wrote, "which we eminently were throughout more than two centuries. What is more, the center of power is absolutely displaced, the influential classes are no longer those who read."[33] Tocqueville's despair earned him the sobriquet of *parnassien* among some modern critics: like Flaubert and Renan, he could console himself for his isolation with the assurance of his own genius and the hope of posthumous recognition.[34]

Tocqueville in the pose of the cursed writer? He no more despaired of being read than he despaired of the future of France. For him, it was largely the ignorant who were guilty, whence his moral duty to enlighten them, or rather to play the national pessimist in charge of public reprimands.[35] As in 1835, he saw himself as confessor and healer. But the healing arts had changed. In 1835 he had thought he could promptly reform French society through a new political science. His 1848–51 failure made him more circumspect. "It is not reasoning, it is passion which leads the world," he wrote, "or at least, reason only makes its way when it meets some passion which by chance wants to keep it company."[36] His ideas were no less effective forming "around every society something like a kind of intellectual atmospheric layer" from which all drew, "often without knowing it, sometimes without seeking it, the principles of their own conduct."[37]

Editorial Strategies

With the book completed in late 1855, a publisher and a title remained to be found, two choices inseparable from the challenge of writing.

No obvious publisher presented himself. Gosselin had retired, and Pagnerre was dead. Tocqueville had been away from the author's trade for years now and knew nothing of how the market had changed. In his doubt, he resorted to his old practice of selling only one edition at a time, watching closely over printing runs, and choosing a solidly established publishing house. On 16 February he opted without excessive enthusiasm for Michel Lévy, publisher of several of his friends, stingy about paying rights but seeming "cleverest at *pushing* a book."[38]

Tocqueville's reputation was more important to him than his author's rights, which were always merely an auxiliary source of revenue.[39] An increase in publishers' political complicity with their authors was characteristic of the second half of the nineteenth century; the choice of Lévy, whose Orleanist sympathies were notorious and who would publish Guizot's *Mémoires* in 1857 and the duc d'Aumale's historical studies the next year, was part of this historical evolution.[40]

Lévy was chosen regretfully. He had not read the manuscript Tocqueville offered him. With a famous author, an Academy man, and ex-minister, there was little risk involved. Yet it fell to Lévy to determine the book's image by choosing its title. As in 1835 and 1840, Tocqueville had not managed to lay hands on a title. He had early on leaned toward *La Révolution,*[41] but that was pretty flat. Then on 17 February 1856, at the advice of Lévy and Ampère, he leaned toward *La Révolution française,* a "vague and hardly new" title "but . . . real, . . . short, and not at all pretentious."[42] Beaumont felt *L'esprit de la Révolution française* more appropriate, though it sounded a bit too much like Montesquieu—even better, *Démocratie et liberté en France.*[43] Yet in a quick switch between 1 and 6 March, Lévy's bookstore catalog appeared with a notice announcing the publication of *The Old Regime and the French Revolution.* We do not know who, Ampère or Lévy, suggested the title. It did more justice to the book's originality than *La Révolution française.*[44] But Tocqueville was still mulling it over anyway, thinking about returning to his first title as better encompassing the overarching project of a history of the Revolution and the empire of which this volume was merely the long preface.[45] Lévy was in favor of the status quo. The inconvenient thing about the title was that it induced the reader to look for some preference for either the ancien régime or the Revolution in the work.[46] For the British edition Tocqueville preferred the more explicit title *On the State of Society in France before the Revolution of 1789 and the Causes Which Led to That Event.* More elegant in its brevity, the French title nonetheless sufficed to indicate the volume's central idea and combined exactitude with the spice of paradox. For contemporaries of the Revolution as for Tocqueville's own contemporaries, the ancien régime's birth date was vague, but its death date of 1789 was well attested. The expression "ancien régime" speaks to the continuity between feudalism and absolutism and to the rupture created by 1789. Yet Tocqueville's entire work shows in fact that absolutism was built on feudalism's ruins and that the rupture of 1789 was incomplete. By bringing the ancien régime together with the Revolution, the book's very title showed the paradoxical quality of its thesis.

Tocqueville's and Lévy's archives allow us to follow the book's sales. Tocqueville signed an agreement for a first edition of 2,000 copies (2,200 including the copies reserved for the publisher known as *doubles passes*) sold for 2,000 francs. Initially planned for April, the book was instead ready in early June 1856, held back a week by the death of Tocqueville's father on 9 June, and published on the sixteenth. Tocqueville promptly conducted his press campaign among all the liberals who gravitated to the Institut, and he saw to it that announcements came out in *Les Débats*, *Le Siècle*, and *La Presse* on 18 June. Then he sent his book on to his friends who were public commentators. By the end of August that edition had sold out,[47] and in October, Lévy hastily reprinted another 2,000 copies (2,200 in fact), not allowing Tocqueville the leisure to make the corrections he felt were necessary. In July 1857 those 2,200 copies had been sold, and a third edition of 2,000 (2,200) went between July 1857 and December 1858, at which point a fourth edition of 2,000 (2,200) copies came out. Public demand for the book remained high until 1900, after which the Calmann-Lévy publishing house sold just over 1,000 copies through 1934, when it had one final printing. From 1856 to 1934 *Old Regime* sold 25,000 copies, 23,600 of them between 1856 and 1900.

Lévy considered these sales extraordinary. They were extraordinary only for a book in the category referred to by one critic as the "thinking person's in-octavo" in the grand manner of Montesquieu. Also in 1856, Lévy launched the Michel Lévy series, subtitled "a selection of the best contemporary works," which as of April 1857 numbered 211 works at one franc apiece. Tocqueville's books never came out in this low-priced series in which most works were fiction. By their nature, they were "not accessible to the masses."[48] This book's audience did not extend beyond the usual audience for history books, and comparing it to Michelet's *Histoire de la Révolution française* is enlightening here. Despite their fairly low price, the first five volumes of *Histoire de la Révolution française* sold only about 3,000 copies between 1847 and 1853.[49] It is true, however, that by wanting to self-publish Michelet deprived himself of the network available to a big publisher. Only after 1880 did Michelet's works form a republican handbook, as Tocqueville's own works sank into oblivion.

A Political Manifesto

Tocqueville's success owed little to a public taste for erudition, as we can well imagine, and in his success Tocqueville correctly read the awakening of the opposition, which had been in a stupor since the coup d'état.[50] Like *Democracy*, *Old Regime* drew partisan praises. Strong censure, though, turned historiography into an opportunity for political polemics. Of course, Bonapartist Forcade de La Roquette, cynical even before becoming minister of the interior, could claim that censure raised the opposition's intellectual level.[51]

The opposition, Orleanists and republicans, were the first to praise the book. Beaumont led off commentaries on 18 June, under the signature of Sacy, editor in chief of the *Journal des Débats*. In June and July, *Le Constitutionnel, La Presse,* the *Journal des Débats,* and *Le Siècle* each devoted an in-depth review to the book, followed in July–August by the magazines and dailies *L'Illustration, Le Correspondant,* and the *Revue des Deux Mondes.*

Within the opposition's united front which used *Old Regime* as a weapon, Orleanist enthusiasm was unsurprising. The Academy was humming with praise for the book from Mignet, Villemain, and Cousin starting in the month of June. Broglie and d'Haussonville, the liberal descendants of de Staël, Constant, and Guizot, shared the general enthusiasm.[52] Among those praising the book, Louis-Philippe's son the duc d'Aumale's comments were even more probing, for he was hardly destined to be enthusiastic about the author. He felt that "one imbibes" in Tocqueville's book "a sincere horror of tyranny, and the enemy lies therein. The *Old Regime* is dead, never to return. Yet we must not believe that on its ruins we can reconstruct only despotism and anarchy. Those are the Revolution's bastards. Liberty alone is its legitimate daughter who with the help of God will chase away those marauders one day."[53]

The republicans were as quick as the Orleanists to seize the occasion for action by the opposition. But their praises were tainted by their political motivations. Tocqueville enjoyed their relative esteem as other liberal historians of the turn of the century did not. Quinet and Chassin, Michelet's republican friend, took abundant notes on *Old Regime,*[54] although they mainly gathered a collection of facts and citations, and although Quinet deemed Tocqueville a "fine but limited mind which only sees the light by chance." Socialist Despois in the *Revue de Paris* approved the work's political direction. All three found material in *Old Regime* to meditate upon regarding the causes of the Republic's repeated failure. It is true that with Professor Despois's resignation, Quinet's exile, and Tocqueville sent back to private life, all three had in common their victimization by the coup. The relatedness of their historical ideas proceeded from their common misfortunes.

Not every republican warmly accepted Tocqueville's idea of an affiliation between the ancien régime and the Revolution. A front for the defense of the Revolution began in 1856.[55] Those for whom 1789 was historically the revelation of freedom, like Lamartine, grew indignant at the idea that one could resort to "little" socioeconomic "explanations"[56] to account for the Revolution. Others more craftily used Tocqueville's severe sketch of the old France to call upon the democratic party to defend its revolutionary heritage. Leon Plée in *Le Siècle* used this strategy with an impudence that made Tocqueville furious. The critique of absolutism was even more precious to Plée because Tocqueville was "a gentleman historian, part of England's liberal governmental family." It made him rejoice to find such an unexpected reinforcement against "those fine men of fusion or legitimacy." The work "is written without much order," Plée commented, but "we will chop it up." Because Tocqueville was not one of their own, republicans like Plée felt tactical indulgence toward Tocqueville but against a ground of fundamental disagreement.

Legitimists and Bonapartists weighed in much later. Beyond Pontmartin (*L'Assemblée Nationale* of June and July), legitimists were silent until the end of August (*L'Union*), and as late as November for the *Gazette de France*. Not that the book was unknown to them.[57] They felt the kind of good feeling for Malesherbes's great-grandson which wise people have toward an enfant terrible. They were quite pleased to see 1789 whittled down to size and the Second Empire lampooned, but they would have liked more indulgence on Tocqueville's part toward the monarchy.[58] Tocqueville was surprised by their moderation:

> I expected primarily to face attacks from all those still attached by their opinions and their memories to the old monarchy and the old royalty, and I thought that on the contrary, ardent allies of the revolutionaries would embrace me. Precisely the opposite has happened. . . . To what to attribute it? Did the former think they had more reason to spare me than the latter? Or would this not instead prove only that on the side of the former, everything has died, both good and evil political passions, and that on the latter, those passions at least remain alive?[59]

The only unitedly hostile groups were the Ultramontane Catholics of *L'Univers* and the Bonapartists, who were in fact united in their common reverence for authority. Their late commentaries were entirely dictated by their need to challenge Tocqueville's unmerited success.[60] In *Old Regime,* Barbey d'Aurevilly heard only a "theme of wailing, muted grace notes for the members of Parliament, a kind of Bridge of Sighs."[61] As Mérimée laconically put it, "Tocqueville's book has just come out. It is said to be excellent, but behind by ten years."[62]

Nastiness from some quarters and delight from others allow us to see how Tocqueville's work was read within the polemics of its time. However, even approval was mixed with reluctance, and the discomfort behind partisan praise was readily visible. With a little more effort, the *Gazette de France* said, the work "could have been a monument raised to national liberty." One more step, and Tocqueville would have been spared the book's "few very bizarre prejudices against socialism," retorted Despois. It was general opinion that Tocqueville "could have done better" (*L'Union*). Because he did not announce his political coloration, he annoyed; his style was found dreary. He was a "halftone Montesquieu" who was "forever playing on the swings," a specialist in evasive history.[63] Sophie Swetchine expressed the general feeling when she wrote, "People reproach you somewhat for not *concluding.* I claim this amounts to reproaching your not *conquering.*"[64] To his readers Tocqueville seemed to excel only at macabre diagnoses, never remedies. His book was a précis of "decomposition."[65] Tocqueville was a doctor who had just told France it had a hereditary illness: "There might have been a way for you to heal; this would mean putting you under my orders. Unfortunately, you are unable to follow them, and I am unable to prescribe to you. I am indeed a doctor, but I studied in the United States, and the Parisian school, which is temporarily against new ideas in medicine, would be hardpressed to grant me a diploma."[66] Tocqueville protested heartily,[67] but he was taken for the "so-sorry doctor" from then on, whence the critic's and the reader's "worried reverie" and "long face[s]."[68]

If Tocqueville disappointed them so, it was by disconcertingly rejecting historiographies that complicitly commemorated either the ancien régime or the Revolution, but not the two together.

Philosophical History and Problem History

The Longue Durée

For everyone, however, *Old Regime* was a work of the already old genre of philosophical history. Tocqueville took up Montesquieu's methods in his *Considérations* on the Romans.[69] "M. de Tocqueville," wrote Lenormant, who

> only allows those thoughts of his which are the most tested and reduced by long travail to reach the public ... does not seek to imitate Montesquieu, but deserves naturally and with real originality to be compared to that great writer. He is satirical and bold without ever compromising himself by being carried away by lan-

guage. One is charmed to read him and feels imperiously called on to reread and meditate upon the book. A great example of a book long and seriously worked upon, in a time when the process of improvisation has become universal.[70]

On the other hand, his detractors sneered at this "*grisaille* Montesquieu," a "pale imitator" and "feeble descendant through the female line" of the great commentator.[71]

But philosophical history as a genre took on new expansion with Tocqueville. Its privileged object in fact was not political history, which lent itself even less than other genres to a history not based on events. In politics, the importance of individuals seemed so great that narrating, as Thiers, Michelet, and Augustin Thierry did, seemed required. The history of the Revolution called even more for narrative than earlier periods. With the Revolution, there was no point from which to achieve legitimate philosophical distance: the historian's destiny seemed to be to spell out origins tirelessly.

Thus Tocqueville distinguished himself immediately in avoiding depicting the debasement of kings at the hands of courtesans, Louis XVI's vacillations, Marie-Antoinette's intrigues, ministers' low deeds, and revolutionaries' grand ones. He was criticized for asking only selective questions of the past and starting with a hypothesis and constructed object, not from the humble level of real history. "One must be terribly capable, in his own eyes or in the eyes of others, to allow oneself to write a volume—or several—of mere historical generalities," noted Barbey.[72] This was especially true for a history many had lived through, and about which there were a number of memoirs and recently published documents.

Tocqueville was thus accused of ignoring his predecessors' works. True, he prided himself on not having read them so they would not influence his judgment. "It is obvious," Sainte-Beuve wrote,

> that this eminent mind has not heretofore done as most martyrs have, who read interesting books as they are published, and that since 1825 he has stopped reading—haphazardly or wrongly or upside down (the preferred method)—the quantity of memoirs and documents that have succeeded each other, as all the young people of his generation did. If he had, he would already have his first layers and the background of his canvas painted in, he would not ask himself all those preliminary questions, he would not set up his equipment so painstakingly as though for a discovery.

According to Sainte-Beuve's summary, which hit the bull's-eye, "He began thinking before learning anything, which means that at times, his thoughts were empty."[73]

From this, some drew an argument that denied Tocqueville all originality and accused him of presenting himself wrongly as the Christopher Columbus of the archives.[74] The assemblies' transcripts, *cahier des doléances,* Arthur Young's *Voyages,* and notarial registries were all well-known sources. As for administrative history, Cheruel's and Raudot's erudite studies had already cleared that terrain.[75] The criticism drew its acrimony from the confusion of readers at a history that ignored official acts and scrutinized practices. No one denied that Tocqueville had exhumed some new documents, but they were deemed of scant interest.[76]

Documentation was not the only disputed territory. Tocqueville was accused of depth by omission only. The criticisms of him we find outlined as early as 1856 are developed by later generations of historians.

Tocqueville's scant interest in international politics was criticized, especially as the war was concerned, where the conflict between liberty and efficiency was played out dramatically. Critics were astonished that he failed to recognize how much the increase in royal powers owed to the wars. In fact, in *Old Regime* Tocqueville attributed that increase to a few slim contingencies: absolutism was born "during the long periods of disorder which had accompanied the captivity of King Jean and Charles VI's dementia"; it grew worse at the end of Louis XIV's reign, under the weight of "financial necessities"—oracular evocation of the Hundred Years' War and the Spanish succession. Doubtless Tocqueville was looking for a way to deny what Jules Ferry later called "the prejudice for dictatorship" that made the exercise of liberty subordinate to security and power. In Tocqueville's thought concern for obedience is always second to concern for autonomy. If he had thought about wars, he would have recognized that absolutism had a few merits. Silence on international political matters was the price to be paid for better promoting solidarity in civil society against state takeover. Still, the absence of reflection that he shares with many liberals, including Hayek, constitutes a blind spot which today continues to disturb historians.[77]

Deliberately incomplete, Tocqueville was not averse to abusive simplifications. It has been observed that he misunderstood the diversity of the nobility. He presented as a single caste the tangled grouping of the nobles of the sword, nobles of the robe, and ennobled bourgeois.[78] He also exaggerated bureaucracy's hold: monarchic administration, held in check by tradition and dominated by the privileged, lacked the oppressive efficiency of modern bureaucracy.[79]

In all of it, Tocqueville gave in to the retrospective illusion of inevitability.[80] Overly fueled by present-day questions, his history in his detractors' eyes was merely a contemporary one which found all the spirit of the Revolution in the *Cahiers* and saw far too much of Napoleon in Louis XIV.

In fact, *Old Regime* is attentive only to resemblances between the Revolution and old society. It is thus a partial history, necessarily distant from the feelings of its actors, and attempts only to revive past "assumptions,"[81] instinctive practices, and unconscious collective representations. The choice of sources, as Rémusat notes, cannot be separated from the question asked.[82]

Metaphors of depth are needed to refer to this new way of writing history. Tocqueville acceded to hidden meanings like a geologist deciphering the history of the earth's revolutions in its deepest strata.[83] At century's end Faguet described this "sociological"[84] way of writing history in terms that would almost turn Tocqueville into a precursor of Braudel's. By offering a "physiology of peoples," *Old Regime* invites the reader to leave "accidental history" for the enduring ground which "within history as such, variable and multicolored, has its own history that follows a more tranquil course, more unified, more assured, which is in consequence more likely to be foreseen and somewhat guaranteed to happen." He added that "between a history overly encumbered with philosophical considerations and a purely epic history, and even a history barely more than a pamphlet or polemic, there was indeed room for a study, both patient and impassioned, of this underside, these deep regions, these sea bottoms over which currents pass, influxes and outfluxes, and the waves' tempestuous agitations."[85]

Proximate Origins of the Revolution

In thinking about the continuity of French history over the *longue durée,* Tocqueville knew that he also had to account for the Revolution's pretension to rupturing the course of history. Thus rather than explaining the Revolution's explosion by poverty, he had looked for the sources of revolutionary radicalism in public passions. The peasant is even more impatient with lordly domination when he becomes a landholder; the third estate even more hostile to privilege when it prospers. In both cases, envy, the daughter of hope, is the source of infinite claims.

Tocqueville's success in this came from his refreshed commonplaces. In 1856 enlightened opinion was concerned with peasant conditions and with landholdings being carved up, which endangered the profitability of farms.[86] This worry was political and sung to a historical tune, as always in the nineteenth century. The Revolution had long been credited with giving peasants the right to own property, making rural history a key point of disagreement between partisans of the Revolution and those of absolutism. Tocqueville as usual found himself between the two camps. He ran counter to the prejudices of democrats by illustrating how old peasant landholding was and how economically prosperous the eighteenth century had been. Legitimists took nasty delight in highlighting this theme. But he ran no less counter to the legitimists by showing that feudal rights were more loathsome because they struck peasants who were already landowners.

Republicans and socialists had a heyday with his demonstration of the iniquity of feudal rights. There were still a few laggards trying to make the poverty explanation of the Revolution serviceable. According to Peyrat, it was purely out of the goodness of their hearts that the prosperous regions joined the Revolution, in order to support the poor regions where the revolt had begun.[87] But most were convinced by Tocqueville, and republican historiography emerged changed. Tocqueville was praised for having studied "social causes, that is, the situation of diverse classes, their interests, habits, and passions."[88] Louis Blanc had studied the industrial arena; Tocqueville is the peasants' Louis Blanc. From Boiteau to Jaurès and then Lefebvre and Godechot, an entire socialist historiography recognized *Old Regime* as the exemplar of a history attentive to social passions.

On the other hand, the Revolution's adversaries had a heyday with Tocqueville's demonstration of the long history of peasant landholding in order to denounce the envy underlying hatred for feudal rights. They believed they could discredit equality by making French history the stage for the triumph of greed. Where Tocqueville had shown the prosperity of peasants and the bourgeoisie, Montalembert's son-in-law de Meaux concluded that "it was not institutions but the human passions which dug abysses between them; inequality did not increase. On the contrary, what grew was disdain from above and envy from below."[89] Envy was thus the most obvious manifestation of the Revolution's "satanic" character and the illegitimacy of passion for equality. Through their moralizing, the Revolution's adversaries made it impossible for themselves to understand the crystallization of the Revolution which was the particular focus of Tocqueville's work.[90]

The Politics of History: French History Inverted

In Tocqueville recourse to "philosophical" history is inseparable from sensitivity to present-day problems. Emulating Montesquieu, Tocqueville, like Guizot, entered what Raymond Aron has called the "English part" of French history. And yet Tocqueville was not another Guizot. Tocqueville introduced a new reading of the past to everyone by showing that the Revolution was absolutism's daughter through those unconscious affiliations steeped in hatred that are the most solid. French history was the showplace for administrative servitude. The idea seemed so new that what happened was that rare phenomenon in the history of ideas— an abrupt shift in general opinion. After having read Tocqueville, "one wonders how, even in the absence of the proofs and documents gathered by M. de Tocqueville, simple common sense had not been enough to reveal to us this fact which the author establishes with such authority."[91]

For Orleanists or republicans, the reversal was complete. Historiography of the Restoration and the July Monarchy had claimed to show that absolutism was the necessary precondition for the establishment of modern representative rule. Absolute monarchy was absolved of its faults in the name of the democratic future that it inevitably engendered. The experience of the coup d'état made the intelligence of Tocqueville's thought possible by challenging the historical optimism of the Doctrinaires.[92] The monarchy was condemned in the name of its Bonapartist offspring. Oppressed, its opponents suddenly discovered the poverty of historicism and used *Old Regime* to denounce the prejudice for dictatorship that, since absolutism, had led France to diminish the importance of the individual in favor of the state. The long-marginalized Tocqueville thus finally found himself in complete agreement with growing disenchantment after 1852, and he received a heightened authority from this precociousness. "He was one of the first," Baudrillart noted in 1865, "to show that liberty and democracy are not necessarily one and the same thing. Much more, he has never ceased saying that there are at the core of democracy and in its very nature tendencies very oppressive to the individual. Therein lies his originality, and there too the enduring import of his work."[93] Reading Tocqueville, those living under the empire learned to reject the idea of linear progress and painfully resolved never again to seek the criteria for legitimacy in history.

This reversal shows most clearly in the new way England began to be seen. Guizot had made English history prefigure French history. In 1856 Montalembert and Rémusat drew proof of missed opportunities in France from English history. *Old Regime* went further by showing that the divergence between absolutist France and liberal, aristocratic England had begun as early as the fourteenth century.[94] From that point on, to Bonapartists and republicans Tocqueville seemed the most extremist of those "manic wits who, needing to write the history of France, always seem sorry not to have to write the history of England."[95]

Among the old Orleanists such praise was doubtless a cover for persistent equivocation. Guizot renounced none of his old differences with Tocqueville and still thought an English-style aristocratic evolution possible. In 1856 he wrote to Tocqueville,

> You paint and you judge modern democracy as a vanquished aristocrat, convinced that his conqueror is right. Perhaps you have thought too commonly of the historical aristocracy, which is indeed truly vanquished, and not enough of the natural aristocracy, which can never be for long and always ends up regaining its rights. Perhaps, if you had more consistently distinguished them, you might have had an easier time, while accepting democracy, contesting what is illegitimate and unsocial in its victory.[96]

But the hour had not yet come for public display of the disagreements that resurfaced after 1870 between the old notables, and only private correspondence showed their reservations toward each other.

The fruits of Restoration historiography were harvested by the Bonapartists. Napoleon III's partisans took Thierry and Guizot's admiration of absolute monarchy as admiration for them—absolutism being the matrix of modernity. For them, too, absolutism was absolved in spite of its vices in the name of the future it engendered. The difference was simply that according to Bonapartists, the modern age was no longer embodied in constitutional monarchy but in the empire. The aims of history differed, not the principle of interpretation. Believing in the necessity of absolutism, Bonapartists took comfort in their illusion that the imperial regime would endure, just as Guizot had taken comfort in his illusion that the July regime would last.

Against Tocqueville's interpretation, Bonapartists contrasted the majestic tableau of the "work of centuries" that had been developed by Augustin Thierry and Guizot.[97] And they pushed Tocqueville off into the counterrevolutionary camp toward de Maistre.

In fact, their hostility did not stem from the old tactics of divide and conquer. It was so hard for them to conceive of democracy without centralization that they did not even understand there might be some beauty to incorporated bodies or state assemblies. "At one point," wrote Nisard in 1856, "I thought I saw a semi-conclusion in M. de Tocqueville's brilliant painting of the prosperity of the old Languedoc province, when it possessed, as a *pays d'état*, a local elected assembly. The writer's severity toward Richelieu, 'who first mutilated Languedoc's freedoms and then abolished them' and against 'the soft and idle Louis XIII who hated them' persuaded me that I had before my eyes at least a portion of M. de

Tocqueville's ideal." His was a retrograde ideal. "As for me," Nisard concluded, "I firmly believe that these freedoms, *hated* by Louis XIII and *mutilated* by Richelieu, were only the final resistance of feudalism."[98]

Republicans understood Tocqueville's discouragement but refused to lose faith in 1789.[99] During that somber period it was hard for them to deny the French taste for despotism. They agreed with Tocqueville in his observation of the continuity between absolutism and revolution, while rejecting his explanation. And they resorted to the old concept of "circumstances" that allowed them to see the Terror as nothing more than the trail of absolutism and to see centralization as merely the youthful malady of a democracy too threatened to abolish all past abuses in one gesture.[100] Not all conceded Tocqueville's postulated noxiousness of centralization. The Jacobins, who hated the memory of privilege so much that any talk of intermediary bodies was suspicious, opposed those who supported self-government, like Quinet. Let Tocqueville carefully glorify in 1856 "that kind of liberty encountered under the ancien régime" among nobles and priests, and republicans and Bonapartists were quick to suspect a sneaky plea for a return to a society divided into those orders.[101] Concern for the residual independence of the eighteenth century seemed to them only "that type of bastard patriotism that is called esprit de corps," and the nobility's grandeur was at best "a kind of seductive absentmindedness which sometimes took on a quite chivalrous appearance."[102]

Old Regime was not part of any particular intellectual lineage. Pleading for independence and for equality, being both Malesherbes's great-grandson and Washington's disciple, was too much by half. But this was the book in which the nation's identity was sought. For all, discussion about the ancien régime and the aristocracy was merely an oblique way of talking about French democracy and the antinomian fears it inspired, fears of decline and social decomposition, as well as of a sly rebirth of exclusivity and inequality. *Old Regime* was a call to liberation through repudiation of France's absolutist heritage. The 1860s would confirm Tocqueville's vocation as national pessimist, making him the posthumous head of the opposition.

European Perspectives

The work's therapeutic virtue and the novelty of its comparative method, often poorly perceived by the French,[103] are much clearer when we examine the reception of Tocqueville's thought abroad. In contrast to *Democracy, Old Regime* was mainly addressed to Europe. "A book on the French Revolution can never excite as much interest in America as in Europe. The French Revolution is a considerable part of the particular history of every people on this continent, and one can say nothing about it that does not immediately cause them to turn and look at themselves," noted Tocqueville.[104]

In fact, in the United States, despite the approval of great historians like Ticknor, Bancroft, and Sparks, the work enjoyed scant success. Translated from galleys by John Bonner and published in 1856, a second edition came out in 1876, with no further editions until the Second World War.

But in Europe the work became an immediate classic. Tocqueville had argued with Lévy, using his international reputation to stipulate retention of his rights to distribute the galleys for translation purposes. In England, through the help of his friend Reeve, he signed a contract with the bookseller Murray for a run of 1,000 copies in 1856. The book was reprinted again in 1873 together with seven chapters from volume 8 of the *Oeuvres complètes* published by Beaumont. A third English edition appeared in 1888 and more editions in 1904, 1916, 1925, 1933, 1947, 1949, and 1952. The press welcomed him very favorably, for the English found in the work a reflection of their virtues, heightened by the comparison with the servitude of the French.

This is how *Old Regime* became an immediate scholarly classic whose influence was great on the next generation of historians and public commentators— among them Lord Acton, Henry Sedgwick, James Bryce, Sir Henry Sumner Maine, and Frederick William Maitland. But *Old Regime* was only read by the English as a history book. Tocqueville himself notes in a letter of 29 August 1856: "In the accounts which have been made of my book in England, it seems that the *free* spirit of the book is what strikes readers least. This is what has struck French critics the most up to this point, as far as I can see: almost without fail they have quoted the parts which show the spirit of liberty most clearly, so that it seems to have been the enslaved people and not the free people who were most moved by what I said in favor of liberty."[105]

Old Regime only had a political impact on the Continent, where equality combined with absolutism. The book was well received in the areas Tocqueville had studied during its genesis. He had sought in Germany and Russia the history of other absolutisms, less complete than the French one. Germans and Russians owed much to reading *Old Regime,* which described the French past but the German and Russian present, as though there had been in Europe one obligatory course of history through which every nation must go at different times, from an ancien régime to a revolution.

Russia was late compared to the rest of Europe. Its ancien régime had developed slowly at the end of the eighteenth century with Peter the Great and then Catherine the Great. Unfortunately for such royalty, the apogee of their ancien régime coincided with the French Revolution whose fascination overtook all Europe. From 1789 until the great reforms of 1861, the Russian state continually distanced itself from the specter of the French Revolution; Catherine II even forbade teaching its history. This dilatory strategy grew increasingly difficult. Nicholas I, czar from 1825 to 1855, was unable to resolve the question of serfdom and unable to make the nobility enter the modern world. When he died, the defeat brewing in the Crimea, to be confirmed by the Treaty of Paris in 1856, led to a crisis which caused his successor Alexander II, czar from 1855 to 1881, to attempt a string of reforms, including the abolition of serfdom (1861) and administrative and judicial reform (1864). More than ever, all minds were obsessed by the French model.

It was precisely during these transitional years that *Old Regime* was read. In Russia, *Democracy* had attracted only limited interest; it seemed to deal only with regimes already democratic. *Old Regime* was the book of the moment. Readers could not know that in writing *Old Regime*, Tocqueville had tried to illuminate the history of France by analogies to Russia. Yet there were many in the 1860s who drew what they needed for their reflections on the Russian social state from *Old Regime*. Tocqueville seemed the commentator Russia needed, as he had seemed the Americans' Montesquieu in 1835. Minister of the Interior Lanskoi asked when the Russians would have their own Tocqueville. The work offered a way to think about the absenteeism of nobles and the difficulties of emancipating the serfs. Tolstoy, who read Tocqueville in April 1857, while preparing the Decembrist novel from which *War and Peace* emerged, sought to understand the reform movement in process by analogy to the history of the French Revolution. He found in Tocqueville the idea that rebellion threatens even more as government lightens its tutelary hold, and that the absenteeism of the nobles was the correlative of growth in centralization, the handmaiden of despotism. In the opposite direction, a Russian magnate like Malkov could gather, from his reading of Tocqueville, that it was time to return to patriarchal order.[106]

Tocqueville's critique of the state apparatus was of even more interest than its sociological look at old France. Despite the anarchy reigning between the provinces before the Crimean War, the Russians had thought little about what institutional changes were needed and even less about the balance of other nations' experiences. *Old Regime* provided a motor for the earliest Russian reform proposals. The French had been especially marked by the state's crushing of civil society, neglecting to think about the virtues of the provincial assemblies suspected of being federalism's own handmaiden. In Russia slavophiles and fans of centralization clashed at precisely the point the French had neglected. Prince Vladimir Sherkasky in a spring 1857 article (*Russkaia Beseda*), proposed putting the Languedoc *pays*'s ideal of self-government into practice in Russia. For slavophiles Tocqueville was an import. On the other hand, those in favor of centralization underscored the risk that national unities would come apart, like Chicherin, who in his *Essais sur l'Angleterre et la France* violently attacked *Old Regime,* especially for its appendix on Languedoc.

In the spring of 1858, while Alexander was calling for reforms, *Old Regime* reminded reformers that there was no more dangerous moment for a prince than when he attempts to comfort his subjects. Among Tocqueville's readers we note Mikhail Saltykov, charged by the Ministry of the Interior with developing the plan for administrative decentralization. He had been a reader of *Democracy* during the 1840s. Another was the Grand Duke Constantine Nikolayevich, named by his brother Alexander II to the head of the secret committee for emancipation and administrative reform.

Tocqueville's success owed much to contemporary urgencies. But the great reforms of 1861–64 made the course of Russian history diverge from that of France. Alexander II, however enlightened he was, continued surveillance of local bodies no less closely, while keeping peasants outside the common law. At the end of the 1860s, just as the history of the French Revolution began to appear on university reading lists and Tocqueville's work began to be the object of a real cult among certain historians, he lost his political hold on progressive minds, a sign of public opinion's general disaffection with the French Revolution, which increased after the crisis of 1905.

In Germany the book was published in 1857 in Leipzig, and a second edition appeared in 1867. In 1909 selected pages annotated by Louis André appeared in Frankfurt, and in 1914 there was a new unabridged edition.

Though Germany had begun its revolution in 1848, long before Russia, it was not completed until 1856. *Democracy* had been the subject of passionate commentary and had met with incomprehension on the part of conservatives. *Old*

Regime incited as much interest but less misunderstanding; Beaumont's publication of Tocqueville's correspondence in the 1860s and especially the appearance of hitherto unpublished chapters on the Directoire revived political interest. During the years before Bismarck established the Reich, *Old Regime* raised questions that had been raised by *Democracy* about the desirable governmental form of modern regimes. After the Reich's establishment, a much more conservative or more pessimistic interpretation of Tocqueville's work emerged. But the attention given *Old Regime* was not limited to such political considerations. Just as in 1835 *Democracy*'s method had been the subject of profound commentary in Germany, *Old Regime* gave rise to a critique of its sources and concepts by professional historians. The pertinence of German analyses contrasted sharply with the absence of a scholarly community in France outside the one surrounding the academies. German historians were sensitive to Tocqueville's explanatory schema. This was true of Heinrich von Sybel, the author of a long, anonymous study of *Old Regime* in the *Augsburger Zeitung* in seven articles published between 10 July and 31 August 1856. Others took up Tocqueville's denunciation of the noxiousness of absolutism, which engendered recurring revolutions. This was true of the *History of France from the Arrival of Louis-Philippe to the Fall of Napoleon III* (1877) written by Karl Hillebrand, who took refuge in France after the Baden uprising of 1849.

Thus continental Europe felt an enthusiasm for *Old Regime* that was at least equal to the enthusiasm that *Democracy* had incited twenty years earlier. The liberal branch of the Anglo-Saxons found renewed evidence of the virtues of self-government in the work. The absolutist and revolutionary branch on the Continent learned from Tocqueville to decipher its future in the past. For the French, Germans, and Russians, the history of the ancien régime and the Revolution, halfway between living memory and scholarly history, was a story whose meaning remained suspended, because the effects of the event were not played out. This explained the tragic character of Tocqueville's thought in their eyes, at the very moment when, throughout Europe, authoritarian regimes radicalized the opposition between states' reasons and common law, sovereignty and self-government. European in conception, for Germany serves in it as a constant point of comparison with France, *Old Regime* was also European in its reception.

4

The Liberals' Posthumous Leader, 1860s

TOCQUEVILLE died on 16 April 1859. Throughout his life he had played the role of solitary opponent. Dead, he became the posthumous leader of the opposition. The path of his renown follows the curve of the progress of the liberal party, to such degree that he was even promoted as a symbol for the pitiful destiny of France. He was imagined as having died not from tuberculosis but from an excessive thirst for liberty, crucified by the bitterness of collective disillusionment. Sainte-Beuve would have preferred him "calmer and cooler" and thereby still alive.[1] A fine Bonapartist! To which Prévost-Paradol retorted that "his friends did not desire Tocqueville other than he had showed himself to them to be, in other words, sad enough to die" from liberty's misfortunes.[2]

Tocqueville's lionizing took place in stages. After the funeral oratory his correspondence appeared and then his complete works, which erected a monument to the great man, clearing the way for biographies and exegeses. To deliver his funeral speech Tocqueville got the genre's greatest master, Lacordaire, in the halls where the genre attains its height of perfection, the Académie Française. Biographies inspired by this memorable speech spread the Tocquevillean stereotype of a noble suffering soul thirsting for justice that always escaped him, the one with which histories and encyclopedias still burden us.

The first in-depth critical studies of Tocqueville were contemporaneous with his obituaries, according to the old tradition that deems only the dead worthy of serious study. Laboulaye, Tocqueville's first great interpreter, admitted as much, ingenuously, as the coffin was closing: "When a talented man, when a patriotic writer leaves this earth, his work takes on the serenity and sanctity of death. The wise of the day no longer set his ideas aside as importunate reverie:

he becomes an authority we invoke, a support we need. Alive, we barely listened to him; dead, silence surrounds him—all the nation, the young generation want to hear this voice emerging from the tomb. . . . His ideas belong to us, his glory is our heritage."[3]

But Tocqueville's glory did not really bloom until the liberal party organized during the 1860s. Let us follow the stages of Tocqueville's ascent to the liberal pantheon.

Funeral Oratory

Obituaries

Tocqueville's death made almost no noise in 1859: a few brief notices in newspapers, a sober ceremony in Cannes, brief presentation of the body in the crypt at the Madeleine, and then burial in familial intimacy at Tocqueville's village. This indifference can be explained by the current rumors of war between Austria and Piedmont.[4] Too, Tocqueville had taken so long to die: his death had been announced in December 1858 and again in early April.[5]

But circumstances do not explain everything. Other than the long obituaries written by his friends Barante, Ampère, and Loménie and Laboulaye's study, which all appeared in opposition publications (the *Revue des Deux Mondes*, the *Correspondant*, and the *Journal des Débats*), announcements revealed cautious reluctance toward Tocqueville, whose political leanings were too unclear to allow his legacy to be glorified. The funeral elegy, used by the living to stand upon the dead, rang hollow; the dead man did not seem exemplary.

Naturally—this was a must in the genre—every elegy strung together all the tired commonplaces about Tocqueville that had circulated since 1835: Tocqueville was a prophet "because what he predicted is happening, and in its history, America writes a new edition of his book every day."[6] He was the public commentator "whose posterity will place his name alongside Montesquieu's";[7] the author who became a "classic" while alive, heir to both the seventeenth-century moralists and the eighteenth-century philosophes.[8]

But other than legitimist evocations of Tocqueville as restorer of the papacy who turns out well in the end, there was not a word about the political man and his works' polemical vigor. Tocqueville's alignment with a Falloux or a Montalembert was normally used to introduce the morality story of his most Christian death and "the general edification" it thus offered.[9] These were perhaps merely the rules of the game, but Tocqueville was more subject to them than others both because of his family's own desires, hardly enlightened as far as piety was concerned,[10] and because of the royalists' stubborn determination to interpret his death as a repudiation of his democratic convictions. The result is that in the tradition of Bossuet, Tocqueville's obituaries spoke more about his effacement before God than about his civic merits in any eighteenth-century elegaic style, more about the creature's pitifulness than the grandeur of his heritage. Funereal rather than funerary, such obituaries buried Tocqueville's memory.

Academic Canonization

Tocqueville received no true homage until 24 January 1861, when Lacordaire succeeded him at the Academy. The Academy was the watering hole for all former notables, carefully increasing their oppositional tribe with each election. Naturally, therefore, Tocqueville was graced with a successor of the same political stripe—Lacordaire, the nineteenth century's Bossuet. "By the words of that funeral oratory, M. de Tocqueville's name now immediately acquires what he lacked during his life, luster and brilliance," Sainte-Beuve commented.[11]

In fact, by a quirk of history, Tocqueville was now in the spotlight of current events. In December 1859 Napoleon III published an officious brochure entitled *The Pope and the Congress* to advise Pius IX to agree to break up his states. Without the pope's consent, on 18 September 1860 Italian troops unseated the pontiff's guard at Castelfidardo. Out of hostility to the emperor, the entire class of notables, from liberal Catholics like Montalembert to agnostics like Cousin and Thiers, and even a Protestant like Guizot, were ready to vote for Pius IX despite his reactionary contagions. Tocqueville, who had scarcely been an enthusiastic restorer of the papacy in 1849, was thus the man of the hour: "a devoted son, though discontented, of the church," to cite Montalembert's phrase. Lacordaire was another devoted, discontented son: hostile to the expedition to Rome, he nonetheless defended the pope's independence, as Tocqueville had.[12] Cousin's and Falloux's efforts to elicit some vibrant praise for the papacy from him made Lacordaire's reception by the Academy a political event. In fact, Protestant Guizot receiving the first monk ever elected to the Academy was an event in itself.

> Imagine the scene: on one side, a Dominican father with M. de Tocqueville as his subject, that is, American democracy as his limitless field; on the other, in counterpoint, the Academy's director, M. Guizot himself, a Calvinist, a heretic, the most eloquent spokesman for the past eighteen years of ordered liberty, regulated, restricted liberty: such antagonism! such antithesis! Add to it the im-

possibility, under the present circumstances, that between such players there could not be talk of Rome, of the pope! Yet one more difficulty, one more source of interest, one more peril: *incedo per ignes* [I go forth amid the flames].... And there is what makes academic speechmaking (about which one may say whatever one likes) a quite modern, quite lively, quite dramatic genre, and one more popular than all the tragedies in the world.[13]

Interviews regarding the event were given a year in advance. A memorable bustle ensued: Parisian women, their noses reddened by the cold, waited hours in line in the Institut's courtyard to attend the much-hyped event.

Lacordaire, already seriously ill, was a disappointment. The Academy did not offer Notre Dame's sonorous vaults, and his declamatory diction and gestures collapsed into melodrama. Worse, his audience's hopes for polemics were dashed. Lacordaire confined his remarks only to brief invocation of the "heroic achievement" of papal restoration and to vigorously applauded allusions to liberty and despotism. Like Tocqueville, Lacordaire deemed only silence appropriate to mourning for freedoms lost. His speech, disappointing to those who had invested it with their partisan expectations, was important for other reasons. Not least, it inaugurated the traditional image of a Tocqueville melting with sickly sweet piety that was long popular in Catholic tradition.[14]

The event's main value was illuminating Tocqueville's thought by confronting it with two doctrinal currents which when alive he had opposed. After his death he was often confused with them: liberal Catholicism, represented by Lacordaire, and the Doctrinaires, whose spokesman was Guizot.

Tocqueville had maintained only distant relations with liberal Catholics, as he suspected them of clericalism. He had read Lamennais, whom he met on the constitutional committee of 1848, and he seems to have met Lacordaire fleetingly during those 1830s dinners which brought liberal youth together. In 1835 he went to hear Lacordaire preach at Notre Dame, as did everyone in good society. In 1848 he graciously compared Lacordaire to a plucked vulture dominating the Assembly; there was nothing in that to indicate any irrepressible sympathy. For his part, Lacordaire must have hastily read Tocqueville's works in order to prepare his reception speech. But the two men are intellectually proximate, both fascinated by America, where Lacordaire had dreamed of traveling during the era of *L'Avenir*, a progressive periodical founded by Lamennais in 1830. Both deemed the advance of democracy irresistible and providential. Both believed it viable only under the protection of some religion. Between Tocqueville and Lacordaire there was thus some fundamental convergence, born of common roots in the traditionalist thought reshaped by Lamennais and of mutual acceptance of the modern world. Lacordaire could easily and without being false integrate Tocqueville into his intellectual genealogy of liberal Catholicism.[15]

In 1861 the movement began which would make Tocqueville the patron saint of democracy's *ralliés*—those who came around to the cause of democracy and especially Catholics for whom such alliance was more difficult. Lacordaire's speech, a vibrant call to Ralliement, was one long parallel drawn between pious American democrats and abominable European ones. In America respect for God is king, as are law, love of liberty, and political liberty joined to civil liberty and well-tempered democracy. In France impiety, envious passion for equality, and license obtain. Results give the measure of these operating principles: "American democracy has founded a great people, religious, powerful, respected, finally free, though not without their trials and perils; European democracy . . . if it is not finally taught and regulated, prepares us for the horrifying alternative of bottomless demagoguery or unchained despotism."

Fine words, but a bit out of date, just when America was slipping into civil war.[16] Lacordaire and Guizot reminded one of the America of the 1830s, the era of early commentaries on *Democracy*. Lacordaire played on contrasts between the taste for liberty and the passion for equality, between the revolutionary democracy of France and the conservative republicanism of the United States, just as Tocqueville had in 1835. To which Guizot responded, as he had in 1837, by alleging the exceptional nature of the United States, with its vast spaces, geographic isolation, and English traditions which allowed it to resist democracy's "natural bad inclinations." But neither alluded to America's dissensions, as though time had stopped for Lacordaire and Guizot—or rather as though those recent events were mere accident, parenthetical. We can suggest biographical explanations for this blindness—illness in Lacordaire's case and innate rigidity worsened by age and political failure in Guizot's. But the resurgence of stale argumentation in Lacordaire also demands a more general explanation. Lacordaire used Tocqueville's argument without changing its terms because the church's own rigidity in the face of modern times continued to make the American model seductive, as disfigured as it was. By following Tocqueville and pleading for a reconciliation of Christianity with popular sovereignty, Lacordaire returned to *L'Avenir*'s doctrines, which had been condemned by Gregory XVI in the *Mirari Vos* encyclical of 1832. But such doctrines had lost nothing of their currency, for the Roman question had merely widened the fault between the church and the democratic universe.

Unchanging arguments and ecclesiastical inertia should not mask the slow shift in Catholic sensibilities. We can see this shift clearly by retracing the intellectual trajectory of Montalembert, Lacordaire's friend and adviser on that speech. In 1835 Lamennais had recommended Montalembert read *Democracy* as an "instructive and very well made book, though a bit tiresome by its formal affectation of the style of Montesquieu."[17] Montalembert found in it only more reason to reaffirm his hesitations toward democracy and his scorn for the American people.[18] Montalembert's intellectual shift began only after the Second Republic, and was to end by the 1860s. Initially, he had supported the coup d'état and thus had fallen out with both Lacordaire and Tocqueville. Montalembert broke publicly with the emperor in December 1852. Only then did he proclaim himself Tocqueville's "intellectual heir," a key reference in his August 1863 speech to the international Catholic congress of Malines, where he opposed Pius IX's reactionary leanings. "Religion, we have said a hundred times, needs liberty; but we have always added: liberty has no less need of religion; and more, a thousand times more, than any other, democratic liberty. . . . This is why Tocqueville, that illustrious contemporary, who is already cited as an elder, pronounced these immortal words: 'The more liberty man gives himself on Earth, the more he should chain himself to heaven.'"[19]

Reading Tocqueville thus accompanied the shift whereby Second Empire liberal Catholics drew closer to the Enlightenment in their hostility toward Ultramontanism. Like Tocqueville, Montalembert and Lacordaire both came to the idea of a separation between temporal and spiritual realms that allowed making the church, founded on the principle of hierarchical authority, cohabit with a democratic society that was founded on individual autonomy.

Nonetheless, Tocqueville's Catholic readers were singularly more optimistic than he was. After 1852 Tocqueville had begun to doubt whether the church was a guarantee against despotism. Religion's logic in effect separated public and private realms, to the degree that it nourished attachment to the beyond and scorn for the temporal. The increase in the number of Christians under the Roman Empire showed that "one of the glories of the Christian faith is that it has produced such men under the worst governments and in eras of the utmost depravity" (*OR*, xiv). The Second Empire was the final demonstration of this. "Why does the Christian religion," Tocqueville asked Albert de Broglie, "which in so many ways has improved the individual and perfected the species, exerted, particularly at its birth, so little influence on the advance of society? Why, as men became individually more human, more just, more temperate, and more chaste, do they seem every day more distant from all public virtues, to such a degree that the great national society seems more corrupt, more cowardly, and more sickly, just as the little society of the family is better ruled?"[20] Such doubts ruined his hopes for any "indirect influence" religion might have on politics and was echoed only by Sophie Swetchine, the nineteenth-century church mother, who reminded Tocqueville that for the church, civic virtue was never anything more than a "sublime and glorious superfluosity."[21] But neither Albert de Broglie, Montalembert, or their descendants shared his doubts about the usefulness of their religion as a fortress against democratic passions.

Thus, the importance of Lacordaire's speech had less to do with its theoretical impact, for there was little innovative about it. Its import was more the new position—an ambiguous one—it assigned Tocqueville in the intellectual genealogy of French Catholicism. For the Catholic party, Tocqueville remained an outsider to the fold.

Lacordaire, echoing Tocqueville's focus on the future, had grown fond of *Democracy.* Guizot preferred Tocqueville's retrospection and *Old Regime.* Guizot's Academy speech was one long sorrowful meditation on recent history and on that long-lived misunderstanding which made his student Tocqueville one of his most determined political adversaries. Just as clearly, in the confrontation between the two men who had been so close, we can read the history of the July regime's failure and Guizot's increasing isolation. "What M. de Tocqueville wished, what he sought for our fatherland," Guizot wrote,

> I wished, I sought as he did. I do not hesitate to say that we felt for public liberties and the institutions on which they are based the same love, inspired by ideas and feelings which for all intents and purposes are very similar and contained within the same limits or nearly so. How then did it happen that in public life, we nearly always occupied opposite camps, and that despite mutual esteem, we spent our time and energy fighting each other while we seemed so naturally called to help and mutually support each other?

As we can imagine, the answer is entirely to Guizot's advantage. The theoretical disagreement stems, according to him, from Tocqueville's political inexperience or, we would say, his being a critical intellectual—in other words, an irresponsible opponent. What did Tocqueville do under the July Monarchy? "In complete liberty, he gave in to the generous ambitions of his thought, freed from any struggle against obstacles and any responsibility for events."

The events of 1848 influenced both Tocqueville's destiny and his thought:

> He had neither desired nor brought about the Republic; he feared it, he doubted it as he saw it coming; but with patriotic, sad devotion, he was one of those who tried seriously to found it; independently of his action in the two great asssemblies of the era, he put his own hand to governing it and for some months was one of the ministers of power. What a difference, what distance, sir, I dare not say what abyss between the two horizons which, twenty years apart, opened before one's gaze! In 1831 he had, as a free spectator, seen and studied the causes that had ensured the success of political and republican liberty in the United States of America. From 1848 to 1851 he struggled, he fought, he succumbed, as a generous actor, to the weight of the causes that on our shores repelled such success. His first mood produced the work on *Democracy;* from the second emerged the volume on the *Old Regime and the French Revolution* . . . a book which reveals all that M. de Tocqueville's mind, already so elevated and so exceptional, had gained in so short a time from the demands of power and under the weight of responsibility.

Guizot was not exempt from preferring to be a spectator. It weighed on him to have succumbed, as Tocqueville had, but long before, to the burden of human mediocrity. Yet regret hardly bothered him, since for Guizot one thought badly when one merely thought; the conceptual rigor of a system was less important than the talent for compromise. According to Guizot, if Tocqueville's acceptance of democracy was more radical than Guizot's, it was because Tocqueville ignored the practical side of politics, scorned the legacy of the past, and underestimated the resistance of the social organism.

As proof, Guizot cited his belated reunion with a Tocqueville finally matured by his trials. In *Old Regime,* Tocqueville had made a carefully nuanced apologia for aristocracy and corporations in order to call for a democratic equivalent to those intermediary social bodies. In this Guizot felt he could recognize his own political art of negotiation between old and new, aristocracy, bourgeoisie, and the people. In this vein he haughtily congratulated himself that Tocqueville had finally caught up with him in eternity.

The hour had come for a tactical union against the empire. The Bonapartists were not fooled, denouncing this "posthumous reconciliation."[22] But the tactic ill masked the persistent antagonism between Guizot and Tocqueville, or rather Guizot and everyone else. By condemning Tocqueville's alliance with democracy, Guizot made his old mistake again. He still wanted to join old with new, aristocracy with democracy. Even worse, he caricatured himself to such degree that one had to wonder if he would not reach back into history and include Charlemagne's cartularies in his desire to represent all the diverse, unequal elements of French society.[23]

For his audience, the divergence between Guizot and Tocqueville was not reducible to misunderstandings arising from political life. The two men were of different schools, as Edouard Scherer shows. Guizot was a Doctrinaire, Tocqueville a liberal. Doctrinaires and liberals differ in their conception of history. The liberal identifies with the course of history and views democracy as a social state we must accommodate. The Doctrinaire fears it like the plague except when only a narrow place is made for it next to monarchy, aristocracy, and the middle classes. Added to this is a philosophical difference: "The Doctrinaire starts with the state, the liberal with the citizen. The Doctrinaire is concerned with social interests; the liberal with individual rights. The former demands order, prepared to add liberty to it thereafter; the latter proclaims liberty as tantamount to order, its condition and foundation." The result is two different systems of government. "The Doctrinaire believes in the need for preventing. The liberal demands that we make do with repressing."[24]

There was no doubt about which school Guizot's audience chose, Guizot's or Tocqueville's. It was the latter. In the second half of the century, even the conservative defenders of the social order accepted democracy, renounced voting tied to landholding, and retreated to a politics of social defense. To make Tocqueville a leading thinker, in this new conjunction of events where liberalism was winning out over conservatism, nothing was lacking but a monument to fill out Tocqueville's rather meager oeuvre—publication of the *Correspondance* and the *Oeuvres complètes*.

A Mausoleum for the Man: The Publication of Tocqueville's Complete Works

Today we seldom read Tocqueville's correspondence; it seems the interminable repetition of his great works. In the nineteenth century, however, letters were not an ancillary genre. They were a literary form tied to the existence of an educated class whose lifestyle—wintering in the city and summering in the country—called to letters by the separations it implied. Letters maintained the dialogue between reasonable people that was the very essence of public commentary. Under the Second Empire letters seemed a substitute for subjugated political discourse. The posthumous edition of Tocqueville's letters, under the durable title *Oeuvres et correspondance inédites* was a part of this same social complicity which nourished the trade in letters.

Tocqueville had doubtless already considered partial posthumous publication of his letters, judging from the care with which he filed his archives. But whatever his intention may have been, there was no premeditated construction of a posthumous self. He accumulated letters without sorting them; innumerable announcements and business letters appear in his archives next to the most intimate correspondence.

The major work of constructing Tocqueville's image thus fell to Beaumont, his longtime friend, with assistance from Tocqueville's widow and Kergorlay, Tocqueville's childhood friend. Beaumont quickly went to work. On 9 December 1860 twenty months after Tocqueville's death, the Bibliographie de la France announced two volumes of the *Oeuvres et correspondance inédites,* with a very long foreword by Beaumont. Then Beaumont contracted with Lévy to publish an edition of the *Oeuvres complètes* in nine volumes (1864–66). To correspondence published once in 1860 and again as volumes 5 and 6 of the *Oeuvres complètes* were added the *Nouvelle correspondance entièrement inédite* as volume 7, a volume of *Mélanges* which brought together historical fragments and travel notes (volume 8), and a volume of economic, political, and literary studies (volume 9). Their success was so great that the comte de Falloux was encouraged in 1866 to publish the *Lettres inédites de Mme Swetchine,* including several letters exchanged with Tocqueville.

Beaumont's publications represent an enormous amount of work. He deciphered Tocqueville's drafts with great accuracy. Finding both familiarity and audacity repugnant, he occasionally effaced some of Tocqueville's expressiveness. But Tocqueville would have approved, for he had similarly cleansed his own writings in his published works.

More seriously, Beaumont censored Tocqueville. In *Democracy* as in *Old Regime,* Tocqueville had taken care never to attack Catholicism directly. He took this caution to the point of falsehood. Yet toward his colleagues in politics, Tocqueville's pen could be ferocious. Beaumont truncated acrimonious remarks.

In fact, this was a smart tactic at a time when the opposition parties were pulling together. Better to make Tocqueville the harbinger of liberal union than the denouncer of those satisfied with bourgeois monarchy.

As much as in his choice of texts, Beaumont's editions were important for their long note opening the 1860–61 letters and the preface to volume 5 of the *Oeuvres complètes* in 1866 before it was published as a separate document in 1897. Here in effect we have a twice-authorized biography: first, by the fussy patronage of Tocqueville's widow and the famous friendship between Tocqueville and Beaumont; second, by the first thorough reading of Tocqueville's papers.

Beaumont could have written an essay, but he preferred to write Tocqueville's life, or *Vie,* as the volume was literally entitled. Thus the theoretical work seems the flowering of the private and public man's own virtues, so that it illustrates Tocqueville's own aphorism: "Life is neither a pleasure nor a pain, it is a serious matter with which we are charged and which we must lead and conduct to our honor." For Beaumont, Tocqueville's theory was never more than practice deferred. Even *Old Regime,* written in retreat, is entirely brought into his design "to oppose material force with moral force, to replace holding power with dignity, action with thought, and in the sphere left to independence of the spirit, however narrow it was, to work for the propagation, or rather the awakening, of ideas which may lie dormant in the world but do not die."[25]

Insisting on the political bearing of Tocqueville's works, Beaumont was naturally led to discuss how they had been received. It was one long song of triumph—*Democracy*'s printers in 1835 avidly deciphering the work as they set it; all sides seeking to claim this impartial author for themselves; fourteen editions all told. France had applauded him, and foreigners joined the chorus: "There is no eminent man in the United States who does not recognize that it is M. de Tocqueville who taught him the constitution of his country and the American *Spirit of Laws.*"[26] Beaumont's preface pulls together all the commonplaces from which collective memory manufactures a classic: spontaneous recognition, public glory, and that hint of unhappiness which is the mark of unusual souls. The transfiguration in public opinion begun by Lacordaire was complete.

The success of *Oeuvres complètes* seemed to confirm Beaumont's affirmations. The first volumes of letters, reprinted in a second edition in 1866, ran to a total of 4,000 copies, of which over 3,000 sold before 1872. The new letters, printed in 1865 in 2,800 copies, sold about 1,400 by the end of 1867. The *Mélanges* appeared in 1865 and then the *Etudes économiques, politiques, et littéraires* the same year, with the same distribution. Public favor did not cool until after 1880.

Portrait: Aristocrat of the Woeful Countenance

Success owed much to lobbying by friends. The *Revue des Deux Mondes* showed particular zeal. After an obituary by Louis de Loménie, the journal offered its readers of 1 December 1860 an excerpt from the *Mélanges* entitled "Quinze jours au désert: Souvenirs d'un voyage en Amérique. Papiers posthumes." Then it opened its columns to Rémusat for an in-depth article on Tocqueville's political doctrine.[27] Such kindness was no mere graveside piety. The authors' Orleanist convictions could not be directly expressed without drawing censure. Praise for the deceased actors of the July Monarchy stood in for personal professions of faith; in 1856 it was common to use literature as a means of political expression. The *Journal des Débats* also excelled in having the courage of its vague allusions. After giving Laboulaye space in 1859, it published Prévost-Paradol's accounts of Lacordaire's reception and Tocqueville's published letters on 4 and 11 January. Bonapartists Sainte-Beuve and Barbey d'Aurévilly thought it well to respond, increasing public rumors about the work. But all this agitation scarcely masks the weak attachment most felt toward Tocqueville the man.

In the eyes of his adversaries, Tocqueville was an author well provided for, even in death. Publication of his correspondence crowned a career which Barbey was indignant to see accruing such honors from the establishment. Tocqueville had had every good fortune. As a "young Montesquieu," welcomed in two academies and then in the Chamber, he surmounted changes in regime without obstacle.

> Thus with two books, with the light baggage of two books, in an era when an abundance of intellectual production seemed to have become literary custom, M. de Tocqueville almost attained the height of consideration which is truly owed only to genius and the tranquil possession of influence which genius does not always have. Of aristocratic family but not going far enough in his opinions to break with men of his class, and yet going far enough for the democrats to be appreciative, he had everyone for him. On both sides there was gratitude toward him, for all he did and all he did not do. . . . Finally, he died—for even fortune can be stubborn, just as misfortune can be—and his successor at the Académie Française is someone we are most surprised to see, Father Lacordaire.[28]

Even those opposed to the empire cast doubt on the glitter of his gold. Tocqueville's thought remained an export article, so exotic did the American model seem in a France that had chosen Bonaparte, not Washington. *Democracy*, a classic in the United States, was merely a curiosity of Americana in France, "a classic in its genre," a minor one. Though Tocqueville as a thinker is a part of both democratic traditions, the French and the American, he was not claimed equally by both. For many on the French side, he was an author merely temporarily in fashion. "It is not useless to recall," wrote Levallois in *L'Opinion Nationale,* "how restricted, how mediocrely efficient M. de Tocqueville's action has been as concerns contemporary events and, even more astonishingly, in the realm of ideas. He influenced little, inspired little, either as a person or as a thinker. His impact on events was never decisive; in going over the history of these past twenty years, one would never find the impress of his will on any important resolution; finally, he gathered neither a group, nor a school, nor a club around his thinking."[29]

Beaumont is partly responsible for such hesitancy toward Tocqueville. He had done what he could to offer an edifying hero, but the means he used were perilous. In its essence the *Correspondance* allows us to measure the gap between the works and the thought trying to locate itself through events, between theory and all that is residual, accidental, fleeting—the disordered abundance of a life that makes letters so seductive. Fluctuations and paths abandoned blur perception of the unity of Tocqueville's oeuvre. Biography and letters are egalitarian genres. They necessarily privilege inheritance over invention, social milieu over singularity, pushing the reader to conclude disabusedly, "So that was all it was," and to think more highly of herself or himself by comparison.

Even when he was alive, Tocqueville seemed irresolute. His letters confirm that sense: "He had an admirably timorous soul."[30] There was almost pity for "this existence which painfully consumed itself, anxious for itself, ungrateful, sterile in others' eyes, whose inner torments kept it from equivocal kinds of greed, errors of system, religious furor, and flights of bad faith." He chose "his ideas to be seen by the public as a woman chooses her dresses for high society, divided between grand designs and small acts."[31] He had only had the "gnawings of ideas," which gave an illusion of impartiality,[32] offering in this way a kind of "fine soul" moaning under the weight of its own impotence.[33]

Some attributed this indecision to physical causes. Under the Second Empire the theory of humors exerted an increasing attraction. Tocqueville, who was always sick, served as a textbook case, arousing "tender compassion for the poor tormented soul who fought for fifty years in a suffering body,"[34] which too much activity used up and which rest killed. To individual determinism can be added the collective determinism of climate, which separates the joyful Montesquieu of Bordeaux from the morosely Norman Tocqueville: "Imagine this nature, coolly polite, more sensitive than expansive . . . place him in his true environment, the

Norman lands, where the earth is rich and fertile but the sky often sad, especially along the coastlines. Consider especially that this mind, which braves political inclemencies as well as those from the sky, is only protected by the frailest of envelopes; is it possible that such a nature could be happy to feel, especially, happy to write?"[35] If Tocqueville was eternally of the political opposition, it was because his thoughts were painful. Can a happy Tocqueville be imagined? Democracy would lose its tragedy.

Others prefer to highlight the social determinism that Tocqueville's aristocratic look clearly showed.[36] His *Correspondance* gave more weight to his noble origins, because it contained a great number of letters to Kergorlay, who had remained a legitimist. Sainte-Beuve tried hard to use the naturalistic method he applied to minds on Tocqueville. Rather than studying the works, which tired him, he studied Tocqueville's family environment and especially the writer's generation of young talents of the same class and the same bright future:

> There was, in that aristocratic and liberal world some thirty years ago, a certain number of young people nobly gifted, enlightened partisans of new ideas, held close by more than one link to tradition, precise, regular in their morals, religious in practice or at least in doctrine, born with these tendencies, exempt from needing to stand out among the crowds and elbow their way up; to be immediately accepted, if they sought it, having only to escape from the front rows and prove their talent or merit in some way.[37]

But this good fortune of high birth had its downside, which deprived Tocqueville of the vigor and realism of those who have tumbled with the times. In the 1830s or 1840s, Royer-Collard and Custine had attributed Tocqueville's fluctuations and hesitancies to his hurry to arrive.[38] In the 1860s people blamed his origins. Tocqueville had wanted to be the representative of an Enlightenment elite; he began to seem the representative of a socioeconomic class, the class of notables. For his biographers, no one escapes his environment, no reason transcends class interests. Tocqueville's image felt the shift created by the Second Republic that laid bare the confrontation between interests. If Sainte-Beuve was more sensitive to this than others, it was because there was still something of Joseph Delorme in him, a poor little penman envious of those who have arrived the day they are born. How can one be modern, Sainte-Beuve commented, with no professional activity, in a world where work is not merely a necessity but the primary tie among social connections? "Without doing every kind of job like Gil Blas, it is good to know what a trade is, even if it is only to be more indulgent toward the poor world, to common, honest people, and so as not to answer necessary *faits accomplis* too often with an absolute veto."[39] By his origins Tocqueville was condemned to be merely a theoretician and a man who reasoned, "to remain in a kind of dilettantism and never emerge a veritable statesman."[40]

The chorus of Tocqueville's friends could not deny that he had been torn between past and present, but this is what, for them, made him exemplary. He was the man of transition who reconnected aristocracy and democracy. His most insignificant actions, overdetermined by the most outrageous symbolizing, became examples for the edification of future democratic elites. Let us cite just one, borrowed from Loménie whose somewhat oafish admiration makes the stereotype obvious:

> With all the virtues of the patronage he exerted, [Tocqueville] joined all the abilities that in our day such patrician status demands. As proof, let us note just one detail we ourselves know. Long ago, in Tocqueville's village church choir, there was a rather sumptuous bench, reserved since time immemorial for the lords of the manor and which had come through the most revolutionary centuries without being removed. This bench, which shocked no one in the community, nonetheless took up a great deal of space, and that it might inspire in someone the notion that it was a disturbance was enough for Alexis de Tocqueville to resolve to have it taken away. On the other hand, as he did not want to seem to be removing it by any special measure which would have made the villagers wonder as to its cause, and in which they might have seen either weakness or a calculated attempt at popularity, he patiently awaited a period of general repairs to the church, and one fine day, following these general repairs, the lords' bench was seen to have been removed and replaced by a much more modest bench placed at the edge of the choir, all to one side and in line with the mayor's and the municipal council's bench.
>
> It was in thus combining the most active devotion to his fellow citizens with scrupulous respect for the dignity of the humblest and an exact knowledge of the spirit of the people of his time, that Alexis de Tocqueville was able to create in his canton, under the empire of the elective principle, a much greater power than that which any of his ancestors had ever enjoyed under the hereditary regime of functions and privilege.[41]

Thus Tocqueville's village offers us a well-tempered democracy where reciprocal consideration is part of the hierarchy of voluntary deference.

These graying or rosy portraits of a man torn between old and new hide within them the interpretation of his oeuvre by its place in literary history. Around Tocqueville, two cultures clashed: the ancient one which the liberals continued, of the seventeenth-century man of honor, and the culture of the romantic, which exalts the uniqueness of the creative self.

A Belated Classicist Exemplar

The gap between Tocqueville and literature's younger generation is nowhere shown more clearly than in Sainte-Beuve. Wishing to recognize Tocqueville's will to change facts that nothing about the young aristocrat could have led one to expect, he noted terms indicating that effort: "target" and "tenacity" in the *Correspondance*. "These forms of language indeed indicate and point out the state and so to speak the common posture of the soul: his own was entirely bound, as Montaigne would have said, to a high and lofty aim."[42] The energy cult seemed to make Tocqueville a romantic hero. But Tocqueville was precisely not a romantic hero, for he did not use his energy to tear down conformity or to show exclusive preference for the self. That energy for him consisted of submitting bravely to norms, bending nobly before the order of things. This was the virtue of "the generous" in classical times. This is why, for the intellectual naturalism of Sainte-Beuve and his followers, Tocqueville descended from Pascal.

Between Pascal and Tocqueville, doctrines differed but not posture or Jansenist ways of thinking. Pascal's anguished search for the City of God in transcendent reality was compared to Tocqueville's anxious turn toward the earthly horizon of providential history. "Tocqueville seems to be as firmly attached to democracy as Pascal was to the cross—with raging passion,"[43] wrote Sainte-Beuve. The idea was developed by Jules Levallois, Sainte-Beuve's secretary between 1855 and 1859, who helped him rewrite his *Port Royal*. Tocqueville had not a loving but "a sad belief, almost one of despair," in democracy. "On every page, reading him, we think again of Pascal's melancholy words, [which Tocqueville] more than anyone would have had the right to make his slogan: 'I blame all equally, those who take the side of praising humanity, those who take the side of blaming it, and those who take the side of entertaining it; and I can only approve those who seek while wailing.'... I would certainly be inclined to see in M. de Tocqueville a kind of political Pascal."[44]

Tocqueville's political Jansenism was echoed by his aesthetic Jansenism. Sadness and banality both describe the author's diaphanous self and his comfortless prose. There is agreement on the paucity of dramatics and colorlessness of style, as much the enemy of fiery expression as of audacity in thought. Tocqueville,

Sainte-Beuve notes, "is too applied," too desirous of transcribing everything in the world of universals to give even a tiny place to the picturesque or the emotionally singular. His is the culture of commonplaces, always seeking what is unanimously acceptable to "good people." Without sharing their ideas, he shared the Doctrinaires' style, the political Jansenists of the Restoration and the July Monarchy, people decidedly too reasonable, "our grave history professors of today, our authors of political considerations after Montesquieu, but sadder than he; all those who seek and claim to give reasons for every deed, the profound explanation for everything that happens, who admit neither the unforeseen nor the play of little causes often as effective as the great on [the events of] this mobile stage, meritorious spirits but dull and laborious, bowed under the weight of maturity."[45] In *Le Figaro,* Jouvin added to critiques outlined in 1856. As a writer, Tocqueville

> had neither color nor personality; the insolent "I" of original prosemakers melted away and disappeared under the graying cloth of phrases draped in monotone uniformity. The most illustrious, to be sure, member of a community of contemporary men of letters whom we might call the Jansenists of the French language, M. de Tocqueville writes with the pen of the convent and seals his style with the stamp of order. He has more views and initiative than most of his coreligionists, but he pours his ideas into the mold whence their productions invariably seem to emerge.[46]

For people of letters Tocqueville was thus henceforth flung onto the heap of the old school born with the century—near his mentor Royer-Collard and far indeed from the new generation.

We could select other quotations. To show how outdated Tocqueville was as a writer, it is better to resort to a romantic roman à clef entitled *Les Pléiades,* published in 1874, in which Gobineau condensed his 1840–60 experiences in conservative and liberal milieus. Here, the character Genevilliers is depicted with the traits of Tocqueville, although some details can only apply to Montalembert. The novelist juxtaposes traits borrowed left and right, forces them and stylizes them but beneath the caricature, its model is easily recognizable.[47] The cuts Gobineau reserved for Genevilliers-Tocqueville bit even more deeply for Gobineau's having been a colleague of Tocqueville's. In 1843 Tocqueville had been asked by the Academy to write a large study on moral progress. He had asked Gobineau to make some philosophical reading notes for him. The work was incomplete in 1848 when the revolution caused the project to be abandoned, and Tocqueville took Gobineau on as the head of his cabinet when he became minister in 1849. Not that he had unconditional confidence in Gobineau. He appreciated his wit, his manners, and his knowledge, while fearing he might misuse them.[48] His fears were valid. In June and July 1853, when Gobineau published the first two volumes of his *Essai sur l'inégalité des races humaines,* Tocqueville felt his "stud farm philosophy" detestable, its "dangerous thoughts expressed in a journalistic style."[49] The next two volumes, published in 1855, aggravated their disagreements. Tocqueville condemned the doctrine in the name of the moral consequences it could not help but have: discouragement before inevitable decline and the oppression of races deemed inferior. On the other hand, Gobineau rejoiced that he had "struck the nerve of liberal ideas at its core."[50] One man loved what brought people together by breathing confidence into them; the other enjoyed the taste of paradox, polemic, and desperate posing. A world separates Tocqueville, a democrat in his mind if not in his heart, from Gobineau, a poet of decadence and aristocratic nostalgia. In the portrait he drew of Tocqueville, Gobineau's surliness is explained by the irreducible opposition between the world of notables and the younger generation of intellectuals more attentive to words and to myth than to the writer's moral magistracy:

> Henry de Genevilliers . . . was of highly honorable character. He belonged to the conservative party. In addition, he was liberal and attached extreme importance, like all wise people, to being able to say to every contradictor, with an attractive smile, "We are less far apart than you seem to believe!" In this way, he had affinities with the legitimists; he had no fewer with the democrats. He kept his balance by leaning in turn toward every side and seeking to agree with everyone, at least a little.
>
> He spent his life seeking the solution to social problems. He worried about statistics, about political economy, about charitable institutions, on which he spent a lot of money. He organized workingmen's societies for the instruction of the lower classes and funded public washhouses, sewing rooms, and savings groups. He was an active member of the Saint Vincent de Paul Society and the Society of Saint François Régis for legal marriages; but above all, he preached the moral transformation of the proletariat who, with the help of healthy doctrines of renunciation and abnegation resulting from religious principles as solid as they were enlightened, would one day become sober, chaste, patient, unselfish, quite uninterested in public dance halls, and the irreconciliable enemies of the cabaret. He did not believe precisely in those things as they must be crudely

stated to be understood. He hoped for them, worked for them, leaned toward them. And *leaning* is a very modern word to describe how one can want a thing without wanting it because it is impossible. In fact, in politics, I repeat, he would have liked to conciliate everything. To suppose of him that he sought a government founded on force would have been to insult him. For nothing in the world did he want what had existed yesterday. In truth, he brushed aside what will perhaps exist tomorrow. Above all, he proclaimed energetically the dangers, poverty, and odiousness of what is today. This way of seeing, common among reasonable people, is called "being conservative." Genevilliers was entirely of this stripe; his convictions were unshakable. All rested upon sand and was composed of great sweetness of soul, timid honesty, pious phrases, much weakness, a few doubts ill interred beneath a layer of trenchant dogmatism. Genevilliers was mayor of his village, a member of the Manche regional (departmental) council, and deputy of his arrondissement.

In the world, he was respected. His name naturally elicited praise. People nowhere like fiery temperaments or those mad for truth who seek it on little-trod paths. Such characters seem to believe and make others understand that commonplaces do not satisfy them. They injure others' self-esteem. Genevilliers injured no one. He took only the best-traveled roads and drew attention only to the points known to all. His wife felt affectionate sympathy for him. As he fluently and approvingly supported the uncontested opinions of the milieu in which he lived, she was persuaded of his value and was proud of him. This method of reducing to well-constructed axioms what was on everyone's lips seemed to her erudition, and she esteemed herself happy to be united with a man whom no one contradicted.[51]

In his condensed version of all the commonplaces about Tocqueville, Gobineau allows us to understand how the gap would grow between Tocqueville and the reactionary movement that attracted the young fin-de-siècle intellectuals. The one had legality and measure on his side; the others had scorn for numbers and dreams of a violence that would give birth to grandeur. Gobineau's portrait is more important as a symptom of the shift in mind-set than for its impact on opinion. Gobineau was not widely read in France, and on top of that, the key to his portrait was not easily found by those who had not known the first half of the century. Only the publication in 1908 of the correspondence between the two men drew public attention to the contrast between Tocqueville's "mental mediocrity," his "timid bourgeois idealism," and "Gobineau, occasionally brilliant but not very nice."[52]

Tocqueville's friends did not challenge the accuracy of the ferocious descriptions hurled by men of letters. But they changed the interpretation of them. Tocqueville's prose was indeed gray, for those who enjoyed eccentricity. But it was through his grayness that Tocqueville rose to the level of the universal solid citizen. "M. de Tocqueville is an easy man to study," Scherer wrote in 1861. "He has none of those infinite complexities, those bizarre contrasts which sometimes make a human being an indecipherable enigma. His personality is perfectly transparent, because it is perfectly unifed. . . . M. de Tocqueville is an admirable kind of moral man. He has the highest sense of human dignity. His existence is a model of order, of conduct, of appropriateness. He is absolutely reasonable."[53] In his austerity Tocqueville thus incarnated liberal rationality, which set great importance on moral duty and placed the principle of responsibility at the heart of the social. He also had the noble liberal style. There was nothing in him of "that sterile intellectual promiscuity which becomes incapable of producing as it ties itself to too many objects."[54]

Inscribing Tocqueville's work in the universe of wisdom made possible the moralizing use of it which became general after the publication of the *Oeuvres complètes*. The *Correspondance* conveys the difficult arguments of the great works in everyday language, making Tocqueville's thought accessible in fragments to a popular readership. *Le Magasin Pittoresque*[55] offered long quotations on fifteen occasions between 1856 and 1876, inserting Tocqueville among philosophers moral (Aristotle, Marcus Aurelius, Cousin, and Lamennais), holy (Saint Augustine and Saint François de Sales), moralist (Montaigne, Chamfort, and Vauvenargues), and historical (Guizot and Macaulay). In this pantheon Tocqueville's particular role was to be democracy's pedagogue. It was recalled that he showed that instruction was necessary to produce national unity, a useful warning, especially after 1870 when that German instructor showed his military superiority.[56] The fine morals in Tocqueville's treatise could be grazed upon, seemingly summed up by one precept: "The world belongs to energy."[57] Tocqueville was the one who took Plutarch's model heroes and adapted them to every situation in the world. By affirming the equal dignity of all social roles, he restored concern for work well done, and duty met, to each person. For example, let us open the volume of 1859: "The feeling which overcomes me," wrote Tocqueville, "when I find myself in the presence of human creatures, however humble their condition, is that of the original equality of the species, and then I am even less concerned with pleasing or serving them than with not offending their dignity."[58] Thanks to him the principle of equality gives the oldest aphorism new youth: "There is no stupid job,"[59] "Woman is made to serve—and what greater mission than serving others,"[60] "There is an art to growing old."[61] Let us not underestimate these moralizing uses made of Tocqueville, who was not the most popular M. Prudhomme. Yet we can see what was so attractive in his work: the taste for sententiousness with reference to a human nature whose essence he never questioned; the affirmation of equality and the virtues of education mixed with social conservatism; the obsession with energy in which Tocqueville's aristocratic heroism joined the courage of humble people. The *Correspondance,* by laying bare Tocqueville's moral process, opened the path to the unregulated practice of worldly-wise quotations beginning, "As M. de Tocqueville said, . . ."

When he was alive, Tocqueville had been a rather posturing, coughing, spluttering personage—indistinguishable from those of his world. In 1859 his death paved the way for his mythologization, without his works, too thin and conventional, exciting passionate attachment. In Tocqueville, readers found not so much intimate charm or seductive surprise but sonorous citations adapted to the twists and turns of French history—just what was needed to beat back Caesarism, venerate liberty, justify equality, and promote virtue.

But the public commentator's glow was heightened by the man's self-effacement and the conventional classicism of his style. Because Tocqueville had expressed himself in the common language of honest people, he could serve as a standard-bearer. This is how we can explain the contrast between the embarrassed biographies (for there was nothing unforgettable about the man) and the post-1860 political commentaries that turned Tocqueville into the inventor of a culture of contestation.

The Inventor of a Culture of Contestation

In effect, on his death in 1859 Tocqueville became the opposition media's great man, from the *Journal des Débats,* prestigious mouthpiece for levelheaded men in which Laboulaye's articles appeared in 1859; to the *Temps,* where Scherer devoted long articles to him; to the *Courrier du Dimanche,* where Prévost-Paradol sang his praises in 1865. Tocqueville's work was no heirloom reserved for old fogies embittered by their exclusion from power. Tocqueville fascinated the younger generation of lawyers who became deputies under the Third Republic. They often joined in the Molé-Tocqueville meetings at which they could hear and practice public speaking. From Rémusat (born in 1797) to Laboulaye (born 1811) and Bertauld (1823),[62] to Savary (1845),[63] three generations of liberals communed in their admiration for *Democracy* and based their political program on it.

Glory has its price. Tocqueville's thought dissolved as it became commonplace, and nothing shows his harmony with the times more clearly than the abundance of casual references and unconscious borrowings. Laboulaye was sensitive to this anonymous trafficking:

> When the poet finished his work, he left us his thought, embalmed, so to speak, in the form in which he created it. His crown tarnishes but does not crumble. Racine has fewer admirers than in the century of Louis XIV, but his theater survives in its entirety, and no one quarrels with him over his *Athalie*. Not so for writers on morals, philosophy, religion, politics. With time, their works diminish, and often posterity wonders whence comes their renown, which it does not understand. The ideas of a Montesquieu astonished and sometimes revolted his contemporaries. The new generation takes them, and the discovery of genius becomes a legacy to all. To writers who once shook their centuries, following eras leave only their errors or uncomprehended ideas. The further ahead these writers have pushed society, the more quickly they are left behind. They are held back by their very success, and ordinarily, ingratitude is rendered in proportion to the degree service was rendered.[64]

Tocqueville's ideas were lost even more in society's incessant chatter because circumstances favored it.

Endurance and Change in the Image of America

Reading *Democracy* was obviously tied to the hazards of American politics—the work was used as a textbook on political America. After 1850 the textbook seems to have become outdated. The Second Republic's failure tarnished the image of its great sister republic. While liberals imputed their failure to America, Napoleon III hated America's "living criticism of his usurpation," and his partisans sought anything that might destroy the American myth of self-government. In the years preceding the Civil War, they had ample ammunition. Tocqueville himself, without joining the chorus of those disappointed in America, wondered after 1850 if America itself had not entered its revolutionary era. Starting in 1856, French newspapers devoted many column inches to the prewar rioting. When the war erupted, French public opinion massively took the side of the South, out of reaction against American imperialism and rejection of the republican model.[65] At the height of the Civil War, there remained an Americanophile, abolitionist current in France. But as this current was reduced to a defensive posture, it began to question the Union's future.

It took the end of the Civil War for initiatives dedicated to the glory of the United States to flourish: a French emancipation committee was formed to aid in the education of black Americans, and plans for the Statue of Liberty gift were begun in 1866. *Democracy in America* immediately once again became the book in which the French regime's opposition sought reasons for hope. Bonapartists could play up the distinction between Tocqueville's America and the America of the 1860s as much as they liked:[66] members of the "liberal union" saw America through Tocqueville's eyes alone. He was lauded as having foreseen the risks of secession, and even more for having perceived the excellence of the American model. Ernest Duvergier de Hauranne, son of the well-known Restoration historian and public commentator and himself a future deputy to the National Assembly in 1871, published *Huit mois en Amérique: Lettres et notes de voyage, 1864–1865* in 1866.[67] The book opened and closed with an homage to Tocqueville. It was one long discourse on Tocquevillean themes, in a travelogue format: the consensual nature of American democracy, individuals' sense of responsibility and taste for risk taking, the absence of envy and the immoderate desire for equality. Like Tocqueville, Duvergier's aim was to present the French with a model of democracy minus revolution. For everyone on the opposition side, "America is the hope of the world."[68]

Thirty years after it came out and despite reservations, *Democracy in America* again seemed an acceptable description of contemporary America. The North's victory appeared merely a return to the equilibrium that had obtained in the United States before the Civil War. The endurance of this image owes much to French ignorance and ensured Tocqueville's fame through the 1880s. But ignorance does not endure unmotivated. Only the America of the 1830s could offer the French an image of liberty sufficiently seductive. For them, America remained the land of small landholders who were also citizens contributing actively to the common interest. They were no more attracted than Tocqueville was to American-style market competition and individualism; like Tocqueville and Jefferson, they could not see how slaves and the economically dependent poor might be integrated into the Republic. Yet this was precisely the challenge America faced after 1860. Capitalist expansion during the latter half of the nineteenth century increased the number of wage earners, people dependent for subsistence on market fluctuations. Blacks may have obtained the right to vote in 1867, but there was no agrarian reform to ensure their economic independence as small landholders. Slavery was indeed abolished but only at the cost of profound political change, because liberty had to cohabit with social inequality. The French had no clear understanding of any of this. The naive praise by Laboulaye and so many others of the American model as drawn by Tocqueville instead meant they required that fantasy for reassurance following France's own misfortunes. This may explain the way *Democracy* was constantly readjusted to meet changing French political demands.

Democracy as Party Platform

There are three phases of these successive readjustments. First, in 1860, a decree of 24 November reestablished the assemblies' right of address. A senate decision of 31 December 1861 then strengthened legislative bodies' fiscal control. The regime grew more liberal. On 10 November 1860 the first issue of the *Revue Nationale* appeared, directed by Laboulaye and with the republican Lanfrey, the Protestant Pressensé, and the economist Baudrillart on its staff. In Nancy in 1861 a group of notables founded the anthology *Varia* to promote provincial liberties. This was the seed of what became the *Comité de Nancy*, the primary opposition publication in later years. Conservative Catholics and liberals at least agreed to call for municipal elections. At this point Tocqueville's *Correspondance* came out, along with a series of works inspired by his thought: *Etudes contemporaines: De la centralisation et de ses effets* by Odilon Barrot (1861);[69] Charles de Rémusat's *Politique libérale* (1860), one of whose chapters reprinted an earlier study on *Old Regime*; and republican Elias Regnault's book *La province*, which showed how far the ideal of self-government had spread beyond the Orleanists.

The second phase was the 30–31 May 1863 elections. The opposition lifted its head. On 11 January 1864 Thiers pronounced a grand speech on "the necessary liberties." Laboulaye published two key opposition books in 1863, *Le parti libéral* and *L'état et ses limites*, in which he reprinted articles on Tocqueville which had come out in the *Journal des Débats* in 1859.

In 1865–66, the liberal union organized. In May 1865 the first edition of the Nancy platform was published. It called for more local liberties and more political participation. "This is the American way," commented Orleanist d'Haussonville, thrilled.[70] Renewed by preparations for local-level elections (in which Tocqueville's authority was often invoked),[71] discussion surrounding *Democracy* took off again with the laws of 18 July 1866 extending the authority of regional (departmental) councils and of 24 July 1867 extending the authority of municipal councils. On all sides, great ancestors were invoked as though the longevity of a doctrine automatically conferred the privilege of its legitimacy. The decentralists combed through history, and *La Presse* invoked the specters of Mirabeau, Robespierre, and Saint-Just and the great American example.[72] But of all thinkers cited, Tocqueville was the only one not suspected of having wavered in his decentralist faith. And of course politically he was ecumenical: legitimist by birth, Orleanist by career before 1848, republican in his alliance. This is why he could be claimed both by the legitimists, who hoped thereby to cleanse themselves of the infamous taint of feudal archaism,[73] and by the Orleanists, indignant that others were stealing their thinker.[74] "Tocqueville said long ago that . . ." became a cliché.

Why Tocqueville? He owed his prestige to having been the first to accept popular sovereignty while at the same time perceiving its possible detour into Caesarism. He was "one of the first, if not the first, to support these two principles at the same time: that democracy is the necessary form of modern society, and that democracy should have as its basis and as its limit all liberties. While political schools of his era were fighting for or against universal suffrage, he was moving forward."[75]

Thus Tocqueville's success came from public opinion siding with political democracy. Universal suffrage lost its exclusive character as a revolutionary claim and came to seem a necessity of the time, so that it was no longer the acceptance of democracy that was debatable but its organization. The *Revue Nationale* emphasized this new pertinence that Tocqueville's works gained from the hiatus of 1848. Under the July Monarchy "the name of Tocqueville was perhaps better known, his book more sought after, his authority as a public commentator better established abroad than in his own country." The bourgeoisie slept in peace, certain that democracy would draw up before wealth, whatever Tocqueville had said about it. In 1848

> it was understood that the Revolution that was thought finished continued; that the movement was not only political but social; that the arrival of democracy might not be an American event but a universal one. With all minds thus violently brought to consider these serious problems, Tocqueville was more widely reread. . . . Far from Tocqueville's writings having aged, we can say that they are of even livelier interest to us today in that they have more direct application than ever to our social and political state. When we reread what he wrote twenty years ago about the tendencies of democracy in modern society, its possible dangers,

its probable future, we are astonished by the prodigious sagacity with which he announced so many things which have since taken place. Then it seemed pure speculation, political philosophy; now, it is history, yesterday's and today's history.[76]

Nothing makes the switch more clear than the sudden interest in Tocqueville's analysis of tutelary despotism.[77] In 1840 people could not imagine despotism in any other form than the Terror. Not until the coup d'état, which turned the Republic into support for Caesarism, was there concern about individual liberty turning to collective dependence or about democratic idolatry of power. Did this mean that, starting in 1851, it was believed, as Tocqueville had, that individualist democracy would naturally corrupt into despotism? Counterrevolutionaries had no problem thinking of individualism as reverting to despotism, but they had no need of Tocqueville to admit what was part of their heritage. No, Tocqueville's notion gave pause only to those who had embraced 1789—and then only grudgingly. The conjunction of material equality and despotism seemed to them a national accident, not in democracies' nature. Suddenly, debate became focused only on when France's problem had been born—under Louis XI, Richelieu, or the Revolution.[78] Hence the equivocal nature of Tocqueville's patronage, glorified by the seniority it conferred on liberal genealogy but obstinately eccentric within French political culture.

Liberty's Eccentric Thinker

Tocqueville's eccentricity comes from his combining defensive liberalism attentive to the modern notion of liberty, i.e., individual independence, with praise for the Ancients' liberty, which was political participation. Or rather Tocqueville construed the Ancients' liberty as guaranteeing that of the Moderns. This caused him to run counter to both Jacobins and liberals in the tradition of Constant.

Defensive Liberalism: Judicial Guarantees

There is nothing unique in Tocqueville about the notion of "necessary guarantees" for protection of the individual. Such a notion is connected to the contractual conception of political links and to the widely shared ideal of preservation of existing interests. Tocqueville is unique only in his insistence on three points: the power of the judiciary to declare laws unconstitutional, the subordination of the state to ordinary courts of law—not specialized ones for administrative law—and belief in juries.

Today everyone knows that Tocqueville pleaded for judicial power to declare laws unconstitutional. This is America's principal contribution to political science in its institution of the Supreme Court and the way citizens are protected from abuses by representatives.[79] Yet Tocqueville's thinking on this was more subtle than is claimed. He felt it impossible to import the American model to France. The principle of judicial control of constitutionality in fact means subordinating law to a higher legal order that is unanimously accepted. Nothing of the kind exists in France, where there is neither consensus on legal norms nor reverence for jurisprudence. Such power invested in the judiciary risked being perceived as trampling on the people's will in a country where one is legally in the wrong when politically in the minority.

Reaction to Tocqueville's idea shows how accurate his fears were. As early as 1835 his readers commented on the risks of usurpation of power by judges.[80] In 1848 constitutional committee members wondered what steps courts would take if a law seemed to them unconstitutional. On 17 August they declared "the opinion that there is danger in foreseeing this evil, that it is very difficult to establish good rules to make it stop, and decide[d] that the plan [for the constitution] will maintain silence on this subject."[81] We might have imagined that the opponents to the Second Empire would have fewer hesitations. Yet they too only weakly called for judicial power as a check on majority power, so associated did it seem with ancien régime parliamentary practices—a shameful memory which seemed to cast a shadow on popular sovereignty.[82] None of the later constitutions of the Third and Fourth Republics introduced judicial control over lawmaking. Hauriou would later provide a good analysis of the reasons for this.

> The truth is that in France, we have not yet realized the danger to the individual liberties of each person represented by the absence of effective controls over laws voted by Parliament. It is not simply that Parliament benefits from the appearance of sovereignty, irreconcilable with the very principle of the national constitution but permitted by memories of the Revolution. It is also that up to this point legislative lapses have only occurred with unusual laws or in unusual circumstances.[83]

Unable to conceive of oversight of legislation as possible, Tocqueville tried to obtain state subordination to ordinary courts of law, on the American model. His argument took the technical form of a critique of the provisions of an article of the constitution on bureaucratic immunity, which forbade submitting to ordinary courts litigation challenging the administration without prior agreement from the Council of State. For Tocqueville the question was central: "The right to sue the agents of power is not a part of liberty—it is liberty itself, liberty at its clearest and most tangible," so that the question of state agents' responsibility furnished a "very precise measure" of liberalism's progress or its decline.[84] The right allowed the state to act as both judge and judged in effect favors the idolatry of public power to which democracies are naturally inclined. Bureaucratic immunity aided democracy's corrupt nature. On the other hand, state submission to ordinary courts was part of the healing art applied to democracies. Opportune in democracies, submission to ordinary courts is desirable in every form of government. No single entity can determine the Good for the entire society. The public good is a hidden good and only shows itself in the debate of freedoms in which no one person's position can claim the Truth. This necessitates recourse to the judiciary to preserve the right to free speech, against the powerful under aristocratic rule and, under democracy, against Power.

The difficulty was obviously how to ensure judges' independence. The ancien régime had achieved it by accident, because members of Parliament purchased their offices. As a result, they were independent and could serve as mediators between the sovereign and his subjects. From an ill came a good.[85] Tocqueville, extremely hostile to the sale of offices, called for finding a democratic equivalent to parliaments. Yet here as on other matters, he confined himself to principles, leaving it to legislators to invent solutions.

Tocqueville's thought had its precedents. The provisions for bureaucratic immunity, drafted under the ancien régime and institutionalized by Article 75 of the Constitution of the Year VIII, was the target of a string of denunciations by Montesquieu, Constant, and the duc de Broglie.[86] And all for naught: in February 1845 a reform proposal by Isambert supported by Tocqueville met with complete indifference. Article 75, in theory abrogated by the decree of 19 September 1870, should in fact have remained law until today. But its political failure did not mean an absence of debate. Between 1860 and 1870 Tocqueville played teacher to a school whose students were Laboulaye, Rémusat in his *Politique libérale*, the Nancy platform, and Savary in his *Projet de loi sur la décentralisation*, all of whom used his authority to plead for doing away with administrative jurisdiction. It is true that the notion appeared even more noxious under the empire when the compressed space of public commentary gave freer rein to abuses by civil servants.[87] Some called for more rigorous pursuit of those who abused power, without going so far as to call for the state to be set below citizens.[88] This sudden interest in a side of Tocqueville's work which had hitherto been little known coincides with the renaissance of administrative law. Administrative law, developed without theory in 1818, underwent a period of disclosure thanks to the collections of laws of Gérando, Macarel, and Cormenin. But from 1848 to 1860 constraints on political liberties caused it to enter a latent phase.[89] The decree of 24 November 1860, which restored freedom in legislative debates, also led the Council of State to increase its openness to appeals. From this arose a great many claims against excesses of power and the flourishing of indexes and great treatises which in classifying administrative jurisdiction defined the central notion of administrative personality and developed a theory of the notion of excess of power.[90] The 1866 publication of Tocqueville's report on Macarel's course in administrative law as part of volume 9 of the *Oeuvres complètes* repositioned Tocqueville at the center of the debate.

Yet challenging the principle of administrative justice under the Second Empire shows not so much adherence to Tocqueville's thought as the desire to do away with the regime. Though dangerous, bureaucratic immunity seemed no less necessary to preserve the public good. Although the selling of public offices by the monarchy might be praised, as Tocqueville had, for its beneficial side effects, no one could see how to make judges independent in a democracy.[91] Even if they were independent, there would remain the risk of subordinating the public good to individuals' egotism. Tocqueville pleaded for the expansion of the legal system and societal self-regulation. His readers had a unitary conception of law: the executive power and the administration, agents of the general will, would only be opposed by illegitimate, factious interests. Hence, his readers feared the denunciation of public officials and condemned the irresponsibility of judges.[92]

The distance between Tocqueville and his readers was not only due to their greater or lesser legitimation of private interest. It was due to divergent political conceptions. Tocqueville was careful to introduce intermediary bodies into the public realm and to partition power. His readers, especially jurists, privileged sovereignty. Nothing shows this fundamental divergence at the core of the liberal camp better than the role which devolved to the jury.

Before Tocqueville, the rationale for the jury had been a commonplace of the liberal tradition. But no one thought about jury practice. In both nineteenth-century America and France, citizens balked at being jurors. The jury was overemphasized theoretically because it dramatically posed—in the specter of judicial error—the problem of the relationship between popular will and the Good, between number and reason. The jury question was thus intertwined with the suffrage question. To one who believed in the virtues of mass suffrage, the popular jury was the means to gain the truth. To one who saw voting as a civil service, both jury and voters must have certain abilities. Tocqueville, who believed in the inescapable dawning of universal suffrage, deemed it logically necessary to resort to a jury in both criminal and civil cases. Serving as voter, juror, and soldier was every man's right and every man's duty, as a consequence of popular sovereignty. Not that jurors were enlightened by nature. For Tocqueville democracy rested on an act of confidence in the ability of humanity to perfect itself—not on the belief in present perfection. The jury perfected its judgment through contact with the elite class of judges. Thus the jury, a republican institution because it places society in the hands of the governed, is the site where the popular will is educated and the conflict between private interest and public welfare is absorbed. There, every man learns "not to recoil before responsibility for his own acts," to fight "individual egoism, which is like rust on society. . . . [The jury] is to be considered a free school, always open, where every juror comes to learn his rights, where he enters into daily communication with the most educated and most enlightened of the upper classes, where laws are taught him in a practical manner."[93] The jury is the institution par excellence in a democracy in which sovereignty is manifested as the exercise of deliberative reasoning. Tocqueville conceived the independence of the judiciary as a bulwark against the excesses of democracy. He took from the state the power to make law only to give it to the sovereign—represented by the jury.

His feeling for the jury, which went almost unnoticed in 1835, became a commonplace around 1848.[94] But if all were aware of the need not to allow the state to make rules unfettered, many feared that the education of citizens would be achieved to the detriment of the accused.[95] In the jury they sought a guarantee against the state, not a way to exercise the Ancients' liberty.

Decentralization: Condition for the Exercise of Liberty

The fight against centralization was as important as the search for an independent judiciary. Both required overturning the transcendent power of French tradition's constitutive sovereignty.

Tocqueville benefited from the sudden interest in decentralization between 1860 and 1866,[96] an interest born of confusion. Weakening the state was confused with weakening the government. Suddenly, using the terms *decentralization* and *self-government* meant rethinking all relationships between government and individuals and even relationships of citizens among themselves.[97]

For all that it was tactical, this sudden adherence to self-government implied no less an intellectual rupture with French tradition. Its earliest signs were in 1856 with the publication of *Old Regime.* To understand this rupture, we can follow the developments in the thinking of Laboulaye, who was often considered Tocqueville's disciple. He was the titled defender of the United States in France between 1860 and 1870, as Tocqueville had been under the July Monarchy. Tocqueville had played the role of adviser in the writing of the constitution in 1848; Laboulaye played the same role in the preparation of the constitution of 1875. Following Laboulaye's hard-won adherence to Tocqueville's ideas provides us a fine example of French wariness toward the American model. In 1843, in an astonishing misinterpretation, Laboulaye declared he had been cured of any admiration for self-government by reading *Democracy.* The interest of all, he felt, was best protected by an impartial administration, recruited democratically by competition and trained in a special school, a kind of Ecole Nationale d'Administration (like today's ENA, whence most of France's politicians emerge) on the Prussian model.[98] Not until 1848 did the concern to defend liberty win out in Laboulaye over the search for governmental efficacy and administrative organization.

In this shift from the Prussian to the American model, the Second Republic's drift toward anarchy and then empire was a determining experience. Named to the chair in comparative law at the Collège de France in 1848, Laboulaye began a systematic study of America. Also in 1848, the new, liberal, Americanophilic generation began to emerge, with Tocqueville as its master. The reversal was so brutal that Laboulaye forgot the lucidity with which Tocqueville had seen Caesarism's shadow as early as the 1840s—when majority opinion was united in Napoleonic fervor.[99] As though the reversal was more pardonable because it was everyone's doing.

Laboulaye's path is a good example. Under the July regime one was suspected of aristocratic nostalgia or federalism in trying to protect a space for civil liberties. In the 1860s Tocqueville's work became the Holy Writ against which one could no longer struggle without seeming a supporter of Caesarism. Celebrating state efficacy and desiring its unity now meant collaborating with despots. The difficulty for all of Tocqueville's heirs was now to find a third path between the minimal state so foreign to the French and the tutelary state which tended toward despotism.

DECENTRALIZATION AND FRENCH HISTORY

Decentralization in effect posed the historical problem of the genesis of the French nation. Between the American experience and the French experience, there was no common ground. This is evidenced in the difference between the terms *self-government* and *decentralization*. To refer to the local level in the United States, the term *self-government* is the only pertinent one, for the colonists constituted themselves into small political societies before they gained sovereignty. In the United States local organization came first, centralization second. On the other hand, in France the local level could only be the result of a process of decentralization because the nation was constituted from the top down. Tocqueville's efforts on behalf of self-government thus came up against the impossibility of referring to a living tradition of local liberties. Anyone making a case for the community was immediately suspected of feudal nostalgia.[100] The weight of memory grew even stronger in nineteenth-century France, with persistent dominance by notables. Defending the local level would not lose its aristocratic character until political parties, particularly France's "radical committees," became established at the local level.

By what arguments from the American experience did Tocqueville prove the need to diverge from French tradition? Or rather, the need to denature the French, so ingrained were the centralist traditions that had given form to the national character.[101]

DECENTRALIZATION: PEDAGOGICAL ARGUMENTS

Decentralization's first merit was that it ensured security. As early as 1848 fear had made the old parliamentarians aware of the charms of the provinces, which were more conservative than the capital. Under the Second Empire very often the only relevant question was whether the state or self-government would provide better prophylaxis against revolutions.[102] The security point of view extended far beyond conservative circles; we find it among liberals like Prévost-Paradol and Laboulaye, as well as among centralist republicans like Elias Regnault.[103] It was far from Tocqueville's own view, though he did tend to set fear on the side of freedom.

To concern for security could be added concern for effective management. In *Democracy,* Tocqueville had contrasted the Americans' spirit of initiative with the deathly somnolence of French society. "There are nations in Europe," he wrote, "whose inhabitants consider themselves a kind of colonist, indifferent to the destiny of the place in which they live" (*DA* 1:92). Cited constantly, Tocqueville's argument was based on the inability of power to inventory and satisfy every need of the social body, but it was fragile, and in 1835 Tocqueville had had to admit "that the villages and counties of the United States would be more usefully administrated by a central authority distant from them and which remained foreign to them" (*DA* 1:92). It is easy to show that a centralized administration is more orderly, more uniform, less battered by corrupting solicitations than locally elected officials. And lack of state interference does not have individual initiative as its unavoidable consequence, as Dupont-White shows in the example of Ireland, where state inertia conjoins with popular apathy.[104] Thinking only about management, the struggle thus remained unclear between public commentators for self-government and partisans of unified government who drew strength from the increasing complexity of modern societies.[105] Indeed, concerns about management more logically led to a weaker central administration than to one decentralized by having decisions made by referenda. This was the conclusion to which turn-of-the-century republicans came. The "town hall revolution" and the great decentralizing laws (5 April 1884 on municipal councils; 22 March 1890 on community syndicates; reform bills relaunched by the decree of 16 February 1895) sought more to increase efficiency by separating special interests than to increase citizen participation. This is why, once the fervor of 1848 was over, self-government's partisans prudently emphasized the pedagogical argument for citizen training over the argument for efficient management, as Tocqueville himself had. Louis de Kergorlay gives us a fine example of return to the pedagogical perspective. A talented legitimist who returned to private life in 1830, Kergorlay was at the head of the legitimist decentralizing movement in 1848. This is how he summed up the balance of his experiences for Tocqueville:

> Although French and German office workers are often stupid, the administrative machine in which they are one of the little cogs functions less maladroitly than do our municipal, and general, etc., councils when they get involved in wanting or organizing something. . . . [In 1848] we did the most awkward thing to my mind, by trying to prove that we could administrate better than a prefect by limiting his sphere of action. . . . I have always thought it would have been better to tear apart the veil and just say simply—we are incompetent, but we want to learn how not to be in future.[106]

Under the Second Empire this notion of a long education in civic-mindedness through common management of small-scale matters had become widespread and was often expressed using Tocqueville's formula, which became a cliché: "Communal governance is to liberty what primary schools are to science."[107]

In Tocqueville, as in his readers, education thus stood in the stead of thinking about political management. This pedagogical utopia is based on an optimistic anthropology. Tocqueville assumed natural sympathy among people. In this, he opposed the Hobbesianism of centralists like Dupont-White. If hatred and fear were natural passions, there could be no progressive pedagogy of civic-mindedness founded on the natural convergence of sentiments and interests. Dupont-White, an obviously simplistic reader of Hobbes, thus objected to Tocqueville that "naturally the more we know each other, the more we hate each other."[108] Within the community is a permanent litigation in which "every difference must be judged by the majority, i.e., by the law of the strongest. . . . Instead of fighting, each side counts its members, and this latter process, for being less violent, is no more reasonable than the other."[109] Then what does the school of local governance teach? Not the management of public affairs—that is an illusion—but the art of profiting personally from the group. Making municipalities independent serves "to educate in universal suffrage, a corrupting education, which teaches the profits of power and how to work sovereignty like a small farm."[110]

Tocqueville had foreseen the objection, and his entire work can be read as a prophylaxis against the fear which is the father of every despotism. It was fear that explains the installation of the Terror, the First Empire, and the Second. After the 1851 coup d'état, Tocqueville noted the nation's immense satisfaction at trembling only at the more limited fear of the government. Tocqueville's hostility toward socialists stemmed largely from his view that once they had taken "among us, the place the devil occupied in the imagination of the Middle Ages,"[111] they precipitated a frightened nation into servitude. There was in effect nothing more dangerous than fear, which by dividing people destroyed the natural feeling of sympathy. Thus Tocqueville inverted the centralists' proposition, for the more we know each other, the more we like each other. His praise for the local level was the institutional side of an anthropology which postulated the coexistence within each individual of concern for private interest and desire for mutual recognition. It was because he affirmed the innate sense of solidarity that local civic-mindedness was the best guarantee against revolutions, which always grow on the mold of class separation. This praise of civic-mindedness's moral virtues attracted many Second Empire public commentators, like Barrot, but even more the Third Republic's neocritics for whom "it was a commonplace to say that public life elevates and ennobles souls. Reducing a people to only their domestic and private preoccupations is taking a source of honor and virtue from them. It is to debase, diminish, and demoralize them."[112]

For local civic-mindedness to serve as the foundation for democracy, education received in the community must efficiently prepare one for general political participation. This does not necessarily follow. The difference of scale brings with it radical differences, as the Bonapartists enjoyed reminding individualists of the American school. According to Tocqueville and his descendants, individuals were prepared, gradually trained for political life, by becoming interested and applying themselves to community affairs. Accustomed to controlling the village budget, they would not find it difficult to supervise and criticize the state's expenditures. The little speeches they made in town council train the orator in them. "Honorable writers who make such strange assertions so coolly," wrote Levallois, "seem not to suspect that the management and discussion of local interests have nothing in common with the complicated difficulties of general politics and, in any case, are hardly likely to expand the spirit, to make it greater, to open broader perspectives to it."[113] For all of Jacobinism's heirs, there was a gap between petty local interests that stemmed from collective egotism and national politics which could only be closed by resorting to the state. Because it was distant, the state was automatically just, "cold as a cipher, entirely devoted to the public good."[114] Tocqueville had not ignored the dangers of corruption. But he thought it possible to mediate between the local and the national in a pyramid of intermediary bodies, for example, associations, newspapers, and local hierarchies whose function was precisely to abolish the distance between the individual and the sovereign.

An Ambiguous Solution: Governmental Centralization and Administrative Decentralization

The difficulty lay in reconciling this pyramid of intermediary bodies with sovereign unity and the building of a national state, a difficulty magnified by Tocqueville's pushing direct democracy to the extreme in which the citizen, in order to be trained, should exercise judgment frequently. Yet citizens could not constantly take part in national decisions, and national interests were not identical to the cumulative juxtaposition of local interests. It was this problem of the necessary hierarchy between national sovereignty and local interests that Tocqueville claimed to resolve through the combination of governmental centralization and administrative decentralization (*DA* 1:86). Deemed brilliant by Sainte-Beuve in 1835,[115] the distinction Tocqueville introduced between the two centralizations—governmental and administrative—became the new liberal party's program. Yet at the same time, its inconsistency and "logomachy" were criticized.[116]

In France the demarcation between administration and government was hazy. As a result, Tocqueville was suspected of having praised governmental centralization only to mask his inadmissible inclination to federalism, which betrayed his criticism of administrative centralization. He had had a brief brush with this suspicion in 1835. In effect, in *Democracy* Tocqueville often defined the nation, on the American model, as "one great association."[117] For the United States the term is accurate: national identity is a political artifact. There is no carnal attachment to the nation in a country where size of the territory, diversity of interests, and multiplicity of races and cultures make achieving the sense of belonging to a community problematic. Nothing was further from the French glorification of the nation as a natural and historic community or from the mystique of nationality. [118]

Tocqueville seemed even more American and even more blind to nationality's mystique in 1849, so indifferent to the "springtime of the peoples" did he appear.[119] Under the Second Empire, republican and Bonapartist Jacobins remarked that Tocqueville and his disciples "are federalist without intending it, without knowing it, but in any case, are so."[120]

It is true that Tocqueville offered no doctrine of sovereignty and that this indifference brings him closer to the American model for which, with the War of Independence ended, the notion of sovereignty was no longer central in national political debate. Yet to accuse Tocqueville of federalism was to misunderstand his thinking. In 1859 Laboulaye recalled that Tocqueville "loved national unity; for him it was the work of time, the natural product of French genius."[121] Between Tocqueville and his readers, therefore, the legitimacy of national sovereignty was not in question, for Tocqueville did not doubt it. Nor did it concern the adoption of a federalist system, which he never envisaged. The accusation of federalism glosses over the opposition between two concepts of national will: one postulating the immediacy and indivisibility of that will, the other insisting on the necessary mediations.

We now see how, in the 1860s, debate was reopened which had been quietly at work in the philosophy of the eighteenth century and in parliamentary debates: Must we admit the preeminence of natural right? Must we subordinate individual interest to group ends? What should be kept from the ancient and the modern notions of liberty? Tocqueville believed it impossible to sever these two forms of liberty. Though he feared the state's lockhold, he was also wary of individualist societies where each person pursued self-interest. Republicans highly attached to the ancient notion of liberty and postulating that the national will was indivisible separated into liberal and Jacobin camps upon reading Tocqueville. The Third Republic deepened the gap between those who did not separate the Republic from individual autonomy and those for whom the Republic had absolute value. Old Orleanists abandoned the idea of a government based on reason which legitimated state control. As a sign of this shift, the very word *individualism* began to take on a positive meaning, and traditional hesitancies toward the market faded, to the point that political and economic liberalism mixed, as in England.[122] Suddenly, the liberal union began to emphasize Tocqueville's defense of human rights rather than his civic humanism, and liberals accorded him an ambiguous place in the intellectual genealogy of liberty's defenders. Tocqueville was indistinguishable from Thermidorian commentators. And Laboulaye saw himself less in Tocqueville than in Benjamin Constant, whose works he reprinted in 1861. It is true that the analogy between the First and the Second Empire was at play, in a century in which historical reminiscence weighed like a nightmare on the spirits of the living. Mme de Staël and Constant seemed closer than Tocqueville to the French of the 1860s, for they too had lived in a Napoleonic France.

Tocqueville was thus only an educator as a critical thinker. People adhered to his way of thinking only out of disappointment. The gray personage his biographers painted had its correlation in the negative character of a doctrine quicker to demonstrate the illegitimacy of the powers than to define the conditions of a state of law. And this opposition culture was only attractive at the cost of confusion between claims for self-governance and praise for individualism. A perilous confusion, for it led liberalism, in the following years, to turn narrowly, frostily inward and cause Tocqueville's work to appear shriveled and bitterly reactionary.

5

Toward Oblivion, 1870–1940

To his readers of the 1860s, Tocqueville had remained a contemporary. *Democracy* described an America the way they still dreamed of it; *Old Regime* gave meaning to their disenchantment. Of course, Tocqueville's public had hardly changed since the 1830s; it was still the academic world of the notables. By driving academies toward the opposition, the Second Empire had even increased their prestige. They had been the intellectual parliaments in the absence of public discourse. Tightly tied to the notables' sociability, could Tocqueville's work outlive it with the advent of the Third Republic and an increased space for public dialogue?

Apparently not, judging from Tocqueville's sales after 1870. *Democracy in America* was reprinted in the *Oeuvres complètes* in 1864 and 1868 (fourteenth and fifteenth editions) in 4,400 copies. These ran out by July 1874, and the book was reprinted in 2,000 copies in August 1874. When that sold out, the book was again reprinted in 1887 in 2,000 copies and again in 1913 in a few hundred copies, most of which were still on the shelves by 1945. After 1913, beyond two collections of excerpts, there was no complete edition of *Democracy* printed again until the Médicis edition of 1947 and the twin publication in 1951 of both the Genin edition revised by A. Gain with a preface by Firmin Roz and the Gallimard edition with an introduction by Harold Laski inaugurating Gallimard's modern collection of complete works.

The fate of *The Old Regime and the French Revolution* was hardly happier. After the 4,400 copies printed in 1866 ran out, *Old Regime* was reprinted in 1876 in 4,400 copies, in December 1886 in 3,000 copies, and in May 1900 in 500 copies. Seven successive printings from 1902 to 1934 apparently totaled fewer than 1,500 copies. Volumes of Tocqueville's *Correspondance* sold more and more slowly. Finally, despite their publisher's long, patient wait, half the reprinted *Mélanges* (1876, 1,000 copies) and the *Etudes économiques* (March 1877, 1,000 copies) were pulped in 1910 and 1920. The rate of decline accelerated as the years went by, starker for *Democracy* than for *Old Regime*. Few new works about Tocqueville compensated for disinterest in the old ones. In 1872 the London publication of economist Nassau Senior's *Conversations* with Tocqueville drew little notice in France. The 2,000 copies of Tocqueville's nephew's *Souvenirs* printed by Calmann-Lévy in 1893 won only ephemeral success. Beaumont's introductory note was reprinted in 1897 in 750 copies, only half of which sold. The *Correspondance entre Alexis de Tocqueville et Arthur de Gobineau,* edited by Schemann and published by Plon in 1908, was more attractive because of Gobineau than because of Tocqueville.

To what can we attribute this disaffection? One might imagine that it was due to a change in the social composition of the works' potential audience. Tocqueville's generation reached its natural end in the 1880s, and the Republic called on new recruits. But the succession of the generations and the regime's installation, whether dated from 1870, from the 1877 crisis, or from the purge of civil servants in 1880, brought about no radical changes in the elites. Gambetta could hail the advent of "new layers" of society as much as he liked, but French society had undergone only slight changes at the end of the nineteenth century. Economic growth was slow, rural life still predominant, social inequalities persisted. Dynasties continued to weigh heavily on the reproduction of social, cultural, and economic elites, including the republican aristocracy. Many of his "heirs" might thus have found Tocqueville's works in their family libraries, and indeed that was where they did find them, for his works were not so much unknown as abandoned. Casual references to them abounded as careful readings became rarer. The explanation for the discrediting of Tocqueville's works is to be found less in an overarching social determinism than in the close relationship of the work to the world it represented.

In fact, Tocqueville's works came up against a difficulty common in political writings whose subject by its very nature is a shifting one. If we reduce political philosophy to the study of "timeless" principles, as Victor Cousin did, we can indeed imagine ourselves spared the intrusion of "real history." But *Democracy* and *Old Regime* were based on the problems of their times. After 1880 French opinion finally noticed that American society had changed. It began to concern itself more with the dangers of lobbying, American imperialism, and trusts than with the merits of self-government. As a result, *Democracy* lost its currency.

Politically passé, Tocqueville was also scientifically outdated with the gradual reorganization of universities. In 1871 Boutmy founded the Ecole Libre des Sciences Politiques which competed first with the law schools that were reforming between 1877 and 1898 and second, after 1890, with sociologists. History became professionalized in 1885–90, followed soon by literary studies. In the thirty-year course of these reorganizations, exchanges and borrowings were marked by ferocious turf wars: delimiting an object of study was inseparable from academic jockeying for position. As a result, the old universe of the belles lettres exploded, and the lines between disciplines were more important than the search for common meaning among them once upheld by the academies; specialists replaced public commentators.

These diverse factors—generational changing of the guard, political shifts, the emergence of new disciplines—each have their own heterogenous historical periods. But the sites where they overlap construct a chronology of Tocqueville's popularity. Between 1870 and 1879 Tocqueville's works were still important; from 1880 to 1893 they were passé; they had sunk into disinterest until they became the object of historical study themselves after the 1893 publication of the *Souvenirs*.

Dying Lights, 1870–77

In 1871 notables did not believe their era had ended. Though it had not had the universal impact of prior revolutions, the Commune had revived memories of the Terror and of June 1848. Its effects were the same, inspiring a robotic need for order and reminding everyone that though there was no turning back from democracy, the Revolution needed to be ended. This aim, which had been Tocqueville's, was now incumbent on his old colleagues to put into effect. These colleagues were Dufaure, Rivet, Laboulaye, Broglie, and Thiers, who had survived the empire's rigors and dedicated themselves to belated better days. Those left behind shared the stage with the young guns.

The end of the notables was a cacophony in many voices: the past was crumbling into revolutionary crises; "new France" was getting used to the Republic. The confused period tempted historians to write it as a suite of dissonant monologues: "One would hear Thiers, MacMahon, Dupanloup of the old school; Gambetta, rejuvenated by the new blood, and many others. Thus did Browning describe Rome in the seventeenth century. But where would one come to? To each his own truth, that is where; in other words, into a new night."[1]

In this darkness Tocqueville offered a point of reference, for he was claimed by the Right (Falloux, de Meaux), the center Right (Broglie), and the center Left (Laboulaye, Dufaure, Rivet).

Political Stakes: The Notables' Last Waltz

Tocqueville's works made little noise between 1870 and 1877. There was no study written on him, and he was rarely cited at the podium. Republicans rarely referred to him, though Tocqueville's brother Hippolyte served in the Assembly, first as a member of the republican Left and then as permanent senator in December 1875.[2]

The legitimists were more devious. They had had to abandon their hope of crowning Henry V when he had refused to give up the white flag on 5 July 1871. The prince was attached to the romantic myth of a divinely ordained, intangible royalty. To shake him from this rigid position, on 23 November 1871 the *Gazette de France* just happened to run Tocqueville's 1852 letter to the comte de Chambord,[3] in which Tocqueville advised the count to personify the principle of regular liberty joined together with order and to grant equitable national representation, public debate, and gradual freedom of the press. He especially urged the count to remember that in the liberals' eyes legitimacy was a means, not an end, and that the hatred inspired by Caesarism gave monarchy, always suspected of absolutist nostalgia, the "marvellous good fortune" of declaring itself liberal. In 1852 there was no more elegant way to say that restoration could come only from reaching out to a hostile nation—and this was even more true in 1871. Thus by appropriating Tocqueville, the *Gazette*'s[4] royalists above all revealed the erosion of legitimacy.

The rarity of Tocqueville citations in speeches should not surprise us. Within the tactical meanderings of speechmakers, there is a difference between families of ideas and the systems of interests in which the parties were embedded. The fertility of Tocqueville's thought only appeared where tactics did not exclude theory, in constitutional books and magazines that sought present intelligence in expansive reflection on democratic transition.

The 1875 constitution was the end point of the process begun by the Revolution, whose constitutional gains it froze until 1940. Preparations for this constitution were made by three successive parliamentary commissions, known as the Commissions of the Thirty.[5]

Tocqueville is the public commentator most often cited in the second commission's works. The second commission was the most important one, though the most parsimonious with theoretical references. In Tocqueville the monarchists found useful arguments to plead for a return to "medieval democracy"[6] or to fight against the seductiveness of the American model.[7] Let us set tactics aside. By this unexpected alliance with Tocqueville, monarchists hoped to confuse moderate republicans like Dufaure or Laboulaye. But their strategy showed how heavily prior regimes and the American model's prestige still weighed. The 1875 constitution was less innovative, for it brought nineteenth-century political culture back into play. The concern to establish a conservative regime led members, often veterans of prior regimes, to reopen questions that had been of interest since the Revolution on the relationship between popular sovereignty and representation, on the risks of corruption of suffrage, etc. These were old questions repositioned in Tocquevillean terms: since universal suffrage is a fact we must accommodate, how can we channel it to avoid Caesarism on one hand and radicalism on the other?

Their answer was like Tocqueville's, that suffrage must be organized to allow a new aristocracy to emerge which would serve as a counterbalance and whose second chamber would offer asylum. The notion of a senate did not inspire the same repulsion in the members of 1875 which it had in 1848. The failure of 1848 had borne fruit, and there was concern to avoid a standoff between the legislative and the executive branches. But though everyone thus referred to constitutionalism, not everyone gave it a democratic meaning.

Some used Tocqueville only to promote a political order seated firmly on social inequalities, in the tradition of constitutional monarchy. They either called for double voting or for the "representation of interests" of the propertied, of commerce, industry, and families. To this would be added certain "intellectual lights," the listing of which incited just as many objections as it had under the July Monarchy. The term *interests* shows just how difficult the conservatives' position was. Because they could not dare to claim they represented general interests or crudely call for a return to property-based voting, they resigned themselves to defending their social difference as constitutive of good order.

Others sought a solution in the recognized abilities of members of the regional (departmental) councils and judges, a form of "expertise" which ill hides its furtive return to notables, or worse, to officially candidates, now almost universally missed but unacceptable as a solution so excessively had they been used by the Second Empire.

Finally, a third group made up of the republican minority tried to channel suffrage through purely functional devices. In the two-phase senate election process, they sought a democratic means of purifying suffrage and selection based on ability. Laboulaye, without citing Tocqueville, used his praises for the American state-level senates as perfect examples of the second democratic chamber in their election procedures, yet aristocratic by their members' abilities.[8]

Thus constitutional debates on the organization of the branches masked fundamental differences of principle. On one side were those who wanted to keep the privilege of legitimate deference based either on wealth or ability. On the other were those who sought a democratic way to regulate society. The reforms called for were sometimes similar, the motivations behind them were opposite, and thus Tocqueville's works, torn between these contradictory strategies, took on an uncertain meaning. In them one could read as much fear of democracy as desire to build democracy. But let us not give undue weight to Tocqueville's authority in these debates, where timing remained the preponderant influence. Everyone referred to the status quo, to necessary sacrifices, to the obligation to keep to the "possible." The constitution prepared was acknowledged to be incomplete, believed ephemeral, and accepted as such. In this for the first time, the members' wisdom was truly inspired by American and Tocquevillean prudence. But it keeps us from clearly seeing what they owed to reading Tocqueville.[9]

Tocqueville's authority becomes more obvious if we examine magazines closer to the political center, where Tocqueville was when alive. Two magazines were then at their apogee, *Le Correspondant* and *La Critique Philosophique*.

In these years during which the Republic was founded, *Le Correspondant* was the voice of the ex-notables who were forced to accommodate democracy. Tocqueville's works never failed to stimulate their thinking, but their version of Tocqueville was revised and edited by Victor de Broglie.[10] Over and over, the magazine reevaluated the advantages and drawbacks of the American model: we are not surprised to find universal suffrage described as a drawback, an inevitable fact[11] but one whose noxiousness the American experience demonstrated,[12] and which Tocqueville was praised for having sensed. All other forms of egalitarian participation in political life were equally condemnable: local self-government, the election of the president of the Republic, the institution of justices of the peace—so contrary to the French notion of hierarchy in law. On the active side were found all the mechanisms that permitted civil society's liberties and in-equalities to reproduce politically: associations, decentralization, bicameralism.[13] It was almost like being back in 1835. For the *Correspondant's* commentators, America had remained an immense and prosperous country without hostile neighbors but lacking in tradition. It had nothing in common with France which was seeking a system appropriate for its national character. The difficulty lay in defining this necessary adaptation. Either one looked to the past and accused Tocqueville of having slandered a monarchy that was reforming itself,[14] or one agreed with Tocqueville's diagnosis of the noxiousness of absolutism but argued for retrofitting by careful introduction of local self-governance.[15]

The *Correspondant's* main contribution was thus not in such reflections on the organization of the government, which reiterated the work of the Commis-sions of the Thirty—demonstrating the astonishing viscosity in speed of politi-cal change since 1830. *Le Correspondant's* contribution was rather a meditation on legal norms. Tocqueville had believed the internal regulation of society pos-sible through the use of judges. He introduced a distinction between legitimacy and legality, justice and majority opinion, but without resorting first to any re-ligious transcendence. There was nothing attractive in this to the *Correspondant's* commentators. The judges' power seemed to them to offer no guarantees, so un-likely they felt it was that reason would transcend partisan preferences or class interests. Constitutional control and state submission to ordinary courts were, in their eyes, merely infantile American "oddities," barely useful in maintaining the influence of an aristocracy of judges in a dangerously egalitarian country.[16] What would they keep from the American example? The model of a religious democracy in which Christianity was dedicated to preserving republican order as it had once preserved monarchic order.[17] This was a great deal—from *Democracy* the *Correspondant's* liberal Catholics had taken the notion that Christian-ity was in fact unconnected with any political regime, an idea which later gave birth to their future Ralliement. But it was also very little, for they refused to imagine that syncretism of Enlightenment and Christianity which gave Ameri-can religion its consensual character. Thus they deprived themselves of the chance to understand the increasingly secular society of their time.

In the 1870s republicans also wondered about legal norms. Ideological dif-ferences ran deep between the veterans of '48 (Quinet, Hugo, Louis Blanc), the disciples of Cousin's eclecticism (Jules Simon), positivists (Littré, Ferry, Gambetta, Clemenceau), and neo-Kantians. We will not spend much time on the veterans of '48 and the eclecticists; these are mere republican vestiges. But it is in the conflict between positivists and neo-Kantians that the building of the republican ideal was played out, along with the future of Tocqueville's work.

Positivists had in common an anticlerical agnosticism, the cult of science, and a historicism tinged to a greater or lesser degree with Darwinism. This separated them radically from Tocqueville, as well as from the neo-Kantians. In the *Critique Philosophique,* which offered a weekly course in political philosophy starting in 1872, neo-Kantians Renouvier and Pillon ceaselessly denounced Darwinism, Hegelian historicism, and positivism[18] as so many immoral theories which overly admired force and the fait accompli. Their originality lay in their rejecting these theories while remaining within a kind of lay, even anticlerical republicanism that presented itself as the democratic version of Christianity and liberalism. Neo-Kantianism saw itself as a secular equivalent of Christianity, which had become too compromised by its political collusions to combat scientism or historicism effectively.[19] It fleshed out a new liberalism to accomplish the mission in which the overly conservative Doctrinaires had failed. The neo-Kantians were even more ferocious toward the Doctrinaires; in Albert de Broglie they saw the political echo of Guizot, and in Taine or Renan, his philosophical echo.

In this attempt the question was what genealogy to claim, against positivist claims to descend from Auguste Comte, a father more easily recognized for being marginal and thus innocent of the entire prior history of France. Renouvier was satisfied with Kant. His old animosity as a veteran of '48 turned him from Constant and Tocqueville. Renouvier's disciple François Pillon did not share his enmity. He found in Constant and Tocqueville denunciation of representatives who seized popular sovereignty, a monopolizing inaugurated by the Revolution and continued thereafter. Pillon traced the conceptual foundations of such monopolizing to its origins—the myth of unity of national will, obsession with federalism, the cult of state reason inherited from Jacobinism. Tocqueville's particular merit was having revealed centralization's absolutist origins and made self-government the heart of true republican doctrine.[20] Thus for Pillon, Tocqueville was the pioneer of real republicans who confronted the secular collusion of conservatives and Jacobins.

> We must consider Tocqueville . . . under Louis-Philippe, in mid-reign of that
> bourgeois liberalism beyond which today, as then, conservatives imagine nothing possible, and where it is so easy for revolutionary ambitions to stop in our

country, so long as a few amendments have been introduced without any result. Scant parliamentary movement and scant parliamentary noise on the surface did not fool [Tocqueville]. Beneath parliamentary freedoms of the press and the courts, he saw the France of royal intendants and Napoleonic prefects unmoving, well organized, well preserved in their traditional connections. And in this administrative praetorianism, which mocked every constitutional guarantee and every effort to apply the principle of the separation of powers, he saw decadence. *France must change its laws and mores; without this it is ripe for conquest:* these are the terrible words our conservatives and our Jacobins would do well to meditate upon.[21]

Tocqueville's popularity went beyond political tactics. For Pillon as for Renouvier, the debate about self-government was more a moral issue than a political one. Decentralization was less important for the facilitation of good management it offered than for the opening it gave human liberty. Tocqueville was the ancestor of neo-Kantianism; he felt society's destiny depended on the state of its mores, and he dealt with the problem of the transcendence necessary through a kind of moral genealogy. As, in addition, his religion seemed closer to a natural one, neo-Kantians believed they had found in his works their own creed formulated in the Declaration of the Rights of Man.[22]

Yet these rationalizing interpretations were difficult to make. Though in agreement with the principles of 1789, Tocqueville was not content with natural law, although he did not articulate the nature of his beliefs.[23] Republicans calling for lay public morals spread by obligatory civic education were far from Tocqueville's belief in religious liberty. Tocqueville believed in the possible liberal evolution of Catholicism. Renouvier and Pillon's only allowance for Christianity was as a precursor to rationalism. Kant and Rousseau were ancestors more to be recommended in their eyes than Tocqueville.

Let us add that at the end of the 1880s, neo-Kantian sympathy for Tocqueville, like neo-Kantianism itself, did not extend beyond the universities. Hegemonic in education, in the Republic's political history Renouvier and his friends lasted merely "the time of an intermission," the time it took for the regime to be installed.[24] After that, their demanding moralism became no more than a critical principle. For opportunists, the neo-Kantians soon seemed no more than a branch of that irritable group within old republicans stubbornly determined to seek minimal government and condemning as monarchical all that smelled of national unity.[25] Johnny-come-lately republicans, those Tocqueville*ains*.

In following the traces of Tocqueville's works during the 1870s, we measure the singularity of his thought. For democrats he was separate from Doctrinaire tradition;[26] for others, like the *Correspondant*'s commentators, he was placed on a line with Guizot, from whom he seemed distant only in his enthusiasm for democracy.

His praise for self-government had begun to seem a commonplace.[27] It was already agreed upon under the empire. But for republicans, self-government was based on the desire to scatter power democratically; for their adversaries, it was based on the desire to maintain inequalities in civil society.

The contrast is no less manifest when we consider public morals. In America consensus was founded on a syncretism between the Enlightenment and Christianity that was difficult for the French to fathom. New republicans found comfort for their attachment to the Enlightenment in such syncretism—when they did not deny the existence of it completely.[28] Conservatives sought in Tocqueville the justification for a religion protecting the established order. On one side the more or less temperate democratic universe; on the other, the solemn hierarchy of dignitaries supporting each other, from the Creator to the lowest rural notable. Only the common struggle against Caesarism had hidden their distance from each other. The opposing interpretations of Tocqueville's work show that the growing political discord between the center Right and the center Left was not one of casual misunderstanding. Thus Tocqueville's renown culminated with the process of installing the Republic. Afterward, while each center was falling apart, Tocqueville's work took a nosedive in popularity. The Republic grew in self-confidence and no longer felt the need to reflect on foreign experiments. "We are forgetting all the principles of liberty only to reassume the authoritarian traditions of despotism; the French Republic grows more and more distant from American ideas."[29]

Early Doubts about Tocqueville's Science

Just as Tocqueville's work lost its political currency, the first doubts began to appear regarding the descriptive pertinence of his analyses.

Through 1875 the French had not perceived American social changes very clearly, and their ignorance benefited Tocqueville. In 1870 the French spoke of America almost as Tocqueville had in 1835. Such inertia in representations is natural in the collective imagination where historical change happens slowly. In his play *L'Oncle Sam,* performed in 1873 at the Vaudeville Theater, Sardou sought to portray a young Frenchman departing for the New World. He showed him with his pocket Tocqueville, America in spun sugar. Tocqueville's book was thus famous enough to serve as a slightly dusty travel guide and a laugh-getter for an audience in the know.

Cultivated opinion was little better informed than the vaudeville audience. Ignorance was encouraged by the absence of university-level courses on American history and by the American Revolutionary centennial, which revived memories of those few years at the end of the eighteenth century when the histories of the two countries had crossed paths. Jefferson's and Tocqueville's America remained the model of a peaceful republic the French could dream of while they hoped for some Washington, reissued Laboulaye, and rewrote Tocqueville.[30] Their American dream was sculpted in the haughty figure of Bartholdi's Liberty.

But the erosion of the American model as *Democracy* had promoted it became noticeable by 1876. The Philadelphia World's Fair of 1876 brought travelers to a nation hounded by political crises (Hayes's contested presidential election, for example) and an economic crisis that was due to fallout from the Civil War. The erosion of the model also was manifested in political ideas. One book created the rupture with Tocqueville—Claudio Jannet's *Les Etats-Unis contemporains, ou Les moeurs, les institutions, et les idées depuis la guerre de Sécession* (1876), reprinted several times, which owed its success largely to Le Play's preface.

For Jannet and Le Play, Tocqueville was still an obligatory reference and America still the figure of France's future, to be scrutinized "as a lost traveler with an anxious eye scans the distant horizon to help determine the road" (1). But although the question asked did not change, the basis for the answer was new. Jannet's book styled itself as an updated *Democracy* in its synthesis of official documents and recent American works that took changes caused by the Civil War into account.

Since 1835, the pertinence of Tocqueville's analyses had been measured by the degree of his ability to prophesy. Jannet upheld this tradition by reproaching Tocqueville for not having predicted the Civil War back in 1835. This failure betrayed what Jannet felt was Tocqueville's false understanding: Tocqueville had seen America only as a new England and had understood nothing of states' rights or of increasing United States centralization. As time wore on, hesitance toward Tocqueville grew. In his second edition (1884), Jannet underscored the increasing role of parties and professional politicians that had been ignored by Tocqueville, whose "complacent judgments about American democracy cannot therefore apply to the current state of things" (130).

Suddenly Jannet could not understand the persistent favor Tocqueville enjoyed, because nothing remained of his analyses, or of the virtue of American women, who had become horribly clever, or of the wisdom of self-government itself, which had been replaced by party convention upheavals. The America of 1880 "resembled much less the one M. de Tocqueville studied than the latter resembled Washington's" (2).

What is astonishing is that Jannet's updating led him to retrogressively invert Tocqueville's historical schema. The democracy Tocqueville had taken as the future of civilization was in fact its infancy. America "is gradually losing the benefit of the exceptional circumstances which seemed to ensure its success, and more and more begins to resemble the revolutionary democracies of the Old World" (93).

Advances in knowledge were thus used by Jannet to facilitate a return to Guizot. This return is even more obvious in the preface. Like Guizot, Le Play saw in Tocqueville, whom he met several times between 1840 and 1855, only an aristocrat resigned to his own defeat, straining his neck forward in the yoke and sublimating his pusillanimity to historical necessity. He "considered the social milieu into which he had been born as struck by irremediable impotency. He had illusions of French liberalism. He believed that the spirit of invention might resolve all of the government's fundamental problems. And he was persuaded that moral reform could only be made in revolutionary France by the lower classes, instructed and guided by new men" (xviii). This led to his blindness in America, whence his servility toward the people in 1848, the servility of vassals toward their king.

In this sociologizing criticism Le Play's conclusions are drawn in stark black and white: Tocqueville was not the fine man he was said to be. Without citing Custine (but had he read him?), Le Play takes up the usual weapons: Tocqueville discouraged the upper classes by his "sophistries" regarding democracy's providential nature. "Since the publication of *The Social Contract,* Tocqueville's book is the one which has exerted the saddest influence over our destinies. . . . Let us not forget about the faults of Lafayette and Tocqueville; let us not forget that good people have hurt us more than ill-intentioned ones" (xvii–xx). Le Play's commentary soon became famous, flattering aristocratic conservatism and seemingly presaging Maurras's doctrine in its attempt to redraw the course of time.

Old Regime did not age as badly as *Democracy*—the Revolution had remained a partisan hot potato. Since the beginning of the nineteenth century, contemporary history had seemed to run a pale second to revolutionary history, like the history of Christianity next to the Old Testament. The Revolution had constituted a repertory of constitutional forms and political roles replayed over and over in each generation, to the point that when historians wrote about it, what they wrote came across as autobiography. The Commune too seemed to have returned to the Jacobins' fold of symbols, renewing fear of the revolutionary sickness as a consequence. This is why the Revolution's history was no more chaste politically after 1870 than before, despite Fustel de Coulanges's remonstrances.[31] Historians just let fly in a new way; rather than insulting either the ancien régime or the Revolution, they worried about the ill effects of their continuance. The new reading of history introduced by Tocqueville in 1856 formed the point of departure for those whose historical vocation was born of the spectacle of the war and the Commune.[32]

This interest in the heritage of absolutism was made manifest by the growing number of erudite works devoted to the ancien régime and the Revolution[33] whose authors seemed the "continuers of M. de Tocqueville."[34] But we see the fascination Tocqueville exerted even more clearly if we leave the domain of erudite history and consider the grand syntheses made by Taine and Fustel de Coulanges.

Taine and Fustel took over Tocqueville's philosophico-historical project, his history rooted in the misfortune of the present and concerned with founding the future. Tocqueville had discovered he was a historian by observing the failure of the Second Republic. Taine and Fustel became historians watching its defeat and the Commune.

By tracing French origins, Taine and Fustel sought to create works that contributed to public health, as Tocqueville had (according to Amiel, Taine smelled more "of the laboratory" than Fustel). They tried to tear the French away from the alienating cycle of repeating their grand revolutionary roles. They wanted to help France achieve that measured transition from aristocracy to democracy which the English had shown by example.

Taine and Fustel owe more to Tocqueville than just this therapeutic view of history—they owe him their method. Like him, they refused to take the actors of the Revolution at their word and sought the deep structure behind official discourses. Many elements in their analysis were borrowed from Tocqueville: the early decadence of feudalism in France, absolutism's role in the disintegration of the social body, class divisions, the abstraction of philosophical doctrines.[35]

But beyond the way they posed their questions, what divergence from Tocqueville! In their hands Tocqueville's gray view of history turned black. Where Tocqueville could pass for a democrat, his successors were conservatives imbued with the spirit of systematization. Taine, Renan, and Fustel were realists and no longer had the respect that spiritualists of the generation before them had felt for the principles of 1789. Nor did they have the faith in the virtues of the Republic that was to animate those of the generation after them such as Monod or Sorel.[36]

This political rupture was paralleled by a revolution in historiography not unlike naturalism among novelists. *La cité antique* by Fustel was closer to Tocqueville's inductive method than Fustel's *Histoire des institutions*. Taine, who criticized Tocqueville for scorning the small factual detail, took a naturalist's approach, depicting the different sorts of revolutionaries, a kind of zoologist of French minds, so that his history becomes a mass of horrible little facts selected with greater taste for sensation than discernment. Like Zola, he was obsessed with the criminal masses, whose collective psychology he described in thick detail.

Thus *Old Regime*, like *Democracy* but to a lesser degree, tended to become buried in the archaeology of the moral sciences as early as the end of the 1870s. But Tocqueville's thought did find an institutional connection which spared it from burial: the Ecole Libre des Sciences Politiques.

Institutional Connections: The Ecole des Sciences Politiques

Overall, the evolution of universities between 1880 and the end of the century was unfavorable to Tocqueville's popularity. This popularity depended on the existence of an intellectual milieu common to academics, journalists, and politicos. The events of 1870–77 had widened the gap between the university and politics. Parliamentarians, needing to focus more on local issues, turned from their studies. In higher education, starting with the Second Empire, the specialization of academic chairs, the fragmentation of knowledge into disciplines, the inordinate lengthening of bibliographies and theses, caused most faculty to give up their roles as public commentators. A victim of this distance between science and politics, Tocqueville's works appeared on the reading list of only one marginal institution, the Ecole Libre des Sciences Politiques,[37] founded in 1872, which continued the cultural traditions of the notables of the nineteenth century.

The school's objective was to educate for democracy but also to legitimate existing social elites by conferring an intellectual distinction upon them. While not purely meritocratic like the Polytechnique, for it left room for patronage, it did break with the tradition of patron-client networks in the civil service system. This was the very system of elite yet democratic patronage Tocqueville had wished for.

The school's promoters came from the constitutional monarchy's circles of notables, and many were close readers of Tocqueville. Founder Boutmy was also Emile de Girardin's godson, a schoolmate of Guizot's son, and student and soon a friend of Taine's. He had scientific endorsement from Laboulaye, Guizot, and Taine. Among the school's subscribers were a number of Tocqueville's friends or descendants, Orleanists by tradition and very moderate republicans, including Boulay de La Meurthe, Duchâtel (Tanneguy's son), Duvergier, J. Favre, Emile de Girardin, the comte de Lanjuinais, Saint-Marc Girardin's widow, and Paul de Rémusat. Among the faculty, many favorable to Thiers's Republic, were most of Tocqueville's commentators: the oldest, like spiritualist philosopher Janet; those writing in the 1880s like Boutmy and historian Sorel; and those of the 1890s like Eugene d'Eichtal, author in 1897 of the first long book devoted to Tocqueville, *Alexis de Tocqueville et la démocratie libérale*. D'Eichtal served as the school's director from 1912 until his death in 1936 at the age of ninety-two, a longevity that sharply marks the school's firm attachment to the past.

The school was Tocquevillean in its program of study, even more than in its objectives and promoters, for its vocation was the production and diffusion of a body of knowledge about the present, in contrast to ossified university practices of the time.[38]

In practice, the institution early on distanced itself from the ambitions of its founders. Boutmy had wanted to train scholars, political men, and men of the world; he trained almost no scholars. Starting in 1873, courses increased that responded to students' desire for professionalization. In 1875 the school began to prepare students for competitive examinations for administrative jobs. The social legitimacy of the school, a seedbed for government ministers, grew, to the detriment of its scientific legitimacy. In its seminars rhetorical cleverness was often more important than concern with proof. "Worldly" speeches? Durkheim made fun of these bastard political sciences, halfway between education and training, science and conversation. But Tocqueville's discourse had also been worldly and well supplied with rhetoric. This explains why the Ecole des Sciences Politiques was the place Tocqueville's work was remembered—a place that preserved it from oblivion but without bestowing on it the intellectual seal of approval of great academic institutions.

In the 1870s, therefore, Tocqueville was not forgotten. He was the man of the transition from old liberalism to republican opportunism, as Albert Sorel showed:

Through him, Montesquieu can still find a hold in contemporary France, wider than one would be tempted to believe. It is thanks to the influence of that very historical and experimental mind, which gradually penetrated institutions and mores, that we abandoned Sieyès's rational mechanics to adopt the applied mechanics of practitioners; that the Republic became parliamentarian, that it was established in France as a result of a constitution the most concise in text, the most traditional in application, the most natural result of the mores and force of events that France has yet possessed.[39]

Was Tocqueville's posthumous destiny linked to the fall of the notables? I know that intellectual history cannot be limited to social or political history. Yet there is confirmation of this way of delineating its periods if we study the image of Tocqueville evidenced in street names and statuary. These two ways of rendering homage mix collective memory (which is drawn out by fund-raising for statues and resident surveys on street naming) with official compulsions to offer the populace a repertory of exemplars of humanity. The decade of the 1870s was a period of massive street naming. Even today, streets and squares place the Third Republic's pantheon on display, with its great men (Thiers, Hugo, and Gambetta) and its less great. The statuary unveiled in the streets between 1870 and 1914 reached such a climax that it provoked snickering about galloping "statuemania." Tocqueville was not among the best endowed: a Tocqueville Street in Valognes in 1865,[40] a Tocqueville Street in Paris in 1877 (and that project had taken four years to come out of storage),[41] possibly an 1879 bust of Tocqueville for the Manche departmental council Tocqueville had served as president.[42] And then a very long period of inactivity, before aborted fund-raising for a statue in 1895[43] and the erection of two busts of Tocqueville in Normandy in 1936. This chronological gap is significant. Honored as a notable—above all a local one—Tocqueville was effaced from public memory until the *Souvenirs* conferred the status of great writer on him in 1893, a status he never fully achieved until 1945.

Oblivion, 1880–93

A Politically Useless Thinker

French wariness toward the United States persisted after 1880. The Statue of Liberty's erection was delayed because the Americans, who had to pay for its monumental base, recoiled at the cost of the gift. Though ready in the spring of 1884, the statue was only shabbily inaugurated in 1886, after two years of sarcasm in the French press about American stinginess. A copy donated by American artists on 4 July 1889 in Paris was unveiled to general indifference. Yet bilateral relations were improving. America had participated in the Paris World's Fair of 1889, and France in Chicago's in 1893. Those who traveled to and wrote about the United States grew less critical. Could the two countries' growing closer revive Tocqueville's prestige?

At first glance Tocqueville's authority continued to be of some importance to young public commentators.[44] All hailed him as a "precursor," even excusing themselves from needing to bring up to date the works of the "Christopher Columbus of American democracy."[45] But these were mere opening flourishes introducing analyses from which Tocqueville was absent. Since Jannet, there was increasing notice of the distance separating turn-of-the-century America from the nation Tocqueville had visited. Comparative legislative studies grew in number. The great book by the Englishman Bryce, *The American Commonwealth,* was published in 1881 and translated into French in 1900–1902. It outdated most of *Democracy*'s constitutional analyses and showed with new precision the English roots of American institutions. All works after 1881 rely heavily on Bryce. Even those which reject his overly English point of view still denounce the "assertions of pure fantasy" and "scaffolding of theories" in *Democracy*.[46]

Stripped of descriptive pertinence, *Democracy* lost its programmatic value at the same time. It had owed its success since 1835 to filling a need which stemmed from worries about the transition to democracy. There is nothing surprising about the success of the movement for democratic conquest taking away its currency, as Scherer showed in *Le Temps* of 30 September 1883.

Scherer has fallen into oblivion himself, although he was significant at the middle level he occupied. A late republican elected in December 1875 to the center Left and a collaborator on the staff of the *Temps* from 1871 to 1887, he was one of the Republic's founding fathers. He shared Tocqueville's indifference to political structures whether republican or monarchic and his moderate's taste for democracy. But he differed from Tocqueville in rejecting Christianity. In his mitigated admiration Scherer is quite representative of the first republican generation. His strength lay in seeing how foreign both he and Tocqueville were to the new republican synthesis opportunists were formulating in the 1880s. The crisis of 16 May and then MacMahon's resignation put an end to the era of political conquest: "Having no more fights to put up against attempts at restoration and reaction, political controversy was soon forced to seek other sources of nourishment, and where would it have found them if not in deduction of the consequences of the principles which had just triumphed, in the ever more rigorous pursuit of the democratic ideal? These are discussional necessities which little by little gave a new importance to the right of suffrage" (*Le Temps*, 30 September 1883) by introducing the principle of popular sovereignty into the society's very economy.

There are some excesses in Scherer's denunciation of Gambetta's rampant socialism. But Scherer clearly shows how one can slip from the conquest of political equality to social conflict. Tocqueville's work had been read as a regretful plea for the republic and for universal suffrage. His objective seems even more outdated given the failure to question the less than perfect institutional forms the exercise of popular sovereignty has taken.

That the movement for democracy exhausted itself can effectively be seen in establishment of a Republic impervious to foreign democratic traditions. Tocqueville's popularity suffered because of this closing of the institutional mind. The Third Republic echoed the Revolution's tendency to eschew popular sovereignty by placing republican legitimacy above it.[47]

Republicans in power henceforth only read Tocqueville tactically. A good example is offered by the Boulanger crisis of 1888. Boulanger won elections on 19 August 1888 in the North, Charente Inférieure, and Somme departments. There were cries of Caesarism, though Boulanger protested he had no other goal than to forge an alternative majority within the republican regime. Boulanger was also suspected of seeking to establish an American-style presidentialism. The two accusations went together, for in America as under the empire, power seemed to flow from popularity—acknowledgment of the primacy of people's sovereignty. At this point, on 15 October 1888 Charles Floquet, minister of the interior and prime minister, a leftist, at the podium chose a quotation from Tocqueville, "a personage of the greatest renown for wisdom, integrity, and liberalism," in supporting a plan to revise the constitution. In 1851, he recalled, Tocqueville had pleaded for revision in "prophetic" terms: "It is no doubt wrong to give in too easily to the current of public opinion; but it is neither always wise nor patriotic to resist it. The rules for the conduct of statesmen in this domain vary with the spirit of the times and the forms of institutions. In free countries, and particularly in democratic ones where good, just like evil, can only be done with help from the masses, one must above all keep their affection and their trust."[48]

Do not cause the worried masses to despair, out of fear they might take sides "with other leaders, another conduct, and other political measures." The principle was Tocquevillean, but its usage a misinterpretation. Tocqueville wished for a revision that would make Louis-Napoléon Bonaparte's reelection possible, to satisfy popular will while remaining within the law. On the other hand, the revision Floquet sought tended to suppress general elections to keep Boulanger out. This meant proclaiming without niceties the need to tame universal suffrage, deepening the divorce between electoral doings and the devolution of state power. The ministry resisted the separation for only four months. Thus, for republicans, Tocqueville's works were no longer more than a collection of quotations to be used by the aged. Floquet's eloquence was solemn and out of style. Tocqueville was useful when national history caught itself stuttering, but only given the proper spin.[49]

Hagiographies: Catholicism and the Democratic Movement

Abandoned by the republicans, Tocqueville's work retained its polemical vigor for only a fraction of Catholics, still fighting the temptation of the Ralliement, and for them, the democratic transition was incomplete. In the 1880s Tocqueville fell prey to a series of pious reactionary biographies which tried to discredit *Democracy*'s "democratic heresy" by contrasting it with Tocqueville's severity toward the Revolution in *Old Regime*, and particularly with his belated obedience to the church. Such revisionist maneuvering betrayed the Catholic hierarchy's reactionary response of grasping at straws while being sucked into the Revolution's hundredth anniversary.

The finest example of this was Monsignor Baunard, legitimist and professor of sacred eloquence at the Catholic University of Lille. In his work *La foi et ses victoires,* the author spears all forms of atheism: Littré's positivism, Naquet and Paul Bert's lay morality, Darwin's and Broca's scientism, the history of Taine, Renan, and Mill. To defend the religion that was being chased from the school, the courts, and the family, he invoked Droz, Bastiat, Le Play, and Tocqueville, the subject of a 125-page note.

In Tocqueville, the writer is too often master of falsehood, scarcely commendable. Of *Democracy,* Monsignor Baunard remembered only the demonstration of the social utility of religions, which Tocqueville developed into a "veritable apologia" with "an eloquence that recalls the language of the seventeenth century, yet with a je ne sais quoi of more emotion in seeming remembrance of [Lamennais's] *Essai sur l'indifférence* with a touch of Jean-Jacques Rousseau's letters" (271).

But Tocqueville's religion was always a "natural" religion, more inclined toward tolerance insofar as it verged on indifference and subordinated the rights of truth to the rights of Man. As for adapting Catholicism to the new democratic tendencies, the idea was hateful. It might be dangerous for the church to ally itself too closely to the throne, Monsignor Baunard would agree because Leon XIII had so ordered. Yet it is circumstantial prudence and "legitimate" that the church should draw closer to governments which "offer it the most assistance in the accomplishment of its divine mission."[50]

So what was the need to exhume the captious Tocqueville? It was because he himself provided the ammunition to refute the fallacious doctrine of *Democracy*. In the second part of his life, Tocqueville pleaded against the first. In 1848 his merit, according to Monsignor Baunard, had been to espouse the conservatives' great fear and restore the pope's power (296). By condemning the Revolution, *Old Regime* drew on the theoretical consequences of this turning point that was Tocqueville's salvation. A bit late in the game, Tocqueville returned to the received truths of his cradle. And with the help of his age, his recovery was speedy. Monsignor Baunard exulted to witness the display of a good man elevating himself all the way to Christianity thanks to "a kind of Jacob's ladder." Family, Christian friends, and then the torment of doubt, "those dull pains of the birth of the divine," raised Tocqueville to the apotheosis of a "good death" in the bosom of the Catholic institution.

The hard part was obviously explaining Tocqueville's persistent hostility to the Ultramontane, illiberal Catholicism of the Second Empire. This was pure reaction, said Monsignor Baunard, to "accidental, absolutely personal fact, common to a few men disappointed" by the church's alliance with the empire (236). Given the spiritualism Tocqueville inherited from the Enlightenment and a church in solidarity with the old, hierarchal order, the gap was thus attributed to accident and youthful explorations, which older wisdom can forgive.

There was nothing surprising in Tocqueville's being ridiculed for breathing the vestry's smoke. On 25 April 1881, at the Comédie Française, Edouard Pailleron's play *Le monde où l'on s'ennuie* [translated and published by Samuel French as *The Art of Being Bored*] was performed—a "study in contemporary morals." It was a huge success, the acting was brilliant, the allusions transparent. In the play a young assistant prefect and his wife are starting out in their Rambouillet house and yard, in that "world of chatting and show, in which pedantry replaces science, sentimentality sentiment, and preciousness delicacy."[51] The young woman diligently serves her husband's career. She cites in the Latin, she quotes

Saint-Evremond, de Maistre, Joubert. She especially punctuates her own personal platitudes with "as M. de Tocqueville says," which makes her seem charming: "What the vulgar person calls lost time is often time gained, as M. de Tocqueville said" (292). "Ah! the voice is the music of the heart, as M. de Tocqueville said" (412).

Of all the boring, respectable cited and unread moralists, Tocqueville was the most recent and the most famous. After 1881, for the mainstream public, he was merely that laughable character from the outdated world staged by Pailleron.

Thus Tocqueville's political glory did not extend beyond the life span of the men of his generation. After 1880 only counterrevolutionaries and aging notables were still interested in him. Almost the same process occurred outside France. In Belgium, Tocqueville was cited in legislative debates during 1830–40 and occasionally from 1870 to 1885, but not after that. In England, Tocqueville was cited in both houses at greater length than any other foreign thinker during debates on electoral reforms in 1866–67. Once the reforms were enacted, Tocqueville's audience decreased; people noticed that establishing mass-supported parties caused neither disaster nor radical change. Democracy began to appear a given, a thing which might be studied technically but which would no longer be the subject of an emphatic moral discourse à la Tocqueville. And in fact, in England, France, and the United States, there was greater sensitivity to persistent inequality than to the threat of class leveling. Even liberalism leaned more toward the providential state and centralization, making Tocqueville's fears outdated.[52]

Scholarly Readings: Political Scientists and Historians

Abandoned by "worldly" discourse, Tocqueville's work might have been claimed by the emerging social sciences. But even the Ecole des Sciences Politiques abandoned it in order to bury itself in scientific writings. Tocqueville was criticized for having "observed the society he saw right under his nose, as the Homeric gods followed the agitation and struggles of mortals from the top of Mount Olympus. To speak more simply, as a philosopher—without being the least concerned to change or improve it." His was an "admirable work of art,"[53] which is to say his talent as an author won out over the scientific side of his words, and he was politically thoughtful, but of no particular era, with nothing useful to offer. This discrediting resulted from a new conception of the object of study. Political science now examined current parliamentary or social questions, from which it drew detailed descriptions of reforms to undertake. Establishing itself by its secession from moral philosophy, it believed it must reject any question of liberty as philosophical or doctrinal. Too pragmatic for the new philosophers, Tocqueville was too philosophical for political scientists.

To new borders established between the disciplines can be added the spread of a new fashion in writing. Tocqueville was very much a stranger to the naturalists' taste for detail; their style influenced every turn-of-the-century social science. Boutmy deplored that Tocqueville's rule had been to "get rid of [the facts] before writing. He shook them off the way a traveler shakes off dust from the road before appearing in good company." This dusting off was what made the old, classical school of the social sciences different from the new one. "The old school," to which Tocqueville instinctively belonged,

> felt that, in the moral and social study of a people, observations relative to individuals or limited to a place and point in time . . . certainly did not in themselves have the rank of proof. They were merely indicators or examples, means of discovering, putting into place, and on occasion *illustrating*—always to be done soberly—the true elements of the demonstration. This demonstration mainly depended on the linkages with major physical and historical causes and their psychological effects, and on the results and unfolding of such effects on the human soul and in society. . . .
>
> "Little facts" merely had a value as points of reference for research and as *specimens,* pungent object lessons which helped to show things in a lively, material way. It was perhaps precisely this final point that upset the consciousness of the austere thinker. Perhaps he feared that the greater vivacity of painting would be taken for greater intensity of its self-evidence and that because the reader had found the painting had more color and greater appearance of perspective, she or he would imagine that there was really more force and solidity in its proof. By his rules of judgment, specific details were thought of as comparable to the depositions of children and domestics, almost always the most striking and closest to the reality described but too often partial, injudicious, and admixed with gossip. The court welcomed them as information but refused to give them legal weight as testimony and did not record them unless they were confirmed by their accord with the general circumstances of the cause.[54]

The insufficiency of *Democracy*'s documentation was gleefully emphasized by all, and the work was admired only as a treatise on democracies in the deceitful form of a monograph on America, as Bryce did.[55] Tocqueville was a "polemical novelist" dreaming of an "imaginary people."[56]

Changes in the disciplines after 1880 were kinder to *Old Regime,* for the Revolution had become a subject of instruction. Throughout the nineteenth century the Revolution had excited passions too greatly to be taught at the respectable Sorbonne. That was left to poets and political men. After the 16 May crisis and despite the Boulanger adventure, the Revolution seemed ended. Opportunism's proclaiming itself the heir of the Revolution achieved the Revolution's political closure. This made it possible to institutionalize teaching the Revolution. And opportunists were the first to benefit from this measure. Even better, teaching revolutionary history was part of a republican strategy to give the Republic the halo of a glorious birth.[57] The stages of this institutionalization are well known. Before 1880, and beyond Michelet's and Quinet's classes at the Collège de France, the Revolution was the subject of only two classes at the Sorbonne in 1848 and 1853–54,[58] although it began to be taught in high schools starting in 1863. During the 1880s the Société d'Histoire de la Révolution and a magazine entitled *La Révolution Française* were founded. In 1886 the creation of a ministerial Commission on Revolutionary History and a chair in revolutionary history at the Sorbonne, inaugurated by Aulard on 12 March, made Revolution studies an academic discipline, with its processes of verification, permission to teach, and carefully delimited field.

This institutionalization froze the Revolution in time and influenced its interpretation. The ancien régime's official ending date became 1789, or 1787 at the earliest, with the prerevolutionary crisis. By the logic of this freezing in time which cut ties to absolutism, there was no *longue durée* to take into account. Its official historian Aulard confined himself to a political history of the Revolution that dealt only with events, and even then studied it from an agreed-upon perspective. By taking the Revolution's official discourse on itself as the truth, Aulard emphasized representation over practice. The very title of his work is revealing: *Histoire politique de la Révolution française; Origines et développement de la démocratie et de la République, 1789–1804* (1901). In so doing, Aulard remained firmly within the intellectual universe of philosophical history. He organized his narrative to serve the present's exigencies and his avowed republicanism, making the history of the Revolution a history of the idea of democracy as traced through the Revolution. But because he thought he was merely giving the facts, he no longer had a philosophy, like the republican historians of the nineteenth century. Instead, he had an impoverished credo popular at the time, the faith of a militant Third Republic radical. Yet for all that, he was exactly as insensitive as Quinet or Lamartine had been to Tocqueville's efforts not to reduce the Revolution to the triumph of an Idea.[59]

In Aulard, narrow focus is compensated for by a scientific asceticism in his writing: he is obsessive about archives, rejecting, he claimed, any economic or social explanation which existing documentation would not have allowed him to discuss with certainty. From this, we see why Aulard does not cite Tocqueville: the two men did not take the same positions or have the same research subject, or even the same conception of historiography.[60]

For Aulard the only beneficiary of the new university history was political history. Under Jaurès's impulse economic and social history quickly and enduringly gained hegemony.[61] Tocqueville was closer to this historiography which dealt with sociological perspectives than was Aulard. In his *Histoire socialiste* Jaurès drew inspiration from Tocqueville's writings on the peasant mentality to the point of imitation. He adopted as his own the notion that absolutism was subversive in nature.[62] Tocqueville owed his survival in the historians' guild to this renewal of rural history at the end of the ancien régime,[63] which was no Left monopoly, moreover, since Le Play's local scholarly disciples also joined in.[64]

Tocqueville was thus not forgotten by official historians. But the fertility of his work appears only when reduced to social history and especially to rural history. His denunciation of the absolutist state was seen as the "shadow" cast by his noble heritage.[65] And even such an oblique reading did not entirely save Tocqueville from scorn by most university professionals, who viewed him as an amateur historian infested by "literature."[66] The mark of rampant scientism perhaps, it was also the mark of professionalization. Historiography as done by writers from Michelet to Tocqueville had not scorned erudition but instead disdained pedantic display. Such display was indispensable to professors quick to level their rivals with a footnote.

But let us not exaggerate the effect of institutionalization on the historical profession. Intellectual legitimacy did not coincide with a high position as *patron* at the Sorbonne. Taine, Fustel, and Sorel had more prestige than Aulard. Beyond a small circle of rural history specialists, Tocqueville was still mostly read by those attached to the old "literary" way of writing history like Brunetière.[67] In a series of articles between October 1878 and November 1885, Brunetière deplored the fact that the younger generation of historians was breaking with Guizot, Thierry, and Mignet and banishing "general ideas from the sanctuary of history to the shadows."[68] Brunetière admired both the local scholars who were modernizing an antique tradition and representatives of a more "philosophical" history.

Tocqueville had had the merit of renewing both branches of history: he had been the first to renew the philosophy of French history by refusing to take 1789 as rupture, and he had been the first to use archives and reject the a priori method practiced by Guizot, Thiers, and Augustin Thierry.[69]

Brunetière was not the only one who wanted to maintain the tradition of historiography by writers. Tocqueville's heritage could be seen in liberal republican Albert Sorel's monumental work, *L'Europe et la Révolution française.*[70] Influential at the Ecole Libre des Sciences Politiques where he taught, Sorel was also an authority to the young historians of the *Revue Historique,* which Monod directed from 1883 to 1898. The magazine gave a lot of space to contemporary history and tried not to separate erudition and historical interpretation. From 1885 to 1898 Taine, Michelet, and Tocqueville were the publication's three great writers,[71] though Michelet was Monod's undisputed favorite. Tocqueville offered an example of history inseparable from political concern for the nation, which joined respect for tradition with the desire for progress.[72] Boulangism, perceived as an avatar of Bonapartism, drew attention to the return to Tocqueville. Distancing itself from commemorating the Revolution in a way which led to confrontation, the magazine traced the genealogy of French political culture, a singular mix of political unfamiliarity with freedom and early calls for egalitarianism. The Catholics' joining the Ralliement in 1893 led them also to Tocqueville's desire to reconcile the two Frances by means of history.[73] But what was Tocquevillean about the magazine was also what condemned it to disabused skepticism and political isolation. Influential through those of its collaborators who entered politics, like Gabriel Hanotaux, in 1895 a member of the Méline government, the magazine remained politically marginal, as Tocqueville had been, whose obsolescence was sadly noted by Lichtenberger in 1897.[74] "Positivist" history did not therefore have the uncontested triumph claimed for it, no more than absolute republicanism stifled the wave of constitutional republicanism. But political constitutionalism, like the liberal historiographic tradition connected with it, remained marginal, and the rejection of Tocqueville is sign of this.

Tocqueville as Minor Classic, 1893–1940

In 1890 Tocqueville's generation had disappeared. Jackson's America was ancient history, and the polemic against Caesarism had lost all meaning. It is time to give Tocqueville his place in the intellectual history of his century: starting as an "old beast," he reached the status of "classic." After the *Souvenirs* was published in 1893, the first great monographs appeared: *L'idée de l'état* by Henry Michel (1896), *Alexis de Tocqueville et la démocratie libérale* by d'Eichtal (1897), and the *Essai politique sur Alexis de Tocqueville* by Pierre Roland-Marcel (1910).

The Souvenirs

Calmann-Lévy had expressed its desire to publish a volume of excerpts from Tocqueville for schoolchildren.[75] Gustave de Beaumont's son Antonin gave the publisher an autographed manuscript of the *Souvenirs* and an abridged version created by his father and Mme de Tocqueville. Publishing the *Souvenirs* replaced the plan to publish the excerpts. The advantage was one of relative opportunity. Antonin said that the memoirs "deal with completely current questions, especially that of socialism and that of regular government." In his short introductory note, Christian de Tocqueville (the author's grandnephew) presented Tocqueville as a posthumous partisan of monarchic restoration, insisting in his turn on the prescient fear Tocqueville had had of socialism.[76] To any temptation to achieve a political coup we must also add the publisher's literary sensibility. Between 1890 and 1910 publishers turned away from cheap popular literature and cultivated a backward-looking, elitist aestheticism. Publishing aristocrats' or politicians' memoirs was part of this shift in sensibility on the part of the large publishers. Thus there is nothing surprising about Calmann-Lévy's ultimately preferring an expensive edition of the *Souvenirs* to a cheap edition of excerpts for use in schools.

Yet the *Souvenirs* was not an easy work to put out. Tocqueville claimed he had not written it with publication in mind.[77] No doubt he had thought of posthumous publication, being "very fond," he wrote, only "of posthumous memoirs; when one no longer has anything to hope for or fear, one gives oneself free rein to bite after one's death those one was obliged to spare while alive."[78] In any case, in his will he authorized publication of the *Souvenirs* only on the condition that it be edited for style and that deletions be made for courtesy reasons. Beaumont and Mme de Tocqueville recopied the manuscript and altered it accordingly. This was the version, along with the original manuscript, which Antonin de Beaumont gave Calmann-Lévy in February 1891.

Since 1855 Calmann-Lévy had submitted their manuscripts to two professional readers.[79] The first favored publication because of M. de Tocqueville's "quite considerable importance" and advised putting the "disconnected" manuscript "back together" by filling in gaps in the narrative and correcting the "sometimes pretentious and slightly Prudhommesque style" as well as "the assessments of contemporaries which stray far from the goodwill with which superior minds must show themselves generous." On the other hand, the second reader favored publishing the manuscript as it was, less out of sympathy for Tocqueville's "spiteful neutrality" toward his contemporaries than out of sensitivity to Tocqueville's literary talent as a memorialist. The *Souvenirs* was "not an entirely new Tocqueville" but "that great man of letters *en déshabillé*," with "no more academic solemnity, no more circumlocutions; that is the language of the memoirs—a lively, acerbic, casual language at times, but always healthy, robust, and direct."

The publisher adhered to the text as abridged by Beaumont and ensured that there was advance publication of the galleys in *Le Correspondant* of October–December 1892 and in *Le Temps* of 15 November 1892. *Le Figaro* of 10 November 1892 announced its publication. The book was printed in 2,000 copies plus the copies reserved for the publisher in late February 1893; 1,880 copies sold from March 1893 to January 1894, and 315 from 1894 to 1927.[80]

Calmann-Lévy had banked on a political success, but the book was above all a literary success. Readers were flabbergasted that Tocqueville was not merely that "reciter of aphorisms for use by bluestockings" whom Pailleron had mocked.[81] He was also full of "destructive nastiness": "Never in the world has a body of work been comprised of two such dissimilar parts: over one reigns the serene religion of science, and over the other, virulent passion. The first reminds us of Montesquieu, the second of Tacitus or Saint-Simon."[82] Tocqueville "has a way of undressing his friends, his best, most intimate friends, and allowing us to read the deepest level of their hearts, which is unfailingly disturbing."[83]

The publication of the *Souvenirs* caused a reinterpretation of Tocqueville's entire body of work. Its haughty severity reinforced the sense of Tocqueville's strangeness, a democrat for being too aristocratic not to despise the bourgeoisie, a prophet only out of archaism: "Through a curious meeting, he was a gentleman and a democrat adrift in bourgeois society. Thus his feelings about the staff of the July Monarchy had something in them of both aristocratic impertinence and popular meanness."[84]

His correspondence, when it came out in 1861, had already given Tocqueville the image of an amazingly timorous soul. From the *Souvenirs* readers concluded that Tocqueville, with little love for the Republic and even less for all other regimes, had never had anything but "negative convictions."[85] There began to be assertions—and still are—that Tocqueville had succumbed under the Second Republic to a growing pessimism, to such a degree he adopted an ironic vision of history which was thought to be found in *Old Regime* and even retroactively in *Democracy*. It is true that *Souvenirs* shows brushes with despair, but this is a matter of circumstances: it was written between June 1850 and September 1851 under threat of a coup d'état, it is private writing and free from a sense of responsibility. It was written at a distance—geographically (near Naples), politically (while on leave from the Chamber), and symbolically. He was writing only for himself. This is why the man who always took pains to leave the future open in his published works in the *Souvenirs* concluded the vanity of all political action.

Showing Tocqueville's impotence, the perennial stubbornness of the privileged, the versatility of the politician, the *Souvenirs* contributed to the enduring disparagement of the July Monarchy, reduced to bourgeois egotism, and of the Second Republic, dismissed as a utopia. The *Souvenirs* also made readers forget that in Tocqueville, optimism of the will always wins over the pessimism in intelligence.

Over the short run a chance conjuncture drew the *Souvenirs* into current events for a brief time, during the heyday of the Panama scandal. A concern for punishing parliamentary corruption led the French to judge the present in the light of the past—as always, using age-old platitudes: There is nothing new under the sun; Since Tocqueville's time our parliamentarians have always been the same, seekers after prestige and sinecures ... On the other hand, there was the opposite reaction, in a historicizing mode: Political life grows uglier every day; Where are the parliamentarians of yesterday ...[86]

Over the long run the *Souvenirs* inspired reflection on patterns of recurrence throughout the century of France's revolution-reaction cycle. But the work did not have a clear impact. One might, as Christian de Tocqueville did following his granduncle, blame the passion for equality, concluding that restoration of the monarchy was urgent. Republicans preferred to read it as a satire of the notables, always just afraid enough to prefer despotism to liberty's upheavals.[87] Tocqueville could be neither the republicans' Mirabeau nor their Lafayette. Yet he was among the first of the *ralliés*. In 1893, when Catholics had to face the issue of the Ralliement to the Republic, he was to gain new luster.

Between the Old Right and the New Right

THE FIRST *RALLIÉ*: TOCQUEVILLE AND "AMERICANISM"

In 1893 only a marginal fringe within the electorate were still tormented by doubt about the timeliness of the Ralliement. Over the course of elections since 1870, the majority of the population had become republican. The morose opposition of the Catholic hierarchy, notables, and the Paris intelligentsia endured. During the years from the Catholic Ralliement in the early 1880s to the Dreyfus affair, turning Catholic tides against the Republic, Tocqueville was the gold ring to be snatched at by both the old, resigned right wing and the new right wing that was formed by the rejection of democracy. A republican, Spuller, Gambetta's friend and minister of public instruction, fine arts, and religion in 1893–94, had analyzed Tocqueville's political importance. Tocqueville had known the Republic would only become stable upon acceptance by Catholics and notables. He had promoted a "new spirit," the "true spirit of tolerance" with which Gambetta's followers then tried to infuse France.[88] He had "the honor of in some degree having founded the *ralliés* party."[89]

Politically, the Ralliement was of little importance. The Right's electoral failure in 1893 and the parish-level clergy's resistance from 1893 to 1898 impeded the formation of any large conservative party which might have allowed for a reorganization of the political chessboard. But this aborted attempt clearly shows that minds had changed, as well as the wake left by Tocqueville.[90]

The Ralliement movement was kicked off by Cardinal Lavigerie's toast of November 1890 to the Republic and was reaffirmed by an encyclical *Au milieu des sollicitudes* of 16 February 1892. The American model served to such a degree as a reference point and lightning rod for discord within the spiritual renewal which went along with the institutional church's changes in position that there was talk of "Americanism."

As in the 1830s, America served as a pretext for developing the notion of Christian democracy. To French reactionaries the American church seemed the flowering of Lamennais's and *L'Avenir*'s liberal heresy. *L'Avenir*'s doctrine had been spread in the United States through the good works of the Sulpicians. Its protagonists succeeded each other along hereditary lines: Montalembert's son-in-law de Meaux who had commented on *Old Regime* in 1856 took up the torch at *L'Avenir* while writing his *L'église et la liberté catholique aux Etats-Unis* (1893).[91]

Americanism was innovative by posing a question in practice which *L'Avenir* and, later on, Tocqueville had only been able to pose theoretically. Lamennais's violent split and the sorrowful submission of Montalembert and Lacordaire had marked the failure of the church to modernize. Tocqueville, Laboulaye, and their followers had been insidiously reduced to seeking the incarnation of their Christian democratic ideal in the Unitarian Channing who resembled a moderate Renan who had remained in the fold.[92] Father Hecker's 1858 founding of the Paulists finally gave Europeans an authentic Catholicism that proclaimed itself democratic, for Father Hecker respected individual independence and the rights of individual conscience, while believing in submission to magisterial authority and even accepting the dogma of papal infallibility. From that point on, Tocqueville's theories of Christianity's shift toward simplified ritual, toward greater respect for individuals' judgment without rejection of magisterial authority, were empirically confirmed by Paulist example. From this development came a renewed fascination with the American model, which de Meaux's book exemplified, by updating Tocqueville's analyses of Catholicism without changing their meaning.[93]

Neo-Tocquevillean Americanism remained marginal. Starting in 1893 and 1894, the Ralliement's adversaries went on the counteroffensive: Loisy was defrocked in 1893; the religious parliament launched in 1895 by Father Charbonnel with the assistance of de Meaux and Leroy-Beaulieu failed because of papal hostility. Publication in 1897 of a book on the life of Father Hecker unleashed a violent anti-American campaign in France. Even Tocqueville's readers, such as Brunetière,[94] who had been seduced by the combination of faith and liberty, turned toward traditionalism out of reaction to the Dreyfus affair and obedience to papal condemnation of Americanism.[95] Americanism's failure demonstrated the persistence in France of the antagonism between Catholic dogma and the Enlightenment,[96] which condemned Catholics to internal exile or embarrassed resignation to the republican regime.

Catholics were wary of any social order based on the rights of the individual. Tocqueville's American model based social order on respect for individual rights and the strength of the associative principle. In 1835 the Christian socialists aligned with Buchez had denounced this as immoral egoism. Those like them at century's end were no less consumed by the communitarian ideal. Let us take just one example, of Father Charles Calippe. Beginning as an Ultramontanist, Calippe began to support democracy after the encyclical *Rerum Novarum* was promulgated in 1891. In 1902 he published the *Journal d'un prêtre d'après demain,* the fictional journal of a monk at work which sketches the ideal of the worker-priest.[97] In 1911 Calippe devoted several pages to Tocqueville in his work *L'attitude sociale des catholiques français au XIXe siècle.* For Calippe, Tocqueville was still the foremost *rallié*, but to his American associations, Calippe preferred the cooperative experiments of the Albi glass factory. In constructing a Christian democracy, Tocqueville counted much less than Le Play or even the socialist Jean Jaurès, whom Calippe admired out of hatred for capitalism and Enlightenment individualism. Tocqueville could hold only a marginal place in the intellectual genealogy of a Catholicism which still hesitated over the notion of law based on individualism.

At the end of the century, Tocqueville's memory survived only within the liberal-conservative movement whose publication was *Le Correspondant.* It is not impossible that Gaullism's intellectual roots may in part be found in this movement's Catholic liberalism.[98] The Gaullist notion of participation may have been an original mixture of the ancient idea of community dear to socially minded Catholics and the Tocquevillean idea of democratic association. But this is merely a later democratic version made possible by the discredit of the reactionary form of the corporate ideal, a discredit caused by the failure of the Vichy regime.

After his ephemeral revival on the wave of Americanism, Tocqueville's work lost all political influence for a long while. The Dreyfus affair in effect simplified the stakes: on one hand were those who rejected parliamentarianism and wanted to see democracy put on trial; on the other, those who were growing used to parliamentary democracy.

DEMOCRACY ON TRIAL

Tocqueville had sought a model for liberal democracy in the United States. It is historical irony that after 1899, antidemocracy advocates found support within the United States for their belief in centralized power and in the nation. America was imperialist: the Venezuela crisis of 1895 and the Spanish-American War over Cuba, which ended with the prompt crushing of the Spanish forces in 1898, clashed with the peaceful character Tocqueville had attributed to democracies.[99]

Was this new America still democratic? French antidemocrats enjoyed emphasizing the aristocracy's eternal renaissance.[100] What remained of Tocqueville? Only error. To the new Right, which slid from repulsion for democracy to the hope of destroying it, Tocqueville, as sad and undecided as he was, became a traitor—even worse, a fabricator. He was accused of having spread a false image of America, the "land of enormous abuses erected as institutions,"[101] a land swept away in the torrent of its magnificent vitality despite its politics. "The person who reestablishes the truth about America in French hearts," wrote Maurras, "will do them the incomparable service of erasing the last vestiges of foolishness and insanity which Franklin, Chateaubriand, Tocqueville, and Laboulaye in turn have written about them, along with a few other liberals of scant brains."[102] Maurras also commented:

> Tocqueville's responsibility cannot be passed over in silence. This sweetest, most innocent, and most dangerous of philosophical malefactors has contributed in immense measure to the general blindness. . . . Through him and his entire school, not forgetting the crazy and specious Laboulaye, all our France has believed in the future of the great pacifist democracy established on the other side of the ocean, constituting, in its order, generosity, and freedom, a salutary counterbalance to the errors of the old continent! . . . A pyramid of dollars, scrap metal, and cold cuts, which was not even the equal of the ruins of Cheops (for those at least have endured) but was like the columns of the Parthenon.[103]

After Maurras, members of Action Française liked to repeat "M. de Tocqueville is a criminal"[104] and classed Tocqueville and his end-of-the-century followers in the defaming categories of anarchist, criminal, and alien—along with Rousseau. Between Tocqueville and Rousseau the difference was only one of an inconsequential democrat versus an impenitent one. No surprise there. When democracy and human rights are both rejected, the distance between liberalism and democracy disappears.

One single attempt was made to retrieve Tocqueville from the pit where Action Française had thrown him along with human rights, capitalism, democracy, and liberalism. Antoine Rédier's great biography, *Comme disait M. de Tocqueville* (1925), was based on considerable erudite research. Between the wars the French mostly viewed Tocqueville through Rédier's eyes. It was a distorting view. Rédier, a member of Action Française, veteran, and head of the legion tempted by fascism,[105] wanted to renew French society through the virtues of a corporate state. His attempt demonstrated how far from fascist criticisms of democracy Tocqueville really was, for Rédier was unaware of the opposition. His whole thrust was to rehabilitate Tocqueville against himself, by making this "miscreant," contaminated by the stench of democratic vapors, into a pillar of righteousness and hierarchy. "In Tocqueville, there are always two men: the one who wrote the preface to *Democracy* and the other who ceaselessly bore witness against that piece written in his youth. One of the two was surely wrong" (222). On one hand, there was the wrongheaded young thinker who had strayed through the perverse influence of liberals like Beaumont and who so thoughtlessly used the language of human rights. On the other hand, there was the "true" Tocqueville, whom the scholar could now reveal, thanks to examination of the family papers. "He was neither American, nor a democrat, but French of the oldest and most aristocratic race to the most intimate depth of his being,"[106] he denounced the Revolution as a "great posturer," he rejected individualism, criticized materialism, sang nationalism's virtues, etc. Rédier quite rightly noted the distance between Tocqueville and Coppet's individualist tradition but only reveals this side while postulating the incoherence of Tocqueville's works, making them no longer interpretable. Rédier could not save Tocqueville from nationalist scorn for that "extravagant gentleman"[107] who represented nineteenth-century stupidity.

In this trial of democracy according to Tocqueville, a republican of the era noted, "Action Française stretches out its hand to the socialist movement. . . . On left and right, it is proclaimed that we must count in groups, and not in heads."[108] Industrial capitalism, individualism, human rights, and parliamentary or bourgeois democracy were all rejected with the same opprobrium. In his 1908 *Les illusions du progrès*, Georges Sorel found Tocqueville guilty of having believed in the predestination of bourgeois democracy and having made use of the rhetoric of progress. In 1919 the *Matériaux d'une théorie du prolétariat* would denounce Tocqueville anew as the most effective promoter of the illusion of democracy's fatal triumph, to which a pusillanimous bourgeoisie resigned itself, out of fear of revolution.

TOCQUEVILLE AND THE REPUBLICAN SYNTHESIS

A criminal to the new Right and the revolutionary syndicalists, Tocqueville did not even have a malefactor's prestige in the eyes of those who crafted the republican synthesis. His memory was "relegated to the dust of those ridiculous pantheons, graveyards of great dreams ill understood by the masses and honored only distractedly. . . . Tocqueville does not figure and will never figure among our national democratic saints."[109]

In the 1880s Tocqueville's works seemed to have been made useless by the achievement of democratic conquest. After 1890 things grew even worse as his works seemed theoretically inconsistent, less archaic than wrong. Like Montesquieu and Constant, Tocqueville had conceived of society as a conglomeration of autonomous individuals. In contrast, politicians, republican philosophers, and sociologists of the 1880s defined society as a system of interdependence, productive of meaning. They thought of the relationships between right and action, individual and state, in a different way.

Between action and right, Tocqueville had believed that a society was threatened with tyranny or decomposition if it was not ordered by a consensual criterion of right anchored in religious transcendence. A regime's form mattered little for no form carried within itself the rule of justice. To republicans, the opposite was true; the Republic was not neutral ground but a doctrinal solution termed "laicity." Laicity provided a way to surpass religions' tendency to divide and reconciled right with history at last. The reformist liberalism that developed around Fouillée, Léon Bourgeois, and Durkheim was a rationalist one. "Philosophy is the religion of democracies," wrote Fouillée.[110] What democracies need is the "intrepid affirmation of the constructive power of the spirit . . . the grand idea of living reason's spontaneity."[111] Democracy is the site of autonomous consciences. Thus Tocqueville's spiritualism seemed inconsistent with the views of those men slipping into free thought or calling for a "new pantheism,"[112] which is to say, secular religion. According to d'Eichtal, Tocqueville had the "illusion" of a religious awakening and was "limited by his Christian liberal and spiritualist point of view."[113]

Concerning the relationship between the individual and the state, Tocqueville was no greater inspiration to the republicans. His concern for decentralizing authority seemed too "American." He was still sometimes cited for polemical purposes,[114] recalling that the local level was "liberty's primary school."[115] But the theme of decentralization, which slid rightward toward regionalism on the Right, was reduced on the Left to an administrative problem of good management. Thus the mistrust of state omnipotence decreased precisely because of relative liberalization in administrative practices. Political liberalism was dying out for having been too successful, "for lack of lists of complaints to write up, major calls to action to proclaim, crying abuses to denounce." The liberal citizen of the Third Republic was often "a citizen against power yet one who trod within its lines."[116] Tocqueville was thus caught in a "natural and necessary demotion and obscurity. . . . The term *liberalism* belongs to the past. Being a liberal is like being a viscountess or a dowager duchess."[117]

The problem was no longer so much one of limiting state intervention out of suspicion but of making it serve general interests. Tocqueville's glory at the end of the Second Empire had rested on his denunciation of the institutionalization of Bonapartist authoritarianism. In contrast, the Council of State's liberal jurisprudence and later the doctrinal efforts of great jurists like Duguit, Hauriou, and Jèze from 1895 to 1905 led to legitimation of exorbitant state rights in the name of guaranteed liberties for all. Suddenly, old-style defensive liberalism seemed only to defend the undue prerogatives of the privileged. For Lanson, "[liberal] solutions, long revolutionary and instruments of progress, have become conservative and instruments of reaction. The liberal party, by maintaining its historical position for the past half century while everything changed, finds itself facing off its former allies next to its enemies of yesterday."[118]

Tocqueville was no less outdated when it came to social problems. True, there were still attempts to "organize democracy." But Tocqueville had found the solution in voluntary associations, charitable societies, academies, parties, and communal and regional assemblies, in which the individuals responsible took their destiny in hand. To republicans, it was doubtless important that citizens not be oppressed, that they deliberate and associate with one another. But the logic of individual responsibility pulled back when faced with the new logic of solidarity that led to the establishment of a providential state. The haughty liberty Tocqueville promoted seemed a Norman aristocratic nostalgia, quite unsuited to resolving social problems.[119] Tocqueville, we were told, had only known democracy in its infantile form, when democracy was identified with the power of the majority, and equality with the universality of rule. In this era at the nineteenth century, democracy seemed to consist more in respecting individuals' infinite diversity through development of societal right. Tocqueville's pessimism can thus be explained by the impotence common to moderates who predict catastrophes without being able to stop them and who define principles without finding the ways to apply them. Tocqueville seemed the precursor of those between-the-wars liberals who went about with perpetual sour faces like Daniel Halévy and Emmanuel Berl, classically "generous" people mired in the depths of human nature and condemned to sterile whining about liberty's decline;[120] among them all was the "same disillusionment, same premonitions, same Cassandra tendencies, same funeral held for liberalism, same pulling back before inevitable democracy, the same intelligent, disabused, distant, and fearful attitude."[121]

Tocqueville in the Sciences: The Birth of Sociology

Likening Tocqueville's work politically to the whining of unhappy consciences did not necessarily mean his exclusion from the scientific field. His exclusion resulted from the organization of the social sciences, which led to the fragmentation of Tocqueville's object of study into distinct and competing disciplines.

It has been said that this fragmentation was the sign that the social sciences were elevated to scientific dignity. Prior indistinction would thus mark the prehistory of the disciplines with indeterminate focus, uncertain procedures, without branches or evaluatory mechanisms in which professionalism was hard to distinguish from amateurism.[122]

This outline is insufficient. The "moral and political sciences" had not remained uncultivated before the institutionalization of university disciplines. They had an institution which legitimated them, the Academy of Moral and Political Sciences, which evaluated their production by awarding prizes to laureates chosen by collective judging procedures. It ordered studies and in so doing defined research priorities; it defined ability in its rules for the recruitment of members and correspondents, and it regularly published the proceedings of its sessions and the scholarly communiqués of its guests. The contrast between the academic world and the university at the end of the century was thus not that of opinion vs. science, or amateurism vs. professionalism, or archaism vs. mature knowledge. They represented two different structurings of the scientific field, one following the other while overlapping. At the Academy of Moral Sciences, "sections" sometimes shared members and collaborated. Commonality of meaning was more important than disciplinary boundaries. On the other hand, by the end of the nineteenth century, boundary rivalries became so essential they in part determined a discipline's focus of study. Boundaries became more important than common meaning, which was reduced to affirming science's positivist character. No doubt the Academy of Moral Sciences survived by welcoming many rejected by the universities. But the university, which controlled the spread of ideas within the educational system through state control of the curriculum, defined disciplinary research focuses and left us an organization of knowledge in which Tocqueville has no place.

Political science was institutionalized in 1872, though its purpose was not clearly defined, with the founding of the Ecole Libre des Sciences Politiques. But the distance between studying events and theoretical reflection that grew noticeable by 1880 became more radical after 1890. The doctrinal political science which stressed moral values and left a large space for discussion of the old doctrines continued to think about Tocqueville. But such activity was a kind of decadence, in which theoretical reflection was no longer nourished by the study of the present.[123]

Might Tocqueville find a readership among sociologists? It has been said that he did. In fact, if we apply a history of ideas approach by trying to isolate the basic ideas circulating among the different doctrines, we can indeed glimpse Tocqueville's influence on Durkheim.[124] But a precursor is only someone identified that way. Though Durkheim wrote about Montesquieu (focusing his Latin thesis on him in 1892) and about Rousseau, he hardly ever cited Tocqueville, and he turned from political studies in 1895. This disinterest had tactical reasons. Durkheim's sociology was built up against neighboring disciplines—it was important to him to demarcate himself from the history of doctrines,[125] from the bastard political sciences because they were infected with empiricism, and from conservative law—whence politics' tiny, shifting place in the *Année sociologique*'s table of contents. There is a biographically motivated reason in addition to these tactical ones. The death in 1895 of his father, a rabbi in Epinal, pushed Durkheim to emphasize religion as a matrix of social linkage. But the reason for his disinterest in politics was mainly theoretical. Political events, for all that they demonstrated individual liberty, seemed to Durkheim to depend too much on chance for him to delineate any signifying structure within them. They were not the object of science except in the limited degree to which they were produced by social morphologies. Durkheim was in thrall to social realism and to the primacy of the whole over the individual, which Tocqueville rejected for reasons of method as much as morality.[126] In doing so, he overlooked liberty and politics. Durkheimians' lack of interest in Tocqueville and in politics was to become even more pregnant with consequence because it was through their influence on the historians of the *Revue de Synthèse* and later of the *Annales* school that many social sciences developed without a political aspect.

There was one exception among the Durkheimians, but he was marginal within their school—Celestin Bouglé. Bouglé was at the confluence of several traditions—neo-Kantianism, Durkheimianism, Proudhonian socialism.[127] He often referred to Tocqueville, whose attention to evaluating regimes according to the degree of liberty they guarantee[128] and wariness toward scientism (then an insidious social Darwinism) he shared.[129]

Bouglé especially shared Tocqueville's primary intuition, to which he devoted his thesis on *Les idées égalitaires.* This was the sense of the democratic nature of modern societies and their fundamental opposition to hierarchical societies whose finest example was India. As Tocqueville had before him, Bouglé devoted an entire work to India. Thus Bouglé is the link connecting Tocqueville with Louis Dumont; he sought to describe the opposition between hierarchal and egalitarian societies in terms of Durkheimian social morphology. It remains to be understood why Bouglé's efforts enjoyed so little future, for Bouglé had nothing of failure about him. He received his doctorate in 1899, was made professor in Toulouse in 1900 and at the Sorbonne in 1908, and became adjunct director (1927–35) and then director (1935–40) of the Laboratoire de Sociologie of the Ecole Normale Supérieure, where he had Raymond Aron as a student. He was also one of the first members of the Ligue des Droits de l'Homme, of which he became vice president from 1911 to 1924, and was an active promoter of solidarism. But between the wars he abandoned political sociology. As a thoughtful man, he turned toward philosophy, and as a man of action, he was consumed by the urgency of reforms to be made. Despite his long-standing ties to Bouglé, Aron did not owe his interest in Tocqueville to Bouglé.

Outside the Durkheimian school, two men seemed possible successors of Tocqueville's, Gustave Le Bon and Gabriel Tarde. Both were outside the university and combined a contested intellectual legitimacy with considerable social, political, and academic legitimacy. Gustave Le Bon, excluded from the university and the academies, was acclaimed by radicalism's opponents who hastened to the banquets he organized starting in 1892. Here Poincaré and Briand were to be found and, after 1914, André Tardieu, Pierre Flandin, Herriot, and Barthou as well. Gabriel Tarde was trained as a judge like Tocqueville and also began in 1886 with a comparative criminological study. He taught at the Ecole des Sciences Politiques and the Collège Libre des Sciences Sociales in 1896 before entering the Collège de France in 1900 and being elected to the Académie des Sciences Morales. Le Bon and Tarde, friends and both writers for Ribot's *Revue Philosophique,* were worried about the advent of mass society and searched for a theory of the elites. Yet their apparent similarity to Tocqueville masked a radical divergence. Even worse, their unfortunate anointing of political sociology with the waters of crowd psychology helped to inter Tocqueville's thought and to render the study of political cultures sterile for a long while.

Gustave Le Bon appeared to be trying to revive the old Orleanist culture by wearing the new suit of nationalist culture so attracted to fascism.[130] But here reviving turns to denaturing. A doctor who was trained in Pinel's and Esquirol's hallucination theory and rubbed shoulders with Darwinism, Le Bon developed a kind of medico-organicist, hodgepodge theory which in fact was not descended from Tocqueville's but its adversary. He reincarnated the biological determinism suspected of racism that Tocqueville had hated in Gobineau. In his introduction to the *Lois psychologiques de l'évolution des peuples* (1894), Le Bon tried to characterize "modern egalitarian ideas and the psychological bases of history." While Tocqueville "believed [he had] found in the institutions of peoples the cause of their evolution," Le Bon's explicit goal was to invert the order of Tocqueville's factors. "I am instead persuaded," wrote Le Bon, "and hope to prove precisely by taking examples from the countries Tocqueville studied that institutions have a very weak impact on the evolution of civilizations. . . . There are great permanent laws which direct the general advance of each civilization. Within these permanent laws, the most general and most irreducible ones flow from the mental constitutions of peoples."[131]

From Tocqueville to Tarde there might seem more continuity. Let us consider Tarde's book, *Les transformations du pouvoir* (1899), his major contribution to political studies. The result of a series of lectures at the Ecole des Sciences Politiques in 1896 and at the Collège Libre des Sciences Sociales in 1898, the book was intended "to give an idea of what political science can be after its sociological baptism."[132] In it, Tarde reexamined many of Tocqueville's theses: the irreversibility of the movement toward democracy; the increase in centralization since the ancien régime; the predominance of customs over laws in the future of societies; a nuanced methodological individualism. But Tarde twisted these theses to serve his apologia for the state, that great producer of harmony.[133] And above all, Tarde used historians at will—Tocqueville in fact less than Taine, Fustel, and Sumner-Maine—taking a list of facts from them which cut across history and obey universal laws: imitation, repetition, opposition. As a result, the democratic tendency could be sighted as much in the Greek city-states as in the Caesars' Rome and the American republic. Centralization was a logical necessity of harmony within collaboration, not the result of a historical process. By reducing everything in this way to everlasting good sense and logical schematics which did little to hide a belief in final causes à la Bernardin de Saint-Pierre,

Tarde misread history and lacked what made for the novelty of Tocqueville's works: attention to the diversity of cultures combined with rupture between the democratic and aristocratic universes.

Thus the democratic culture that had captured Tocqueville's attention was not history's, political science's, or Durkheimian sociology's object of study. Abandoned to such semi-amateur sociologists as Tarde and Le Bon, his works became the blind spot in scholarship's field of vision. This is why, after having lost their currency in 1880, Tocqueville's works only limitedly attained classic status.

The period between the wars did not noticeably increase this tiny space conceded Tocqueville. As the years went on, he seemed ever more American than French. Nothing shows this more clearly than the homages given him in 1935 and 1936, on the occasion of the first *Democracy*'s hundredth anniversary. Two committees were formed, the France-Amerique committee and the Alexis de Tocqueville committee. A bust of Tocqueville was given in the name of France to President Franklin Roosevelt,[134] and another two busts were unveiled in August 1936, one in Cherbourg, the second at Tocqueville's château. Both bronzes were erected in symbolic sites. At Cherbourg, it was in the entryway to the maritime port's great hall, to welcome American travelers with a familiar face, not least the American squadron whose presence in Cherbourg that August gave its own luster to the ceremony. At Tocqueville, the cortege left the village square to place the bust in the château, clearly connoting Tocqueville's aristocratic image[135] and the preponderant place of his descendants in the commemoration's organization. But French opinion remained cool. The same feeling that affected the centenary ceremonies could be seen in the rare scholarly works devoted to Tocqueville between the wars:[136] Tocqueville's name was more important than his works, the hardly readable vestige of an era when democracy was still unstable, and political language was overinflated by the remnants of grandiloquence. Tocqueville survived in memory only as an old Norman notable and a link in the history of Franco-American friendship: a "philosopher Lafayette with boredom added."[137]

6

Tocqueville's Return

THE END OF the nineteenth century had propelled Tocqueville from the rank of prophet to that of thunderously dull sermonizer who seemed ready-made, as Barbey said, "to maintain the human jawbone in [the] vigorous and moral gymnastic of yawning." The beginning of the twentieth century remembered only his morosity. In the 1930s this grew worse: even for liberals, the choice was between an imperial state and a democratic one, not between self-government and state control, and Tocqueville did not allow them to think about the rise of totalitarianism.[1] Tocqueville's recent renaissance strikes us as an enigma. How can we explain the work's presence today and its earlier absence? Could the same reasons explain both old reticences and new enthusiasm? And what sudden shift in French culture reveals Tocqueville's great return?

Today in France, Tocqueville is the object of a kind of consensus hardly disturbed by the irritated grumblings of those who denounce the emergence of a new democratic bible. Tocqueville's château is a pilgrimage site for successive French presidents and ministers. The highest authorities in the land participate in Tocqueville Prize ceremonies, and few writers have had the privilege of being the object of citations during ministry meetings, as Tocqueville has.[2]

The publishing history of Tocqueville's complete works allows us to trace the paths to this renaissance. After Tocqueville's long period of oblivion between the wars, the *Souvenirs,* which had been out of print for some time, was reprinted in 1942 in the Mémoires du passé pour servir au temps présent series. Tocqueville, whose works appeared with the likes of Sully and Napoleon in this collection, was still just a nineteenth-century author thanks to whom one learned to explain the continuity of the country's sad history and the recurrence of internecine wars which at the moment were disturbing Vichy France.[3] Commentaries on the book were directly aligned with those of the nineteenth century: some, fascist or Pétainist (the only ones who could freely express their opinions), deplored that at a time when paper was scarce, anyone had thought to take that "dusty Tocqueville" out of the box. Of course, Tocqueville did a judicious job of criticizing bourgeois individualism, but he "didn't do it on purpose." It was pure chance that the knight-errant of liberty at certain points approached the fascist criticism of democracy.[4] Vichyites especially appreciated Tocqueville's depiction of the pathological nature of socialism and the narrow-mindedness of parliamentarians.[5] As for democrats, publicly they stuck to cautious analysis of the literary merits of Tocqueville,[6] who survived in memory only as a witness to a democratic transition now in the process of becoming complete. Serious and moderate, and thus predestined to defeat, Tocqueville was part of a past in which all old parliamentarians were laid to rest, republicans included. His exclusively literary superiority was as the brilliant, clever prophet of his world's decadence.[7] The questions he asked were those of the nineteenth century, and his dialectic was aimed at the notables, with no hold on the opinion of the masses hounded by modern propaganda techniques.[8]

Tocqueville's renaissance in France thus dates only to after the war. Curiously, this followed the rediscovery of his work in countries crushed by totalitarianism. In Italy the *Souvenirs* was published in 1939, and fragments on the Revolution in 1942. The following year Croce wrote a short article on Tocqueville. Starting in 1949, Tocqueville's thought was taught at the Croce Institute for Historical Studies. Then studies devoted to Tocqueville followed one another without interruption.[9] In France, for lack of French scholars who wanted to do so, J. P. Mayer, a German Marxian specialist who had taken refuge in England in 1939, launched the monumental enterprise of editing the *Oeuvres complètes* for Gallimard. Over time the edition received the necessary support. Encouraged by governments, the complete works are now partially known abroad thanks to translations.

Yet beyond a circle of specialists, the complete works are more significant as indexes of Tocqueville's fame than for the material they supply intellectual debate. Sold in about a thousand copies, neglected by many talented Tocqueville scholars, the series had scarcely influenced Tocqueville's image in 1984 before André Jardin's biography of Tocqueville was published by Hachette, condensing what was known about the writer. We would be wrong to see this as merely one more proof of French dislike for true scholarship, distasteful to the public and disdained by academics—as though the complete works ironically illustrated what Tocqueville himself said about democratic preference for easy pleasures, quickly made careers, and vast systems. No, if the *Oeuvres complètes* is mostly used by historians, it is rather that the collection emphasizes how Tocqueville's works are inscribed in time, for the preference today is to read them for the light they shed on the present. The renaissance or rather the renaissances of Tocqueville since 1950 have all interpreted him in present terms and have all postulated his currency. This explains the gap between the confidential distribution of some of his writings and the extraordinary aura surrounding *Democracy* and *Old Regime*, which have sold hundreds of thousands of copies and remained in print since 1951.[10] Nothing shows more clearly that the reputation of his works prospers as much for his vices as for his genius. The generality of his ideas seems to authorize every anachronism of interpretation, and many readers have a taste for the charm of Tocqueville's vagueness. It might be amusing at this point to examine the multifarious treachery committed by some commentaries, but it is better to notice how fertile the works' contribution is to new thinking. Let us attempt a chronology.

We can distinguish three periods in the history of rereadings of Tocqueville—the 1950s, when around Raymond Aron there developed critical reflection on governments which centered on rereading the first *Democracy;* the 1960s, when questions about democratic culture led sociologists, philosophers, and anthropologists to emphasize the second *Democracy;* and the 1970s, during which François Furet and his circle gave *Old Regime* a major place in the interpretation of French history. These three rereadings were sequential but overlapping as well because all belonged to the same intellectual universe. All were born of a fruitful encounter with American culture and made comparison between Europe and America central to their thinking. All sought to reposition liberty as a central criterion in the social sciences, which had developed holding too tightly to a blind positivity.

The 1950s: The End of Ideology

Rereading Tocqueville is made possible by the very slow disaffection with Communism's messianic ideology that marked the period of 1955–65. The stages of this disaffection are well known: the de-Stalinization launched by Khrushchev's report of February 1956 to the Twentieth Congress of the Communist Party and then the shock of the Soviet invasion of Budapest in November 1956. At this point "the end of ideology" theme appeared in both France and the United States, launched at a large conference on the future of freedom held in Milan in 1955.[11]

On both sides of the Atlantic, Tocqueville became the author of a single page of *Democracy,* the page on the parallel between the two modern world powers, the democratic United States and despotic Russia. In the nineteenth century the parallel had been striking only by its force of expression. Memory of Cossack brutality in Paris and the astonishment caused by the rapid rise of the United States reduced this powerful geopolitical vision to a modest commonplace.[12] The Cold War gave the parallel a descriptive pertinence even more admired for being prophetic. Thanks to Tocqueville, confrontation between the two blocs took on the majesty of a historical necessity.[13] It was Tocqueville against Marx, a philosophical Cold War, to each camp its eponymous hero. The duel even took on diplomatic form at the summit where Eisenhower called on Tocqueville in an 4 April 1959 speech, while Khrushchev in *Pravda* mocked the "natterings of that French reactionary from the last century."[14] The duel also took academic form, in fact canonically so, as Tocquevillean hermeneutics often became reduced to parallels between Tocqueville and Marx.[15]

But Tocqueville's work was much more fertile than casual references to his prophesizing might indicate. In the United States, *Democracy* had lost its descriptive pertinence at the end of the nineteenth century in a world in which centralization, urbanization, and class struggle seemed the common characteristics of modernity.[16] Tocqueville's work was read only as a history of constitutional law or a standard against which to measure ground covered since 1830.[17] The undertow of the Communist ideal had pulled against attempts to cut American history out of the same cloth as European history, with its own class struggle and even the Civil War for a revolution, as Charles Beard had done. Compared to European societies, America revealed itself a consensual society, with rival pressure groups but no class struggle, a democratic culture but not a revolutionary one, with respect for authority but no cult of reason of state. Suddenly the ever-valid analysis of America's exceptional nature was found again in Tocqueville.

We can follow Tocqueville's path in America in the field of history: Louis Hartz, in *The Liberal Tradition in America* (1955), which bears an epigraph by Tocqueville, shows how the absence of an ancien régime in the United States also explained the absence of conflict between religion and the Enlightenment and a more moderate class struggle. Following Tocqueville, sociologists also showed the specificity of American culture in the bargaining among a plurality of interest groups engaged in permanent negotiation with no class attaining hegemony.[18]

In Tocqueville one at last could find a philosophy which emphasized the dividing line between pluralistic and totalitarian societies. In this perspective Tocqueville's thought sometimes is poorly distinguished from Burke's conservative liberalism.[19] Against a European culture suspected of totalitarian constructivism, English-style liberalism is exalted, and an apology for the market is constructed without nuance. The cooptation of this heritage is most clearly shown by the 1974 interpretation of Tocqueville by Nobel Prize–winning economist Hayek, the defender of extreme liberalism. An Austrian emigré when Nazism arrived, Hayek borrowed the title of his first famous work, *The Road to Serfdom* (1994), from Tocqueville's 1848 speech against socialism. Hayek's work culminated in his thinking about classical liberalism, in which he updated seventeenth- and eighteenth-century authors like Locke, the Scottish moralists, the Old Whigs, and their descendants Macaulay and Burke. From the Continental tradition infested with Cartesianism and Rousseauianism, he salvaged only Kant, Constant, and above all Tocqueville, denatured in his elevation to British dignity.[20]

Hayek saw two merits in Tocqueville. First, he had denounced constructivism and the notion of social law, which leads to totalitarianism via socialism. And second, he had, as Burke did, defended intermediary bodies, families, towns, and groups that allowed social consensus to develop. Hayek found Tocqueville inconsequential at times, for example, when he gave an entirely arbitrary and upsettingly negative meaning to the word *individualism*. What Hayek deems "arbitrary" is precisely what separates him radically from Tocqueville. For Hayek, liberty is only negative. It is not to be confused with either political participation (which Tocqueville identified with democracy) or national independence. The nation is a vestige of our primitive tribalism. Tocqueville was assuredly a primitive, according to Hayek's terminology—imperialist by his national passion, as attached to political responsibility as he was to the superior form of the good life, and wary toward the market virtues, which he sought to regulate so that the weakest would not be forced to alienate their freedom. What Hayek had in common with Tocqueville was the nominalism that led him to interpret social phenomena starting from an understanding of the individual. The two also share a mistrust of those who claim they alone hold the secret of the public good and an attachment to social regulation by law. But Hayek departs from Tocqueville in his narrow attachment to the modern notion of liberty, making him more Constant's heir than Tocqueville's.[21] Yet Tocqueville's thought owes much of its glory in modern America to this uncertain affiliation.

In the 1950s the tragic memory of totalitarian experience conferred more radical urgency on thinking about democracy in Europe than in the United States. Tocqueville's return, so evident in Italy and Germany, was even more so in France. We can evaluate the writer's fame by the way his birthday was celebrated. Tocqueville, who until this point had hardly been remembered, suddenly gained the status of a great national writer. His 150th birthday and then the centennial of his death were celebrated during the 1950s.[22] By this point, the expansion of the French middle class made it clear that France would not see a revolution; it was a time when cautious reforms were preferred to French revolutionary politics, while political stakes had shrunk to mean simply the art of growing used to well-being. In later years Tocqueville became the emblem of a party, the head of the lineage of conservative liberal thought invoked while campaigning to tip the scales, amid forgetfulness of the reticence Tocqueville had had toward the bourgeois melting pot Guizot had set to simmer, which melted liberalism down to the defense of private interests.[23] The recent disintegration of Communism since 1989 has increased Tocqueville's prestige by awarding him a victory over Marx which is proclaimed definitive.

Tocqueville's rediscovery in Europe cannot be reduced to the maladjusted match between his thought and party politics or to post–Cold War ideological jousting. Among intellectuals, his rediscovery also benefited from the prestige of the social sciences, which dominated the intellectual universe during the 1950s and 1960s, even winning over history, thanks to the *Annales* school.[24] Following American sociology, the French social sciences began to emphasize the increasing importance of the middle classes. The nineteenth century had felt social separations sharply as it drew to a close. The prosperity of the 1960s shrank the gulf between poor and rich. As Aron noted, the society of the 1930s resembled Marx's vision, and the society of the 1960s, Tocqueville's.[25] Tocqueville suddenly regained his stimulating power, as the person who had positioned the notion of equality centrally in his thinking about modernity without having imagined democracy necessarily succeeded by some kind of socialism.

We can understand this reopening of the Tocquevillean question of the relationship between equality and liberty by studying Raymond Aron's reading of Tocqueville. Aron presided over the publication of Tocqueville's works from 1979 to 1983 and is often considered the twentieth-century Tocqueville. Aron is exemplary of the renewal in interpretations even in the unexpectedness of his encounter with Tocqueville.[26] Aron did not receive Tocqueville from a tradition of sociologists or French philosophers, though no one was better placed to collect the final vestiges of a nonpositivistic sociology. A student and then collaborator of Celestin Bouglé's, Aron's path to *Democracy* nonetheless was not through him. Elie Halévy might have been the link but was more of the lineage of English utilitarians than of Tocqueville. Like so many others, Aron received his training in German philosophy, especially in Marx. The major part of his works were devoted to a critique of Marx. He discovered Tocqueville only late in life, after 1950, as a consequence of his dissatisfaction with Marxism[27] and his contacts with American sociologists R. Dahl and Daniel Bell. While Aron proclaimed himself the "delayed descendant" of the lineage that went from Montesquieu to Tocqueville and then to Halévy, which he referred to as "the Anglo-Saxon school of our sociology," we must understand that this affiliation is reconstructed to give nonpositivistic sociology a genealogy.

This belated encounter explains the slightly casual use Aron makes of Tocqueville, whose works interest him as a prelude to writing and a stimulus to his own thinking. "Mother ideas" are more important to him than grasping Tocqueville's coherence, lucky premonitions more important than the complexity of Tocqueville's ideas.[28] In the historicist vision of Aron's *Etapes*, Tocqueville appears as an incomplete sociologist, an ancient stratum of a discipline that grows by successive sedimental layering; a "worldly" and hardly rigorous sociologist because he still writes in the common language of ordinary, educated people.[29]

Yet the reading of Tocqueville was no mere stratum in the archaeology of knowledge. It led Aron to place or rather replace the relationship between equality and liberty at the heart of modernity. In Tocqueville's works, Aron was indeed less sensitive to details of argumentation than to the convergence of all the analyses around the two ideas of equality and liberty. As Bergson has written, each philosopher only has one question to ask, always the same. Marx sought a way to reknit social linkages in societies torn apart by class struggle. Tocqueville, according to Aron, sought only the answer to this single question: "All modern Western societies are of an egalitarian tendency: what will be their social and political nature?"[30] Thus reading Tocqueville allowed Aron to retrace the steps that in the nineteenth century had led from concern about democracy to the concern about class struggle. "For us," Aron wrote, "impregnated with Marxism, what refreshed us in the Tocqueville we came back to in the 1950s, capitalism's Indian summer, was the speculation on history centered in social equality and political liberty—not on class struggle or ownership of the means of production."[31]

The speculation centered first of all on social equality. Certainly, "Tocqueville's return" did not do away with the historic distance separating us from him. Mill had criticized Tocqueville for deducing everything from equality while forgetting the role of motor played by the progress of civilization. In his turn, though more subtly, Aron accused Tocqueville of having misunderstood the industrial character of modern societies and the inventiveness that comes from technology. Tocqueville "had the tendency to combine two images, of fundamentally stable societies and societies fundamentally concerned with well-being, but what he did not see clearly enough was that a concern for well-being, combined with the spirit of science, causes an uninterrupted process of discoveries and technical innovations. A revolutionary principle, science, is at work within democratic societies, which are in other regards essentially conservative."[32]

Thus equality does not explain all of modernity. Tocqueville's sin was his penchant for explaining all with a single cause—as the nineteenth century had already said. Even worse, he also sinned by conceptual confusion. By *equality*, we understand legal equality, social equality, and the egalitarian imagination. Tocqueville emphasized the latter realm. He was less interested in social equality than in the appearance of an egalitarian norm which ruled passions, customs, feelings, and ideas. He thus dealt only marginally with pauperism, a side effect— in fact an irremediable one—of industrialization. In his theory, poverty is residual. Aron was not so easily satisfied with democratic abstractions. We are all "Marxists in a sense," said Aron, and we all reread Tocqueville through the experience of a century of calls for social equality. As new Prometheuses, we believe in the possibility of abolishing poverty and illness by technology and science. Retracing Marxism's steps does not mean forgetting how far it had come. For Aron, equality is not so self-evident as Tocqueville believed; it is a gauntlet thrown down to all we are capable of.

From this comes a paradox, that Tocqueville prospered in the twentieth century through the "relative blindness to . . . the social question" that had caused him to be forgotten in the nineteenth century. He

> had essentially leaped over the century of class struggle between the proletariat and industrialists, over the pauperization of the working masses, and he foresaw the society of petty bourgeois concerned with their own small affairs, indifferent to their peers and to larger concerns. . . . Was he right on this central point? Were today's people peers and equals? Was Tocqueville the victim of a double illusion, confusing the equality of the pioneers of 1835 with the legal equality of citizens, confusing aristocratic inequality with inequality par excellence? Modern society puts all young people into the same schools, gives them rights to all jobs, promises them the same opportunities and the same happiness, but re-creates hierarchies of income, prestige, and power that weigh no less heavily on people for not being set down in law, and that refute the implicit thesis of the crowd of innumerable, similar beings.[33]

History had led Aron to reopen questioning Tocqueville on equality; it also caused the problem of liberty to reemerge. "It took the schism between totalitarianism and pluralistic democracies for sociologists finally to discover the historical impact of the problem posed by Tocqueville."[34] Antagonism between the two blocs brought human responsibility in the choice of political regimes up-to-date. Suddenly the tradition of political moralists from Montesquieu to Tocqueville found a new life after the long discredit the social sciences had burdened it with. But for Aron rediscovering Tocqueville did not mean passively adopting Tocqueville's analysis. Tocqueville had feared the tutelary providential state, but modern totalitarianism was neither kind nor protective, and was oppressive in a way that Tocqueville could never have foreseen. Though Aron certainly believed, as had Tocqueville, that modern societies were only liberal out of tradition or survival, he rejected anachronistic readings that sought in Tocqueville's works distinguished patronage for the whining of the well-endowed about too much state and for displeasing denunciations of the providential state.

Above all, from Tocqueville Aron inherited deep repulsion toward historicism.[35] Doubtless, the adversary had changed. Tocqueville struggled against Thiers's and Guizot's historical fatalism; Aron confronted Marxist determinism and Durkheimian sociology. But using different means, both Aron and Tocqueville developed a systematic critique of historical reason and refused the comforts of millenial thinking. The two men might well differ in social origin, professional status, and intellectual points of reference,[36] but both were called to show the virtue of caution. In analyzing totalitarianism, Aron was wary of ideology. As a historian of the Revolution, Tocqueville rejected the philosophes' abstractions. Both made politics more a layering of practices than a realized utopia.[37] As wary of reactionary outbreaks as they were of millenial utopianizing, both were democratic with a hint of skepticism. They had the same style, now exasperated, now ironic, and the same repugnance toward partisan positions, the same repulsion toward revolutionary bandwagons, whether of 1848 or 1968, which condemned them to isolation in spite of themselves. But the rediscovery of the virtue of prudence, which Aron called to the attention of French public opinion, was done in a melancholy mode. Tocqueville, born in a historicist century, believed history's providentialism acted in such a way that democracy mysteriously participated in divine justice; Aron secularized and disenchanted politics. Tocqueville believed in the Enlightenment; Aron participated in the Enlightenment's spirit, but its light had dimmed.[38] This is why it seemed to him that the third party, whether Tocqueville's or Halévy's or his own, "had probably little chance of finding satisfaction, even a quarrelsome satisfaction, with the course of French politics."[39]

Though Aron picked up Tocqueville's question, "Under what conditions can societies neither frugal nor small, which have erased social distinctions, be free?"[40] he did not accept the answer. Tocqueville thought it was possible to prevent the risk of despotism by protecting laws and civic participation. But this apology for self-government masked the role of bureaucracy in modern societies and was silent about authority, which caused war and international politics to be relegated to the level of circumstance. Aron was less afraid of individualism than of the rending of the social body in the conflict of classes, races, and nations. As a result, he felt that the distance between power and civil society which Tocqueville sought to shrink was actually necessary. Aron deemed bureaucracy inevitable as a way to manage the complexity of modern societies and ultimately was more interested in the mechanisms of representation and the play of institutions than in local-level democracy. This is why he preferred the first *Democracy*'s institutional analyses to the study of democratic culture Tocqueville did in 1840.

Each of these two thinkers reveals his strengths and weaknesses in contact with the other, and each betrays the weight of historical experience that changed the premises of the problems the two men posed in like terms. Both posed the question of equality. But Tocqueville admirably analyzed the unending work of democracy and wrote about democratic abstraction at the risk of not seeing the incessant resurgence of real inequalities. Aron, heir to a half century of the providential state, was an attentive analyst of social stratification but, on the other hand, misunderstood the power of the egalitarian imagination and the strength of democratic universalism. Both were concerned about liberty. But Tocqueville constructed his praise for self-government on not discussing sovereignty; Aron explored sovereign national rivalries without dealing with the insidious peril of political bodies coming apart.

The astounding thing is that the two men together gained public recognition at the end of the 1970s, Aron pulling Tocqueville behind him, Tocqueville conferring upon Aron the luster of an intellectual lineage rooted in the Enlightenment. It is an irony of history that both thinkers about differences between free and servile societies had founded their own kind of ecumenism, Tocqueville even more than Aron. The liberalism that today claims Tocqueville as its own is that era of good feeling, universal centrism, and the third party which Aron despaired of miraculously becoming a majority. The cost has been the loss of its impact. Liberalism is now merely that vaguely charming word indicating a weariness with social control, attachment to the negative liberty of the individual, and celebration of civil society.

In Search of Democratic Culture, 1960s–1980s

Aron had stressed the problem of institutions, especially admiring the first *Democracy*. In later years questions about democratic culture arose that led to a rereading of the second *Democracy*.

This new questioning was not limited to one specific school or movement. We see it among thinkers as diverse as ethnologist Louis Dumont, philosopher Claude Lefort, and sociologists Michel Crozier and François Bourricaud. All came to read Tocqueville, as Aron had, from other intellectual perspectives. All had been stimulated by the American social sciences. François Bourricaud, who had read Tocqueville in 1950 at Aron's suggestion, only discovered the importance of his works while living in the United States where Tocqueville was a classic.[41] Lefort combined his uninterrupted deciphering of the great texts of political philosophy with a critical interest in ethnology, especially Kardiner's notion of culture and basic personality.[42] Crozier's references were American organizational sociology (Merton, Parsons), Bell's idea of the end of ideologies,[43] and cultural anthropology. Dumont came out of the same anthropological lineage. None can simply be lumped into the Aronian movement as Tocqueville's heirs often are. Lefort and Crozier began their intellectual journeys in the Temps Modernes group; seated to the left of the intellectual parliament, they drew near Aron in a way both partial and unlikely.

Among such a diverse group of men and Aron, beyond mutual esteem, was a common intellectual universe revealed by their interest in Tocqueville. They shared an interest in the nature of democracy, a distance from ideologies, and the desire to bring the criterion of liberty back into study of society and politics. In this they broke with a conception of the social sciences which assigned sociologists only Durkheim or Auguste Comte as their legitimate intellectual genealogy. Let us take Dumont and Crozier as examples, for their encounter with Tocqueville seems the most improbable.

Louis Dumont renewed Tocqueville's contrast between the two ideal types of democratic and hierarchical people.[44] This contrast, which appears throughout Tocqueville's work, emerges in Tocqueville from both feeling and intellect. It stemmed from his painful perception of the rupture between hierarchal society and the new era but took the form of a systematic intellectual exploration. On one hand, Tocqueville studied inegalitarian societies like England, Algeria, and India; on the other, egalitarian ones like America and France. But the systematic character of his process was hidden by the fact that his texts were published in a scattered way, or not published at all.[45] In 1899 Celestin Bouglé was inspired by *Democracy* in his own *Les idées égalitaires*, and then in 1908 he considered inegalitarian ideas in his *Essais sur le régime des castes*. He followed Tocqueville's path through India without even realizing it. Inspired by Bouglé, whose works he was editing, and by Tocqueville, whose heir he claimed to be, Louis Dumont seemed not to know Tocqueville's works on Algeria and India any better than Bouglé. But like Bouglé he was interested to find in *Democracy* an interest in collective representations and a desire for self-understanding through reflection in the mirror of the other.[46]

Dumont took from Tocqueville the elements he needed to deal with both democratic and hierarchal society. Crozier found the basis for a comparison of French and American democracies. The comparative method in Crozier predates his reading Tocqueville, for he had studied American labor unions very early on and from this study had formed an analysis of French culture that was woven of remnants of the revolutionary spirit, the rejection of social confrontation, and the appeal to tutelary protection by the state.[47] Writing *Le phénomène bureau-cratique* (Seuil, 1963) led Crozier to work with the writings of Tocqueville, whom he cites more than any other noncontemporary author.

Crozier turned to Tocqueville in retracing the tradition of the social sciences. Tocqueville had opened up the path to the study of administrative practices in their relationship to a cultural system. Later sociology did not follow him. The psychology of nations became shallowly deterministic. Taine, Le Play's social reformers, the regionalists of the 1910s, and public commentators until Michel Debré at times attempted analysis of French cultural specificity but with aims that were always narrow, partisan, and conservative. According to Crozier, it was not until the new organizational sociology that studies of collective customs were again undertaken.

In Tocqueville, Crozier found a way to resituate within the *longue durée* the French cultural characteristics he had observed in public organizations of the 1960s. Tocqueville demonstrated "the logical link between individual isolation and the lack of cooperative spirit, on one hand, and the isolation of different social categories and their perpetual struggles for artificial privileges, on the other" (284). The obsession with equality led to eliminating all direct relations of dependency and to accepting only the combination of abstract rationality and arbitrariness that characterized absolute monarchy. From this arose the difficulty of changing the system without resorting to revolutions. Like Tocqueville and the nineteenth-century public commentators, Crozier could not separate sociological research from reformist aims. He in effect placed his expertise at the service of developing a new, more flexible kind of organization through which French democracy would converge with American democracy and set himself the task of education for democracy that was distanced from longing for the past or for communism's utopian attraction.

Interest in democratic culture is not confined to university circles. Today, many general readers seek out Tocqueville's analysis of the grandeur and erring ways of the democratic idea: the grandeur of human rights finally recognized, the errant individualism that inclines citizens to set themselves apart from each other.

The conjuncture of causes of this rediscovery is reduced national particularities and the 1960s' weakening of the sense of belonging to a nation. The grand imperialist politics of France, England, and America encountered so many Third World liberation movements that the nation ceased to be the obligatory framework for feeling one belonged to a whole. The entire Western world faced the same problems—the crisis of the nation, challenges to the providential state—while movements of "minorities" calling for the right to difference took over from discredited messianic hopes. Henceforth, it was less a question of totalitarianism opposing democratic pluralism than of the need to call for both the right to universal equality and the right to difference. History thus justified Tocqueville against Aron's reticence toward him, but not without equivocation.

In Tocqueville we find happy formulas for denouncing the illusions of individuals who believe themselves complete and solitary while in reality being nothing more than monads whose tastes change with those of the day. Popular anger about modernity, into which psychoanalysis, feminism, progressive education, moral laxity, and the decline of culture can be read in no particular order, goes far beyond popular readings of Tocqueville and has become a commonplace.[48] But Tocqueville confers the dignity of a historical law upon this commonplace.

Like Tocqueville, many willingly point fingers at the providential state, which transforms citizens into eternal children withdrawn into themselves. But the tutelary state's sweet despotism has soured, while over its head the shadow of totalitarianism still lurks. Tocqueville thus has become the prophet of all the state's detractors, in a confused, exaggerated, anachronistic reading of his works. Here we must denounce, if not "Tocqueville's error," at least his exaggerated fears.[49] Tocqueville's worries fed on the spectacle of the embryonic politics of public assistance he witnessed, which he feared even more because he lacked the conceptual tools of an economic analysis. Tocqueville's prophecy was untimely, and what is more, it has been disproved, for today the state is harassed by contradictory claims and called on to exercise responsibilities that citizens ordinarily deny it the means to pay for. We demand much, we obey little, and living comfortably as we please, we are slaves only metaphorically.

Tocqueville and Revolutionary Historians

Historical perspective is secondary but not absent in Aron, Bourricaud, Lefort, Crozier, and Dumont. They focus on Tocqueville's analysis of democracy in gestation. In fact, before 1980, few scholars wondered as Tocqueville had about the origins of a French democratic tradition which thought itself exceptional. It was the crisis in the idea of the Republic which invited scholars to rewrite the origin story by reworking Tocqueville's thinking.

In France the time seems to have come to envisage the nineteenth century extended until after the Second World War as a single period. Republican historiography long reduced the nineteenth century to insignificance in the linear transition to the present. Today we are more attentive to revision than to continuity. Suddenly, Tocqueville's work has acquired the power to give our history back its strangeness. There is no better example than Tocqueville's sudden glory in 1989, the commemorative year in which France by celebrating itself had to choose its identity. The Revolution's centennial, commemorated in 1889, forgot Tocqueville, made useless by the triumph of the Republic. In one gesture, the bicentennial in 1989 made use of both renewed interest in Tocqueville and thoughts about the end of French exceptionality.

Rather than surveying historiographical debates, it is better to stick to a single reader of Tocqueville's. In the 1950s Raymond Aron had restored Tocqueville to sociologists, philosophers, and political scientists. François Furet, who had succeeded Aron as the head of the publication of the complete works, restored Tocqueville to the historians of the 1970s.[50] In fact, there are many similarities in the paths of the two men. Aron had discovered Tocqueville out of theoretical disenchantment with German philosophy of history. Furet came to Tocqueville out of political disenchantment with revolutionary messianism. In fact, it is a constant that since Laboulaye and the Second Empire liberals, thinkers develop a taste for Tocqueville only out of disillusionment.

For both men, disillusionment had its origin in the shock of experience with totalitarianism; both Aron and Furet deciphered this using the light shed by Tocqueville. One made the contrast between totalitarianism and democracy central to his thinking; the other sought the historical roots of the contrast. Radicals' reverence for the Revolution taken as a whole and then the historical affiliation between 1789 and 1917 established by Mathiez had led to thinking of the French Revolution, including the Terror, as the universal matrix for human emancipation. It took the collapse of Communist regimes in thought and then in action for the Revolution's fascination to dissipate. In leaving Communism behind and repudiating the Jacobin heritage, Furet began to doubt that the Revolution was in fact the basis of a universal history. Rupture in the link of identity between the French Revolution and the Russian Revolution allowed comparison with other revolutions, first the English and then the American, which made the singularity of French tradition's obsession with the general will stand out in contrast.[51] The thinking about totalitarianism that Aron had begun thus found its extension in a historical meditation on French exceptionality.

As he aged, public opinion had accorded Aron a delayed respect for his defense of liberty which marked French conversion to the liberal politics promoted by Tocqueville. Long contested, the theses of François Furet in turn met with general assent in 1989, sign of a shift in opinion which he preceded and in part led.

What did Furet take from Tocqueville? Not so much facts as hypotheses. This did not mean replacing the study of history with the study of interpretations of it, though such a temptation can be seen in writings derived from Furet's works. Every generation of historians outdates some of the works of those who came before, and we can no longer unreservedly subscribe to Tocqueville's sketch of ancien régime society.[52] But the cumulative nature of scholarship does not imply that we must reject all questions or hypotheses developed in the past.

From Tocqueville, Furet mainly took an idea: that the Revolution can be explained upstream, by absolutism. It was absolutism that produced the nation, imposing equality by sapping the aristocracy. Thus we must seek the seeds of egalitarian passion and the uniquely French obsession with the cult of state reason in the system of absolutist representations and practices.

Furet recognized Tocqueville's merit of not reducing the Revolution to a rebound. Tocqueville tried to think about the gulf separating Enlightenment rationalism from obsession with the general will. Between Louis XIV's administrative vision of the state as manager and Robespierre's state which sought to institute a new society, he saw a difference in kind. True, his study of the Revolution's lurch forward was hardly fleshed out. Tocqueville foresaw the mystery of the event without having the time to get close to it, and perhaps without wanting to. The revolutionaries' radicalism ranked in Tocqueville's thought only as a secondary cause. It was absolutism, by depriving the French of political experience, which was the first cause of the Revolution's outrages.

This is where Furet splits from Tocqueville. Both start with the problem of the deregulation of democratic politics and the wrong turn taken by the passion for equality. Both try to describe the rupture of old links of dependency and the emergence of modern individualism. But Tocqueville examined the prevalence of despotism in France, manifested in the transition from absolutism to Caesarism. Furet scrutinized the appearance of the obsession with the general will.

One emphasized absolutism as continuous with the empire; the other stressed the rupture created by the revolutionary period in which the entire nineteenth century according to him became intelligible.

Tocqueville had seen the philosophical character of the Revolution and admired 4 August's sublime folly, but without going into it. And can one explain human nature? To him, the Revolution seemed to make the natural taste for liberty arise, hidden but not destroyed in the dark night of absolutism. Furet begins where Tocqueville left off: what intrigues him in the Revolution is its philosophical character, "the dignity of an idea and the nature of a beginning" which it confers. "The idea of human universality" creates "the intellectual unity of a Revolution founded on human rights."[53] Moving away from his experience with the Second Empire to the study of absolutism, Tocqueville sought the causes of French complacency toward Caesarism. In the same movement, which leads from concern for the present to knowledge of the past, Furet seeks in the Revolution the origins of claims to rights that today define Western egalitarian culture.

Explanatory system determines method. Making the Revolution, as a philosophical event, the matrix for French history, Furet emphasizes the genealogy of ideas. What is said or thought is more important than events, *mentalités,* and the variegations of practice. Marxist political shake-ups led an entire generation of historians trained after the war to slip from studying economic or social infrastructures to studying the history of *mentalités.* Today we witness the radicalization of this movement, renewing the long-decried history of ideas. By neglecting this history, Tocqueville missed a way to explain the Revolution's utopia. But he explained something else, often hidden by modern scholars' slippage from the skeptical reading of administrative archives Tocqueville did to devote themselves to the history of texts, even to the study of "great texts": the weight of the everyday, of conformism, of mechanical adherence to power. Tocqueville believed that only a small part of our awareness was at work in our everyday actions, that our actions said more about the social than our discourse, and that the commonplaces of an era were more instructive than its philosophical canon. Though he did not explain the seductive power of revolutionary radicalism, he explained its decomposition well—the cynical thinking of some who legitimated their particular impulses by rational discourse in which they no longer believed and the nauseating adherence and passive terror of others who supported despotism for want of the ideas, courage, or power to do otherwise. He introduced us to a history of cultures which would account for the consent to servitude. That is why he allows us to think today not about the establishment of Communism but about its duration and how long it took to fall apart.

Tocqueville and Us

Whatever disagreements there are within historical analysis, scholars agree in finding in Tocqueville's work a meditation on French exceptionality.[54] Tocqueville's return today is the symptom of a partial escape from this exceptionalness.

We return to Tocqueville's emphasis on the preservation of individual initiative; we like his critique of state reason and his denunciation of the confusion between law and right. In the nineteenth century Tocqueville had pleaded in vain for administrations to be subject to ordinary courts and for critical examination of the notion of public interest. Between the American tradition founded on individual rights and a procedural conception of justice and the French tradition that stressed distributive justice and public interest, no compromise seemed possible. Tocqueville's thought today is at the heart of debates on constitutional control. This questioning of French tradition grows with contestation of the legitimacy of administrative courts. Yet it would be excessive to speak of a conversion to the American model. In answer to cheerleaders for an American judicial system who gain new authority from the system of European law now under construction,[55] French jurists can retort that the administrative jurisdiction of the Council of State has not been shown to be less protective of the individual than the Supreme Court, while having avoided relegating the state to impotence and reducing universal suffrage to a subsidiary role. In so doing, they underscore the risk of a detour of which Tocqueville was aware and which his successors have not always escaped. Human rights language tends to disqualify any assertion of collective aims and any search for the common good. From exalting human rights, it is easy to slide into a civil society cult of spontaneity. If we retain from Tocqueville only his critique of collective power, we risk making him a partisan of a democracy in which we all pursue our own personal dreams, where democracy, for lack of a common ideal, is torn between competing interests, while the abstaining state stands by and watches. In opposition to those who, thinking they follow Tocqueville, proclaim that liberty begins where politics ends, Tocqueville did not believe that the preservation of the private sphere could be the sole criterion for a free society. Thus denouncing the state was less important than restoring the political vocation of citizens.

A "new kind" of liberal, Tocqueville in fact was as mistrustful of individualism as he was of state despotism and refused to choose democracy over the republic or civil society over politics. The idea of rights was for him "simply that of virtue introduced into the political world" (*DA* 1:244). In this, Tocqueville was part of the Aristotelian and Christian tradition in which virtue is the accomplishment of human telos as a social being and a member of the lineage the Americans call communitarianism, which since the nineteenth century has accompanied individual liberalism, serving as its corrective.[56] Thus there is nothing surprising today in our searching Tocqueville for the means to rehabilitate public virtue compromised by too much Jacobin excess. Doubtless, he does not leave us a theoretical reflection, but he analyzes the collective practices in which such virtue is exercised.

Yet there is an urgency, now more than in the nineteenth century. The generations after the Revolution had trembled at the thought of the disintegration of the social body. There is much greater fear of it today, in France as in America. Mobility in modern societies often makes political commitment and pursuit of a career conflict. How can the political model of the self-governing polis be made to coexist with the economic model of the market? Is civic feeling merely vestigial now, and hope of restoring it utopian? The end of our century thus seems to embody Tocqueville's most somber prognoses[57] and calls us to seek in his footsteps the means to renew political culture. Some give themselves over to nostalgia, forgetting that the idyllic image of bygone communities hides a chilly conservatism and social control by notables.[58] Others seek new forms of civic humanism needed to prevent equality from slipping into uniformity. For them, the discredit that strikes national politics today does not include religious, cultural, ecological, and charitable associations. They wonder whether civic activism must not now take place through plural networks of belonging, and whether the dramatic expansion of public debate is no longer coextensive with the exercise of voting rights.[59] There is nothing surprising in Tocqueville's relevancy being proclaimed from every corner.[60]

For Aron the world of the 1930s resembled the universe of Marx's class struggle, and the world of the 1960s, Tocqueville's egalitarian dream. The latter has been so emphasized that we cannot escape hearing about Tocqueville's prophetic powers. Anachronism plays its part in such posthumous glorification. Yet it remains true that Tocqueville foresaw the shift in our egalitarian societies: the hedonistic individualism of democracy that henceforth reigns uncontested; the end of the revolutionary spirit and accompanying lack of civic commitment; the attraction to the market, God's long agony, etc. It is all enough to feed a bittersweet bitterness among those who deplore the insipidity of the modern world without really missing the era of poverty and patriotic furor. Tocqueville did not share the bitterness of some of his heirs. He believed modern societies compatible with the passion for liberty. One of the paradoxes of Communism's recent collapse is that it proved Tocqueville's correctness compared to Marx and to his own heirs, by showing that human beings can call at the same time for freedom of the imagination and freedom in the marketplace, civic participation and equality.[61] In addition, Tocqueville allows both western Europe—materially satisfied but worried about democracy's ills—and eastern Europe—drunk with having won its own freedom—to restore the threads of a shared tradition. He had wanted to be the bridge between France and America, and in his final incarnation, he reappears now as the tutelary divinity who presides over exchanges among Europeans reconciled in their quest for an equality within liberty.

Conclusion: Tocqueville in French Culture

SINCE 1946 Tocqueville has come back to us from America miraculously spared by the ravages of time. And the thinker's freshness, drawing new strength in the undertow of Communism, is so apt we call him a prophet. The only deduction to be made is that in the nineteenth century he was misunderstood or at least delivered unto the nattering of fools.

But Tocqueville was never such a loner. I shall not here reemphasize his contribution to knowledge. From 1835 to the 1880s, *Democracy* was the unrevised Baedeker to political America, and everything admirable about American institutions was to be learned from its pages. But the enduring glory of the work resulted in part from French ignorance. It was ultimately inevitable that the French would discover its inadequacy in describing America after the Civil War. *Old Regime* suffered less from advances in scholarship, without completely escaping obsolescence. For it was less its data that had become stale than the stance Tocqueville took in writing it. Starting with the end of the nineteenth century, public commentators gave way to specialists, and moralizing language to the positivism of science.

But Tocqueville's contribution to French culture lies less in his scholarship than in his new way of thinking about modernity. In France, and even more broadly in Europe, his works' reception went hand in hand with the fortunes and misfortunes of the democratic transition upon which they conferred such dramatic pathos.

Tocqueville was seen as the eloquent prophet deploring democratic failings in the biblical tradition of jeremiads and seeking to smooth democracy's path. In fact, he used the prophets' declamatory and eschatological rhetoric: "Soon it will be too late . . ." The descent into barbarity threatens careless democracy, as hell gapes open for the sinner too slow to repent. Neither *Democracy* nor *Old Regime* was read with indifferent serenity, as nice conversational works. Their anxiety over the health of democracies, their insistent proclaiming that humanity had "embarked" upon democracy and that it was urgent to side with grandeur, brought Tocqueville ever closer to Jansenism and gave his words the dignity of a speech on ultimate ends.

Unfortunately, the prophet's position is an ungrateful one. Sermonizers grow dull over time with their inexhaustible speeches; the will is weak, resistance against the Truth stubborn, and thus the duty to continue writing interminable, whence the formidable yawns of Tocqueville's readers from Balzac to Barbey. To liberalism's adversaries, Tocqueville seemed the knight of lost causes whose proclamations struck only those distracted deaf ears spoken of in the Bible.[1] Once the Republic was established, eschatological rhetoric and calls to liberty lost any practical impact. There was laughter when the doughty Lemercier opened the parliamentary session of 12 January 1897 by crying out, "We must, my dear colleagues, speak the great names of Montesquieu and Tocqueville so as to repeat as they did that democracies have greater need than other forms of government of practicing Virtue." Tocqueville's chagrined moralism seemed henceforth to exude an aristocratic odor, and his optimism toward will, which won out over his pessimism toward reason, was misunderstood.

Though Tocqueville was the thinker of the democratic transition, he was above all a critical one. Even during his time of glory, he was criticized for proposing an opposition culture more than a government. Indifferent to all political forms, he seems reduced to a sterile Cassandra, unheard and powerless. This led to the cyclical character of the attention given him. Though he had been masterful in troubled times, once the Republic was well established, he was merely a worn-out thinker. The French never raised him to the rank of founding father in the republican pantheon.

In French tradition Tocqueville was much more than a democratic philosopher—he was the philosopher of the "natural" corruption of democracy. His strength lies in having shown that Jacobinism, socialism, and Caesarism drew their seductive power from their resemblance to democratic liberty. For like liberty, they flatter the taste for grandeur though they satisfy it only by proxy, making popular will or state will the exclusive beneficiary of autonomy. From this came the ascendance of Tocqueville's work in the dark hours of the Second Empire: he made French history intelligible, a history which appears to be that of great exploited men who unfailingly reaffirm servitude while believing they are founding liberty.

Does this mean that he left nothing constructive to the French?

He left them all his thinking on structural guarantees and norms of justice by the central place he accorded religion, whose function was to preserve a kind of transcendence which made a place for the protestations of moral conscience. Of course, at a practical level, his thought was of little help. For religion to be a goad to the spirit of liberty and not the rampart of moral order, dogmatic, social, and institutional distance between the churches and politics had to be maintained. The American example had led Tocqueville to believe that this autonomy of religion from politics was possible. This separation between arenas was uneasy in France. The Catholic Church's principle of consubstantial authority linked it to oppressive regimes. And Protestantism was never to be a majority religion in France. Tocqueville's skill at never speaking of anything beyond an indeterminate religion could not spare his work from suffering the lamentations of an intellectually bloodless Catholic Church and hostility from the republicans. If the pages Tocqueville devoted to religion were such an irritatant to thinking, it was less by their positive content than by the tragic uncertainty they contained: the anguish of the death of God which Tocqueville was afraid he deciphered democracy presaged by its advance; the persistent quest for a transcendence which might tear humans away from idolatrous satisfaction with themselves.

Tocqueville's political science was no less distant from French tradition than his religious thought. He mistrusted both abstraction and the philosophical temptation to rebuild society from the ground up. The public good for him was neither determinable a priori by common reasoning, as it was for Guizot, nor embedded in the system of interests, nor a miraculous extract from the alchemy of the general will. Tocqueville radicalized the critique of constructivism so much that he took issue with the very notion of the state as teacher to society, popular from the Revolution to Ferry. Since 1789 French tradition had continued to dream of training new citizens through uniform national education. Tocqueville unmasked the unholiness of the human creature who sought to rival God's order and offered only a sinister parody of it. For "God, therefore, stands in no need of general ideas"; he "discerns in each man the resemblances that assimilate him to all his fellows, and the differences that distinguish him from them" (*DA* 2:13). The state's pedagogues, in contrast, advanced like barbarians, and in their desire for uniformity, they acted on brains like "those peoples of the eastern coast of Africa [who] had the custom of placing the heads of newborn babies in a kind of mold which gave all of them the same shape. There everyone has either a very high or a very flat crown depending on the rule adopted during the era of their birth."[2]

Logically, because he was more sensitive to individual autonomy than to the search for the public good, Tocqueville developed no doctrine of sovereign authority. Instead, he substituted for the French notion of a single, indivisible authority the American notion of a group of communities. No doubt he was trying to combine self-government with the concern for national unity by drawing a distinction between governmental centralization and administrative centralization. This initially famous distinction became illusory. Yet for all its theoretical weakness, it has still been politically effective in advancing the idea of a local independence which would not threaten sovereignty. To say that the local level and the jury were "liberty's primary schools" meant capturing the seductive pedagogical utopian legacy of the Revolution to benefit self-government. Tocqueville thus influenced common opinion by separating his praise for self-government from praise for the aristocracy,[3] which allowed certain sons of the Revolution to surmount their Jacobin prejudices. It is obviously difficult to tell how much reading Tocqueville was responsible for shifts in mind-sets and practices. Tocqueville's cause triumphed only when his thought became lost in the anonymity of public opinion. But in this he had reached the aim he had set for himself, of spreading within public opinion some ideas "in the hope that, if they be accurate, they will end little by little transformed into passions and deeds."[4] In French history he left a long trail of protest against the tutelage of Power.

Tocqueville's work thus has been far more than a link in the historical chain of liberalism after Montesquieu and Constant and before modern democratic liberalism. The word *liberal* is only attractive in its vagueness. One cannot be simply a liberal. One can be an authoritarian liberal, a conservative liberal, a monarchist liberal, a republican liberal, a democratic liberal, a wise old liberal, a "new kind of liberal" like Tocqueville, or even under the Third Republic, "liberalish" or "liberawful." There are liberal practices, liberal sensibilities, liberals who were on the Left and on the Right, and sometimes, with the help of age, both in succession—but there is no French liberalism. The lineage in which we place Tocqueville's work is less important to us than its exoticism. An aristocrat by instinct and a democrat by reason, at the crossroads of French and American democratic cultures, Tocqueville has been the repressed side of French democratic tradition.

Notes

Abbreviations

BN = Bibliothèque nationale

Boesche = Roger Boesche, ed. *Tocqueville: Selected Letters on Politics and Society.* Trans. James Toupin and Roger Boesche. Berkeley, Los Angeles, and London: Univ. of California Press, 1985.

DA = Alexis de Tocqueville. *Democracy in America.* 2 vols. Trans. Henry Reeve. Ed. Phillips Bradley. New York: Knopf, 1976.

MU = *Moniteur universel,* France

NRF = *Nouvelle revue française*

OC = Alexis de Tocqueville. *Oeuvres complètes.* France: Gallimard, 1951–. See list of individual volume contents in Bibliography.

OC (Bmt) = Alexis de Tocqueville. *Oeuvres complètes.* Ed. Gustave de Beaumont. 9 vols. France: Michel Lévy, 1864–66. See list of individual volume contents in Bibliography.

OR = Alexis de Tocqueville. *The Old Regime and the French Revolution.* Trans. Stuart Gilbert. New York: Doubleday Anchor Books, 1955.

PUF = Presses universitaires de France publishing house

RDM = *Revue des deux mondes,* France, 1835–1914

RMM = *Revue de métaphysique et de morale,* France, 1896–1923

Introduction: The Transition to Democracy

1. This research was part of a dissertation, "Tocqueville dans la culture française," supervised by F. Gerbod and done at the University of Paris X-Nanterre in 1991. The present work is result of that dissertation. I would like to thank Louis Audibert, Marie-Claire Bancquart, François Furet, Françoise Gerbod, André Jardin, Lucien Jaume, Jacqueline Lalouette, René Rémond, and Pierre Rosanvallon, whose remarks were especially precious to me.

2. Unpublished [prosecution address], Tocqueville Archives.

3. [Hervé] de Tocqueville, *Histoire philosophique du règne de Louis XV* (Paris: Amyot, 1847), and *Coup d'oeil sur le règne de Louis XVI*, 2 vols. (Paris: Amyot, 1850). These two works, a century out of date, are overly wedded to chronologizing and limited to analysis of the role of key people. Alexis de Tocqueville cites them nowhere. See Jardin, *Alexis de Tocqueville*, 18–39, and Robert R. Palmer, *The Two Tocquevilles, Father and Son: Hervé and Alexis de Tocqueville on the Coming of the French Revolution* (Princeton, N.J.: Princeton Univ. Press, 1987).

4. Gaston Deschamps, *Le temps*, 17 Jan. 1897.

5. See the testimony of his friend Jean-Jacques Ampère: "Making an estimable book would not have satisfied him; he rightfully looked much higher, first so that the popularity of his book would make it more useful, and also out of desire that the book be popular in its own right" (*OC* 11:444).

6. Open letter, 31 Oct. 1837, *OC* 3, 2:46.

1. The New Political Science, 1820s-1830s

1. Letter to Kergorlay, 4 Sept. 1837, *OC* 13, 1:472.

2. In the famous words of Royer-Collard, speech of 22 Jan. 1822.

3. Royer-Collard, speech of 17 May 1820, in Prosper de Barante, *La vie politique de M. Royer-Collard: Ses discours et ses écrits*, 2 vols. (Paris, 1851).

4. Guizot, *Mémoires* 1:159, cited in Rosanvallon, *Le moment Guizot*, 26–28.

5. See his notes on Thiers, *OC* 16:537–40.

6. Class notes on Guizot, *OC* 16:439–534.

7. *OC* 16:68.

8. See his pamphlet, "De la charte provinciale."

9. "La vérité, 1830: Un mois avant la révolution du 28 juillet," and "Conversations assez curieuses de moi-même avec MM. Guizot et Boinvilliers," *OC* 16:397–408.

10. "La vérité," *OC* 16:400.

11. Reprinted in *Mélanges philosophiques* and again 1 Nov. 1841 in the first issue of *Revue indépendante*, published by Pierre Leroux. It was in relation to Jouffroy's skepticism that Tocqueville sought to clarify his position in a letter to Francisque de Corcelles, 12 Apr. 1835, *OC* 15, 1:54.

12. He recounted his youthful crisis of skepticism to Sophie Swetchine in a letter dated 26 Feb. 1857, *OC* 15, 2:315.

13. Unpublished letter to Charles Stöffels of 21 Apr. 1830.

14. *Souvenirs* in *OC* 12:86.

15. "Connected to the royalists by a few common principles and by a thousand familial ties," he wrote, "I see myself in a sense chained to a party whose conduct often seems to me scarcely honorable and almost always extravagant" (unpublished letter to Chabrol, 18 Oct. 1831).

16. Custine, *Letters*, 420–21.

17. See Curtius, *La littérature européenne et le Moyen Age latin* (Paris: PUF, 1956); Maria Piwinska, "Le vieillard désespéré et l'histoire," *Romantisme* 36 (1982): 3–14.

18. Rémusat admits ingenuously that if England "had not had its institutions, I would not have dreamed of crossing the channel" (Charles de Rémusat, *Mémoires de ma vie*, ed. Charles Pouthas, 5 vols. [Paris: Plon, 1958–67], 2:160).

19. See letter to Beaumont, 5 Oct. 1828, *OC* 8, 1:57.

20. See René Rémond, *Les Etats-Unis devant l'opinion française* (Paris: Armand Colin, 1962), 2:547–52.

21. See *Voyage en Amérique* in *OC* 5, 1:89, 92.

22. Cited in Rédier, *Comme disait M. de Tocqueville*, 92–93.

23. Unpublished letter to Charles Stöffels, 4 Nov. 1830.

24. Letter to Eugène Stöffels, 21 Feb. 1831, *OC* (Bmt) 6:411–12.

25. Letter to Kergorlay, 18 May 1831, *OC* 13, 1:224.

26. *OC* 5, 1:202.

27. Unpublished letter to Orglandes, 24 Nov. 1834.

28. *DA* 1:7, 93–94.

29. Boesche, 62.

30. *OC* (Bmt) 7:476–77.

31. See letter to Corcelle, 22 July 1854, *OC* 15, 1:108.

32. *DA* 1:211–12, 2: 241: Men are "once again equal and alike."

33. References to political or administrative texts became increasingly scarce, while literary references (Chateaubriand, La Bruyère, Lamartine, Montaigne, Pascal, Racine, Madame de Sévigné) increased. Their function was ornamental. The notes which remain concern either the first three chapters on American geography and history or the chapter on the "current state and probable future" of the Union.

34. Merely an allusion. *DA* 1:259.

35. See just a few allusions: *DA* 1:15–16, 230–31, 262, 297–98, 302, 317, 340–41. Only in his chapter on the future of the United States does Tocqueville give the date of his trip (334).

36. Letter to Beaumont, 6 Jan. 1839, *OC* 8:1, 330.

37. Draft of the second *Democracy*, in the critical edition of *De la démocratie en Amérique* published by Vrin, 270.

38. "Mémoire sur le paupérisme," in *OC* 16:132.

39. There is a "hidden incline which impels the aristocracy to seek the welfare of the smaller number and the democrat to favor interests identical to his own" (*DA* 1:244).

40. *Voyages* in *OC* 5, 1:121.

41. Letter to Eugène Stöffels, 24 July 1836, *OC* (Bmt) 6:431.

42. Tocqueville himself did not escape the nightmares of French history. He presents the tyranny of opinion in the United States as the basis of a legislative despotism not unlike Jacobinism.

43. *DA* 1:184–85.

44. In the United States senators "accurately represent the majority of the nation," "but they represent only the elevated thoughts that are current in the community and the generous propensities that prompt its nobler actions rather than the petty passions that disturb or the vices that disgrace it" (*DA* 1:205).

45. In Jan. 1836 Tocqueville specifically chose the galleys of his chapter on the "point of departure" to read to the Academy (Archives of the Institut de France).

46. See his letter to Mill of June 1835: "A French democrat is, in general, a man who wants to place the exclusive direction of the society not in the hands of all of the people, but in the hands of a certain portion of the people and who, to arrive at this result, only understands the use of material force" (Boesche, 101).

47. *DA* 1:7, 12.

48. "It is impossible, after the most strenuous exertions, to raise the intelligence of the people above a certain level. Whatever may be the facilities of acquiring information, whatever may be the profusion of easy methods and cheap science, the human mind can never be instructed and developed without devoting considerable time to these objects. The greater or lesser ease with which people can live without working is a sure index of intellectual progress" (*DA* 1:200).

49. On Gosselin, see Nicole Felkay, *Balzac et ses éditeurs, 1822–1837: Essai sur la librairie romantique* (Paris: Promodis, 1987). Gosselin was born in Paris in 1795. His father was a cook. In 1810 he went to work for the bookseller Nicolle whose shop he took over in 1820. He had a reputation as a greedy editor, one not shy of lawsuits.

50. Unpublished letter to Stöffels, 14 Apr. 1842.

51. Letter to Beaumont, 14 July 1834, *OC* 8, 1:141.

52. Letter to Beaumont, 1 Apr. 1835, *OC* 8, 1:151.

53. See the anonymous article in *La dominicale*, "De la presse en 1835," 1836, 412, which notes the exceptional nature of Tocqueville's success: "Works about politics are surely few and far between, and will become scarcer everyday, because of great discussions about politics in the press, which does not allow a political question the time to mature. Thus we cannot count, in this realm of ideas, more than 275 works or brochures, printed on average in fewer than 1,000 copies."

54. Letter to Beaumont, 14 July 1834, *OC* 8, 1:149.

55. Yet Tocqueville hastened to publish in order to benefit from the temporary resurgence of hostile interest in the United States caused by Franco-American disputes over payment of indemnities for damages caused by the Napoleonic blockade.

56. The success of the first edition incited Gosselin to a certain level of activity. Out of its own coffers the government paid for twenty copies of *Democracy* for the kingdom's libraries to encourage the arts and sciences (decree of 30 Apr. 1835, National Archives, ser. F 17, 2899). On 25 July Gosselin solicited a new subscription from the government in vain (F 17, 2896, information furnished by Nicole Felkay). The point was not so much the tiny number of copies purchased as it was publicity. Early on, Gosselin began announcing the new Tocqueville on England in the press (*Le courrier français*, 17 June 1835), to the author's fury. Tocqueville intimated to Gosselin that he should "abstain from such announcements in the future, for they not only might serve no purpose whatsoever but might be harmful, by giving [him] the air of a literary charlatan who wants to keep his public panting" (letter to Reeve, 24 July 1837, *OC* 6:39). Gosselin did not stop at that; see *MU,* 10 Jan. 1837.

57. Letter to Reeve, 5 June 1836, *OC* 5, 1:33.

58. See Louis Huart, "La philanthropie à la mode," *Le musée pour rire* 2 (n.d.):69: "Especially in the past few years, philanthropy has become the general mania, a universal fashion. . . . Not only philanthropy but *specialization* is again in fashion. . . . All modern philanthropists get along marvellously on one point, and that is the *publicity* they give to their philanthropy. There is no soup given out, no drunk improved, no bottle drained by drinking to the abolition of slavery, without the entire world being informed of it through notices sent to the journals. . . . And as another general rule, specialist philanthropists only care for their particular brand of unfortunate."

59. See *Le national*, 7 Dec. 1844: "We have no great confidence in the doctrinaire illuminations of M. de Tocqueville, and this importer of "pensilvanian" cells has made us very wary of both his sentiments and his ideas." See also *Les guêpes* 11 (Mar.–June 1843): 18, in which Alphonse Karr exhorts spring to "return the flowers and take back the philanthropists who invented government by cells and mutiny in the prisons."

60. William B. Sarsfield, ed., *Democracy in America*, vol. 1 (abr. British ed., London: Taylor, 1833; unabridged German ed., Berlin: Th. Enslin, 1833; Belgian ed., Brussels: Société Belge de librairie, 1837; U.S. ed., Philadelphia: Francis Lieber, 1833, rept. 1868, 1964, 1970, 1979, 1981).

61. *Le rénovateur*, 28 July 1834.

62. *Le national*, 5 July 1833.

63. *Le semeur*, Mar.–May 1833.

64. Vail, *Réponse*; Poussin, *Considérations*; G. Duden, *Die Nordamerikanische Democratie und das von Tocqueville'sche Werk darüber als Zeichen des Zustandes der theoretischen Politik* (Bonn, 1837).

65. *Considérations* follows *Democracy*'s organization so closely that Gosselin, who published both Tocqueville and Poussin, thought it would be wise to get Tocqueville's endorsement of it. "This book," responded Tocqueville, "marries mine as completely as possible; I see that he has taken my chapter headings to make his own. After citing or analyzing the body of each of my chapters, he approves or blames, giving to reinforce his opinions or mine often curious details, which his long stay in the United States has positioned him to know much better than I" (unpublished letter to Gosselin, 1841, Beinecke Library).

66. Letter to Royer-Collard, 3 June 1836, *OC* 11:16.

67. Only *Le foyer: Journal de la littérature et des arts* devoted a brief positive notice to *Democracy* on 18 Feb. 1835.

68. See Sainte-Beuve, *Le temps* (7 Apr. 1835), rept. in *Premiers lundis* 2 (1874): 277–90; Abel Villemain, "Rapport sur les concours de l'Académie française en 1836," *MU* 19 Aug. 1836, published in *Discours et mélanges littéraires* (1856), 275–85.

69. Balzac, *Monographie de la presse parisienne*, 66–67.

70. But Tocqueville was of no interest to economists: Blanqui and Sismondi's *Revue d'économie politique* did not mention him; the *Journal du commerce* contented itself with derisory mention on 30 Mar. 1835. This shows that in the first half of the nineteenth century, political liberalism in no way coincided with economic liberalism.

71. *Le national* used Tocqueville to launch an argument with the *Journal des débats* on 19 Jan., 3 May, 7 and 29 June, 21 Aug., and 1, 3, 7, and 21 Sept. 1835.

72. At least over the longer term. Until 1842 Tocqueville found his colleagues too ideological. So he gave no public readings, finding it too dangerous "in a time of industry and intellectual greed to give ideas to a body of knowledgeable people" (letter to Beaumont, 7 May 1838, *OC* 8, 1:294).

73. See the proclamation *A MM. les électeurs de Valognes*, Valognes, 13 Feb. 1839. "No one has made more efforts than I to show that we must, without departing from monarchy, arrive at government of the country by the country. I have not couched these opinions in obscure words which can be explained or retracted or denied according to the needs of the moment, but in writings which remain and which engage me in the eyes of my friends as well as those of my adversaries" (*OC* 3, 2:52).

74. Letter to Beaumont, 7 Oct. 1837, *OC* 8, 1:239.

75. See the campaign in favor of Tocqueville in the *Courrier français* and the *Siècle* in Oct. 1837.

76. The comte de Montlosier, an old Gallican monarchist, cited *DA* in the Chamber of Peers on 15 June 1835 to illustrate Tocqueville's clear opposition to those partisans of emancipation who misunderstood the persistence of racial prejudices and free blacks' poverty! Montalivet's citation in the Chamber of Deputies on 10 Jan. 1838 follows the same logic. To defend the pressure exerted by the administration during the elections, Montalivet compared it to the American system of spoils so "remarkably" analyzed by Tocqueville.

77. Beaumont to Tocqueville, 17 Jan. 1838, *OC* 8, 1:276.

78. In Boesche, 99–100. Not long beforehand, Tocqueville had received praise from Royer-Collard, Chateaubriand, and Lamartine.

79. Blanc, "De la démocratie en Amérique," 116.

80. Dupin, *Le siècle*, 16 Nov. 1837.

81. *Le rénovateur, L'écho français,* the *Gazette de France,* and the *Gazette du Berry* published accounts as early as Feb. 1835, and then the *Revue européenne, L'ami de la religion, L'écho de la jeune France,* and *La dominicale* took over.

82. *La quotidienne* was content to announce the work on 24 Jan. *La France* alluded to *Penitentiary System* on 24 Feb. 1835 but never mentioned *DA*, while stretching out hostile allegations throughout rest of the year.

83. BN, Cabet papers, NAF 181555, vol. 10, fol. 158–202, and Proudhon papers, NAF 18257, fol. 35–45.

84. Regarding the centrality of the question posed by Tocqueville to republicans, see Duquesnel, *Du travail intellectuel,* chap. 6, "Le parti républicain et la démocratie en Amérique." Duquesnel and Lacordaire were close friends.

85. Salvandy, warm toward *Penitentiary System,* was cool in the *Journal des débats,* 23 Mar., 2 May 1835; Rossi, in the *Journal général de l'instruction publique,* May 1835; L.M. [Anon.], in the *Moniteur du commerce,* Dec. 1835, was reticent; *MU* waited until Dec. 1836.

86. Carné, "De la démocratie aux Etats-Unis." At the start of 1837, financial contribu-

tions had ensured Guizot support from *RDM*, which until that point had favored the opposition.

87. Guizot's pamphlet *De la démocratie en France* shows the extent of the disagreement in his rejection of even the term *democracy* and his interest in the American model's aristocratic component. Yet Tocqueville had offered Guizot an autographed copy of the four volumes of *DA* in 1840 (Union Catalogue, Library of Congress).

88. Resurgence of debates about Tocqueville was contemporaneous with Guizot's two great speeches in the Chamber on 2 May, when he glorified rule by abilities against "envious, jealous, worried, pestering democracy which seeks to bring everything down to its level."

89. Desessarts, *La France littéraire*, Feb. 1835, 388–93.

90. Corcelle, "De la démocratie en Amérique."

91. See René Girard, "Stendhal and Tocqueville," *American Society of the Legion of Honor Magazine* 31 (1960): 73–83; René-Louis Doyon, "Notes inédites sur l'Angleterre et l'Amérique," *La table ronde* 72 (Dec. 1853): 9–28; James F. Marshall, "Stendhal and America," *French-American Review*, Oct.–Dec. 1949, 240–67; Michel Crouzet, preface to Stendhal, *Lucien Leuwen*. We find references to Tocqueville's works in *Lucien Leuwen* where Stendhal accuses Tocqueville of having been stipended by the French government to promote a negative image of America (363) and in the *Mémoires d'un touriste* where Stendhal includes Tocqueville among difficult good authors, after Montesquieu.

92. See Chateaubriand, *Mémoires d'outre-tombe*, bk. 44.

93. Custine, *L'Espagne sous Ferdinand VII* 2:319. Custine devotes several pages to examining the introduction of *DA* in a postscript dated 1836 to the 31st letter. I owe the discovery of this text to D. Lichtenhan.

94. Ibid., 317–19.

95. Ibid., 320.

96. Annual article in the *Revue française*, Oct. 1837, "De la démocratie dans les sociétés modernes." To fight against Tocqueville, Guizot employs arguments that began figuring in his works at the end of the Restoration—one sign among others of a closed mind, incapable of perceiving changes in mind-sets.

97. See Carné, "De la démocratie aux Etats-Unis," 667.

98. See the controversy in the *Journal des débats*, 16 Dec. 1835, and the *National*, 8, 9, 23, 29 Dec. 1835.

99. *Gazette de France*, 3–13 Feb. 1835.

100. Boyer, *De l'état des ouvriers et de son amélioration par l'organisation du travail*. But Boyer does not accept the idyllic view of a feudalism where lords, "without seeing their equal in the poor man, watch over his destiny like a parcel placed in their hands by Providence." On Boyer, see Jean Maitron, *Dictionnaire biographique du mouvement ouvrier français*, vol. 1 (Paris: Editions de l'Atelier, 1964).

101. Blanc, "De la démocratie en Amérique," 162.

102. Peyrat, *La presse*, 17 Dec. 1860, and Barbey, *"L'Ancien Régime et la Révolution."*

103. BN, Cabet papers, unpublished notes NAF 18155, vol. 10, fol. 58–202.

104. Ibid., fol. 179.

105. Ibid., fol. 198. See also the conclusion of fol. 199: "The United States of America is the country in the world where there is the most liberty, equality, average education, and prosperity, the fewest poor and least poverty. It is the country which has the fewest imperfections and the greatest means for becoming perfect—and all of this is a result of democracy. Yet it contains great imperfections, inequality of fortunes, great landholders and poor people, powerful capitalists and indigent people, an ignorant and turbulent populace of workers and sailors, of impoverished freedmen and slaves, racial prejudice, vanity and hatred against people of color, an excessive avidity for gold and gain, in a word, for property which produces all these evils. Here as elsewhere, the community will be the only remedy; nowhere else will it be as easy to establish it. No government can so easily as the American Congress *give* vast territories *to the poor* both black and white, and civilize the *savages* by giving them the necessary *capital* to then establish *community*."

106. Sorel attributes Proudhon's providentialism in his *De la célébration du dimanche* (1839) to Tocqueville's influence. Yet it is important to note that providentialism is a common trait of what Paul Bénichou has called "the prophets' era." Proudhon did not use Tocqueville's book in his *Qu'est-ce que la propriété?* because Tocqueville's America could not help resolve that question. In the United States a quite relative equality resulted from a gift of nature which gave Americans territory immense in proportion to their population. Proudhon cites Tocqueville's analyses of Native American issues at length (BN, Proudhon papers).

107. Sainte-Beuve, *Le temps,* 7 Apr. 1835, praised his "excellent manner both experimental and philosophical."

108. The connection is made by Cerisé, Champagny, Daireaux, Chassériau, Salvandy, Eckstein, and the *Siècle*'s critic. There is hardly any comparison made with other authors like Delolme or Blackstone.

109. The absolutist paper *La France* noted on 28 Oct. 1835 that its legitimist competitor, the *Gazette de France,* "has always professed the greatest admiration for *Montesquieu,* who is its political oracle, and it is in fact because of its idolatry for the celebrated sophist that the *Gazette* professes such great veneration now for what it calls the *beautiful movement* of '89."

110. Edouard Lemoine, *Le siècle,* 28 May 1837.

111. Carné, "De la démocratie aux Etats-Unis," 655.

112. *Le national,* 7 June 1835.

113. See Anon., *Bulletin littéraire* (Librairie A. Cherbuliez, 1835), 29–30; Blosseville, *Le rénovateur,* 9 Feb. 1835; *L'écho de la jeune France,* 1 Mar. 1836; Sainte-Beuve, *Le temps,* 7 Apr. 1835.

114. Tocqueville was consulted by parliamentarians (see *OC* 16:85–87), and his book was used in the press to understand American politics (see *Le national,* 3 May).

115. The similarity between Tocqueville and Proudhon has often been discussed, because both are, in the French tradition, defenders of the breakup of sovereignty and anti-Marxist heroes. See Adolphe Blanqui, "Communication à l'Académie des sciences

morales," session of 29 Aug. 1840; Georges Sorel, *Les Illusions du progrès*, 258; Mayer, *Prophet of the Mass Age*, 159; Lamberti, *Tocqueville et les deux démocraties*, 206. Long intuitive, the similarity is confirmed today by Proudhon's reading notebooks, which contain a dozen pages of unpublished notes from 1839 on the first *DA* (BN, NAF 18257, fol. 35–45). According to his usual practice, Proudhon meticulously copied long passages which he punctuated with personal commentaries. The quotations' disorderliness shows that the notes were written during a thoughtful reexamination of the work.

116. "There are two chapters on the people's sovereignty, without one's getting very far on this matter after having read M. Tocqueville. I begin to think that the man is a phrasemaker and talker" (Proudhon, MS notes of 1839, BN, NAF 18257).

117. Proudhon, *Qu'est-ce que la propriété?* , 148.

118. See this commentary of Proudhon's on *DA* 1, chap. 2: "What proves the most how far M. Tocqueville is from the truth is the way he calls 'singular,' sometimes 'atrocious,' often 'meticulous' and 'rigorous' the early colonists' legislation because, in imitation of the Bible, they punished all moral violations. He often says that the legislator, after being concerned with sublime ruling, concerns himself with objects 'unworthy'" of him. He cites as proof an ordinance against 'tobacco' and the 'worldly luxury of long hair.' On those two points the legislator may have been mistaken in how to approach the thing—but we could not say that the subject was 'small' and 'unworthy' of his attention—there is no such thing for the legislator'" (BN, Proudhon papers).

119. Notes of Jan. 1839, commentary on book 29 of the *Esprit des lois*, BN, NAF 18256, fol. 21.

120. The only allusion to Proudhon is found in his talk of 12 Sept. 1848 on the right to work (*MU*, 13 Sept.): "Since the first socialist who said, fifty years ago that 'property was the origin of all the evils of this world,' to the socialist we have just heard at this tribune and who, less charitable than the first, going from property to the property-owner, tells us that 'property is theft,' all socialists, all I dare say, attack individual property either directly or indirectly."

121. See Proudhon, *De la capacité politique des classes ouvrières*, 284. "Those fine folk freely admire Swiss and American freedom; they regale us with tales of it in their books, they use it as a mirror to make us ashamed of what we adore, but for nothing in the world would they touch this fine unity which according to them is our glory, and which is the envy of the nations, they assure us."

122. See *Le moniteur du commerce*, 27 Dec. 1835: "You are proud of the freedom to say and think anything out loud; the law of the majority protects you: you pass by, you are arrested, your throat is cut."

123. Carné, "De la démocratie aux Etats-Unis," 658.

124. The Doctrinaires had a strong taste for the argument that American virtues were attributable to vestiges of English morals, and American vices to democratic institutions. See Allart, *La femme et la démocratie de notre temps*, 71.

125. See Corcelle in *RDM*, 14 June 1835, 752; *L'ami de la religion*, 29 Aug. 1835, 498; Chasseriau, *MU*, 22 Dec. 1836.

126. Carné, "De la démocratie aux Etats-Unis," 677.

127. A good example of collusion in matters of theory between Catholics and Jacobins is found in *L'univers religieux*, 11 Oct. 1840. Martial Guillemon rejects the associative remedy prescribed by Tocqueville. Liberty "is not contained in mere individual franchise, nor even in very extensive practice of association. Democratic liberty is the ability of the people to make laws and institutions." When readers grew indignant, *L'univers* editors felt not that they had to defend Tocqueville but that they should distinguish Guillemon's position from that of Rousseau.

128. *L'Européen*, 25 Dec. 1835, 98.

129. Ibid., 52, 54.

130. See Chassériau, *MU*, 22 Dec. 1836.

131. See Sacy, *Journal des débats*, 9 Oct. 1840, who contrasted representative government by property holders with party democracy: "The guarantee of liberty for us is the property census, which establishes in election itself a hierarchy, an order; which means that one arrives by degrees through work, saving, morality, and enlightenment to the exercise of sovereign right. The principle of the greatest number will only lead the nation to one result: tyranny!"

132. Regarding the passionate debates inspired by *Democracy*, see Eschenburg, "Tocquevilles Wirkung in Deutschland," xxxiii–xxxvi.

133. Rosmini left thirty-five manuscript pages of notes on *DA*. They served only as a memorandum and contained almost no details. The passages copied are not those which inspired Rosmini's reflections in *La società ed il suo fine*. See also Mario Tesini, "Rosmini: Lettore di Tocqueville," *Rivista rosminiana de filosofia e di cultura*, ns, 21 (July–Sept. 1987): 265–87. In 1848, when Rosmini tried unsuccessfully to strengthen the liberal leanings of Pius IX, Tocqueville expressed regret over his failure.

134. Rosmini, *La società ed il suo fine* 20:193, 525–27.

135. All the same, the idea of a prudent temporary separation between state and church is not foreign to the most conservative Catholic tradition. It corresponds to the distinction between hypothesis and thesis. See *L'ami de la religion*, 25 Aug. 1835, 465–67, 29 Aug. 1835, 497–99, 8 Sept. 1835, 561–65.

136. See *Le semeur*, 25 Mar. 1835: the Puritans "borrowed their code from the books of Moses, without recalling that by the order of God Moses expressly destined his laws only for the Israelites."

137. In 1835, see the legitimist *Gazette de France*, *Gazette du Berry*, *Ami de la religion*, *Revue européenne*, but also Orleanists like Villemain, Sacy, or Salvandy.

138. See *DA* 1:164, 174, 238, 252, 426.

139. Their strategies varied. The most hostile denied this prosperity, like *La France*, 26 Jan. 1835. Most refuse to see political importance in prosperity. See Barbey, *Nouvelliste*, 26 Dec. 1838: "For some time, we have been advised to consider the United States as necessarily having an imminent and formidable effect on the destinies of Europe. We do not share these terrors. The United States politically exists only for itself; commercially, it exists for the rest of the world."

140. *RDM*, 15 Sept. 1840, 903–4.

141. *Le national* on 3 May thought it saw in Tocqueville the "feeling . . . that French nationality had reached its decadent period; that power belongs to Russia, in the Old World, and that England, in becoming democratic, has allowed to escape the oceans' scepter which can only be grasped by America"—all predictions that were injurious to France, "queen of modern nations."

142. See *Des idées napoléoniennes* (1839) in the *Oeuvres* published by Plon (1856–69), 1:24–25. "I say this regretfully, I cannot see today but two governments which fulfill their providential mission well, these are the two colossi who are at opposite ends of the earth, one at the far end of the new World, the other at the far end of the Old. While our old European middle is like a volcano consuming itself in its crater, the two eastern and western nations go, without hesitation, toward their own perfection, one by the will of a single person, the other by freedom." Louis-Napoléon then wonders what France's mission is.

143. Speech made at Tocqueville's reception into the Academy, 21 Apr. 1842, *OC* 16:279.

144. See Ott, "Centralization," in *Dictionnaire des sciences politiques et sociales.*

145. See letter to Beaumont, 3 Sept. 1848, *OC* 8, 2:38, "France is only legitimist when it despairs it is right."

146. On 19 Oct. by the democrat Pascal Duprat and the conservative Pierre Jouin. On 18 and 20 Oct. *Le national* deplored Tocqueville's silence on the Commune.

147. See Eugene Newton Curtis, *The French Assembly of 1848 and American Constitutional Doctrines* (New York: n.p., 1917).

148. This is when the young Taine read Tocqueville: "It is a bit bombastic, sententious, pretentious. It is above all too abstract, it seems to me. . . . But it is well thought out and teaches much. M. de Tocqueville seems to me to be Montesquieu's best student" (letter of 15 Oct. 1851 to Cornelis de Witt, *RDM*, 15 Dec. 1903, 772).

149. See the vicomte d'Arlincourt, *Dieu le veut.*

150. *L'opinion publique*, 3 July 1848.

151. Dréolle, ibid., 28 Nov., 10 and 19 Dec.

152. These transcripts are in Piero Craveri, ed., *Genesi di una costituzione* (Naples: Guida Editori, 1985).

153. *Souvenirs* in *OC* 12:181.

154. From the earliest commentaries on Tocqueville through 1875 we find the same misunderstanding: the Union's Senate, a congress of diplomats, was often confused with state senates which could alone offer a possible model for France. Tocqueville remarked on this in the constitutional committee of 1848, as did Laboulaye during preparation for the constitution of 1875. In 1835 confusion on this matter was being impelled by the legitimist *Rénovateur* and by Louis Blanc in the *Revue républicaine.*

155. See Louis Blanc, *Revue républicaine*, 10 May 1835, 141–44.

156. The idea of recourse to a senate as a crucible for formation of a national consensus which could not take place immediately is only taken up systematically by Laboulaye, "La question des deux chambres," *RDM*, 1 June 1871, 459, 471.

157. Boesche, 263.

158. See report of 8 July 1851 on the revision of the constitution in *OC* 3, 3:433–53.

159. Hippolyte Fortoul, *Une page de l'histoire contemporaine: La révision de la constitution* (1851), 71.

160. Sessions of 27, 31 May and 15 June.

161. Sessions of 14 and 15 June. During the debate in the Assembly, Martin allied himself nonetheless with the nomination of the president by the Assembly because he failed to gain the president's right to dissolve it.

162. Tocqueville's speech, 5 Oct., *OC* 3, 3:219.

163. This is why conservatives accuse him of having been a surreptitious republican. Parieu denounces what he sees as "contradiction" in Tocqueville's allegiance to the monarchy, and even a "lack of consequence." "By seeking to the development of liberty and equality to which he gave almost no limit, was M. de Tocqueville not trying to maintain in his ideal society the name of a monarchy that would survive the ruins of its past existence?" (*Revue contemporaine* 53 [1860] :576).

164. Session of 15 June.

165. See letter to Beaumont, 9 Sept. 1850, *OC* 8, 2:296.

2. Moralist for Modern Times, 1840s

1. Letter to Mathieu Molé, Aug. 1835, *OC* (Bmt) 7:133–36.

2. Draft cited in Schleifer, *Making of Tocqueville's Democracy*, 21.

3. Letter to Beaumont, 8 Oct. 1839, *OC* 8, 1:380.

4. *OC* 2, 2:58.

5. Boesche, 106. On this point see Drescher, *Tocqueville and England*.

6. *OC* 5, 2:49.

7. Draft cited in Lamberti, *Tocqueville et les deux démocraties*, 180.

8. Letter to Bouchitté, 26 May 1836, *OC* (Bmt) 7:149.

9. *DA* 2:175, 237.

10. Boutmy, *Eléments d'une psychologie du peuple américain* (1902; rept. 1911), 11.

11. D'Eichtal, *Tocqueville et la démocratie libérale*, 35.

12. See, for example, *DA* 2:58.

13. "Penchants," *DA* 2:290, 325; "inclinations," 57, 79; "slopes," 63, 144, 222; and all verbs of inclination or movement, 3, 10, 22, 53, 145, 284, 325.

14. For the lexicon of obscurity, see *DA* 2:29, 69, 79, 104, 166, 238, 289, 294, 313.

15. *DA* 2:9, 22, 29, 46, 77, 79, 89, 98, 166, 290, 313.

16. *DA* 2:46, 89, 98, 290, 313.

17. See this 1838 draft: "Somewhere dare to give L[ouis]'s idea that one must distinguish between absolute affirmation and Pyrrhonism, that the system of probabilities is the only true one, the only *humane* one, provided that probability can make people act as energetically as certainty can" (cited in critical edition of *DA* published by Vrin, 280).

18. Thus in democracy, a man is "almost always unhappy with his fortune," so that "most wealthy people . . . naturally turn their attention toward commerce and industry"

(*DA* 2:161). Tocqueville then concludes that wealthy people "are thus *all* inclined toward commerce" (162).

19. In fact, Tocqueville appeared to his readers to have an analytic mind in the spirit of Aristotle. See Wilhelm Dilthey, *Aufbau der geschichtlichen Welt in den Geisteswissenschaften* (Berlin: Verlag der königlich preussichen Akademie der Wissenschaft, 1911).

20. See letter to Kergorlay, Feb. 1838, *OC* 13, 2:12–18.

21. Letter to John Stuart Mill, 19 Nov. 1836, *OC* 6, 1:314.

22. Letter to Reeve, 21 Nov. 1836, *OC* 7, 1:35.

23. Letter to Royer-Collard, 30 Aug. 1838, *OC* 11:71.

24. The subprefect of the Manche sector of France commenting on Tocqueville's electoral difficulties, cited in Jardin, *Alexis de Tocqueville*, 278.

25. Letter to Royer-Collard, 21 July 1838, *OC* 11:66.

26. Letter to Royer-Collard, 8 Aug. 1839, *OC* 11:79: "What I saw from inside the political world for the past few months has caused me to feel I must rewrite certain parts of my work which I had thought were finished."

27. *OC* 3, 2:132.

28. *Souvenirs* in *OC* 11:30.

29. See discussion of the 1842 address in *OC* 3, 2:197–207.

30. Unpublished letter to Langlois, 4 Jan. 1838.

31. *DA* 2:193–94.

32. Letter to Beaumont, 8 July 1838, *OC* 8, 1:311.

33. *DA* 2:26, 130. The very word *bien-être* (well-being) appeared and was socially accepted in the nineteenth century. See Jean Dubois, *Le vocabulaire politique et social en France de 1869 to 1872* (Paris: Larousse, 1962), 277.

34. Which Tocqueville was aware of. See *DA* 2:127.

35. *DA* 2:123. In an unpublished letter of 25 July 1838, Tocqueville criticized philosopher Charles Stöffels for having preached a very unappetizing kind of Christian stoicism: "Our contemporaries' weak temperaments require no heroic remedies. I do not even know if in another era, the Christian stoicism you depict with eloquence and passion has ever served as a guide to most men. Believe me, the moralists, while demonstrating the charms of virtue, never lose sight of its utility, for they did not write just for the great souls but also for the small ones. As for me, I combine both those truths in one. I believe virtue is beautiful, and I deem it useful. Experience proves it to me every day." And then Tocqueville shows—not without platitude—that giving up greediness preserves one from stomachaches!

36. Draft of *DA* 2 (Vrin ed.):114.

37. Ibid., 115.

38. *OR*, 168. Yet Tocqueville will resort in every economic crisis to utilitarian arguments, as they alone seemed effective to him when dealing with great numbers of people. See the letter to Circourt, 17 Mar. 1859, *OC* 18:540: "What has sustained this government for the past ten years is the idea that it is the necessary guarantee of material well-being and benefits. Yet recent trials have demonstrated clearly that such was not the case at all, that

despotism was as dangerous to the interests that are dear to us as extreme freedom. This is a practical education that the French have just been given, and it is a good one."

39. See his commentary on Poussin's painting at the Académie française, 13 Apr. 1858, *OC* 16:310–11.

40. Letter to Corcelle, 1 Aug. 1850, *OC* 15, 2:29.

41. See *OR*, 7, 12, 149, 153–54.

42. Boesche, 49.

43. Tocqueville borrowed the technique of reduction "en cascade" from Catholic apologetics. He had read Bossuet's *L'histoire des variations des églises protestantes* and Lamennais's *Essai sur l'indifférence en matière de religion,* both of which use this technique. Maret's *Essai sur le panthéisme* (1840) used the same argument to condemn democratic tendencies in intellectual life. But from the theological concept of indifference to the "true" religion, Tocqueville moved to the sociological concept of indifference to any religion.

44. Boesche, 357.

45. On 14 Nov. 1839 Tocqueville again gave his title to John Stuart Mill as "Influence of Equality on Human Ideas and Sentiments" (*OC* 6, 1:326). The chapter titles mostly refer to American experience, hardly mentioned in the body of the work.

46. Letter to Beaumont, 8 Oct. 1839, *OC* 8, 1:379.

47. Boesche, 119.

48. See letter to Reeve, 5 June 1836, *OC* 6, 1:33: "Instead of a whole volume, I will be *forced* to publish two. I say 'forced,' for on this point I do not follow booksellers' opinions and hold to my plan to put myself out in the smallest format possible. But there is a limit after all to conciseness, and I was not able to put in what I had to say in a single volume." (Booksellers pushed for publishing two volumes, which could be sold more expensively.) He resisted the publisher's pressures to pad the volume of notes in order to raise the price: "I have since yesterday carefully looked to see if I could attach notes of any importance to my text, and I find none which would be *motivated,* and I think that it would be beneath the seriousness of the book to add notes to fill it up whose goal would obviously be to increase the number of pages while teaching nothing" (unpublished letter to Fournier, 8 Jan. 1840).

49. In Sept.–Oct. 1839 Tocqueville had negotiated with Alexandre Paulin, Thiers's publisher and director of *L'illustration,* who proposed a price of 70,000 francs to him. These negotiations were not followed up, as Paulin did not offer sufficient financial guarantees (letter to Beaumont, 14 Oct. 1839, *OC* 8, 1:387). Between Nov. and Dec., Tocqueville wrote to Gosselin to suggest payment of 10,000 francs for 2,500 copies, reserving for himself all English and American rights and proposing future negotiations on an in-18 edition, more limited and in smaller format (unpublished letter to Gosselin, n.d.).

50. *Journal des débats,* 22 Apr., *Le national, Le siècle, La quotidienne, La gazette de France,* and *Le commerce,* 24 Apr., *Le constitutionnel* and *Le courrier français,* 26 Apr., *Le journal de Valognes,* 3 May.

51. *Le voleur,* 30 Apr.; *L'espérance,* 2 May; *L'écho de la presse,* 3 May; and *Le constitutionnel,* 26 Apr.

52. Democratization did not include publishing an illustrated edition, which would have been ill suited to a book with so little narration. In an unpublished letter, 10 Jan. 1852, Gustave Barba, bookseller and publisher, suggested an illustrated edition of *La démocratie en Amérique* to Tocqueville in his Panthéon populaire series, but there was no follow-up.

53. American Vail was up in arms against Tocqueville's severe criticism of American lack of culture in *De la littérature et des hommes de lettres*; Poussin's *De la puissance américaine* plagiarizes entire pages from the second *DA.*

54. See Rossi, *RDM,* 15 Sept. 1840. As in 1835, the work gave rise to polemics: on 13 Oct. 1840 the *Gazette de France,* reprinting excerpts from a very critical article that had run in the *Journal des débats* on 9 Oct., was happy to see ministerial officials joining legitimists in the horror of modernity.

55. The first to comment on *DA* was in fact the Protestant paper *Le semeur,* 29 Apr. 1840.

56. See hesitation toward the second *Democracy* in the writings of Saint-Simonian economist Michel Chevalier. He praised Tocqueville's "finesse" only to regret in the next breath that Tocqueville had strayed from the terra firma of economics from which morality stems (*Journal des débats,* 15 Sept. 1851). Chevalier's hostility is but a sign of the rivalry that made its way into the Académie des sciences morales, those upholding political economy against those for classical moralism.

57. Whence the considerable impact of Louis Reybaud's work on the reformers, which explained to leading citizens everything they needed to know about those dangerous doctrines. The praises given Reybaud as an "enlightened and impartial man" (*Le commerce,* 21 Aug.) contrast with Balzac's mockery of his dull gravity and remind us of those given Tocqueville in 1835.

58. See *OC* 8, 1:426–27.

59. See Armand Cuvillier, *Hommes et idéologies de 1840* (Paris: M. Rivière et Cie, 1956).

60. See the articles outlined by Tocqueville when planning for the new edition in *OC* 3, 3:397–402.

61. See the articles entitled "Individualisme" and "Libéralisme" in Pagnerre's *Dictionnaire politique.* See also Louis Blanc, *Revue du progrès* 4 (1840): 276: "For some, 'liberalism' encompasses all the glorious fights sustained against the triple tyranny of kings, noblemen, and priests; it is Voltaire followed through with intelligence, it is congregationalism vanquished, Loyola's society disarmed.... For others, 'liberalism' is hatred, blind in its exaggeration, of the authority principle; it is ties between souls broken, the individual freed but with that liberty that isolates and leaves him to die, if he is poor, in a corner of a field; it is a universal negation: finally, eunuchs made potent!"

62. See Aug. Billiard's article, "Etats-Unis," in Garnier-Pagès's *Dictionnaire politique.*

63. The Jan. 16 speech was published in *OC* 3, 2:197ff. The reception speech was in *OC* 16:251–69. The year 1841 was marked by serious trouble, the most salient episode being

Quenisset's attack on the duc d'Aumale of 13 Sept. 1841. The right to set foot on French boats, which Guizot wanted to concede to the English to facilitate stopping the slave trade, incited left and legitimist nationalist ire, whence Tocqueville's moral and patriotic virulence.

64. *La mode*, Jan.–June 1842, 123–24.

65. *La phalange*, a socialist publication, 21 Jan. 1842, article by Aug. Colin. On 30 Jan. and then on 27 Apr. 1842, ibid., Charles Pellarin responded critically to Tocqueville's "vain and even puerile recriminations" "which attacked people instead of institutions." While appreciating Tocqueville's opposition to ministry officials, Pellarin denounced his vague conception of liberty, as well as the lukewarmness of his taste for equality and his "mean-spirited" social observations.

66. Rossi, "De la démocratie en Amérique," 893.

67. Sacy, *Journal des débats*, 9 Oct. 1840, proposed as a title, "De l'avenir de la démocratie dans le monde et particulièrement en France."

68. *RDM*, 25 Sept. 1840, 899.

69. Letter to Eugene Stöffels, 14 July 1840, *OC* (Bmt) 6:441.

70. "M. de Tocqueville has only an observer's patience and timidity: what he has seen, he writes. But what takes place in the supernatural world of ideas, those brave syntheses which surge up inflamed and harmonious in the world of the intellect, like stars in space, he does not know, he does not even suspect them—M. de Tocqueville has something of Cuvier's mind, the fear of going beyond facts" (Eugène Pelletan, *La presse*, 4 Sept. 1840).

71. Letter to John Stuart Mill, 18 Dec. 1840, *OC* 6, 1:330.

72. Villemain, *Journal des savants*, May 1840, 263.

73. See Molé, speech receiving Tocqueville at the Académie, 21 Apr. 1842, *OC* 16:277–78: "Your book is perhaps one of the most systematic that has been written. . . . While admiring it, I would say to you that the art and power with which, not turning aside for a moment for four volumes, you cause all the facts, all your most ingenious or profound observations, to converge toward one selfsame demonstration, I said to myself that in such sustained study, with such an exclusive preoccupation, the spirit sometimes ends up completely absorbed in a subject on which it has so long concentrated all its efforts; the better to possess it, it allows itself to be possessed."

74. Félix de Courmont, *L'opinion publique*, 3 July 1848.

75. *Edinburgh Review*, 1840. Tocqueville's friend John Stuart Mill had published a first article on *DA* in the *London [and Westminster] Review* in 1835. These two articles are reprinted in *Dissertations and Discussions* 2 (1859): 1–83.

76. Unpublished letter to Stöffels, 21 Apr. 1830.

77. *OC* 16:117–39. Above all, Tocqueville owes much to having read Jean-Paul Alban, vicomte de Villeneuve-Bargemont, *Economie chrétienne*, 3 vols. (1834).

78. Boesche, 336.

79. See his note on the Cherbourg dike in 1847 in *OC* 16:349–96, and his letter to Gobineau, 19 Jan. 1855, *OC* 9:228: "I often have feeling against humanity . . . but not against the

century which, after all, will be set down as one of the greatest in history, the one in which man has most subjected nature and achieved his conquest of the globe."

80. *DA* 2:181. Cournot refers to Tocqueville in his *Essai sur les fondements de nos connaissances et sur les caractères de la critique philosophique*. Like Tocqueville, Cournot feels humanity gradually comes to discover its uniformity in the course of history (214).

81. Guillemon, *L'univers religieux*, 11 Oct. 1840.

82. Faucher, *Courrier français*, 20 Jan. 1841.

83. Letter from Royer-Collard, 29 Aug. 1840, *OC* 11:93.

84. Travel plans for a trip to Germany in 1837 show this. "Absolutist governments are for me terra incognita," wrote Tocqueville, "and every day I notice that such understanding is necessary to me. My mind is too concentrated within one sphere" (letter to Reeve, 21 Nov. 1836, *OC* 6, 1:36). The trip was interrupted in 1849 and not undertaken until 1854.

85. Pelletan, *La presse*, 4 Sept. 1840, and Faucher, *Le courrier français*, 20 Jan. 1841, note with good reason that pantheism was a German and not a democratic phenomenon. The critique of Tocqueville's abusive generalizations was particularly acerbic from America specialists like Poussin, who, reserving his attention for "examining American subjects" (*Considérations*, 201), was led to skip the chapters on pantheism, individualism, the industrial aristocracy, relationships between master and servant, the craving for public positions, five chapters on military society, and ultimately the entire fourth part, for he "found nothing in the author's considerations which dealt exclusively with [American] democracy or which caused it to be better understood" (307).

86. Letter from Leo Thun, 15 July 1841, Tocqueville Archives.

87. Rousiers, *La vie américaine*, and Demolins, *A quoi tient la supériorité*.

88. See letter to Corcelle, 2 Sept. 1837, *OC* 15, 1:86.

89. *RDM*, 15 Sept. 1840, 899.

90. See Ampère, *Promenade*; Duvergier de Hauranne, *Huit mois*; and the letters of André Siegfried, *Deux mois en Amérique du Nord* (Paris: Armand Colin, 1916).

91. *L'univers*, 11 Oct. 1840. See also *Journal des débats*, 18 Jan. 1844: "'France is bored,' cried M. Tocqueville. Oh! I think so, and let us tell you, it will not be your speeches that wake us up! France is asleep! And how could it not be, with the monotonous noise of your empty, pretentious sentences trying to sound like Montesquieu."

92. See Gustave de Beaumont, *Oeuvres et correspondance inédites* (Paris: Michel Lévy, 1861), 50: Tocqueville studied no writer "with more constancy and love than Pascal. The two minds were made for each other. The incessant obligation which Pascal inflicts on one to think was for him one full of charm; perhaps one might find in this predilection the origin of the single defect which has been criticized in him, of leaving his reader too little respite."

93. Sainte-Beuve, *Nouveaux lundis* (1868), 10:320–21.

94. *Journal des savants*, May 1840, 263.

95. See Deschamps, *Le malaise de la démocratie*, which notes that "long hopes and vast

thoughts were no longer in fashion," and had been replaced by the "cult of the I," "the religion of Bibi" (95–96), the cult of the dilettante.

96. "Epitre à M. de Tocqueville," *Revue de Paris*, 20 Sept. 1840.

97. In 1900 Faguet noted in his *Politiques et moralistes* 3:82 that *DA*'s "sharp spice of paradox" was "applied to events. This is like saying, 'democracy is peaceful, democracy is conservative, democracy is kind in its customs' to men to whom the word *democracy* inevitably recalls the French Revolution and who could hardly think of democracy in other terms than those of the Revolution; by exciting readers' sense of contradiction, it excited their interest. It took a certain courage." But Faguet here commits an anachronism: in 1840 paradox inspired no interest at all.

98. Rossi, *RDM*, 15 Sept. 1840, 898.

99. See Michel Chevalier, *Journal des débats*, 1 Oct. 1851. In the Second Empire among economists, only Baudrillat, Sacy's son-in-law, was interested in Tocqueville's work. But Baudrillart specifically subordinates the search for utility to the idea of justice as Christianity and natural law develop it. See his article "Démocratie" in Block's *Dictionnaire général de la politique.*

100. See *Le semeur*, 4 Mar. 1835, 163: "We do not believe . . . that the doctrine of Enlightenment self-interest is another means of combating individualism, or that it raises the species while lowering a few individuals. Even less will we try to reconcile this doctrine with religious beliefs. Nothing is more opposed to the devotion that love inspires." Among ministry officials Chassériau saw "health for European societies only in a return we hope is still possible to the spirit of sacrifice, the essence of Christianity" (*MU*, 9–22 Dec. 1836). Guizot himself used interest as a politician, but whenever he wanted to philosophize, he turned to the authority of reason.

101. *Nouveaux lundis*, 318.

102. Janet, *RDM*, 1 July 1861, 128.

103. Michel, *L'idée de l'Etat*, 336.

104. Draft of *DA* 2 (Vrin ed.):15.

105. *DA* 2:24. *Democracy* outlined a democracy akin to the pastoral practices of priests, thrifty with symbols and rituals, prudently resorting to those who would intercede and to the mysteries. Very early on, in 1845, Tocqueville grew alarmed by the campaign for the proclamation of papal infallibility, which went against democratic trends. See the session in the Chamber of 5 Mar. 1845, Tocqueville's address to the archbishop of Lyons preaching in favor of the pope's infallibility, *OC* 3, 2:605: "What! You are confronted with an unquiet century which denies and contests authority wherever it finds it; you live in a skeptical nation which only with difficulty supports the empire of laws it itself has made, and which has no respect for any power, even the powers it has created, and among all the forms Catholicism can take, you choose the one in which authority appears the most absolute, the most arbitrary, and it is that one you wish to impose on belief."

106. *L'espérance*, 7 Nov. 1840.

107. BN, NAF 20764, fol. 135b and 20765, fol. 128a: "The wave which M. de Tocqueville

has set into motion with his questions on religion has something despairing about them. No light can pierce these clouds which pile up one on top of another.... In this method, which is the opposite of any method, there is no difference any longer, no temperament, but an agreed-upon formula, religion, which dispenses us from having to examine anything in either its fact or its idea."

108. Laurentie, *L'union*, 4 Sept. 1856.

109. See Mgr. Baunard, *La foi et ses victoires dans le siècle présent* 2:245.

110. *Journal des débats*, 26 Jan. 1861.

111. See letter to Corcelle, 15 Nov. 1843, *OC* 15, 1:174: "Catholicism, which produces such admirable effects in some cases, [and] which one must support with all one's power because in France the religious spirit can only exist together with it, Catholicism ... will never adopt the new society."

112. "My finest dream in entering political life was to contribute to the reconciliation of the spirit of liberty and the spirit of religion," he wrote his brother Edouard on 6 Dec. 1843 (unpublished letter).

113. Speech of 17 Jan. 1844, *OC* 3, 2:493.

114. Ibid., 488.

115. Letter to Edouard, 6 Dec. 1843. See also *Le commerce*, 11 Dec. 1844: "There is only liberty, regulated but real liberty, which can serve as a guarantee for the world" (in *OC* 3, 2:586).

116. Tocqueville himself notes that the leaders of the Catholic party allowed themselves to be led astray by their old absolutist tendencies. "They called for the right to direct education as one inherent to the Church.... They put forward principles by virtue of which not only should they be free to teach but to control education they did not provide, principles they had neither the will nor the ability to apply in our present society. This meant awakening all the old philosophic passions without the least need for it" (letter to Edouard, 6 Dec. 1843).

117. *L'univers*, 29 Nov., 4, 6, 8 Dec. 1844.

118. *Le commerce*, 29 July 1844; *OC* 3, 2:512.

119. Regarding his expedition to Rome, see *Correspondance d'Alexis de Tocqueville et de Francisque de Corcelle* in *OC* 15; *Correspondance étrangère* in *OC* 7; and my article "Tocqueville et la restauration du pouvoir temporel du Pape (June–Oct. 1849)," *Revue historique* 271:1 (1984): 109–23.

120. See the short work by Quinet, *La croisade autrichienne, française, napolitaine, espagnole contre la république romaine*, and Giuseppe Mazzini's two open letters to Tocqueville, in Mazzini, *Scritti editti ed ineditti* (Imola: P. Galeati, 1906–43), 38:301–7, 39:139–65.

121. Roland-Marcel, *Essai politique sur Alexis de Tocqueville*, 267.

122. During the Second Empire, Tocqueville, together with the American Unitarian preacher Channing, became the founding father of a new Christianity linked to the Enlightenment that was as concerned with liberty as it was with social justice. See Laboulaye, *L'Etat et ses limites*, 79.

123. Only Daumier's caricature of Tocqueville, in his 1849 "Les Représentants Représentés" series, and Chassériau's drawing and portrait seem to have received widespread distribution.

124. Anon., *Profils critiques et biographiques des 750 représentants du peuple à l'Assemblée législative par trois publicistes* (1849), 291–92: "In M. de Tocqueville, the political man is a faithful copy of the writer," i.e., equally soporific. "He's done his time; his liberalism is nothing but the old liberalism made new." He represents "a schism in the party which favors order." To the ambiguity of the minister's political choices was added his aristocratic appearance. *La silhouette*, 30 Sept. 1849, presents Thiers as spreading the rumor that "Toc-Toc is retiring from his affairs to devote himself exclusively to raising and being friends with his greyhounds."

125. Fortunate Mesuré, known as Fortunatus, *Le rivarol de 1842*, 182. See also *Le globe*, 3 June 1842: "As for ourselves, we have only one complaint against M. de Tocqueville, but it is serious. This is the perpetual molting to which he appears subject. A relentless Carlist, to the point of being threatened with requisitions from the king's procuror, he became a ministerial candidate in M. Molé's conservative cabinet, and today affects democratic postures and is puffed up by the opposition papers. Changing three or four times in four or five years is a lot."

126. See Lourdoueix, *Profils critiques et biographiques des 900 représentants du peuple* (Paris: Garnier, 1848), and *Le charivari*, 2 Aug. 1849.

127. Lourdoueix, *Profils critiques et biographiques.*

128. See *Le charivari*, 26, 27 June 1849, 2, 7, 31 Aug., 19 Oct. 1849.

129. *La silhouette*, 29 Aug., 9 Sept. 1849.

130. Saint-Arnaud, *Lettres du maréchal Saint-Arnaud* 2:120.

131. Rémusat, *Mémoires* 4:44–46.

132. Versailles Museum.

133. In François Furet's well-turned phrase, *La Révolution* (Paris: Hachette, 1988), 372.

3. In Search of France's Identity, 1850s

1. *OC* 2, 1:31–68.
2. *OC* 16:251–69.
3. Letter to Montalembert, 10 July 1856, *OC* (Bmt) 7:388–90.
4. See "Why Great Revolutions Will Become More Rare," *DA* 2:251–63.
5. *OC* 16:274.
6. *Souvenirs* in *OC* 12:87.
7. Even Molé later recognized his mistake. See *OR* 2:291.
8. *OC* 12:75.
9. Letter to Mme de Circourt, 19 June 1850, *OC* 18:34.
10. Unpublished letter to Charles Stöffels, 30 July 1852.
11. Boesche, 252.
12. *OC* 2, 2:291.
13. Tocqueville had sketched a few notes which have remained unpublished.

14. Letter from Kergorlay, 22 Aug. 1856, *OC* 13, 2:305.

15. Letter to Kergorlay, 28 Aug. 1856, *OC* 13, 2:309.

16. *Souvenirs* in *OC* 12:50.

17. Whence Tocqueville's ability to speak of the Revolution in terms of intensity. See use of the notion "more and more," 73–74, "increase," 58–59, 77, and "in the degree that," 75, 77, 185.

18. Boesche, 292.

19. Unpublished letter to Z. Gallemand, 28 Aug. 1852.

20. Letter to Gobineau, 30 July 1856, *OC* 9:268.

21. Tocqueville Archives. On the 1854 trip to Bonn, see Märker, "Alexis de Tocqueville und Deutschland," and Seidel, "Tocquevilles Forschungsaufenhalt in Bonn 1854."

22. Mandeville, "dissolute and anti-Christian writer" (!), Tocqueville Archives.

23. See *OR*, 134: "Nevertheless, the ideas of the age were beginning gradually to seep into the minds of the French peasantry and in those cramped, obscure retreats they often assumed peculiar forms."

24. *OR*, 47–49. The idea of affiliation between the "feudal constitution" and the American federation can be found in the United States in *Federalist* no. 17 and in France in Royer-Collard, for whom feudal government "left us the balance of powers, judgment by juries, rights which come from reciprocal obligations, loyalty rather than passive obedience, an admirable feeling which the ancients did not know. And if feudal government in turn had had its own philosophers, would those philosophers have told it that it would bear in its loins the constitution of the United States of America?" (Barante, *La vie politique de M. Royer-Collard*, 2:40).

25. In studying medieval Germany, "I felt sure that if I searched long enough I would find its exact parallel, or something substantially the same, in France and England—and thus it always was, with the result that each of the three nations helped me to a better understanding of the other two" (*OR*, 15).

26. Unpublished notes of 1854 on August Ludwig von Reyscher, *Das gesamte württembergische Privatrecht*, 3 vols. (1837–48), Tocqueville Archives.

27. Letter to Beaumont, 3 Nov. 1853, *OC* 13, 3:164, commentary inspired by Aug. von Haxthausen's book, *Etudes sur la situation intérieure de la vie nationale et les institutions rurales de la Russie*, 2 vols. (1847–52). Tocqueville filed his notes on this work (*OC* 16:562–68) in his *Old Regime* file.

28. Unpublished preparatory notes to *Old Regime*.

29. Cited in Maurice Agulhon, *Histoire vagabonde* (Paris: Gallimard, 1988), 2:225. Tocqueville copied Caesar's portrait of the French nation into his preparatory notes for *Old Regime*.

30. Speech to the Académie Française, 24 Jan. 1861, *OC* 16:343.

31. *Le pays*, 29 July 1856, rept. in Barbey d'Aurevilly, *Les oeuvres et les hommes*, 3d ser., 21:125. Tocqueville was consistent throughout his works in limiting his study of the aristocracy to examining its decadence. Whether he was studying Algeria, India, or American Indians, he was only interested in the decomposition of hierarchic society due to abrupt confrontation with a modern colonial power.

32. *OR*, xi, 118–19, 148, 155.

33. Letter of 29 July 1856, *OC* 13, 2:303.

34. See Kelly, "Parnassian Liberalism."

35. See letter to Corcelle, 15 Nov. 1856, *OC* 15, 2:186: "I was not able to claim to paint a pleasant picture, only a likeness, persuaded as I am that the only opportunity nations, like individuals, have to heal is to first study the reality of their illness. Then it sometimes happens, it is true, that after having seen and known it, one succumbs to it nonetheless. But without knowing it, one is certain not to heal. Few men would persist in their failings if they could have a clear view of them, see their source, and measure the results of them."

36. Letter to Beaumont, 9 Sept. 1850, *OC* 8, 2:296.

37. Speech to the Académie des Sciences Morales, 3 Apr. 1852, *OC* 16:233.

38. In 1855 Lévy had published Ampère's *Promenade en Amérique* and Louis de Loménie's *Beaumarchais et son temps*. Loménie introduced Tocqueville to Lévy.

39. Letter to Reeve, 6 Feb. 1856, *OC* 6, 1:160: "However wretched I am, and I often am like any small landholder who has imagined outfitting his hut and ornamenting his garden, I don't give a hang about any money earned through poor-quality work. I care above all about my reputation, not about my purse."

40. See Jean-Yves Mollier, *Michel et Calmann-Lévy ou la naissance de l'édition moderne* (Paris: Calmann-Lévy, 1984).

41. Letter to Reeve, 6 Feb. 1856, *OC* 6, 1:161.

42. Letter to Beaumont, 17 Feb. 1856, *OC* 8, 3:370.

43. Letter to Beaumont, *OC* 8, 3:372–73.

44. The title *L'Ancien Régime et la Révolution* does not seem to have been used beforehand, except for a work obscure by 1842.

45. Letters to Beaumont, 17 and 22 Mar. 1856, *OC* 8, 3:379, 384.

46. See letter to Beaumont, 8 Mar. 1856, *OC* 8, 3:378.

47. BN, Calmann-Lévy registers.

48. Letter to Ampère, 9 July 1856, *OC* 11:326.

49. The printing and sales of the work, which Michelet had given over to Chamerot, a simple bookseller, broker, and wholesaler, were noted by an undated inventory that was doubtless written before July 1853 (Historical Library of the City of Paris, Michelet section, information given by D. Bellos). Copies sold: vol. 1, 3,000; vol. 2, 2,500; vol. 3, 1,533; vol. 4, 1,429; vol. 5, 1,186; 5,000 copies of vols. 5 and 6 were printed.

50. "For a book as filled as mine was with the sentiment of liberty to meet with such rapid sales, this very sentiment must not be as dead as many among us believe and as some hope" (letter to Mrs. Austin, 29 Aug. 1856, *OC* 6, 1:192).

51. *Revue contemporaine*, 15 Dec. 1956.

52. See the Beaumont-Tocqueville correspondence, July–Aug. 1856, *OC* 8, 3:420–22.

53. Correspondence between the duc d'Aumale and Cuvillier-Fleury. See note by Peter Mayer, "Histoire de l'influence de l'Ancien Régime," in *OC* 2, 1:342.

54. BN, Quinet papers; Chassin, Historical Library of the City of Paris, ms 1443, fol, 48–51.

55. It showed up most emphatically when Quinet's book on the Revolution appeared in 1865. See François Furet, *La gauche et la Révolution au milieu du XIXe siècle* (Paris: Hachette, 1986).

56. Lamartine, *Cours familier de littérature*, vol. 2, course 9 (1856). See also Lanfrey, *Essai sur la Révolution française*.

57. See *OC* 18:317, 2 Sept. 1856 in *OC* 18:333, and *OC* 18, 3:452.

58. When Kergorlay criticized him for having written "the most terrible censures of the ancien régime ever to have seen the light of day" (22 Aug. 1856, *OC* 12, 2:306), Tocqueville answered, "The kind of violence truth did to me gave to that violence an impartial character, which seemed an even greater blow for that period [the ancien régime] than all that revolutionary passion could have made me say" (28 Aug., *OC* 13, 2:310).

59. Letter to Kergorlay, 28 Aug. 1856, *OC* 13, 2:310.

60. On 2 Aug. 1856 Barbey d'Aurevilly wrote: "This evening, I will send off a fourth article on that born eunuch called *Tocqueville* whose reputation is one of the most disgusting things of this disgusting reign of mediocrity which will go down in history as 'Louis Philippe.' My article on this lucky louse, on that man who has worked so hard to be nothing so he can be all, is the first blow to him. By his family, he belongs to the Faubourg St. Germain; by his academic title, to the Institut and its clientele; by his opinions, to *Le siècle* and the bourgeoisie. But what is all that to me, I who care only about one thing—the holy truth!" ("Lettres à Trébutien," in *Oeuvres complètes* [Paris: F. Renouard, 1926–27], 7:200–201). The article is the one which appeared in *Le pays*.

61. *Le pays*, 29 July 1856.

62. Mérimée to Miss Senior, 22 June 1856, *Correspondance générale, 1856–1858*, 58; Forcade de La Roquette, "Le gouvernement impérial et l'opposition nouvelle," 17.

63. *Le pays*, 29 July 1856.

64. Letter to Sophie Swetchine, 13 Aug. 1856, *OC* 15, 2:289.

65. Letter to Gobineau, 29 Nov. 1856, *OC* 9:272.

66. Jouvin, *Le figaro*, 26 Oct. 1856.

67. Letter to Gobineau, 30 July 1855, *OC* 9:265–66: "If my doctor were to come tell me one of these mornings, 'My dear Sir, I have the honor to tell you that you have a mortal illness, and as it is one of your very constitution, I have the advantage of being able to add that there is absolutely no chance to avoid it in any way,' I would first be tempted to beat the doctor. Second, I would find no other thing to do than to put my head under the covers and await the predicted end, or if I had the kind of temperament which animated Boccacio's characters during Florence's plague, I would care only to abandon myself effortlessly to all my tastes while awaiting that inevitable end so that life at least had been, as they say, short and good. Or I could benefit from my sentence to prepare myself for life eternal; but societies have no eternal life. Thus your doctor would decidedly lose my business. I would add that doctors, like philosophers, often err in their prognoses, and I have seen more than one man condemned by them do very well later and grow angry at the doctor who had so uselessly frightened and discouraged him."

68. Jouvin, *Le figaro*, 26 Oct. 1856.

69. Without lying to himself about the enterprise's risks, for "many praise Montesquieu in quotation, but few read him. I would even say this is so among serious people. Most of his ideas are of such a general character that the reader can almost always find several specific cases in which they appear false, and this turns them away. One must raise oneself almost to the author's own height, encompass with one's gaze as wide an expanse of facts as he does in order to perceive that the maxim proved false by many specific applications made of it is profoundly true in its generality" (unpublished letter to Freslon, 29 Dec. 1855, Tocqueville Archives).

70. *Le correspondant,* 25 July 1856, 693–94.

71. Barbey d'Aurevilly, *Le pays,* 29 July 1856.

72. Ibid.

73. The phrase was borrowed from "someone very judicious and very respectable" whom Sainte-Beuve did not name (*Causeries* 15:104–5).

74. Peyrat, *La presse,* 7 July 1856. Tocqueville himself was aware of the debt he owed his predecessors: "Every day," he wrote, "brings some intelligence into the area surrounding my subject, and there are already many facts which were entirely new two years ago and which, scientifically at least, are new no longer" (letter to Ampère, 1 Feb. 1856, *OC* 11:307).

75. Published in 1855, Cheruel's *Histoire de l'administration monarchique en France* had been presented to the Academy of Moral and Political Sciences in 1847 as a memoir. Tocqueville, whom Cheruel had helped in his preparation of *OR,* would necessarily have known about it.

76. At the close of the century, d'Eichtal, *Alexis de Tocqueville,* 185–92, and Roland-Marcel, *Essai politique,* 114, criticized Tocqueville for having used legal and administrative sources too much and memoirs and philosophical ones too little.

77. After de Meaux and Pontmartin in 1856, see Heinrich von Sybel, "Der alte Staat und die Revolution in Frankreich," in *Deutsche Rundschau* (1878).

78. De Meaux, *Le correspondant,* Nov. 1856, 264.

79. In an unpublished letter of 16 Dec. 1856, the old Etienne Pasquier accused Tocqueville of having misunderstood the persistence of aristocratic influence through 1789. Tocqueville saw only vague opinions on this, though it was one of the major themes in criticisms of his work (letter to Corcelle, 13 Nov. 1856, *OC* 15, 2:184; letter to Ampère, 7 Jan. 1857, *OC* 11:359). His overestimation of the weight of bureaucracy before 1789 was especially noticed by the Bonapartists, concerned with valorizing Napoleon's works: see Forcade, "Le gouvernement impérial et l'opposition nouvelle," 13.

80. See Coquille, *L'univers,* 11 Aug. 1856.

81. See Despois, *Revue de Paris,* 1 Oct. 1857, who, after enumerating archival sources consulted by Tocqueville, concludes: "The official and materially true picture of the state's diverse powers in the eighteenth century might be a perpetual source of error concerning number, civil servants' attributions, etc. This book is like Father Galiani's—what we must read in it is not only what is written but what is assumed, the *blanks,* as the clever abbé said. And in these blanks are practices. M. de Tocqueville has read them, translated and

commented upon them in these intimate documents. That is where he found, in intelligible and lively form, those unappreciated assumptions" (58).

82. *RDM*, 1 Aug. 1856, 657.

83. Edmond Scherer, *Etudes critiques sur la littérature contemporaine* (Paris: Michel Lévy, 1895), 10:226.

84. Faguet, *Politiques et moralistes* 3:75–76.

85. *Ibid.*

86. See the article entitled "Morcellement," *Dictionnaire d'économie politique.*

87. Peyrat, *La presse*, 30 June–7 July 1856.

88. Despois, *Revue de Paris*, 57.

89. See *Le correspondant*, Nov. 1856, 269.

90. It was blindness to these mechanisms of the democratic imagination that gave rise to the thesis of spontaneous reform of the monarchy which might have avoided the Revolution in Léonce de Lavergne, *Les assemblées provinciales sous Louis XVI*. See 114, "M. de Tocqueville's entire book is directed against the centralizing despotism of the old monarchy; how is it that Louis XVI's very noble efforts find no grace with him? No one has painted a crueller and more accurate picture of the intendants' administration, and when the monarchy itself abandons them, he begins to defend them, at least in appearance." The same thesis could already be found in de Meaux in *Le correspondant*, 1856.

91. Despois, *Revue de Paris*, 59. The demonstration seemed obvious only because it had been so long in coming, as Peyrat notes in *La presse*, June 30–July 7. The denunciation, if not of centralization itself (the term does not appear until the end of the eighteenth century), at least of royal power's encroachments, had made the rounds among aristocrats since the time of the monarchy's opponents—Fénelon, then the duc de Saint-Simon and the comte de Boulainvilliers. Under the Restoration, belief in the continuity between absolutism and postrevolutionary society was already common. The charter had claimed it established continuity between old France and the new by its respect for tradition and liberties. In a famous book, *De la monarchie française depuis son établissement jusqu'à nos jours* (1814), François-Dominique de Reynaud, comte de Montlosier, turned this argument on its head, showing the seed of revolutionary tyranny in absolutism. Under the July Monarchy, the Academy had in turn encouraged study of the ancien régime's administrative centralization. But the Lansonian method of hunting for the sources of an idea here shows its own limits. We can enumerate Tocqueville's "precursors" forever, but that will not tell us why people after him have said, "since Tocqueville."

92. Yet some did not make this reversal. The historian Mignet, Tocqueville's friend, in his "Notice historique sur la vie et les travaux de M. Alexis de Tocqueville," did not understand the work, because he remains faithful to the centralizing historiography developed by his friend Thiers and himself under the Restoration. He thought he read in it that France "is the admirable and slow work of a family, which in the surprising course of its existence over eight centuries has had the merit and glory . . . to gather up its parts, introduce unified organization, bring its minds together at the same time as its territories, melt its diverse populations into a single people, prepare its subjects by means of simi-

larity in obedience to equality before the state." The explanation for this revolutionary genesis as due to French political inexperience is only an "ingenious insinuation" (25).

93. *Journal des débats*, 27 July 1865.

94. See Rémusat, *RDM*, 1 Aug. 1856, 658: "Our nation is the least Germanic of all Germanic nations. For diverse reasons, among which the Roman civilization in the Gallic seems to me the principal one, it was in France that the distinctive characteristics of the conquering race were most promptly attenuated. France is in consequence the country where the aristocratic establishment was least developed, where in any case it was soonest modified by other elements basic to society, and for that reason it was because the aristocracy was less strong that it was less supported. The same causes which made it weak and passing made it unpopular; it didn't take, you might say."

95. Limayrac, *Le constitutionnel*, 29 June 1856. Through this shift Tocqueville and his readers returned to the Thermidorian tradition. In 1856 the subject of *Old Regime* evoked Mme de Staël's *Considérations sur la Révolution*. True, Tocqueville fails to cite them, but that is not a decisive argument, for Tocqueville does not cite secondary sources, a common practice in his era. Yet Tocqueville was too distant from the romantic tradition to owe much to Mme de Staël. On this connection see Kergorlay's letter to Tocqueville, 7 July 1856, *OC* 13, 2:300–301.

96. Guizot's letter to Tocqueville, 30 June 1856, Tocqueville Archives.

97. See Forcade de La Roquette, *Revue contemporaine*, 15 Dec. 1856, 13, 18.

98. Nisard, *Etudes d'histoire et de littérature,* 135–37.

99. See Hauréau, *L'illustration*, 17 July 1856.

100. See Regnault, *La critique française*, 15 Jan. 1961, 106.

101. See Limayrac, *Le constitutionnel*, 29 June 1856: "Where then is M. de Tocqueville seeking to go? He does not miss the aristocracy such as it was, such as he has just depicted it; that is impossible. He misses it as it must have been. This is no longer history nor politics, it is imagination and fantasy."

102. Despois, *Revue de Paris*, 1 Oct. 1856, 70, 75.

103. Neither the Bonapartists nor the republicans were in effect sensitive to the comparative study of revolutions that Tocqueville initiated, so counter did the comparative perspective run to their reverence for a national tradition in which they could read the universal. See Lamartine, course 9 in *Cours familier*, 196, 197: "And the word was made people . . . and this people was France." For Hauréau, *L'illustration*, 17 July 1856: "The French Revolution's particular character is an energetic tendency toward universality. England, Switzerland, and still other countries in old Europe had had national revolutions; the 1789 uprising sought a much more general aim than the emancipation of a nation; it was a veritable religious revolution that sought to save all peoples by proclaiming a new dogma. Thus do not keep the innovators from going toward the sons of Samaria, for it is in the name of the rights of man that they took up arms, for it is in the name of eternal justice that they, philosopher revolutionaries, set their hands to the oldest establishment of iniquity."

104. Letter to Sedgwick, 14 Oct. 1856, *OC* 7:182.

105. Letter to Mrs. Austin, 29 Aug. 1856, *OC* 6, 1:192.

106. See Feuer, "Tocqueville and the Genesis of War and Peace," and Diestelmeier, "Tocqueville lu par un magnat russe."

4. The Liberals' Posthumous Leader, 1860s

1. *MU*, 31 Dec. 1860, rept. in *Causeries du lundi* 5:93–121.

2. Regarding that polemic, see *Nouveaux lundis* 1:148–49. Sainte-Beuve concludes: "In truth, Tocqueville's political friends are strange. They seem to love him better in death than in life, for that is their fine theme and makes him a saint as well."

3. *Journal des débats*, 4 Oct. 1859, rept. in *L'Etat et ses limites*.

4. Tocqueville died on 16 Apr. On 19 Apr., Cavour accepted disarmament after five weeks of negotiation between the great powers in Paris. On 27 Apr., Austrian troops crossed the Ticino River.

5. On 1 Dec. 1858 western French newspapers, then *La patrie* and the *Gazette de France* announced his death. Tocqueville had to let them know otherwise, but from that point on, people in the know spoke of that "poor Tocqueville." On 13 Apr. 1859 there was a second announcement of his death in *Le constitutionnel*, followed on 14 Apr. by *La patrie*, which published his obituary on 15 Apr. On 16 Apr.—the day he did die—the family was denying earlier reports.

6. Augustin Cochin, *Le correspondant*, 25 Apr. 1859, 759.

7. Limayrac, *La patrie*, 15 Apr., attributes the origin of this comparison to Armand Carrel, a sign that the cliché had traveled so far that its true origins had been forgotten.

8. Cochin, *Le correspondant*, 25 Apr. 1859, 759.

9. Riancey, *L'union*, 19 Apr.; *L'univers*, 20 and 25 Apr., etc.

10. Starting with the funeral. While politicos had been asked kindly to keep their mouths closed, the family had called on "the poor, and the different charitable associations of Cannes, the Pénitents blancs, the Société des dames de la miséricorde and the Conférence de Saint Vincent de Paul" (*L'univers*, 25 Apr.). Then Edouard de Tocqueville protested on 8 Feb. 1861 in *La France* against a notice read by Mignet at the Academy in which Tocqueville was presented as a deist. Mme de Tocqueville destroyed the letter in his published correspondence in which Tocqueville expressed his religious doubts to Sophie Swetchine. Beaumont's preface was changed, at the family's request. See Jardin, *Alexis de Tocqueville*, 500–501.

11. *MU*, 25 Jan. 1861.

12. See his leaflet of 25 Feb. 1860, *De la liberté de l'Eglise et de l'Italie*.

13. Sainte-Beuve, *MU*, 25 Jan. 1861. Lacordaire and Guizot's speeches, also published in *MU*, 25 Jan. 1861, were reprinted in *OC* 16:312–45.

14. Lacordaire very accurately recalled Tocqueville's rational faith but added, so as to achieve the edifying effect he sought in his biography: "It was death which gave him the gift of love. He received as an old friend the God who visited him and, touched by his presence to the point of tears, finally free of this world, he forgot what he had been, his

name, his service, his regrets, desires, and even before bidding us adieu, there remained of this soul nothing more than the virtues it had acquired on earth during its stay." This myth was recirculated by Catholic tradition; see, for example, Henry Bordeaux, *Mémoires secrets du Chevalier de Rosaz (1796–1876)* (Paris: Plon, 1958).

15. See Lacordaire's letter of 23 Feb. 1861 in Rémi Brocart, "Alexis de Tocqueville et les catholiques libéraux" (M.A. thesis, University of Paris IV, 1988), 201–2: "Chateaubriand, O'Connel, Frédéric Ozanam, Tocqueville—these were, in the generation which has just closed, our fathers and our leaders." On 26 Feb. 1863 Albert de Broglie, Lacordaire's successor, emphasized what aligned his two predecessors: "Both thought the same way. But whereas one, afflicted with common impotence, confined himself to observing and predicting, the other drew confidence and the right to act from the inalienable liberty of faith."

16. See Prévost-Paradol, *Journal des débats*, 26 Jan. 1861.

17. Lamennais, *Correspondance générale* 6:828.

18. "What portrait does [Tocqueville] draw of this democracy, in that country in the world where it was seen in its most favorable conditions and where, in the greatest contrast to France, democracy had committed no crime and had always depended upon religion? He formally declares that it had destroyed the *spirit of family*, that it produced the most complete degradation and enslavement of the intelligence to mass passions at the same time as unbridled greed. . . . From all this I conclude that . . . the spirit of modern democracy is an infernal one" (letter to Lacordaire, 28 Feb. 1840, Lacordaire-Montalembert, *Correspondance inédite*, 478–79).

19. *Le correspondant*, 25 Aug. 1863.

20. Letter to A. de Broglie, 20 July 1856, *OC* (Bmt) 6:323.

21. Letter from Sophie Swetchine, 26 Sept. 1856, *OC* 15, 2:294.

22. Léopold Monty, *Revue européenne*, Mar.–Apr. 1861.

23. Felix Solar, *La presse*, 8 Dec. 1861.

24. Scherer, *Etudes critiques* 4:85–106.

25. *Correspondance et oeuvres posthumes* in *OC* (Bmt) 8:78–79.

26. Ibid., 42.

27. *RDM* 35 (1861): 777–813.

28. *Le pays*, 22 Jan. 1861.

29. *L'opinion nationale*, 5 May 1861.

30. Ibid.

31. *Augustin Cochin, 1823–1872* 2:93.

32. Leon de Wailly, *L'illustration*, 19 Jan. 1861: "He indeed sought to give a hand to liberalism and philosophy, without abandoning legitimacy and religion. . . . These were in truth merely intellectual pulls from different directions, but the result was a propitious balance in which reigned, though one might miss it, moderation, impartiality, and supreme reason."

33. See Abbé Ulysse Maynard, *Bibliographie catholique*, 1872, 81–82: "When alive, Tocqueville was overestimated because he was known more for his aspirations than his

true acts; because the moral man in him had too often pleaded beyond criticism, in favor of the literary and the political man … as a man of letters, Tocqueville wrote only one book, whose second part he was not even able to cause to agree with the first, and then sketches, always in breathless pursuit of a masterpiece, which fled on ahead of him; as a man of action, he never had an aim, or never reached it."

34. Monty, *Revue européenne*, Mar.–Apr. 1861, 61.

35. Louis Etienne, *Le constitutionnel*, 18 Jan. 1861, 3.

36. See Arbaud, *Le correspondant*, 25 Jan. 1866, 18. "There was in Tocqueville's rather thin personage and in the fine, angular, and regular lines of his face that indefinable aristocratic imprint that showed in everything, even in his reserve and silences, and which was in him not only the result of native elegance of morals but testimony of his exquisite delicacy of feeling and the elevation of his mind."

37. *Causeries du lundi* 15:100.

38. See letter from Royer-Collard, Dec. 1842, in the duchesse de Dino, *Chronique de 1831 à 1862* 2:438: "I fear that out of impatience to arrive, he has strayed onto impracticable paths, seeking to reconcile what cannot be reconciled. He is using both hands at the same time, giving the right hand to the left, the left hand to us, sorry he does not have a third he would give invisibly."

39. Sainte-Beuve, *Causeries du lundi* 15:100.

40. Mourin, *Revue de l'instruction publique*, 9 May 1861, 82.

41. *RDM*, 15 May 1859, 420–21.

42. Sainte-Beuve, *Causeries du lundi* 15:103–4.

43. Sainte-Beuve, *Cahier vert*, 165.

44. Jules Levallois, *L'opinion nationale*, 5 May 1861.

45. *Causeries du Lundi* 8:508.

46. *Le figaro*, 3 Jan. 1861.

47. See Jean Gaulmier's introduction to *Les Pléiades* in *Oeuvres de Gobineau* 3:972–76.

48. See letter to Gobineau, 8 Aug. 1843, *OC* 9:43.

49. Letters to Beaumont and to Corcelle, *OC* 8, 3:186, 15, 2:104–5.

50. Gobineau to Prokesch, 20 June 1856, cited in note by Chevallier in *OC* 9:30.

51. *Oeuvres de Gobineau* 3:136–37.

52. Rolland to A. de Chateaubriant, 10 Oct. 1920, cited in Jean Gaulmier, *Gobineau et sa fortune littéraire* (Saint Médard en Jalles: Editions Ducros, 1971), 10.

53. Scherer, *Le temps*, 7 May 1861.

54. Ampère, *Le correspondant*, 2 June 1859, rept. in *OC* 9:447.

55. An encyclopedic publication with woodcut illustrations whose aim was to provide a complete popular education, *Le magasin pittoresque* (1833–1938) was directed by Saint-Simonian Edouard Charton and proved a great success.

56. *Le magasin pittoresque* 30 (1862): 203, 41 (1873): 114, and 44 (1876): 179.

57. Ibid., 34 (1866): 254.

58. Ibid., 27 (1859): 306.

59. Ibid.,32 (1864): 402: "If I had children, I would tell them every day that we are in a time and a society where we must be apt for everything and prepared for everything, for none of us is sure of our destiny. And I would above all add that in this country it is well to count upon nothing anyone can take from you, but only to acquire what one can never lose except upon ceasing to live: energy, courage, knowledge, and good conduct."

60. Four long quotations in 1862 and 1875.

61. Especially see ibid., 35 (1867):182, "to be active in old age": "The firmest principle in my mind is that there is never a period in one's life when one can lie back; that effort beyond one's means, and even more within oneself is as necessary and even more necessary as one ages as when one was young. I compare people in this world to travelers who walk unceasingly toward a land growing colder and colder, and who thus must move even more as they advance. The great malady of the soul is the cold; to fight this fearful evil, we must not only keep up the mind's lively activity through work but even more through contact with one's peers and the affairs of this world."

62. See Bertauld, *La liberté civile.* Born in 1812, died in 1885, a lawyer at the bar of Caen in 1844, and professor of civil procedure and civil law at the law school of Caen, president of the bar on six occasions, he became a deputy to the Assembly in 1871 and president of the center Left.

63. Savary, Quenault's grandson, a political adversary of Tocqueville's in the Manche region, and one of the founders of the Molé-Tocqueville talks, devoted his opening speech to Tocqueville at the talk of 10 Dec. 1867. He was a center-right deputy and undersecretary of state for justice in Dufaure's cabinet (Feb. 1877–Jan. 1879).

64. Laboulaye, *Journal des débats,* 30 Oct. 1859.

65. See Prévost-Paradol, ibid., 11 June 1865. In French admiration for the southern United States, he saw "no other excuse than that falsely religious and blindly conservative passion, than that disgust for liberty and democracy in any form, than that exaggerated sense of our own misfortunes which make one part of French society instinctively defiant and spiteful toward all free states."

66. See Bonapartist L. Derome, "Une phase nouvelle de la crise américaine," *Revue contemporaine* 45 (May–June 1865): 159: "It was the regime before 1861 which excited the enthusiasm of public commentators the world over. This was what M. de Tocqueville spoke of, and what M. Laboulaye today speaks of, without adding that it has been destroyed by its clients."

67. First published in twelve parts in *RDM,* 15 Aug. 1865–1 Apr. 1866.

68. Allain-Targé, *La République sous l'Empire,* 51.

69. Regarding Tocqueville's influence on Barrot (who does not cite him), see Beaumont's letter of 8 July 1856, *OC* 8, 3:422. The relation between the two works was often brought up in 1861.

70. Letter to Laboulaye, 5 June 1865, in P. Legendre, "Méditation sur l'esprit libéral: La leçon d'Edouard de Laboulaye juriste témoin," *Revue du droit public et de la science politique* 1 (1971): 117.

71. *La presse,* 22 July 1865.

72. 5 and 7 Sept. 1865.

73. *La France,* 11 Sept. 1865.

74. Nefftzer, *Le temps,* 8 Sept. 1865.

75. Janet, "Alexis de Tocqueville et la science politique au XIXe Siècle," 112.

76. E. Poitou, *Revue nationale* 21 (May–July 1865): 66.

77. See Gigot, *Le correspondant,* 25 Dec. 1860, 694; Poitou, *Revue nationale* 21 (May–July 1865): 73; Laboulaye, *Journal des débats,* 30 Oct. 1859.

78. See Bertauld, *Philosophie politique,* chap. 10.

79. See *DA* 1:101, and the account of Sedgwick's work on the American Constitution (1858) in *OC* 16:243.

80. Champagny, *Revue européenne,* 1 Apr. 1835. Louis Blanc admits the moderating role of the judiciary which, attacking "the legislature with a small cry and small blows, . . . holds back the legislature's excesses" (*Revue républicaine,* May 1835, 146). But he only found virtue in judicial control as a way to oppose the creation of a second chamber.

81. Constitutional committee minutes in Craveri, *Genesi de una costituzione,* 301.

82. See Poitou, *Revue nationale* 21 (May–July 1865): 77–78.

83. See Maurice Hauriou, *Précis du droit constitutionnel* (Paris: Sirey, 1929). Rept. as "Il reste à conquérir les juges et l'opinion," *Commentaire* 36 (Winter 1986–87): 690.

84. *Le commerce,* 16 Feb. 1845; *OC* 3, 2:156–57.

85. See Benjamin Constant, *Principes de politique . . .* (1815; new ed., Paris: Hachette, Pluriel, 1989), chap. 19: "A removable or revocable judge is more dangerous than one who has purchased his job. Having bought one's position is a less corrupting thing than always fearing one will lose it."

86. *Esprit des lois* 11:11; "acte additionnel aux constitutions de l'Empire," written by Benjamin Constant (even though he had been a fierce opponent of Napoleon I during the first empire) during the Hundred Days, which was then published on 1 June 1815; anonymous article by Broglie in the *Revue française,* Nov. 1828, 58–132. Broglie's article led to provisions for the responsibility of agents of power in the charter. Despite the creation of a commission on 20 Aug. 1830 for the purpose of reorganizing the Council of State and various reports in 1832, 1834, and 1835, no law was enacted.

87. See Casimir-Périer, *L'Article 75 de la constitution de l'an VIII sous le régime de la constitution de 1852.*

88. Notably Dupont-White and Bertauld, *Philosophie politique.*

89. On such periodicity, see Maurice Hauriou, *De la formation du droit administratif français depuis l'an VIII* (1893).

90. Especially Anselme Batbie's great treatise, *Introduction générale au droit public et administratif* (1861); Rodolphe Dareste de La Chavanne, *La justice administrative en France* (1862); Théophile Ducrocq, *Cours de droit administratif* (1861); Léon Aucoc, *Conférences sur l'administration et le droit administratif* (1869).

91. Faguet, *Politiques et moralistes* 3:107, notes that the problem "had been resolved under the old monarchy in an accidental manner and by a shameful accident which, as happens in our poor world, had had excellent results," but in a democracy how could one

conceive of a "factitious class" of magistrates who would escape the state's and the parties' hold? "This organization has no chance of being tried out among a people who find the Institut and the bar too aristocratic and on the whole clashing with democratic institutions" (108).

92. See Louis Blanc, *Revue républicaine*, 10 May 1835, and Block's *Dictionnaire de l'administration française*, 2d ed. (1862), 15.

93. *DA* 1:285. That is why when judges are elected, as in America after 1850, there is no more civic "school." See Tocqueville's speech against the election of judges on 6 June 1848 to the constitutional committee. Here as elsewhere, Tocqueville vacillated between theoretical audacity and fear of going too fast. In 1848 he wanted to restrain the jury's expansion into the civil sector. See the constitutional committee minutes of 5 June 1848: "The jury is a difficult, complicated machine which we do not know how to set in motion in France. Judges and citizens are not ready to make it work, we must thus take our time." After Barrot, the commission moved more boldly in favor of expanding juries to deal with civil issues.

94. In Block's *Dictionnaire général de la politique* the article on the "Jury" by Gaston de Bourge is a gloss of *Democracy*. Favor for the notion of the jury can be found in Laboulaye, Jules Simon, Prévost-Paradol, Odilon Barrot, Girardin, and Proudhon.

95. See summary of the debate in Bertauld, *La liberté civile*, chap. 19.

96. The very word *decentralization*, which as late as 1863 Littré considered a neologism, became widespread. See Elzéar Lavoie, "La décentralisation discutée par la presse politique parisienne de 1860 à 1866" (university paper, Paris, 1963), xx. From 1840 to 1850 four works had the word *centralization* or *decentralization* in their titles, three of them in 1849; from 1850 to 1860, there was one work; from 1860 to 1870, 30 works; from 1870 to 1875, 12 works, 8 of them in 1870. The same trend can be seen if we examine works whose title refers to community administration: 11 from 1840 to 1850, 13 from 1850 to 1860, 38 from 1860 to 1870.

97. See Bersot, *Journal des débats*, 6 July 1861: "Words do not always say what they seem to say; they have different meanings according to the period in which they are spoken; if I am not mistaken, the word *decentralization*, repeated on all lips today, only means this: We want to act. We are experiencing an awakening of the individual, as elsewhere an awakening of nationality is experienced."

98. See "De l'enseignement et du noviciat administratif en Allemagne," *Revue de législation et de jurisprudence* 18 (1843): 513–611.

99. See Laboulaye, *Journal des débats*, 16 July 1865, notice in Block's *Dictionnaire général de la politique*: "The true heads of the new party, those who have given it its watchword and its flag, are the few writers enlightened by the Revolution of 1848, Tocqueville leading them all."

100. See Limayrac, *La patrie*, 8 May 1861.

101. Edouard Dupont-White, opponent of the empire, an economist, and the one who introduced Mill to France, specifically disagrees with the neo-Tocquevillean gospel in the

name of French nature. He criticizes Tocqueville for having introduced "a new way of reading history. In this past we see only the baleful creation of laws and customs which seem incompatible with political liberty" (*La centralisation*, 198). Yet for Dupont-White French centralization was adapted to the French "race," whereas the Anglo-Saxon race was characterized by individualism. Though Dupont-White concedes Tocqueville's diagnosis on the longevity of the tendency toward centralization, he thus refuses its explanation: the cause is neither in laws nor in the kings' perverse actions. The French are by nature "the most communistic of peoples" (125). Dupont-White's only success was in attracting paternal approval from the Bonapartists and disapproval from their opponents.

102. On the "revolutionary" dangers of state tutelage, see Barrot, *Etudes contemporaines*, chap. 6, "De l'influence de la centralisation sur la stabilité des gouvernements." The notion became a commonplace of the opposition, whence Dupont-White's line of argument in his *Centralisation*, 125: "A country where political powers are centralized will perhaps have revolutions with their natural effect of disturbing order, harming justice, compromising peace, and making the nation vulnerable. A country with powers distributed does not run these risks, and I well know the reason why: it has neither order, nor justice, nor peace, nor national connection."

103. In the *Dictionnaire politique* of Garnier-Pagès, Regnault wrote an article very favorable to centralization. In 1861 he published *La province* where he appeared to be a disciple of Tocqueville.

104. Dupont-White, *La liberté politique*, 81.

105. See Littré, *Fragments de philosophie positive et de sociologie contemporaine*, 206–29. Littré contrasted Dupont-White with "distinguished public commentators" who promoted self-government: "The modern advancement of civilization demands that the study and management of general interests be in the hands of an authority enlighted enough by positive knowledge to apply them, that it have enough foresight to embrace the whole and be impartial, and be strong enough to triumph over fragmentary resistances."

106. 11 Aug. 1857, *OC* 13, 2:329–30.

107. *DA* 1:60–61. This formula is found in the Nancy program, in Laboulaye's *Le parti libéral*, in Prévost-Paradol, *La France nouvelle*, and even in the report of Feb. 1865 to the legislature on the bill regarding decentralization.

108. Dupont-White, *La centralisation*, 10.

109. Dupont-White, *La liberté politique*, 213.

110. Ibid., 230.

111. Boesche, 306.

112. *La critique philosophique*, 3 Oct. 1872, 129.

113. *L'opinion nationale*, 7 Aug. 1865.

114. Dupont-White, *La centralisation*, 7.

115. *Le temps*, 7 Apr. 1835.

116. Girardin, *La presse*, 22 Jan. 1864.

117. *DA* 2:113, 1:169. He also referred to temporary groupings of opinions and interests as a "nation." Speaking of parties, he wrote, "they constitute, as it were, a separate nation in the midst of the nation, a government within the government" (*DA* 1:192).

118. Whence Louis Blanc's early reservations in *Revue républicaine*, 10 May 1835, 136.

119. In 1949 Maxime d'Azeglio noted that Tocqueville called the nationality question "political poetry," in an undated letter published by Cura di Nicomede Bianchi, *Lettere inedite di M. D'Azeglio al marchese E. D'Azeglio* (1883–84), 24–25.

120. Jules Levallois, *L'opinion nationale*, 7 Aug. 1865.

121. *Journal des débats*, 1 Oct. 1859.

122. Ibid., 16 July 1865, in an account of Block's *Dictionnaire*: "It is not this new [liberal] party's least merit that with the sole principle of individual liberty, it resolves political as well as political economy problems."

5. Toward Oblivion, 1870-1940

1. Daniel Halévy, *La fin des notables* (Paris: Grasset, 1930), 2:196.

2. Nonetheless, see Ferry's speeches of 10 Apr. 1870 and 3 June 1876.

3. See *OC* 3, 3:465–70, document written at the request of the duc de Levis. A copy is kept in the Montalivet papers and bears the note, "letter consulted by the princes d'Orléans." Its expression "marvellous luck" was not included in the *Gazette*.

4. During the second attempt at restoration on 24 Sept. 1873, in the *Correspondant*'s "political chronicle," Boucher once more returned to Tocqueville's letter.

5. The minutes are archived at National Archives, series C* II, 607–18. The first commission focused on the question of regime. The second and third commissions examined constitutional laws that defined the shape of the regime. The second commission met from 5 Dec. 1873 until May 1875. Batbie was its president, and its vice presidents were Kerdrel and Talhouet. Among its members were Dufaure, Laboulaye, Waddington, Lacombe, de Meaux, comte Daru, Chesnelong, Lefèvre-Pontalis, and Vacherot. Conservatives were dominant.

6. Kerdrel, 22 Dec. 1873, 9 Feb. 1874. As representative to the constituent assembly and the legislative assembly in 1848 and 1849 and as deputy to the legislature in 1852, Kerdrel had cited Tocqueville at the podium. He was a representative to the National Assembly in 1871 and a senator in 1876. Kerdrel was one of the main speechmakers of the legitimist party and was elected vice president of the Assembly in 1874.

7. 28 Mar. 1874, by vice president of the cabinet Broglie, heard during the commission's discussion of the senate.

8. 13 Jan. 1874 session of the subcommission.

9. See Broglie's speech, 28 Mar. 1874, "The more simplicity with which we can act, the better. The country is tired of declarations of human rights."

10. Victor de Broglie, *Vues sur le gouvernement de la France* (Paris: Michel Lévy, 1870).

11. See Léopold de Gaillard, "L'obstacle," *Le correspondant*, Oct.–Dec. 1876, 19. "It is no longer the right time to argue for or against the institution invented twenty years ago which has been in practice since then. The best is to accommodate oneself to it."

12. See F. de La Coste, "La loi électorale et le scrutin d'arrondissement," ibid., Apr.–June 1875, 1269–90, and H. de Larcy, "La décentralisation de 1789 à 1870," ibid., 10 Apr. 1870, 5.

13. See H. de Lacombe, "Le suffrage universel et la représentation des intérêts," ibid., 25 Nov. 1876, 593–650, and Carné, "La Commission des Trente," ibid., 25 Jan. 1873, 201–20.

14. H. de Larcy, "La décentralisation de 1789 à 1870," 5.

15. Gaillard, "L'obstacle."

16. Anon., "Les mœurs judiciaires et les crimes en Amérique," *Le correspondant*, 10 July 1873, 152–61.

17. Boucher, ibid., 9 July 1873, advised Gambetta to "read those true and profound maxims of M. de Tocqueville": "Despotism can do without faith, not liberty. Religion is much more necessary in a republic than in a monarchy, and in democratic republics above all others."

18. See "La doctrine républicaine ou ce que nous sommes, ce que nous voulons être," *La critique philosophique*, 8 Aug. 1872.

19. See Renouvier, "Le progrès et la morale," ibid., 8 Feb. 1872: "Evil is in a philosophy which reigns throughout, in Germany more than in the Latin nations, against which Christianity now seems powerless to fight, and whose fearful invasion only criticism can combat."

20. "Le dilemme: Césarisme ou république," ibid., 18 July 1872; "Décentralisation et Self-Government," ibid., 5 Sept., 3 Oct. 1872; "Maires et préfets," ibid., 13 Apr. 1876.

21. "Décentralisation et Self-Government," ibid., 3 Oct. 1872, 131.

22. Michel, *Questions du temps présent*, 17–20, 64; Michel, *L'idée de l'Etat*, 318–19.

23. Tocqueville's conceptual vagueness is highlighted by Michel, *L'idée de l'Etat*, 326, 338, and by Roland-Marcel, *Essai politique*, 122.

24. Halévy, *La fin des notables*, 231.

25. Ferry attacked Pillon starting 31 Dec. 1868 in *L'électeur libre*.

26. See Scherer, *Le temps*, 17 Aug. 1876; "We must keep . . . from confusing Tocqueville with the Doctrinaires, and especially with those who followed them, the conservatives of our time. Tocqueville is different from both of them in his political principles and his religious tendencies. It is enough to convince oneself to compare those writings where Guizot is determined to represent democracy as a plague with those where Tocqueville applies himself to understanding it as a fact."

27. See Flaubert, *Dictionnaire des idées reçues* (written between 1872 and 1880): "America: Go into a tirade on self-government."

28. Planning a course on the United States in 1866, Allain-Targé wanted "to prove that M. de Tocqueville and M. Laboulaye were wrong, and that they had provided a false argument for a detestable theory by claiming that America was the result, the work of the Protestant religious spirit, and the development of Saxon institutions brought from England by New England's early Puritans. On the contrary," he sought to "demonstrate that the founders of the United States were all freethinkers, men of the eighteenth century, from Franklin to Jefferson" (*La République sous l'Empire*, 39).

29. Laboulaye to Miss Mary Booth, 11 July 1880, cited in Simon Jeune, *De F. T. Graindorge à Barnabooth* (Paris: Didier, 1963), 100.

30. See Frout de Fontpertuis, *Les Etats-Unis*. This is the only important synthesis before Jannet's 1876 book. It is based on Chevalier, Tocqueville, Laboulaye, Bancroft, and Story, all old sources at the time. Frout's book is often mentioned in the histories and dictionaries of the 1870s.

31. "La manière d'écrire l'histoire en France et en Allemagne," *RDM*, 1 Sept. 1872.

32. See Gabriel Hanotaux, *Sur les chemins de l'histoire* (Paris: Champion, 1924), 2:220, and Courcelle-Seneuil, *L'héritage de la Révolution*.

33. See Charles-Olivier Carbonell, *Histoire et historiens: Une mutation idéologique des historiens français, 1865–1885* (Toulouse: Privat, 1976), 159–60. Two-thirds of the biographies and monographs published from 1870 to 1875 focused on France from the end of the ancien régime to the Revolution.

34. Title of Lavollée's article in *Le correspondant*, Jan. 1874.

35. See Salmon, *Revue des questions historiques* 19 (1876): 606; Sorel, *Revue historique* 2 (1876): 283–84; Hillebrand, *Deutsche Rundschau* 12 (1877). In several places Taine's correspondence shows that he read Tocqueville. See Taine, *Vie et correspondance* 3:266, 300, 319. Though Fustel does not cite Tocqueville, he uses the apology for the Middle Ages' local freedoms shaken by monarchy and destroyed by the Revolution; the wariness toward our modern bureaucracy "which only the French find admirable" (*RDM*, 1 July 1871); and the apology for the judiciary as a "safeguard" against legislative excesses (*RDM*, 1 Oct. 1871). But these developments are influenced by an aristocratic perspective.

36. Gabriel Monod, in Fustel's obituary, *Revue historique* 41 (Sept.–Dec. 1889): 284–85: "M. Fustel de Coulanges is of the family of Tocqueville and Montesquieu. He is superior to both, not only as an artist and writer but also as a scholar . . . but more than they were, he was ruled by a spirit of systematization."

37. Regarding the Ecole des sciences politiques, see Anon., *L'Ecole libre des sciences politiques, 1871–1889* (1889); Pierre Rain, *L'Ecole libre des sciences politiques* (Paris: Fondation nationale des sciences politiques, 1963); Pierre Favre, *Naissance de la science politique en France, 1870–1914* (Paris: Fayard, 1989).

38. When Taine established the program of study in 1871, he proposed a comparative study of political constitutions from the founding of the American republic in the manner of Tocqueville and Laboulaye, but with the scientific rigor of a Le Play or the zoologists (*Journal des débats*, 17 Oct. 1871).

39. Sorel, *Montesquieu*, 166.

40. National Archives, F1C1 156, Manche.

41. National Archives, F1C1 168, Seine. In 1873 the Paris city council had made plans for a Tocqueville Street in the sixth arrondissement, later aborted.

42. National Archives, F21 4383, Manche.

43. See the *Gazette de France*, 21 Mar. 1896.

44. Let us set aside anachronistic texts which, though published in the 1880s, are part of the July Monarchy's conceptual universe. These include the very critical posthumous work of Gaillardet who lived in New Orleans for ten years from 1837 to 1847, *L'aristocratie en Amérique* (1883), and Auguste Carlier's *La République américaine*, posthumously published in 1890 through Jannet's offices, which follows Tocqueville's path, hating and den-

igrating him all the more as an unsurpassable rival. Notary Carlier went to the United States from 1855 to 1857 and met several of the people Tocqueville talked with: Gilpin, E. Everett, G. Ticknor, Longfellow, Josiah Quincy, Charles Sumner.

45. Portalis, *Deux républiques*; Noailles, *Cent ans de république aux Etats-Unis.*

46. Carlier, *La République américaine* 1:72, 146.

47. Portalis, *Deux républiques.* Portalis, who dabbled as a public commentator, was sent to prison and punished with fines under the empire and the Republic. He had traveled in the United States during the 1860s. His entire work tries to show how, since the Revolution, France had distanced itself because of its specific notion of sovereignty from "good" American tradition and adopted a more representative than democratic form of government.

48. The annals of the National Assembly, 26:4–6.

49. Concern with how democracy was to be organized never disappeared. But it resurfaced in the residual milieu of the "moderates," at the Ecole des sciences politiques and in the thinking of Paul Laffitte, a friend of the d'Eichtals. Thinking in *Le suffrage universel et le régime parlementaire* about what Boulanger's success revealed about French society, Laffitte faulted the distance between France and the American model. In France there was no local life except at the township level. French democracy was not yet delivered of its revolutionary heritage. Laffitte felt France must return to Tocqueville, "at the risk of seeming to some a little behind the times" (230–31).

50. Baunard, *La foi*, 284. In the same vein, see Nicolas, "Le vicomte A. de Tocqueville." Father Baraud, the prolific author of pious biographies and tales of the Vendée "martyr," took Monsignor Baunard's strategy to a radical extreme and plagiarized him shamelessly in his *Chrétiens et hommes célèbres au XIXe siècle.*

51. Pailleron, *Le monde où l'on s'ennuie.*

52. See Frans van Kalken, "L'influence de Tocqueville en Belgique," *Livre du centenaire*, a colloquium in 1959 (Paris: CNRS, 1960), 115–20, and Drescher, *Tocqueville and England*, 217–21.

53. Gabriel Alix, review of *La réforme sociale* by Le Play in *Annales de sciences politiques* 7 (1892): 722–33.

54. Boutmy, *Eléments d'une psychologie politique du peuple américain*, 11–13. This, together with ideological divergences, explains the paucity of references to Tocqueville among the members of Le Play's social economy society. Le Play used Tocqueville in *La réforme sociale* to show the moderating weight of religion (1:65), the effect of laws governing succession (1:105), the rise of envy (1:204–5), and the role of towns (2:284), while criticizing his partiality. Le Play's successors kept greater distance. In the Le Playsian movement's periodical *La réforme sociale*, founded in 1881, only one article is devoted to Tocqueville: Paul Nourrisson, *La réforme sociale*, 1–16 July 1915, 492–95.

55. See James Bryce, "The Predictions of Hamilton and de Tocqueville," *Johns Hopkins University Studies in Historical and Political Science*, Sept. 1887.

56. Roland-Marcel, *Essai politique*, 102, and Boutmy, *Eléments d'une psychologie politique du peuple américain*, 10.

57. The anthologies of articles by Georges Avenel which initially appeared in Gam-

betta's *La République française* before 1875 were followed by those of Marcellin Pellet, *Variétés révolutionnaires*, 3 vols. (1885–90), and by Eugène Spüller, *Hommes et choses de la Révolution* (1896). See Paul Farmer, *France Reviews Its Revolutionary Origins* (New York: Columbia Univ. Press, 1944).

58. See Paul Gerbod, "L'enseignement supérieur découvre la Révolution française au XIXe siècle," in *La légende de la Révolution* (Clermont-Ferrand: Faculté des lettres et sciences humaines de l'Université Blaise Pascal, 1988), 597–604.

59. In this, Alphonse Aulard was hardly different from most historians who confined themselves to the philosophes' intellectual history. See Charles Aubertin, *L'esprit public au XVIIIe siècle* (Paris: Didier, 1872); Felix Rocquain, *L'esprit révolutionnaire avant la Révolution* (Paris: Plon, 1878); Champion, *Esprit de la Révolution française*; Roustan, "Les philosophes et la société française au XVIIIe." Only Daniel Mornet in *Les origines intellectuelles de la Révolution française* tries to analyze the effect of social tendencies on ideology, but with only initial and scornful reference to Tocqueville.

60. Aulard cites Tocqueville in *Taine, historien de la Révolution française* but only to deplore that Taine had "taken Tocqueville at his word, only because Tocqueville was grave," 48.

61. On 27 Nov. 1903 Jaurès presented a resolution to the Chamber to publish documents on the Revolution. The commission, presided over first by Jaurès and then by Aulard, published 27 volumes of the *cahiers de doléances* drawn up by the three estates in 1789 (1905) and then 11 volumes on sales of *biens nationaux* (1906 and 1908).

62. Jaurès, *Histoire socialiste*, 77, 82.

63. *OR* is cited by the Russian Ivan Vasilévitch Loutchiski, *La petite propriété en France avant la Révolution* (1897) and *L'état des classes agricoles en France à la veille de la Révolution* (Paris: Champion, 1911), and later by Georges Lefebvre, *Les paysans du Nord* (Lille: O. Marquant, 1924).

64. See Father Lemonnier, "De la propriété foncière du clergé et la vente des biens ecclésiastiques dans la Charente-Inférieure," *Revue des questions historiques*, Jan. 1906.

65. Georges Lefebvre, preface to *OR* in *OC* 2, 1:57.

66. Seignobos, chap. 5 in *Histoire de la langue*, ed. Petit de Julleville, vol. 8.

67. See also the comte de Chambrun, who spoke of "our historians Guizot, Tocqueville, Thiers" in a Sept. 1888 lecture. Chambrun, a disappointed Anglophile and republican who represented the conservative right wing, played an essential role in the founding of the Musée social.

68. Brunetière, *Histoire et littérature* 1:209. Article dated 1878.

69. See ibid., 1:103, 215, and the *Manuel de l'histoire de la littérature française*.

70. Sorel used Tocqueville's explanation of hatred for feudalism, the idea of the growing similarity between the bourgeoisie and the nobility, and that of increasing discontent due to prosperity. Sorel even displayed the same astonishment at the events of 1789: "The reign of freedom was what would have been truly extraordinary in the Revolution" (*L'Europe* 1:233).

71. See Alice Gérard, "Histoire et politique: La *Revue historique* face à l'histoire contemporaine (1885–1898)," *Revue historique* 255: 2:353–405.

72. Ibid., 1879, 414: "M. de Tocqueville was the first to try to develop the national conscience in this direction."

73. Ibid., 1895, 364–70.

74. Ibid., 1897, 350–51.

75. Letter from Antonin de Beaumont to Calmann-Lévy, 7 Feb. 1891, made known to me by Jean-Yves Mollier.

76. See preface by Antonin de Beaumont in Tocqueville, *Souvenirs*, ed. Christian de Tocqueville, pp. iii–iv.

77. Boesche, 253.

78. Letter to Reeve, 5 Apr. 1857, *OC* 6, 1:217.

79. Reports of 17 Feb. 1892, Calmann-Lévy Archives, made known to me by Jean-Yves Mollier.

80. BN, Calmann-Lévy records.

81. See *Le temps*, 15 Nov. 1892.

82. Lanzac, *Le correspondant*, Apr.–June 1893, 165.

83. Michel in *Histoire de la langue*, ed. Petit de Julleville, 7:630.

84. Lanzac, *Le correspondant*, 164.

85. Lautier, *Le temps*, 3 Mar. 1893.

86. See H. Rabusson, *L'univers illustré*, 18 Mar. 1893, and Gaston Deschamps, *Le temps*, 4 June 1899.

87. See Louis Farges, *Revue historique*, 1893, 345.

88. Spüller's speech of 3 Mar. 1894.

89. Eugène Spüller, *Figures disparues* (1894), 3:26.

90. See Houtin, *L'américanisme*, and Alexander Sedgwick, *The Ralliement in French Politics, 1890–1898* (Cambridge, Mass.: Harvard Univ. Press, 1965).

91. First published as articles in *Le correspondant*, 23 Apr. and 23 Aug. 1890.

92. See Guillaume de Chabrol, "Un prêtre américain, Le Révérend Père Hecker," ibid., 25 May 1897. After recalling, like Tocqueville, that American democrats were not anti-Christian like the European ones, Chabrol notes: "In Paris, Channing would perhaps have been debased to the level of a Renan. Channing has been compared to a magnificent belltower calling, in a harmonious tone, the faithful to a nonexistent church. Yet a belltower and a bell are still something; the faithful can ultimately find sanctuary in themselves" (675).

93. The letter is published in the second edition of Marie, vicomte de Meaux's book, *L'Eglise et la liberté catholique aux Etats-Unis.* Cardinal Gibbons compared de Meaux to Tocqueville. Like Tocqueville, de Meaux emphasized the beneficial influence of a democratic clergy on society's right order (342), the role of women in social mores (191), and the double tendency of Protestants toward Catholicism and atheism (341). Like him, too, de Meaux sought to end the Revolution by destroying irreligiosity, the final remnant of the revolutionary spirit (408).

94. Brunetière had praised the American church in "Le catholicisme aux Etats-Unis," *RDM*, 1 Nov. 1989, 140–81. He affirmed, as Tocqueville had, that Catholicism might survive in democratic times and praised the combination of Catholicism and self-interest prevalent in the United States.

95. See Léon XIII's letter to Monsignor Gibbons in "Testem Benevolentiae," of 22 Jan 1899.

96. Houtin, *L'américanisme* 1:276. In 1835–40, "those who fought to gain political and social liberties may even have drawn all their weapons from a book written by a Catholic, Tocqueville, *Democracy in America*. But that work, as famous as it was, seemed false and dangerous to the clergy, who were very certain that democracy would never become established in France and that the principles of 1789, disapproved of by the church, could never triumph for long. M. de Tocqueville's authority seemed even more importunate to the clergy because he was not afraid to give them advice. A layman really does not have the state of grace sufficient to deal with reserved questions." American Catholicism, less concerned with dogma and ritual than with morality and social practice, respects rights of conscience. But precisely for that reason it is close to what the French consider a kind of "Protestantism" (160).

97. Reprinted by E. Poulat, 1961, 22–211, and initially published in nine installments in *Démocratie chrétienne* beginning in Feb. 1902.

98. See de Gaulle's 1916 notebooks, *Lettres, notes, et carnets, 1905–1918*. De Gaulle knew indirectly of Tocqueville by reading Boutmy, A. Sorel, and Catholic literature (Lacordaire, Sophie Swetchine, *Le correspondant*). I owe to Odile Rudelle this notion of the possible lineage of nineteenth-century liberalism.

99. See *Le temps*, 10 Mar. 1904.

100. See Paul de Rousiers dissenting from Le Play's school, *La vie américaine*.

101. Maurras, *Gazette de France*, 8 Feb. 1903, rept. in the *Dictionnaire politique et critique* 1:61–62.

102. *L'action française*, 27 Aug. 1913, rept. in the *Dictionnaire politique et critique* 1:62.

103. *L'action française*, 30 Apr. 1910, rept. in the *Dictionnaire politique et critique* 1:63.

104. Montesquiou, *L'action française* [bimonthly] 92 (Apr. 1903): 169–78. Montesquiou cites Le Play's judgment at length. In Apr. 1911, while Action française seemed the titled defender of the papacy and royalism, and connections were severed with the liberal Right, Léon de Montesquiou reminded d'Haussonville—who was related to the Broglie dynasties—that "the error of good people is more dangerous than that of rogues" (ibid., 30 Dec. 1911). A courteous preliminary controversy had exploded in July–Sept. 1902 in *Le gaulois*, a publication read by the fashionable society Action française was trying to court. When d'Haussonville pleaded that it was impossible to "mak[e] an overflowing river retrace its path," Bourget criticized [him] for being a poorly informed disciple of Tocqueville's. For like Tocqueville, d'Haussonville had allowed himself to be fooled by the "idol" of democracy. Criticism of supporting liberal democracy went beyond Action française. Charles Benoist, who denounced the era's political sophistry in *Sophismes politiques de ce temps*, attacked the "political romance" which tended to posit that democracy was rising like a fast stream.

105. In the fall of 1925, Rédier created a militant group, the Legion, and he claimed to have acquired Maurras's support for it. The Legion's program showed real fascination with Italian fascism. It merged in 1926 with Taittinger's traditionalist group the Jeunesses

patriotes, of which Rédier became vice president. Rédier tried to make them join Le Fais-
ceau, created by Valois. Taittinger, helped by a right-wing coalition, managed to expel
Rédier. See Zeev Sternhell, *Ni droite ni gauche: L'idéologie fasciste en France* (Paris: Seuil,
1983), 116–20.

106. Antoine Rédier, *Comme disait M. de Tocqueville*, 239.

107. Lucien Dubech, *Le gaulois*, 18 Nov. 1925. See also Orion, *L'action française*, 16 Nov.
1925: "It was through an act of intelligence that Tocqueville made himself the prophet
of democracy, but an intellectual act entirely consonant with that stupid nineteenth century, and an illustration of it."

108. Guy Grand, "Le procès de la démocratie," *RMM*, 1910, 132.

109. Lucien Maury, "Les lettres, oeuvres, et idées de Tocqueville," *Polybiblion*, 1910,
376–79.

110. Cited in William Logue, *From Philosophy to Sociology: The Evolution of French Liberalism, 1870–1914* (DeKalb: Northern Illinois Univ. Press, 1983).

111. Parodi, *RMM*, 1912, 320.

112. Grand, "Le procès de la démocratie," 579. See also "The Christian democrats, disciples of Tocqueville or Brunetière, and the [1848]-style socialists were indeed happy; they
marched in Providence's wake, knew that democracy was heaven-ordained and that it
would triumph over and against all, sooner or later, but as sure as the church with which
it had so much affinity. . . . We must, not without regret, abandon these aimable theological fictions. They have great force for those whom they enchant, but this force fails
us" (707).

113. D'Eichtal, *Alexis de Tocqueville*, 53, 112, 190.

114. In the Chamber during the Dreyfus affair, Jaurès reminded Cavaignac that a free
democracy has everything to fear from a vast army. "These are the words of M. de Tocqueville, in the tradition of all liberals" (24 Feb. 1898 session).

115. See Deschanel, *La décentralisation*, 9, 59.

116. Albert Thibaudet, *Les idées politiques de la France* (Paris: Stock, 1932), 54–55.

117. Thibaudet, "Le politique et le philosophe."

118. "La crise du libéralisme," *RMM*, 1902, 748.

119. See Maxime Leroy, "Alexis de Tocqueville," *Politica* 1:4 (Aug. 1935): 392–424. The
same Maxime Leroy was much less critical of Tocqueville in 1962 in his *Histoire des idées
sociales en France*.

120. See Faguet's imaginary dialogue with Tocqueville concerning the constitutional
committee of 1848 in *Politiques et moralistes* 3:66: "You did nothing whatsoever?" "Nothing." "Nor said anything?" "Almost nothing." "Why?" "Insufferable malaise. There was a
chatterbox and a schemer." "As on all commissions." "The chatterbox kept me from
putting in my ideas. The schemer took advantage of the exhaustion the chatterbox had
caused us to pass his own little proposals schemed in advance, one by one, at the end of
every session. We would have had to outscheme the schemer and conquer the chatterbox.
I let things go." "In fact, you lacked firmness." "In the presence of fools." "That is what it
means to be ill suited for public life."

121. Thibaudet, "D'Alexis de Tocqueville à Daniel Halévy," 317.

122. Favre, *Naissances de la science politique en France*, 9.

123. The genre's stagnation became noticeable in reprints like *Histoire de la science politique dans ses rapports avec la morale* by Paul Janet, published in 1855 and three times thereafter until 1913. Henry Michel renewed the genre but distanced his normative history of ideas (see *L'idée de l'Etat*, 1896) from his work as a public commentator for *Le temps.*

124. See Robert Nisbet, *The Sociological Tradition* (New York: Basic Books, 1966).

125. See Philippe Besnard, "La formation de l'équipe de l'*Année sociologique*," *Revue française de sociologie* 20:1 (Jan.–Mar. 1979): 7–31. Besnard shows *L'année sociologique*'s founders' desire in 1896 to distinguish themselves from Renouvier's and Pillon's old *Critique philosophique*. The split was even more important because Durkheim had been a student of Renouvier.

126. "I think the realists are wrong; but especially, I am certain that the political tendency of their philosophy, dangerous in any era, is very pernicious in the era in which we live. The great peril of democratic eras . . . is the destruction or excessive weakness *of the parts* of the social body in the presence of the *whole*" (letter to Henry Reeve, 3 Feb. 1840, *OC* 6, 1:52–53). Tocqueville's "methodological individualism" is the epistemological side of his political liberalism.

127. Bouglé, a student at the Ecole normale supérieure, placed first in the *agrégation* in philosophy in 1893. He made a study trip to Germany in 1893–94 where he met up with Simmel, who had read Tocqueville. He began a thesis under the direction of Henry Michel, received advice from Paul Janet, and as a friend of Elie Halévy's wrote the sociology column for the *Revue de métaphysique et de morale*, founded in 1893. In 1896 he founded the *Année sociologique* with Durkheim.

128. Bouglé is one of those rare people to have taken a position in the name of liberty against anticlerical politics. See his article, "La crise du libéralisme," *RMM*, 1902, where he claims Constant, Tocqueville, and Durkheim as his influences.

129. See "Le Darwinisme en sociologie," *RMM*, 1910, 79–92. Against sociological Darwinism, Bouglé proposed a return to Tocqueville, that is, to a veritable experimental sociology which combined observation and "idealism."

130. See Robert A. Nye, *The Origins of Crowd Psychology: Gustave Le Bon and the Crisis of Mass Democracy in the Third Republic* (London and Beverly Hills: Sage, 1975), chap. 7.

131. Le Bon, *Les lois psychologiques*, 6. Le Bon only uses *DA*'s chapter on the possible emergence of an industrial aristocracy. Where Tocqueville discerns marginal risk, Le Bon sees confirmation of his theory on the growth in consubstantial inequality as civilization progressed, 39.

132. Tarde, *Les transformations du pouvoir*, foreword, v.

133. "It is fortunate, in sum, that, as it grows, i.e., as it becomes more intense and more irresistible as well as more extensive, power becomes more impersonal through distance which increases between government and governed" (ibid., 209).

134. See the *New York Herald*, 6 Aug. 1936.

135. Through the efforts of comte Jean de Tocqueville, the bust was later placed in the village square.

136. Beyond Rédier, we can cite Charles Cestre, professor of American literature and civilization at the Sorbonne, who devoted several courses to Tocqueville in 1932–33, published in the *Revue des cours et conférences* 34:1 and 2 (1933), 35:1 (1934). Cestre deplored Tocqueville's indulgence toward Christianity and the ancien régime. He stated that Tocqueville had exaggerated the importance of America's Puritan beginnings. "With such general statements, one could make a whale come out of protozoa" (525). The only other important work was solely concerned with Normandy: Edmond L'Hommedé, *Un département français sous la Monarchie de Juillet: le conseil général de la Manche et Alexis de Tocqueville* (Paris: Boivin, 1933).

137. P.G. [Anon.], *Livres et revues*, 12 Nov. 1925.

6. Tocqueville's Return

1. Elie Halévy, *L'ère des tyrannies* (Paris: Gallimard, 1924; rept. 1938, 1990).

2. Created in 1979 by Godefroy, deputy from Valognes, with the support of the Manche regional (departmental) council, the prize has been presented by such distinguished personalities as former French presidents Valéry Giscard d'Estaing and Mitterrand and poet and former president of Senegal Léopold Sédar Senghor. It is awarded by a jury presided over by Alain Peyrefitte and has been given to Raymond Aron (1979), David Riesman (1980), A. Zinoviev (1982), Sir Karl Popper (1984), Louis Dumont (1987), Octavio Paz (1989), François Furet (1991), Leszek Kolakowski (1994), and Michel Crozier (1997).

At the cabinet meeting on 19 Nov. 1986, François Mitterrand made reference to the *Système pénitentiaire* to fight a plan for private prisons, to which Minister of Justice Albin Chalandon retorted that the president had not read his Tocqueville very well (*Le monde*, 21 Dec. 1986).

3. Charles Rist used a Tocquevillean denunciation of class hatred which causes the French to tear each other apart. See *Une saison gâtée*, 333–43.

4. Cousteau, "Alexis de Tocqueville, Quarante-huitard en peau de lapin."

5. See Ramon Fernandez, *La gerbe*, 10 Dec. 1942; Pierre Masteau, *L'appel*, 11 Feb. 1943.

6. See Pierre MacOrlan, *Les nouveaux temps*, 18 Dec. 1942.

7. André Thérive, *Demain*, 16 Dec. 1942.

8. See Ramon Fernandez, *NRF*, 1 Dec. 1942, 724–34. Fernandez analyzed Tocqueville's style with great subtlety and noted the overly serious, outdated character "of those solid, fine reflections which shaped awareness of public life, and which modern propaganda's overkill has made us lose the habit of" (734).

9. See Michela Dall'aglio, "Contribution to an Italian Bibliography on Alexis de Tocqueville," *Tocqueville Review* 13 (1992): 1.

10. In *La presse de la Manche* (26 May 1978), Mayer indicated that Gallimard had sold 80,000 paperback copies of *Ancien Régime*, 50,000 copies of *Démocratie* in its abridged edition, and 30,000 copies of the *Souvenirs*. To which we must add the 10/18 series in paper of *Démocratie* (abridged ed., 1963); the edition of *Démocratie* published by Flammarion

(unabridged, 1981), the one published in 1986 in the Folio-Gallimard series, and the edition published together with *Souvenirs* and *Ancien Régime* in the Laffont's Bouquins series. *Ancien Régime* was published in 1960 by Amiot and also as part of the series, Club du livre d'histoire. It was published by the Club français du livre in 1963, and in a Folio-Gallimard edition in 1988.

11. See Raymond Aron, *L'opium des intellectuels* (Paris: Calmann-Lévy, 1955)(the last chapter is entitled "Fin de l'âge idéologique"); Daniel Bell, *The End of Ideology* (New York: Collier, 1962; French trans., Paris: PUF, 1997).

12. We find close parallels in de Pradt, Custine, Thiers, and Ségur. See Fabian, *Alexis de Tocqueville Amerikabild.*

13. See Mayer, *Prophet of the Mass Age* ; Karl Pisa, *Tocqueville, Prophet des Massenzeitalters: Eine Biographie* (Stuttgart: deutsche Verlagsanstalt, 1984).

14. See *Le monde,* 16 Apr. 1959.

15. See Aron, "La définition libérale de la liberté," and the second lesson of *Dix-huit leçons*; Geiss, "Tocqueville und Karl Marx"; Mayer, "Alexis de Tocqueville und Karl Marx"; Benson, "Group Cohesion."

16. See 1898 ed. of *Democracy in America* with a preface by Daniel C. Gilman.

17. This type of interpretation was long-lived. See Eugene J. McCarthy, *America Revisited 150 Years after Tocqueville* (Garden City, N.Y.: Doubleday, 1978); Thomas Molnar, *Le modèle défiguré: L'Amérique de Tocqueville à Carter* (Paris: PUF, 1978), which ends with a chapter entitled "Tocqueville revu." Richard Reeves has retraced Tocqueville's journey step by step, interviewing descendants of those Tocqueville interviewed; see *American Journey: Traveling with Tocqueville in Search of Democracy in America* (New York: Simon & Schuster, 1982). All of these interpretations have been made possible by the remarkable scholarly work of George W. Pierson, *Tocqueville and Beaumont in America.*

18. Connections between Tocqueville and American thinkers on consensus has been highlighted by Birnbaum, *Sociologie de Tocqueville,* 137–47. Similarities to David Riesman are the most frequently noted, though Riesman criticized Tocqueville for ignoring the weight of inequality in America in "Tocqueville as Ethnographer." Similarities to Seymour Lipset, Daniel Bell, and R. Dahl have also been noted.

19. See Kirk, *The Conservative Mind.* Chapter 6 brings Macaulay, Cooper, and Tocqueville together under the heading of "liberal conservatives."

20. See Friedrich Hayek, "Individualism: True and False," *Individualism and Economic Order* (Chicago: Univ. of Chicago Press, 1980).

21. See Aron's critique of Hayek, "La définition libérale de la liberté," in *Etudes politiques* (Paris: Gallimard, 1972), 195–215.

22. On the 150th anniversary of Tocqueville's birth, see Jean-Jacques Chevallier's lecture at the Académie des sciences morales, *Le monde,* 26 Apr. 1956. For the hundredth anniversary of Tocqueville's death in 1959, there was an exhibit and a colloquium at the BN (*Hommage à Alexis de Tocqueville: Manuscrits, portraits, souvenirs* and the *Livre du centenaire, 1859–1959* [1961]), as well as a special issue of the *Revue internationale de philosophie* 13:49 (1959), and a celebration at the Académie des sciences morales, with a speech by E. Mireaux (*Le monde,* 9 Dec. 1959).

23. In *Le monde*, 7 May 1981, "Tocqueville au second tour" was the heading for an article by Maurice Ligot on the coming presidential election's second stage.

24. See Braudel's belated recognition in his preface to the 1978 *OC* edition of the *Souvenirs*: Tocqueville "can without difficulty be placed on the side of what is known as the *Annales* school (27). "Does he not always return, as though to his mind's center of gravity, toward a deep history, slow to pass, which he distinguishes from the history of events—he calls it 'the accidental'" (16). Yet the *Annales* school, which neglects political history, has reserved only a very minor place for Tocqueville.

25. Aron, *Etapes*, 229.

26. See Stanley Hoffmann, "Aron et Tocqueville," in *Raymond Aron, 1905–1983: Histoire et politique* (Paris: Plon, 1985), 200–212, a special issue of *Commentaire*.

27. See Aron, *Etapes*, 21: "I owe nothing to the influence of Montesquieu or Tocqueville, whose works I only seriously studied within the past ten years.... I came to Tocqueville from Marxism, from German philosophy, and from observation of the present world." The meeting of the minds with Tocqueville was easier for Aron than for others because Aron, as early on as his thesis, *Introduction à la philosophie de l'histoire: Essai sur les limites de l'objectivité historique* (Paris: Gallimard, 1938), had rejected the positivism and scientistic rationalism dominant in the French university system since the end of the nineteenth century.

28. See *Etapes*, 21: "I continue, almost despite myself, to be more interested in *Capital*'s mysteries than in the limpid, dispiriting prose of *Democracy*."

29. Tocqueville "as a sociologist, is still of Montesquieu's tradition: he writes in the common language, he is understandable to all, more concerned with giving ideas literary form than with developing concepts and discriminating among criteria" (Aron, *Etapes*, 234).

30. Aron, *Dix-huit leçons sur la société industrielle*, 36–37.

31. "Tocqueville Retrouvé," *Tocqueville Review* 1 (1979): 16.

32. Aron, *Etapes*, 259.

33. "Tocqueville Retrouvé," *Tocqueville Review* 1 (1979): 16.

34. Aron, *Etapes*, 639.

35. Ibid., 262: "Tocqueville, like Montesquieu, wanted to make history intelligible, not to erase it. Knowing history before it happens takes away its truly human dimension of action and unforeseeability."

36. See Aron's radio interview, "Alexis de Tocqueville: L'historien ou la tentation du pouvoir," France-Culture, 20 Feb. 1980. Aron recalled that political vocation had come earlier to Tocqueville than his desire to write and was determinative in him. On the other hand, Aron, who was born to a middle-class Jewish family and "impassioned in an almost exclusive way with philosophy ... accidentally became a commentator of events" with no other link to politics than a brief sojourn in Malraux's cabinet in 1945–46.

37. In his interview with France-Culture, Aron noted that he shared with Tocqueville the fear of "historical fallout from undefined hopes."

38. According to Marc Fumaroli's expression, in "Raymond Aron, 1905–1983: Histoire et politique," *Commentaire*, 1985, 81.

39. Aron, *Etapes*, 261.

40. Ibid., 633.

41. See the conversation between François Bourricaud and Roger Stéphane, *Commentaire*, Summer 1992, 437.

42. See Claude Lefort, *Les formes de l'histoire: Essais d'anthropologie politique* (Paris: Gallimard, 1978).

43. See Pierre Grémion, "Michel Crozier's Long March: The Making of the Bureaucratic Phenomenon," *Political Studies* 40:1 (Mar. 1992): 5–20.

44. See Louis Dumont, *Homo hierarchicus: Le système des castes et ses implications* (Paris: Gallimard, 1966; rept. 1973; Dumont, *Homo aequalis I: Genèse et triomphe de l'idéologie économique* (Paris: Gallimard, 1977).

45. Trips to and political writings on Algeria, like his unrealized work on India in 1842, were only published in the *OC* in 1962.

46. Speech on receiving the Tocqueville Prize (1987).

47. See *Syndicats et ouvriers d'Amérique* (1951) and "La France terre de commandement," *Esprit* 25 (Dec. 1957): 256, 779–97.

48. The success of analyses of decadence in France has its analogue in America, with bestsellers by Christopher Lasch, *The Culture of Narcissism: American Life in an Age of Diminishing Expectations* (New York: Warner Books, 1979), and by Allan Bloom, *The Closing of the American Mind*, which when it came out in France was called "neo-Tocquevillean."

49. See Jean-François Revel, chap. 3, "L'erreur de Tocqueville," in *Comment les démocraties finissent* (Paris: Grasset, 1983),

50. Tocqueville has never been forgotten by historians. On this see, among the historians of the Sorbonne, who seem to have nothing to do with Tocqueville, Georges Lefebvre's preface to *OR* in *OC* 2, and Marcel Reinhardt, "Tocqueville, historien de la Révolution," *Livre du centenaire* (1961), 171–80. But François Furet repositions Tocqueville at the center of his interpretation; see *Penser la Révolution française, L'atelier de l'histoire*, and his article "Tocqueville" in the *Dictionnaire critique*.

51. Daniel Roche, "1789: A chacun sa Révolution," *Etudes*, Sept. 1988, from page 197 on, clearly highlights the intricate connection between new historical interpretation and the critique of totalitarianism. Comparison between the French Revolution and the English Revolution, common among nineteenth-century liberals, is discussed by Aron in his *L'opium des intellectuels*. Comparison to the American Revolution was one of the Bicentennial's required memory "sites" (per Pierre Nora's notion of the *lieu de mémoire*).

52. According to François Furet's reservations in *Penser la Révolution*, Tocqueville emphasized continuity between absolutism and postrevolutionary France and "deductively" reconstituted "the imaginary actors in the process described" (188) because his class analysis was weak.

53. Furet, *Dictionnaire critique*, 7, 12, 13.

54. See François Furet, Jacques Julliard, Pierre Rosanvallon, *La République du Centre: La fin de l'exception française* (Paris: Calmann-Lévy, 1988).

55. See Laurent Cohen-Tanugi, *Le droit sans l'Etat: Sur la démocratie en France et en Amérique* (Paris: PUF, 1985).

56. See the book by Robert Bellah et al., inspired by Tocqueville: *Habits of the Heart: Individualism and Commitment in American Life* (Berkeley: Univ. of California Press, 1985), and commentary inspired by that book, Charles H. Reynolds and Ralph V. Norman, ed., *Community in America: The Challenge of* Habits of the Heart (Berkeley: Univ. of California Press, 1988).

57. See Sennett, "What Tocqueville Feared."

58. Regarding these interpretations, see Richard Taub, *American Society in Tocqueville's Time and Today* (Chicago: Rand McNally, 1974).

59. Beyond the American works cited above, see Besnier, *Lectures de* De la démocratie en Amérique.

60. See Roland Drago, "Actualité de Tocqueville," *Revue des sciences morales et politiques* 139:4 (1984): 633–49.

61. See François Furet, "L'importance de Tocqueville aujourd'hui," *Cahiers de philosophie politique et juridique* (Caen), 19 (1991): 144–45.

Conclusion: Tocqueville in French Culture

1. Jouvin, *Le figaro*, 31 Jan. 1861.

2. *Le commerce*, 11 Dec. 1844; *OC* 3, 2:586.

3. Laboulaye showed how important it was to the republicans to substitute the American model for the English model: "North America is an emigrated England, but having left royalty behind in the Old World the church established peerage, nobility, and privilege. If I may say it, it is a free England made over to our weaknesses and prejudices" (*Journal des débats*, 1 Oct. 1859).

4. Letter to Barrot, 18 July 1856, *OC* (Bmt) 7:295.

Bibliography

Abbreviations

MU = Moniteur universel, France
NRF = Nouvelle revue française
PUF = Presses universitaires de France publishing house
RDM = Revue des deux mondes, France, 1835–1914

I. Sources

1. Manuscripts

Archives départementales de la Manche (press files)
Archives départementales des Yvelines (judicial archives, archives of the Société académique de Versailles)

Archives nationales
    Série AP (Private Archives)
    Série BB6 (Personal files of judges; Tocqueville file)
    Série C*, C* II 611–18: transcripts of the second and third Commissions des trente, concerning the organization of government entities, Dec. 1873–Dec. 1875
    Série F1C1: F1C1 156, Hommages publics, Manche 1859–1910; F1C1 168, Hommages publics, Paris, 1860–82
    Série F 17: police de la librairie
    Série F 21 4383: Beaux-Arts, Manche
Archives of the Académie des sciences morales and the Académie française
Archives privées de Tocqueville
Beinecke Library, Yale Univ., Tocqueville collection
Bibliothèque historique de la ville de Paris: papiers Chassin
Bibliothèque nationale
    Cabinet des estampes, séries chronologiques
    Département des manuscrits: registres Calmann-Lévy, papiers Cabet, Fustel de Coulanges, Proudhon, Quinet

2. Works by Tocqueville

There are two editions of Tocqueville's complete works. The first, by Gustave de Beaumont, was published by Michel Lévy frères from 1864 to 1866. The second, begun in 1955 and still unfinished, is published by les éditions Gallimard.

2.1. *Oeuvres complètes* **of Alexis de Tocqueville published by Mme de Tocqueville. 9 vols. Michel Lévy frères, 1864–66.**

Because the Gallimard edition is still incomplete, it is often necessary to refer to certain volumes of the first edition. This edition, designated by the acronym *OC* (Bmt), is comprised of the following volumes:

Vols. 1–3: *De la démocratie en Amérique*, 14th revised ed. with a preface by Gustave de Beaumont, rept. separately as a booklet by Calmann-Lévy in 1897, Dec. 1864, 3 vols. in 8.
Vol. 4: *L'Ancien Régime*, 7th ed., Mar. 1866.
Vols. 5 and 6: *Correspondance et oeuvres posthumes*, Nov. 1866.
Vol. 7: *Nouvelle correspondance entièrement inédite*, Oct. 1865.
Vol. 8: *Mélanges: Fragments historiques et notes sur l'Ancien Régime et la Révolution et l'Empire; voyages; pensées; entièrement inédits*, Apr. 1865.
Vol. 9: *Etudes économiques, politiques, et littéraires*, Dec. 1865.

2.2. Gallimard edition of the complete works (1951–).

This edition is designated by the acronym *OC*

Vol. 1, book 1: *De la démocratie en Amérique*, 1951 .
  book 2: *De la démocratie en Amérique*, 1951.
Vol. 2, book 1: *L'Ancien Régime et la Révolution*, 1953.
  book 2: *Fragments et notes inédites sur la Révolution*, 1953.
Vol. 3, book 1: *Ecrits et discours politiques: Ecrits sur l'Algérie, les colonies, l'abolition de l'esclavage, l'Inde*, 1962.
  book 2: *Ecrits et discours politiques sous la Monarchie de Juillet*, 1985.
  book 3: *Ecrits et discours politiques* [Second Republic], 1990.
Vol. 4, books 1 and 2: *Ecrits sur le système pénitentiaire en France et à l'étranger*, 1984.
Vol. 5, book 1: *Voyage en Sicile et aux Etats-Unis*, 1957.
  book 2: *Voyage en Angleterre, Irlande, Suisse, et Algérie*, 1957.
Vol. 6, book 1: *Correspondance anglaise, avec Reeve et J. S. Mill*, 1954.
  book 2: *Correspondance et conversations d'Alexis de Tocqueville et William Nassau Senior*, 1991.
Vol. 7: *Correspondance étrangère d'Alexis de Tocqueville (Amérique-Europe continentale)*, 1986.
Vol. 8, books 1, 2, and 3: *Correspondance Tocqueville-Beaumont*, 1967.
Vol. 9: *Correspondance Tocqueville-Gobineau*, 1959.
Vol. 10: *Correspondance et écrits locaux*, 1994.

Vol. 11: *Correspondance Tocqueville-Ampère et Tocqueville-Royer-Collard*, 1970.

Vol. 12: *Souvenirs*, 1968.

Vol. 13, books 1 and 2: *Correspondance Tocqueville-Kergorlay*, 1977

Vol. 15, books 1 and 2: *Correspondance Tocqueville-Corcelle et Tocqueville–Mme Swetchine*, 1983.

Vol. 16: *Mélanges*, 1989.

Vol. 18: *Correspondance Tocqueville-Circourt et Tocqueville–Mme de Circourt*, 1983.

De la démocratie en Amérique, 2 vols. Critical ed. by Eduardo Nolla. Paris: Vrin, 1990.

Beaumont, Gustave de. *Les lettres d'Amérique, 1831–1832*. Ed. A. Jardin and G.-W. Pierson. Paris: PUF, 1973. Supplementing Toqueville's travel notebooks.

2.3 Works by Tocqueville Available in English

Democracy in America, 2 vols. Ed. Phillips Bradley. Trans. Henry Reeve. New York: A. A. Knopf, 1976.

The European Revolution and Correspondence with Gobineau. Trans. and ed. John Lukacs. Gloucester, Mass.: P. Smith, 1968.

Journeys to England and Ireland. Trans. George Lawrence and K. P. Mayer. Ed. J. P. Mayer. New Brunswick: Transaction Books, 1988.

Journey to America. Ed. J. P. Mayer. New Haven: Yale Univ. Press, 1959.

The Old Regime and the French Revolution. Trans. Stuart Gilbert. Garden City, N.Y.: Doubleday , 1955.

On the Penitentiary System in the United States and Its Application in France by Alexis de Tocqueville and Gustave Beaumont. Trans. and annot. Francis Lieber. New York: A. M. Kelley, 1970.

Recollections. Garden City, N.Y.: Doubleday, 1970.

Selected Letters on Politics and Society. Trans. James Toupin and Roger Boesche. Ed. Roger Boesche. Berkeley: Univ. of California Press, 1985.

3. Commentaries on Tocqueville's Work, 1831–1951

3.1. Periodicals (consulted systematically)

Annales de sciences politiques

Le correspondant

La critique philosophique, 1872–84

Journal officiel

Magasin pittoresque

Musée des familles

Revue de métaphysique et de morale, 1896–1923

Revue des deux mondes, 1835–1914

Revue des questions historiques

Revue historique

Le temps

3.2. Reviews of Système pénitentiaire

Consultation was limited to the references provided by "L'argus de presse," published in an appendix to the book.

Anon. *Le constitutionnel*, 28 Aug. 1833.

——. *La France nouvelle*, 7 Jan. 1833.

——. *Le rénovateur, courrier de l'Europe*, 28 July 1834.

——. *Le semeur* 2:30 (27 Mar. 1833): 236–37 and 2:36 (8 May 1833): 285–87.

Bl[osseville]. *Le courrier de l'Europe, journal de la France royaliste et constitutionnelle*, 9 Jan. 1833.

L.P.C. [Anon.]. *Le national*, 5 July 1833.

Marie. *Gazette des tribunaux*, 5 Oct. 1833.

3.3. Reviews of the Two Editions of *Démocratie*

For the first and second *Démocratie* (1835 and 1840), as for *L'Ancien Régime* (1856), all national newspapers were consulted for up to one year after the date of publication. Articles that only make reference to Tocqueville are not included here.

FIRST EDITION OF *DA*

Anon. *Le bon sens, journal de la démocratie*, 5 Feb. Extracts of the introduction, 9 Feb.

——. *Bulletin littéraire: Revue critique de tous les livres nouveaux*, pp. 29–30. Librairie A. Cherbuliez, 1835.

——. *Le cabinet de lecture*, 30 Jan. 1835.

——. *Le constitutionnel*, 18 May 1835.

——. "De la démocratie en Amérique," *Gazette de France*, 3, 13 Feb. 1835.

——. "De la presse en 1835," *La Dominicale*, 1836, 412.

——. *Gazette du Berri*, 21 Feb. 1835.

——. *Revue de Paris* 17 (May 1835): 69–70; bulletin littéraire 31 (3 July 1836): 65.

A.C.T. [Anon.]. "Mouvement de la presse française en 1835," *RDM*, 4th ser., 6 (1836): 79–82.

Blanc, Louis. "De la démocratie en Amérique," *Revue républicaine*, Apr. 1835,14–16, 10 May 1835, 129–63.

Blosseville, Ernest de. "De la démocratie en Amérique," *L'écho français*, 11 Feb. 1835, and *Le rénovateur*, 9 Feb. 1835.

Carné, Louis de. "De la démocratie aux Etats-Unis et de la bourgeoisie en France," *RDM*, 15 Mar. 1837, 635–82.

Cerisé. L. *L'européen*, 25 Nov., 25 Dec. 1835, 52–58, 92–98.

C[hampagny], Franz de. "Politique: De la démocratie aux Etats-Unis par M. de Tocqueville," *Revue européenne*, 1 Apr. 1835.

Chassériau, F. *MU*, 9, 22 Dec. 1836.

Corcelle, Francisque de. "De la démocratie en Amérique," *RDM*, 14 June 1835, 739–61.

Custine, A. de. *L'Espagne sous Ferdinand VII* 2:347–61. Paris: chez Ladvocat, 1838. New ed., Paris: François Bourin, 1991.

Daireaux. "De la démocratie en Amérique et de M. Alexis de Tocqueville," *Phare de la Manche,* 9 Dec. 1838. Commentary in *Phare de la Manche,* 30 Dec. 1838.

Desessarts, Alfred. *La France littéraire,* 17 (Feb. 1835): 388–93.

Eckstein, baron d'. "De l'ouvrage de M. Tocqueville intitulé de la démocratie aux Etats-Unis," *Le Polonais,* Apr. 1836: 235–63.

F. [Anon.]. *L'ami de la religion et du roi,* 25, 29 Aug. and 8 Sept., 1835, 465–67, 497–99, 561–65.

Faucher, Léon. "De la démocratie aux Etats-Unis," *Le courrier français,* 24 Dec. 1834.

Granier de Cassagnac. "Publicistes et philanthropes: M. Alexis de Tocqueville," *Revue du XIXe siècle,* 2d ser., 6 (Jan.–Mar. 1840): 129–41, 257–68.

Guizot, François. "De la démocratie dans les sociétés modernes," *Revue française,* Oct. 1837.

J. [Anon.]. *L'écho de la jeune France, journal des progrès par le christianisme,* 1 Mar. 1836, 205–12.

L.M. [Anon.]. *Moniteur du commerce,* 27 Dec. 1835.

[Lutteroth, H.] *Le semeur,* 25 Feb., 4 Mar. 1835, 59–61, 65–68.

Rossi, Pellegrino. "Sciences politiques: De la démocratie en Amérique," *Journal général de l'instruction publique et des cours scientifiques et littéraires,* 21 May 1835.

Sainte-Beuve, Charles-Augustin. "Alexis de Tocqueville: *De la Démocratie en Amérique,*" *Le temps,* 7 Apr. 1835. Rept. in *Premiers lundis* 2:277–90. Paris: Michel Lévy, 1874.

[Salvandy, Narcisse-A.]. *Journal des débats politiques et littéraires,* 23 Mar., 2 May 1835.

S[tapfer?], A. *Le national,* 7, 29 June 1835. Cited 19 Jan., 3 May, 21 Aug., 3, 7, 21 Sept. 1835.

Villemain, Abel. "Rapport sur les concours de l'Académie française en 1836," *MU,* 19 Aug. 1836. Reproduced in *Discours et mélanges littéraires,* pp. 275–85. Paris: Didier, 1856.

Second edition of *DA*

Extracts

"Des révolutions dans les sociétés nouvelles," *RDM,* 15 Apr. 1840.

Le constitutionnel, 26 Apr. 1840.

"Les femmes aux Etats-Unis," *L'écho de la presse, gazette des villes et des campagnes,* 3 May 1840.

"Les femmes aux Etats-Unis," *L'espérance,* 2 May 1840.

"Les femmes aux Etats-Unis," *Le voleur, gazette des journaux français et étrangers,* 30 Apr. 1840, 369–70.

Anon. *Le constitutionnel* (22 May 1840).

——. *L'écho français* (29 Nov. 1840).

——. *L'espérance,* 7 Nov. 1840.

——. *Journal de l'arrondissement de Valognes,* 10 July 1840.

——. *Revue de bibliographie analytique,* Dec. 1840, 1067–72.

——. *Le semeur,* 29 Apr., 20 May, 5 Aug. 1840.

Ampère, Jean-Jacques. "Epître à M. de Tocqueville," *Revue de Paris,* 20 Sept. 1840. Rept. in *Littérature, voyages, et poésies* 2:53–58, Paris: Didier, 1850, and in *OC* 11:139–44.

[Beaumont, Gustave de]. *Le siècle,* 26 Aug. 1840.

Bl[osseville]. *La quotidienne,* 25 June 1840.

Chassériau, Frédéric. "De la démocratie en Amérique," *MU,* 14, 26 Aug. 1840.

Chevalier, Michel. *Journal des débats,* 1 Oct. 1851.

Courmont, Félix de. *L'opinion publique,* 3 July 1848.

F.R. [Anon.]. "De la démocratie en Amérique," *Bibliothèque universelle de Genève* 29 (Oct. 1840): 209–26.

Faucher, Léon. *Le courrier français,* 20 Jan. 1841.

Guillemon, Martial. *L'univers religieux,* 11 Oct. 1840.

[Pelletan, Eugène]. Signed "Un inconnu." *La presse,* 4 Sept. 1840.

Rossi, Pellegrino. "De la démocratie en Amérique." *RDM,* 4th ser., 23 (15 Sept. 1840): 886–904.

Sacy. "*De la démocratie en Amérique* par M. A. de Tocqueville," *Journal des débats,* 9 Oct. 1840. Rept. in *Variétés littéraires, morales, et historiques* 2:107–18. Paris: Didier, 1858.

Saucié, D. *Bibliographie catholique* 12 (July 1852–June 1853): 61–66.

[Tocqueville, Hervé de]. *L'écho français,* 29 Nov. 1840.

Töppfer, Rodolphe. "D'un nouvel album de M. Calame," *Le fédéral,* 31 Dec. 1841.

Villemain, Abel. "*De la Démocratie en Amérique* par Alexis de Tocqueville," *Journal des savants* 3–4 (May 1840): 257–63.

3.4. Reviews of *l'Ancien Régime et la Révolution*

Extract

    Journal de Toulouse, 18 July 1856. Extract of the appendix on the states of Languedoc, selected by Lavergne.

Annuaire des deux mondes, 1856, 120–21.

Journal de Valognes. Reproduction of Pontmartin's articles in *L'Assemblée nationale,* 27 June, 7, 18 July, 1 Aug. 1856.

Ampère, Jean-Jacques. "*L'Ancien Régime et la Révolution* d'Alexis de Tocqueville," *Rivista contemporanea* (Turin) 7 (25 July 1856): 256–60. Rept. in *OC* 11:429–37.

Barbey d'Aurevilly, Jules. "*L'Ancien Régime et la Révolution,*" *Le pays,* 29 July 1856. Rept. in *Les oeuvres et les hommes,* 3d ser., 21:119–34. Paris: Lemerre, 1906.

Barthélemy, Edouard de. "*L'Ancien régime et la Révolution* par M. de Tocqueville," *Le Nord,* 1 Mar. 1857. Rept. in *Les livres nouveaux: Essais critiques sur la littérature contemporaine* 1:33–35. Paris: Didier, 1859–67.

[Beaumont, Gustave de]. Signed Sacy. *Journal des débats,* 18 June 1856.

Belloy, Auguste de. *Revue française* 6 (Aug. 1856): 52.

Bouchitté, Louis-Firmin-Hervé. *Union de Seine et Oise,* 17 Dec. 1856, 7, 14, 21 Jan., 18, 25 Feb. 1857.

Coquille, Jean-Baptiste-Victor. *L'univers,* 11 Aug. 1856.

Despois, Eugène. *Revue de Paris,* 1 Oct. 1856.

Forcade de La Roquette, Adolphe. "Le gouvernement impérial et l'opposition nouvelle," *Revue contemporaine,* 15 Dec. 1856, 5–29.

Grandmaison, Charles de. *Bibliothèque de l'école des Chartes,* 4th ser., 3 (1857): 178–80.

Hauréau, Jean-Barthélémy. *L'illustration,* 17 July 1856.

Jouvin, B. *Le figaro,* 26 Oct. 1856.

Lamartine, Alphonse de. In *Cours familier de littérature* 2:186, 9:142. Paris: the author, 1856–69.

Laurentie, Pierre-Sébastien. *L'union,* 16, 17, 29 Aug., 4 Sept. 1856.

Lavertujon, André. *La Gironde,* 2, 5 Sept. 1856, 29 Jan. 1857.

Lenormant, Charles. *Le correspondant* 38 (25 July 1856): 693–95.

Limayrac, Paulin. *Le constitutionnel,* 29 June 1856.

Lourdoueix, Jacques-Honoré Lelarge de. *Gazette de France,* 15, 17 Nov. 1856.

Maynard, U. *Bibliographie catholique,* 20 July–Dec. 1858, 238–46.

Mazade, Charles de. "Bulletin bibliographique," Chronique de la quinzaine, *RDM,* 1 July 1856, 216–17.

Meaux, Marie-Camille-Alfred de. *Le correspondant* 39 (Nov. 1856): 254–82.

Nisard, Désiré. *La patrie,* 6 Mar. 1857. Rept. in *Etudes d'histoire et de littérature,* pp. 132 ff. Paris: Michel Lévy, 1859.

Passy, Frédéric. *Journal des économistes,* Jan. 1857.

Peyrat, Alphonse. *La presse,* 30 June, 7 July 1856.

Plée, Léon. *Le siècle,* 6, 18,19, 21, 27 July 1856.

Pontmartin, Armand de. *L'Assemblée nationale,* 20 June, 5, 12 July 1856. Rept. in *Causeries du samedi,* 2d ser., 1:181–207. Paris: Michel Lévy, 1859–66.

Pressensé, Edmond de. "Etudes contemporaines" [revue de l'année], *Revue chrétienne* 4 (1857): 14–30.

Rebitté. *Le sémaphore de Marseille,* 19 Sept. 1856.

Rémusat, Charles de. "*L'Ancien Régime et la Révolution,* à propos du livre de M. de Tocqueville" *RDM,* 1 Aug. 1856, 652–70. Rept. in *Politique libérale ou fragments pour servir à la défense de la Révolution française,* pp. 164 ff. Paris: Michel Lévy, 1860.

Verusmor. *Le phare de la Manche,* 22 Sept. 1856.

Villemain, Abel. *Journal des débats,* 1 July 1856.

3.5. Biography

Satirical Newspapers

Le charivari
Les guêpes

Le journal pour rire
La silhouette

BIOGRAPHICAL COLLECTIONS

Bibliothèque nationale, series Ln6 and Ln2

TOCQUEVILLE AS A MEMBER OF THE ACADÉMIE FRANÇAISE

Le commerce, 22 Apr. 1842.
La mode, Jan.–June 1842.
Musée des familles, Oct. 1841–Sept. 1842, 128.
La phalange, 27 Apr. 1842.
Cassou, Charles. *Le Biographe universel: Revue générale biographique et littéraire* 15 (Apr. 1842): 60–98.
Molé. Discours de réception de Tocqueville, 21 Apr. 1842. Published in *OC* 16:270–80.

OBITUARIES

Académie des sciences morales et politiques, speech by Reybaud, *Séances et travaux* 48 (20 Apr. 1859): 475.
Année littéraire et dramatique (Vapereau), 1859.
Annuaire des deux mondes, 1858–59: 127.
Le constitutionnel, 20 Apr. 1859.
Journal des débats, 19 Apr. 1859.
La patrie, 14, 15, 16, 20 Apr. 1859.
Le pays, 16, 20 Apr. 1859.
La presse, 25 Apr. 1859.
Revue chrétienne, May 1859, 320.
Le siècle, 16, 20 Apr. 1859.
L'union, 20, 25, 26 Apr. 1859.
L'univers, 20, 25 Apr. 1859.
Ampère, Jean-Jacques. *Le correspondant* 47 (2 June 1859): 312–35. Rept. in *OC* 11:438–55.
Barante, Prosper de. "Notice biographique sur M. le comte Alexis de Tocqueville, membre de l'association normande, de l'Académie française, et de l'Institut des provinces," read before the Société d'histoire de France, 3 May 1859. Published in *Bulletin de la société de l'histoire de France,* 1859–60, 68–77, and in *Annuaire de Normandie* 26 (1860): 536–47.
Cochin, Augustin. "Monsieur de Tocqueville," *Le correspondant,* 25 Apr. 1859, 759–60.
Laboulaye, Edouard de. *Journal des débats,* 30 Sept., 1, 2, 4 Oct. 1859. Rept. in *L'Etat et ses limites, suivi d'essais politiques sur Alexis de Tocqueville, l'instruction publique, etc.,* pp. 138–201. Paris: Charpentier, 1863.
Loménie, Louis de. "Publicistes modernes de la France: Alexis de Tocqueville," *RDM,* 15 May 1859, 402–28. Rept. in *Esquisses historiques et littéraires,* pp. 397–439. Paris: Calmann-Lévy, 1879.

3.6. Reviews of the *Correspondance* (1860–61) and of the *Oeuvres complètes* (1864–66)

This list was established using the following sources: first, an unpublished file of Beaumont; second, the letters received by Beaumont (in Tocqueville's archives) during the preparation of the *Oeuvres complètes*; third, bibliographic surveys.

Journal des savants, "Oeuvres et correspondances inédites," Feb. 1861, 120.

RDM, "Quinze jours au désert: Souvenirs d'un voyage en Amérique, Papiers posthumes," extracts, 1 Dec. 1860.

Revue britannique, Aug. 1861.

Arbaud, Léon. "Tocqueville, ses oeuvres posthumes," *Le correspondant*, 25 Jan. 1866, 1–25.

Barbey d'Aurevilly, Jules-Amédée. "Littérature épistolaire: Alexis de Tocqueville, Oeuvres et correspondance inédites," *Le pays*, 22 Jan. 1861. Rept. in *XIXe siècle: Les oeuvres et les hommes*, 2d ser., 13 (Paris: Lemerre, 1892): 165–79..

Barthélemy, Edouard de. "Oeuvres et correspondance inédites d'Alexis de Tocqueville," 28 Feb. 1861. Rept. in *Les livres nouveaux: Essais critiques sur la littérature contemporaine* 2:306–13. Paris, Didier, 1859–67.

Baudrillart, Henri. *Journal des débats*, 27 July 1865.

Bertauld, Alfred. *De la philosophie politique à l'occasion des oeuvres posthumes de M. Alexis de Tocqueville*, Mémoire de l'Académie impériale des sciences, arts, et belles lettres de Caen. Caen: F. Le Blanc-Hardel, 1865.

Delord, Taxile. "Oeuvres et correspondance inédite d'Alexis de Tocqueville," *Le siècle*, 21 Jan. 1861.

Douhaire, Pierre-Paul. *Le correspondant*, Apr. 1865, 908–11.

Duplessy, "Oeuvres et correspondance inédites," *Bibliographie catholique* 25 (1861): 236.

Etienne, Louis. *Le constitutionnel*, 18 Jan. 1861.

Falloux, Alfred de. "Mme Swetchine et M. Alexis de Tocqueville," *Le correspondant*, 25 Feb. 1866, 265–300.

Gigot, Albert. "M. de Tocqueville," *Le correspondant*, 25 Dec. 1860, 690–726. Rept. as a booklet in 1861.

Janet, Paul. "Alexis de Tocqueville et la science politique au XIXe siècle," *RDM* 34 (1 July 1861): 101–33. Rept. in *Histoire de la science politique dans ses rapports avec la morale*, pp. 37–130. Paris: Ladrange, 1872.

Jourdan. *Le progrès de Lyon*, 12 Jan. 1860.

Kergorlay, Louis de. "Etude littéraire sur Alexis de Tocqueville," *Le correspondant*, 25 Apr. 1861, 750–66. Rept. in *OC*, vol. 13, bk. 2, pp. 351–67.

Lacordaire, Dominique. Discours de réception à l'Académie française au fauteuil d'Alexis de Tocqueville, 24 Jan. 1861. Published in *MU*, 25 Jan. 1861. Rept. in *Oeuvres complètes de Lacordaire* 8:325–61, Paris: Poussielgue, 1872; ed. and annot. Françoise Gallouédec-Genuys, as "Lacordaire à l'Académie française," *Politique*, ns, 15–16 (Oct.–Dec. 1961): 315–35. See also the summaries of this speech in *MU, Journal des débats, Le figaro, La revue nationale, L'illustration, La revue européenne,* and Legouvé's review, *La lecture en action.* Paris: 1881.

Larcy, Roger de. *Gazette de France,* 11 Apr. 1865.

Levallois, Jules. "Oeuvres et correspondance inédites d'Alexis de Tocqueville," *L'opinion nationale,* 5 May 1861.

Maynard, Ulysse abbé. "Oeuvres et correspondances inédites d'Alexis de Tocqueville," *Bibliographie catholique* 25 (Jan.–June 1861): 236–39.

Mignet, François-Auguste. "Notice historique sur la vie et les travaux de M. Alexis de Tocqueville lue à la séance publique annuelle du 14 juillet 1866," *Le temps,* 16, 17 July 1866. Rept. in *Nouveaux éloges historiques,* pp. 59–103. Paris: Didier, 1877.

Monty, Léopold. "Alexis de Tocqueville," *Revue européenne,* Mar.–Apr. 1861, 38–64.

Mourin, Ernest. "Oeuvres et correspondance inédites d'Alexis de Tocqueville," *Revue de l'instruction publique de la littérature et des sciences en France et dans les pays étrangers* 21 (9 May 1861): 81–84.

Mouy, Charles de. "Nouvelle correspondance inédite d'Alexis de Tocqueville," *La presse,* 10 Jan. 1866.

Parieu, Félix Esquirou de. "La philosophie politique de M. Alexis de Tocqueville," *Revue contemporaine et athenaeum français* 53 (1860): 561–85.

Peyrat, Alphonse. "Oeuvres et correspondances inédites d'Alexis de Tocqueville," *La presse,* 17 Dec. 1860.

Poitou, Eugène. "Alexis de Tocqueville, oeuvres complètes, correspondance, et fragments inédits," *Revue nationale* 21 (May–July 1865): 66–84. Rept. in *Portraits littéraires et philosophiques,* pp. 199–234. Paris: Charpentier, 1868.

Prévost-Paradol, Lucien-Anatole. "Mélanges et fragments historiques," *Courrier du dimanche,* 4 June, 5 Nov. 65.

———. "Oeuvres et correspondances inédites d'Alexis de Tocqueville," *Journal des débats,* 4, 11 Jan. 1861. Rept. in *Nouveaux essais de politique et de littérature,* pp. 58–83. Paris: Michel Lévy, 1863.

Regnault, Elias. "Oeuvres et correspondances inédites d'Alexis de Tocqueville," *La critique française: Revue philosophique et littéraire,* 15 Jan. 1861, 102–9.

Rémusat, Charles de. "L'esprit de réaction: Royer-Collard et Tocqueville," *RDM* 35 (15 Oct. 1861): 777–813.

Riancey, Henri de. *L'union,* 27 Apr. 1865.

Sainte-Beuve, Charles-Augustin. "Nouvelle correspondance inédite de Tocqueville," *Le constitutionnel,* 18, 19, 25, 26 Dec. 1865. Rept. in *Nouveaux lundis* 10:280–334. Paris: Lévy, 1868.

———. "Oeuvres et correspondance inédites de M. de Tocqueville," *MU,* 31 Dec. 1860, 7 Jan. 1861. Rept. in *Causeries du lundi* 15:93–121. Paris: Garnier, 1862.

Savary, Charles. *Alexis de Tocqueville: Sa vie et ses ouvrages.* Paris: Retaux, 1868.

Scherer, Edmond. *Le temps,* 14 Dec. 1861. Rept. in *Etudes critiques sur la littérature contemporaine* 1:1–15. Paris: Michel Lévy, 1863.

Wailly, Léon de, *L'illustration,* 19 Jan. 1861.

3.7. Reviews of Works That Were Published Posthumously

Masson G. *Revue des questions historiques* 12 (July–Dec. 1872): 556.

Nassau Senior, W. *Correspondence and Conversations of Alexis de Tocqueville with W. Nassau Senior*, 2 vols. Ed. Mrs Simpson. London: King, 1872.

TOCQUEVILLE, ALEXIS DE. *SOUVENIRS*. ED. CHRISTIAN DE TOCQUEVILLE. PARIS: CALMANN-LÉVY, 1893.

Extracts

    Le correspondant, Oct.–Dec. 1892, 401–20, 633–48.

    Le temps, 15 Nov. 1892.

Anon. *Revue encyclopédique* [later *Encyclopédie Larousse*], 1894, 11–13.

Biré, Edmond. *Mémoires et souvenirs, 1789–1830: La Révolution, l'Empire, et la Restauration* 2:300–317. Paris: Victor Retaux, 1895–98.

Boudet de Puymaygre. "Les *Souvenirs* d'Alexis de Tocqueville," *Revue des questions historiques* 54 (1893): 232–45.

Crue, F de. *Revue critique d'histoire et de littérature* 2 (1893): 260–61.

Farges, L. *Revue historique* 53 (1893): 345–47.

Lanzac de Laborie, Léon de. "L'amitié de Tocqueville et de Royer-Collard," *RDM* 63 (1930): 876–911.

———. "Les livres Barante-Tocqueville-Target," *Le correspondant*, Apr.–June 1893, 162–68.

Lautier, Eugène. "Actualité politique, histoire, littérature," *Le temps*, 3 Mar. 1893.

Pierre, Victor. *Polybiblion* 68 (1893): 148–50.

Rabusson, Henry. *L'univers illustré*, 18 Mar. 1893.

Spuller, Eugène. *Revue politique et littéraire* (*Revue bleue*), Dec. 1893, 787–92. Rept. in *Figures disparues, portraits contemporains, politiques et littéraires* 3:15–47. Paris: F. Alcan, 1894.

EICHTAL, EUGÈNE D'. *ALEXIS DE TOCQUEVILLE ET LA DÉMOCRATIE LIBÉRALE*. PARIS: CALMANN-LÉVY, 1897.

Chapter 1 appeared in the *Revue politique et parlementaire* 8 (Apr.–May 1896): 47–66, 350–76. In the appendix there is a partial translation by Mrs. Simpson of conversations between Tocqueville and Nassau Senior.

Deschamps, Gaston. "Pourquoi M. de Tocqueville est-il ridicule?," *Le temps*, 17 Jan. 1897. Rept. in *Le malaise de la démocratie*. Paris: A. Colin, 1899.

Grandmaison, Geoffroy de. *Polybiblion: Revue bibliographique universelle* 80 (1897): 350–52.

Lichtenberger, André. *Revue critique d'histoire et de littérature* 1 (1897): 173–75 and *Revue historique* 63 (1897): 350–51.

Weill, G. *Revue historique* 66 (1898): 414–16.

CORRESPONDANCE ENTRE ALEXIS DE TOCQUEVILLE ET ARTHUR DE GOBINEAU, *1843–1859,* PUBLISHED BY LUDWIG SCHEMANN. PARIS: PLON, 1908–9.

Driault, E. *Revue historique* 103 (1910): 104.
Grandmaison, Geoffroy de. *Polybiblion: Revue bibliographique universelle* 115 (1909): 352–53.
Marsan, J. *Revue d'histoire moderne* 13 (1909–10): 373–75.
Rubat du Merac. *Revue des questions historiques* 86 (Oct. 1909): 788–89.
Weill, G. *La Révolution française* 56 (1909): 278–79.

ROLAND-MARCEL, PIERRE. ESSAI POLITIQUE SUR ALEXIS DE TOCQUEVILLE. PARIS: ALCAN, 1910.

Crémieux, A. *Revue d'histoire moderne* 17 (1912): 330–32.
Driault, E. *Revue historique* 106 (1911): 113–14.
Eichtal, Eugène d'. "Alexis de Tocqueville," *Revue politique et parlementaire* 64 (1910): 99–106.
Maury, Lucien. "De Tocqueville," *Revue politique et littéraire* (*Revue bleue*) 48 (1910): 376–79.
Mazel, Henri. *Mercure de France,* 1 Sept. 1910, 117.
[P.C.] [Anon.]. *Revue d'histoire des doctrines économiques et sociales,* 1911, 297–98.

RÉDIER, ANTOINE. COMME DISAIT M. DE TOCQUEVILLE. PARIS: PERRIN, 1925.

Rédier had first published an article in *Le correspondant,* July 1905, 239–45.

L'action française (Orion), 16 Nov. 1925, and (Interim), 20 Nov. 1925.
La croix (Amoudron), 11 Oct. 1925.
L'écho de Paris, 23 Nov. 1925.
Le gaulois, 18 Nov. 1925.
Livres et revues, 12 Nov. 1925.
Revue angloaméricaine, Oct. 1925.
Revue du Nord et de l'Est, 1 Oct. 1925.
La vie catholique, 21 Nov. 1925.

REVIEWS OF *SOUVENIRS,* 1942–43

Cousteau, P. A. "Alexis de Tocqueville quarante-huitard en peau de lapin," *Je suis partout,* 24 Dec. 1942.
Fernandez, Ramon. *Itinéraire français.* Paris: éd, du Pavois, 1943. First published in *NRF* 1 (Dec. 1942): 724–34.
———. "Tocqueville," *La gerbe,* 10 Dec. 1942.
Mac Orlan, Pierre. "*Souvenirs* d'Alexis de Tocqueville," *Les nouveaux temps,* 18 Dec. 1942.
Masteau, Pierre. "Alexis de Tocqueville aristocrate de la démocratie," *L'Appel: Pour la France unie dans l'Europe unie,* 11 Feb. 1943.
Thérive, André. "Un témoin," *Demain,* 16 Dec. 1942.

3.8. Books and Various Articles

Baraud, Armand abbé. *Chrétiens et hommes célébres au XIXe siècle*, 3 vols., 3:308–11. Paris: Tequi, 1890–91.

Baunard, Louis Mgr. *La foi et ses victoires dans le siècle présent*, in *Quatre maîtres de la science sociale: Joseph Droz, Frédéric Bastiat, Alexis de Tocqueville, Frédéric Le Play* 2:229–354. Paris: Poussielgue, 1884.

Calippe, Charles abbé. *L'attitude sociale des catholiques français au XIXe siècle*. Paris: Bloud, 1911.

Cestre, Charles. "Alexis de Tocqueville témoin et juge de la civilisation américaine," *Revue des cours et conférences* 34–35 (1933–34).

——. "Comment Tocqueville a vu et prévu le mouvement intellectuel aux Etats-Unis," *Revue angloaméricaine* 3 (1925): 1–19.

Chambrun, J.-D.-A. Pineton de. *Nos historiens: Guizot, Thiers, Tocqueville*, pp. 30–34. Paris: Calmann-Lévy, 1888.

Delerot, E. "La correspondance d'Alexis de Tocqueville," Société des sciences morales, des lettres, et des arts de Seine et Oise, *Mémoires* (Versailles), 11 (1878).

Deries, Léon. "Les idées d'Alexis de Tocqueville: L'égalité et la démocratie," *Revue d'études normandes*, Nov. 1908, 13–19.

Faguet, Emile. *RDM* 121 (1 Feb. 1894): 641–72. Rept. in *Politiques et moralistes du XIXe siècle* 3:65–114. Paris: Lecène, Oudin et Cie, 1900.

Giraud, Jean. "Quelques idées pédagogiques et morales de Tocqueville," *Revue pédagogique*, July–Dec. 1912, 201–14.

Janet, Paul. *Philosophie de la Révolution française*. Paris: G. Baillière, 1875.

Lanzac de Laborie, Léon de. "L'amitié de Tocqueville et de Royer-Collard d'après une correspondance inédite," *RDM* 58 (July–Aug. 1930): 876–911.

Le Grin, Adrien. "Etude relative au mémoire d'Alexis de Tocqueville sur le paupérisme," Comité des travaux historiques, *Bulletin des sciences économiques et sociales* 12 (1910): 127–31.

L'Hommèdé, Edmond, *Un département français sous la monarchie de Juillet: Le conseil général de la Manche et Alexis de Tocqueville*. Paris: Boivin, 1933.

Maynard, Ulysse abbé. "L'Académie française et les Académiciens. Le XVIe fauteuil. Tocqueville," *Bibliographie catholique* 45 (Feb. 1872): 81–95.

Michel, Henry. *L'idée de l'Etat*. Paris: Hachette, 1896.

——. "Note sur la constitution de 1848," *La révolution de 1848*, May–Jun. 1904, 41–56.

Montesquiou, Léon de. "M. de Tocqueville est un criminel," *L'action française* 9, 92, 15 (1903): 169–78.

Nicolas, J. "Le vicomte A. de Tocqueville," *Biographies du XIXe siècle*, pp. 197–248. 3 vols., 1st ser., Paris: Librairie Bloud et Barral, 1888.

Nourrisson, Paul. "Alexis de Tocqueville et la guerre actuelle," *La réforme sociale: Bulletin de la Société d'économie sociale et des unions de la paix sociale* 70 (1915): 492–95.

Rolland, Romain. "Le conflit et deux générations: Tocqueville et Gobineau," *Europe* 3 (1923): 68–80.

Thibaudet, Albert. "Le politique et le philosophe: Tocqueville et Gobineau," *NRF* 42:1 (1934): 215–22.
———. "Réflexions: D'Alexis de Tocqueville à Daniel Halévy," *NRF*, 1 Aug. 1931, 317–26.

4. General Works Consulted

4.1. Biographies

Grande Encyclopédie 31:136–37.

Asse, Eugène. "Tocqueville," in *Nouvelle biographie générale depuis les temps les plus reculés jusqu'à 1850–1860*, ed. Hoefer, vol. 45, cols. 452–59. 1866.
Rosenwald. "Tocqueville," in *Biographie universelle ancienne et moderne*, ed. Michaud, 41:627–32.

4.2. Specialized Dictionaries

Block, Maurice. *Dictionnaire général de la politique*. Paris: O. Lorenz, 1863–64. 2d ed., 1884.
Coquelin and Guillaumin. *Dictionnaire de l'économie politique*. Paris: Guillaumin, 1852–53.
Dictionnaire de l'administration française. Paris and Strasbourg: Vve Berger-Levrault, 1856. 2d ed., 1862.
Garnier-Pagès. *Dictionnaire politique: Encyclopédie du langage et de la science politique rédigé par une réunion de députés, de publicistes, et de journalistes*. Paris: Pagnerre, 1842.
Ott, Auguste. *Dictionnaire des sciences politiques et sociales: Encyclopédie Migne*, 3 vols. Petit-Montrouge, 1855–66.

4.3. Textbooks

Lavisse, chap. 23 in *Histoire générale du IVe siècle à nos jours* 9 (1848–70):899–900. 2d ed., Paris: A. Colin, 1905.
Petit de Julleville, L., ed. *Histoire de la langue et de la littérature française*, 8 vols. Paris: A. Colin, 1896–99.

4.4. On America

Ampère, Jean-Jacques. *Promenade en Amérique: Etats-Unis, Cuba, Mexique*, 2 vols. Paris: Michel Lévy, 1855.
Bourget, Paul. *Outremer: Notes sur l'Amérique*, 2 vols. Paris: A. Lemerre, 1895. Trans. as *Outre-mer: Impressions of America*. New York: C. Scribner, 1895.
Boutmy, Emile. *Eléments d'une psychologie politique du peuple américain*. Paris: Colin, 1902.

——. *Etudes de droit constitutionnel (France, Angleterre, Etats-Unis)*. Paris: Plon-Nourrit, 1885. Trans. from the 2d ed. by E. M. Dicey as *Studies in Constitutional Law: France, England, United States*. New York: Macmillan, 1891.

Brunetière. "Le catholicisme aux Etats-Unis," *RDM*, 1 Dec. 1898, 140–81. Rept. in *Questions actuelles*. Paris: Perrin, 1907.

Carlier, Auguste. *La République américaine*, 4 vols. Ed. C. Jannet. Paris: Guillaumin, 1890.

Chasles, Philarète. "Les Américains en Europe et les Européens aux Etats-Unis," *RDM* 1 (1843): 446–76.

Chevalier, Michel. *Lettres sur l'Amérique du Nord*, 2 vols. Paris: Gosselin, 1836. Trans. as *Society, Manners, and Politics in the United States*. New York: A. M. Kelley, 1966.

Cochin, Augustin. *L'abolition de l'esclavage*, 2 vols. Paris: J. Lecoffre, 1861. Trans. Mary L. Booth as *The Results of Emancipation*, 2 vols. 2d ed. Boston: Walker Wise, 1863, 1869. Rept., Miami: Mnemosyne Publishing Co., 1969.

Demolins, Edmond. *A quoi tient la supériorité des Anglosaxons?* Paris: Firmin Didot, 1897. Trans. Louis Bert as *Anglo-Saxon Superiority: To What It Is Due*. Freeport, N.Y.: Books for Libraries Press, 1972.

Duvergier de Hauranne, Ernest. *Huit mois en Amérique: Lettres et notes de voyage, 1864–1865*, 2 vols. Paris: A. Lacroix, Verboeckhoven et Cie, 1866.

Estournelles de Constant, Paul Henri d'. *Les Etats-Unis d'Amérique*. Paris: Colin, 1913. Trans. as *America and Her Problems* [1915]. Rept., New York: Arno Press, 1974.

Franqueville, comte de. *Les Etats-Unis du centenaire*. Paris: Soye et fils, 1889.

Frout de Fontpertuis, Adalbert. *Les Etats-Unis de l'Amérique septentrionale*. Paris: Guillaumin, 1873.

Gaillardet, Frédéric. *L'aristocratie en Amérique*. Paris: Dentu, 1883.

Gigot, Albert. *La démocratie autoritaire aux Etats-Unis: Le général Andrew Jackson*. Paris: Calmann-Lévy, 1885.

Haussonville, comte Othenin d'. *A travers les Etats-Unis: Notes et impressions*. Paris: Lévy, 1883.

Jannet, Claudio. *Les Etats-Unis contemporains, ou Les moeurs, les institutions, et les idées depuis la guerre de sécession*, preface by M. Le Play. Paris: Plon, 1876.

Laboulaye, Edouard de. "De la constitution américaine et de l'utilité de son étude," speech of 4 Dec. 1849, booklet, extract from the *Revue de législation et de jurisprudence*, 1850.

——. *Les Etats-Unis et la France*. Paris: E Dentu, 1862.

——. *Union francoaméricaine*. Speeches by Henri Martin, E. B. Washburne, Ed Laboulaye, and J. W. Forney delivered at the banquet of 6 Nov. 1875.

Meaux, Marie, vicomte de. *L'Eglise catholique et la liberté aux Etats-Unis*. 2d ed. Paris: V. Lecoffre, 1893.

Noailles, Paul, duc de. *Cent ans de république aux Etats-Unis*, 2 vols. Paris: Calmann-Lévy, 1886–89.

Ostrogorski, Moisei. "De l'organisation des partis politiques aux Etats-Unis," *Annales de sciences politiques* 3 (1888):43–72, 235–67, 520–38, and 4 (1889):12–30. First version of a part of *La démocratie et les partis politiques*, 1902.

Portalis, A. Edouard. *Deux républiques*. Paris: Charpentier, 1880.

Poussin, Guillaume Tell. *Considérations sur le principe démocratique qui régit l'Union américaine et de la possibilité de son application à d'autres états*. Paris: Gosselin, 1841.

———. *De la puissance américaine*. Paris: Guillaumin, 1843.

Rousiers, Paul de. *La vie américaine*, 2 vols. Paris: F. Didot, 1892.

Roz, Firmin. *L'énergie américaine: "Evolution des Etats-Unis."* Paris: Flammarion, 1910.

Sardou, Victorien. *L'Oncle Sam*. Paris: Michel Lévy, 1875. Four-act comedy in prose, performed 6 Nov. 1873.

Tardieu, André. *Notes sur les Etats-Unis: La société, La politique, La diplomatie*. Paris: Calmann-Lévy, 1908.

Vail, Eugène A. *De la littérature et des hommes de lettres des Etats-Unis d'Amérique*. Paris: Gosselin, 1841.

———. *Réponse à quelques imputations contre les Etats-Unis énoncées dans des écrits et journaux récents*. Paris: Delaunay, 1837.

Weiller, Lazare. *Les grandes idées d'un grand peuple*. Paris: F. Juven, 1903.

4.5. On the Old Regime and/or the Revolution

Aulard, Alphonse. *Histoire politique de la Révolution française: Origines et développement de la démocratie et de la République, 1789–1804*. Paris: A. Colin, 1901.

———. *Taine, historien de la Révolution française*. Paris: A. Colin, 1907.

Avenel, Georges. *Lundis révolutionnaires, 1871–1874*. Paris: Ernest Leroux, 1875.

Babeau, Albert. *Le village sous l'Ancien Régime*. Paris: Didier, 1878.

Champion, Edme. *Esprit de la Révolution française*. Paris: C. Reinwald, 1887.

Chassin, Ch. L. *Le génie de la Révolution: Histoire des idées et des institutions démocratiques, 1789–1795*. Paris: Pagnerre, 1863.

Cochin, Augustin. *La crise de l'histoire révolutionnaire: Taine et M. Aulard*. Paris: Champion, 1909.

Jaurès, Jean. *Histoire socialiste de la révolution française*, vol. 1. New ed. Paris: Ed. sociales, 1983.

Jullian, Camille. *Extraits des historiens français du XIXe siècle*. Paris: Hachette, 1896.

La Farelle. *Un pays d'état sous l'Ancien Régime. Etude sur les institutions politiques, municipales, et économiques de l'ancienne province du Languedoc*. Orléans: 1857.

Lanfrey, Pierre. *Essai sur la Révolution française*. Paris: F. Chamerot, 1858.

Lavergne, Léonce de. *Les assemblées provinciales sous Louis XVI*. Paris: Michel Lévy, 1864.

Leroy-Beaulieu, Anatole. *La Révolution et le libéralisme: Essais de critique et d'histoire*. Paris: Hachette, 1890.

Loutchisky, J. *L'état des classes agricoles en France à la veille de la Révolution*. Paris: Champion, 1911.

Mornet, Daniel. *Les origines intellectuelles de la Révolution française (1715–1787)*. Paris: A. Colin, 1933.

Pressensé, Edmond. *L'Eglise et la Révolution française: Histoire des relations de l'Eglise et de l'Etat de 1789 à 1802*. Paris: Meyrueis, 1864.

Quinet, Edgar. *La Révolution*. Paris: Lacroix, 1865. New ed. Belin, 1987.

Roustan, Marius. "Les philosophes et la société française au XVIIIe siècle." Thesis, Lyon, 1906.

Sorel, Albert. *L'Europe et la Révolution française*, 9 vols. Paris: Plon, Nourrit, 1885–1911. Vols. 1–2. Vol. 1 trans. by Alfred Cobban and J. W. Hunt as *Europe and the French Revolution: The Political Traditions of the Old Regime*. London: Collins, 1969.

Taine, Hippolyte. *Les origines de la France contemporaine*, 6 vols. Paris: Hachette, 1876–94. New ed., 2 vols. Paris: Laffont, 1986. Selected chapters trans. as *The Origins of Contemporary France: The Ancient Regime, the Revolution, the Modern Regime*. Ed. Edward T. Gargan. Chicago: Univ. Press of Chicago, 1974.

4.6. Works by Public Commentators

Collective works

> *Bulletin de l'Institut français de Washington* (Dec. 1935).
> *Cahiers de politique étrangère* (1936).

Anon. *Un projet de décentralisation*. Nancy, 1865.

Allart de Meritens, Hortense. *La femme et la démocratie de nos temps*. Paris: Delaunay, 1836.

Alletz, Edouard. *De la démocratie nouvelle, ou Des moeurs et de la puissance des classes moyennes en France*, 2 vols. Paris: F. Lequien, 1837.

Arlincourt, vicomte d'. *Dieu le veut*. 5th ed. Paris: Garnier, 1848.

Aucoc, Léon. *Conférences sur l'administration et le droit administratif faites à l'école impériale des ponts et chaussées*, 3 vols. Paris: Dunod, 1869.

———. "Les controverses sur la décentralisation administrative: Etude historique," *Revue politique et parlementaire*, Apr. 1895, pp. 7–34; May 1895, pp. 227–54.

Balzac, Honoré de. *Monographie de la presse parisienne*. Paris: Bureau central des publications nouvelles, 1842.

Barrot, Odilon. *Etudes contemporaines: De la centralisation et de ses effets*. Paris: H. Dumineray, 1861.

Benoist, Charles. *Sophismes politiques de ce temps*. Paris: Perrin, 1893.

Bertauld, Alfred. *De la philosophie sociale: Etudes critiques*. Paris: Germer-Baillière, 1877.

———. *La liberté civile: Nouvelles études critiques sur les publicistes contemporains*. Paris: Didier, 1864.

———. *Philosophie politique de l'histoire de France: Etude critique sur les publicistes contemporains*. Paris: Didier, 1861.

Beudant, Charles. *Le droit individuel et l'Etat: Introduction à l'étude du droit*. Paris: A. Rousseau, 1891.

Boudet de Puymaygre, Théodore, A. de Circourt, and Victor Vaillant. *Décentralisation et régime représentatif.* Metz,: 1863.

Bouglé, Célestin. *Les idées égalitaires: Etude sociologique.* Paris: Alcan, 1899.

Bourget, Paul. *Etudes et portraits,* vol. 3, *Sociologie et littérature.* Paris: Plon-Nourrit, 1905–6.

Boyer, Adolphe. *De l'état des ouvriers et de son amélioration par l'organisation du travail.* Paris: C. Dubois, 1841.

Broglie, Albert de. Discours de réception à l'Académie française et réponse de Saint-Marc Girardin, meeting of 26 Feb. 1863, impressions de l'Académie.

Broglie, Victor de. *Vues sur le gouvernement de la France.* Paris: Michel Lévy, 1870. Completed in 1861 and published in 1870.

Brunetière, Ferdinand. *Histoire et littérature,* 3 vols. Paris: Calmann-Lévy, 1884.

——. *Manuel de l'histoire de la littérature française.* Paris: Delagrave, 1898.

Casimir-Périer, Auguste. *L'Article 75 de la constitution de l'an VIII sous le régime de la constitution de 1852.* Paris: A. Le Chevalier, 1867.

Courcelle-Seneuil, J.-G. *L'héritage de la Révolution: Questions constitutionnelles.* Paris: Guillaumin, 1871–72.

Cournot, Antoine Augustin. *Essai sur les fondements de nos connaissances et sur les caractères de la critique philosophique,* chap. 7 in vol. 2 of *Oeuvres complètes de Cournot,* ed. Jean-Claude Pariente. Paris: Vrin, 1975.

Deloge, Albert. *Causes de révolutions périodiques.* 2d ed. Paris: 1871 [Extracts of *Démocratie*].

Deschanel, Paul. *La décentralisation.* Paris: Berger-Levrault, 1895.

Dupont-White, Edouard. *La centralisation.* Companion vol. to *L'individu et l'Etat.* Paris: Guillaumin, 1860.

——. *L'individu et l'Etat.* Paris: Guillaumin, 1858.

——. *La liberté politique considérée dans ses rapports avec l'administration locale.* Paris: Guillaumin, 1864.

Duquesnel, Amédée. *Du travail intellectuel en France depuis 1815 jusqu'en 1837.* Paris: W. Coquebert, 1839.

Faguet, Emile. *Le libéralisme.* Paris: Société française d'imprimerie et de librairie, 1902.

——. *Propos littéraires.* Paris: Société française d'imprimerie et de librairie, 1902–10.

Farcy, Charles. *Etudes politiques: De l'aristocratie anglaise, de la démocratie américaine, et de la libéralité des institutions françaises.* Paris: Chamerot, 1842.

Fave, General Ildefonse. *La décentralisation.* Paris: E. Dentu, 1870.

Ferron, H de. *Théorie du progrès,* 2 vols. Rennes: Impr. A. Leroy, 1867.

Flaubert, Gustave. *Dictionnaire des idées reçues,* vol. 2 of *Bouvard et Pécuchet.* Ed. G. Bollême. Paris: Denoel, 1966. Trans. by Jacques Barzun as *Dictionary of Accepted Ideas.* New York: New Directions, 1968.

Fouillée, Alfred. *L'idée moderne du droit.* Paris: Hachette, 1878. 2d ed. 1883.

Gobineau, Arthur de. *Les pléiades.* In vol. 3 of *Oeuvres.* Ed. Jean Gaulmier. Gallimard, nrf la Pléiade, 1987.

Guizot, François. *De la démocratie en France*. Brussels: Wouters frères, Jan. 1849.

Guy-Grand, Georges. *Le procès de la démocratie*. Paris: A. Colin, 1911.

Houtin, Albert. *L'américanisme*. Paris: E. Nourry, 1904.

Laboulaye, Edouard de. *De l'Eglise catholique et de l'Etat*, booklet, extract from the *Revue de législation et de jurisprudence*, 1845.

———. "De l'enseignement et du noviciat administratif en Allemagne," *Revue de législation et de jurisprudence,* July–Sept. 1843.

———. *La liberté antique et la liberté moderne*, booklet, extract from the *Revue nationale*, 1863, 3–24.

———. *La liberté religieuse*. Paris: Charpentier, 1858.

———. *Le parti libéral: Son programme et son avenir*. Paris: Charpentier, 1863. Rept. five times until 1871.

Laffitte, Paul. *Le paradoxe de l'égalité et la représentation proportionnelle*. Paris: Hachette, 1887. 2d ed. 1910.

———. *Le suffrage universel et le régime parlementaire*. Paris: Hachette, 1888.

Lanson, Gustave. *Enseignement et démocratie*. Paris: n.p., 1905.

———. *Histoire de la littérature française*. Paris: Hachette, 1895.

———. *Trois mois d'enseignement aux Etats-Unis: Notes et impressions d'un professeur français*. Paris: Hachette, 1912.

Lebon, Félix. *La décentralisation*, Cannes: impr. de H. Vidal, 1870.

Le Bon, Gustave. *Les lois psychologiques de l'évolution des peuples*. Paris: F. Alcan, 1894. Trans. as *The Psychology of Peoples* [1924]. Rept., New York: Arno Press, 1974.

Le Play, Frédéric. *La Réforme sociale en France*, 2 vols. Paris: Plon, 1864.

Littré, Emile. *Fragments de philosophie positive et de sociologie contemporaine*. Bureaux de "La philosophie positive," 1876.

Luçay, comte. *La décentralisation: Etude pour servir à son histoire en France*. Paris: Guillaumin, 1895.

Maurras, Charles. *Dictionnaire politique et critique*, 2 vols. Ed. Pierre Chardon. Paris: St. Dizier, impr. A Brulliard, 1931–32.

Ménard, Louis. *Rêveries d'un païen mystique*. Ed. Rioux de Mayllou. Paris: Georges Crès et Cie, 1911.

Michel, Henry. *Questions du temps présent: La doctrine politique de la démocratie*. Paris: A. Colin, 1901.

Montalembert, Charles de. *Des intérêts catholiques au XIXe siècle*. Paris: J. Lecoffre, 1852.

Montégut, Emile. *Essais sur l'époque actuelle*. Paris: Poulet-Malassis et de Broise, 1858.

———. *Libres opinions morales et historiques*. Paris: Hachette, 1888.

Nettement, Alfred de. *Histoire de la littérature française sous le gouvernement de Juillet*, 2 vols. 2d ed. Paris: J. Lecoffre, 1859.

Pailleron, Edouard. *Le monde où l'on s'ennuie*, in *Théâtre complet d'Edouard Pailleron* 3:271–99. Calmann-Lévy, 1911. A comedy performed for the first time at the Comédie-Française, 25 Apr. 1881. Trans. by Barret Harper Clark as *The Art of Being Bored: A Comedy in Three Acts*. New York: Samuel French, 1920.

Poitou, Eugène. *La liberté civile et le pouvoir administratif en France.* Paris: Charpentier, 1869.

———. *Un projet de décentralisation.* Nancy, 1865.

Prévost-Paradol, Anatole. *La France nouvelle* [1868]. New ed. by Pierre Guiral. Series les classiques de la politique. Paris: Garnier, 1981.

Proudhon, Pierre Joseph. *De la capacité politique des classes ouvrières,* vol. 3 of *Oeuvres complètes.* Paris: Marcel Rivière, 1924.

———. *Qu'est-ce que la propriété?* vol. 4 of *Oeuvres complètes.* Paris, 1926. Trans. by Donald R. Kelley and Bonnie G. Smith as *What Is Property?* New York: Cambridge Univ. Press, 1994.

Quinet, Edgar. *Le Christianisme et la Révolution française* [1845]. New ed. Paris: Fayard, 1984.

———. *La croisade autrichienne, française, napolitaine, espagnole contre la république romaine.* 1849.

Raudot, Claude-Marie. "La décentralisation," *Le correspondant,* Nov. 1858, 459–81, and June 1861, 242–82.

Rémusat, Charles de. *Critiques littéraires: Passé et présent,* 2 vols. Paris: Didier, 1859.

Sainte-Beuve, Charles-Augustin. *Le cahier vert, 1834–1847.* Paris: NRF, Gallimard, 1974.

———. *Causeries du lundi,* 15 vols. 3d ed. with index. Paris: Garnier, 1857–72. Trans. by William Mathews as *Monday-chats.* Chicago: S. C. Griggs, 1877.

———. *Nouveaux lundis.* Paris: Michel Lévy, 1863–70.

Saint-René Taillandier. "La confession du parti conservateur," *RDM,* 15 July 1878, 332–64.

Savary, Charles. *Un projet de loi sur la décentralisation.* Paris: G. Pichon, Lamy et Dewez, 1870. Work submitted to the Tocqueville conference, 3 Nov. 1866.

Scherer, Edmond. *La démocratie et la France.* Paris: Librairie nouvelle, 1883.

———. *Etudes critiques sur la littérature contemporaine.* Paris: Michel Lévy, 1863.

Simon, Jules. *La liberté civile.* 5th ed. Paris: Hachette, 1881.

———. *La liberté politique.* 5th ed. Paris: Hachette, 1881.

Stendhal. *Lucien Leuwen.* New ed., with preface by M. Crouzet. Paris: G.-F., 1982. Trans. as *Lucien Leuwen.* New York: New Directions, 1961.

———. *Mémoires d'un touriste.* New ed. Paris: Maspero, 1981.

Sorel, Albert. *Montesquieu.* Paris: Hachette, 1887. Trans. as *Montesquieu.* Port Washington, N.Y.: Kennikat Press, 1969.

Sorel, Georges. *Les illusions du progrès.* Paris: études sur le devenir social, 1908. Trans. as *The Illusion of Progress.* Berkeley: Univ. of California Press, 1969.

———. *Matériaux d'une théorie du prolétariat.* 1919. 2d ed., 1921. Rept., Geneva: Slatkine ressources, 1981.

Taine, Hippolyte. *Histoire de la littérature anglaise,* 4 vols. Paris: Hachette, 1863–64. Trans. as *History of English Literature.* New York: F. Ungar, 1965.

Tarde, Gabriel. *Les transformations du pouvoir.* Paris: Alcan, 1899.

Thureau-Dangin, Paul. *Histoire de la Monarchie de Juillet,* 7 vols. Paris: Plon, 1892.

Vacherot, Etienne. *La démocratie.* Paris: F. Chamerot, 1860.

Vigny, Alphonse de. "Journal d'un poète," in vol. 2 of *Oeuvres complètes*. Ed. Baldensperger. Paris: Gallimard, La Pléiade, 1948.

———. *Oeuvres complètes*, vol. 1. Ed. François Germain and André Jarry. Paris: Gallimard, La Pléiade, 1986.

Villemain, Abel. *Rapport à l'Académie française*, 25 Aug. 1859.

4.7. Correspondence, Memoirs, Journals

Allain-Targé. *La République sous l'Empire: Lettres (1864–1870)*. Paris: B. Grasset, 1939.

Barante, Prosper-Amable de. *La vie politique de M. Royer-Collard: Ses discours et ses écrits*, 2 vols. Paris: Didier, 1861.

Barbey d'Aurevilly. *Oeuvres complètes*, vols. 3, 4, 7, 15 (*Lettres à Trebutien* et *Memoranda*). Paris: F. Renouard, 1926–27. Rept., Geneva: Slatkine, 1979.

Biré, Edmond. *Mémoires et souvenirs*, vol. 2. Paris: V. Retaux, 1896.

Carné, Louis de. *Souvenirs de ma jeunesse au temps de la restauration*. Paris: Didier, 1872.

Chateaubriand, François-René de. *Mémoires d'outre-tombe*. New ed., Paris: Gallimard, La Pléiade. Trans. by Robert Baldick as *The Memoirs of Chateaubriand*. Harmondsworth, U.K.: Penguin, 1965.

Cochin, Augustin. *Augustin Cochin, 1823–1872: Ses lettres et sa vie*, 2 vols. Paris: Bloud et Gay, 1926.

Custine, Astolphe de. *Lettres du marquis A. de Custine à Varnhagen*. Brussels: C. Mocquardt, 1870.

De Gaulle, Charles. *Lettres, notes, et carnets, 1905–1918*. Paris: Plon, 1980.

Dino, duchesse de. *Chronique de 1831 à 1862*, 4 vols. Vols. 1–3. Paris: Nourrit, 1909.

Guizot, François. *Mémoires pour servir à l'histoire de mon temps*, 8 vols. Paris: Michel Lévy, 1858–67.

Gobineau, Arthur de. "Arthur de Gobineau et Albert Sorel, correspondance inédite (1872–1879)," *Revue d'histoire diplomatique* 3–4 (July–Dec. 1977).

Lacombe, Charles de. *Journal politique*, 2 vols. Published by the Société d'histoire contemporaine, 1907–8.

Lacordaire-Montalembert. *Correspondance inédite, 1830–1861*. Ed. Louis Le Guillou. Paris: Cerf, 1989.

Lamennais, Félicité de. *Correspondance générale*. Ed. Louis Le Guillou. Paris: A. Colin, 1971.

Lanfrey, P. *Correspondance de P. Lanfrey publiée par Othenon d'Haussonville*, 2 vols. Paris: Charpentier, 1885.

Meaux, Camille de. *Souvenirs politiques, 1871–1877*. Paris: Plon-Nourrit et Cie, 1905.

Mérimée, Prosper. *Correspondance générale, 1856–1858*. Ed. Maurice Parturier. Toulouse: Privat, 1955.

Montalembert, Charles de. *Correspondance inédite, 1852–1870, avec le P. Lacordaire, Mgr de Mérode, et A. de Falloux*. Paris: Cerf, 1970.

Nisard, Désiré. *Souvenirs et notes biographiques*. Paris: Calmann-Lévy, 1888.

Ollivier, Emile. *L'Empire libéral: Etudes, récits, souvenirs*, 18 vols. Paris: Garnier frères, 1897.

Passy, Louis. *Le marquis de Blosseville: Souvenirs.* Evreux: Herissey, 1898.

Récamier, Juliette. *Souvenirs et correspondance tirés des papiers de Madame Récamier.* Ed. Mme Lenormant. Paris: Michel Lévy, 1859.

Rémusat, Charles de. *Mémoires de ma vie.* Ed. and annot. Charles H Pouthas. Paris: librairie Plon, 1958–67.

Rist, Charles. *Une saison gâtée: Journal de la guerre et de l'occupation, 1939–1945.* Ed. and annot. Jean-Noel Jeanneney. Paris: Fayard, 1983.

Saint-Arnaud, Armand Jacques de. *Lettres du maréchal Saint-Arnaud, 1832–1854.* 3d ed. Paris: Michel Lévy, 1864.

Taine, Hippolyte. *Vie et sa correspondance,* 4 vols. Paris: Hachette, 1902–7. Vol. 3, 1905.

II. Studies of Tocqueville

The bibliography on Tocqueville since 1950 is considerable. Included here are only those titles used for this particular work which are relevant to the place of Tocqueville in European culture in the nineteenth and twentieth centuries. For a detailed bibliography, see Françoise Mélonio, "Tocqueville dans la culture française," thesis available on microfiche, Paris X, 1991.

1. Collective Works

Bibliothèque nationale, *Hommage à Alexis de Tocqueville: Manuscrits, portraits, souvenirs.* Paris, 1959.

Livre du centenaire (1859–1959). Paris: CNRS, 1960.

Magazine littéraire, special ed., Dec. 1986.

Revue internationale de philosophie 13:49 (1959).

2. Individual Works

Aden, Hanna. *Wesen und Unterschiede in der Darstellung der Französischen Revolution bei Alexis de Tocqueville und Hippolyte Taine.* Nuremberg: Erlangen, 1959.

Aron, Raymond. *Dix-huit leçons sur la société industrielle.* Paris: idées Gallimard, 1962. Trans. as *Eighteen Lectures on Industrial Society.* London: Wiedenfeld & Nicolson, 1967.

———. *Essai sur les libertés.* Paris: Calmann-Lévy, 1965. Trans. as *An Essay on Freedom.* New York: World Publishing Co., 1970.

———. *Les étapes de la pensée sociologique.* Paris: Gallimard, 1967. New ed. Gallimard, 1976. Trans. by Richard Howard and Helen Weaver as *Main Currents of Sociological Thought,* 2 vols. Garden City, N.Y.: Anchor Books, 1968.

———. *Mémoires.* Paris: Julliard, 1983.

———. "Raymond Aron, 1905–1983: Histoire et politique," *Commentaire.* Julliard, 1985.

Battista, Anna Maria. *Lo spirito liberale e lo spirito religioso: Tocqueville nel dibattito sulla scuola.* Milan: Jaca Book, 1976.

———. *Studi su Tocqueville.* Florence: Centro editoriale Toscano, 1989.

Bergin, Martin. *Tocqueville as Historian: An Examination of the Influences on His Thought and His Approach to History.* Ann Arbor, Mich.: Univ. Microfilms International, 1986.

Besnier, Jean-Michel. *Lectures de* De la démocratie en Amérique. Paris: Belin, 1985.

Birnbaum, Pierre. *Sociologie de Tocqueville.* Paris: PUF, 1970.

Boesche, Roger. *The Strange Liberalism of Alexis de Tocqueville.* Ithaca and London: Cornell Univ. Press, 1987.

Bradley, Phillips. "An Historical Essay in Tocqueville's Democracy in America," appendix to *Democracy in America* 2:389–487. New York: Vintage, 1954–60.

Diez del Corral, Luis. *La mentalidad politica de Tocqueville con especial referencia a Pascal: Discorso de reception del Academico de numero y contestation de Alfonso Garcia Valdecasas.* Madrid, 1965.

Diggins, John. *The Lost Soul of American Politics: Virtue, Self-Interest, and the Foundations of Liberalism.* Chicago and London: Univ. of Chicago Press, 1987.

Drescher, Seymour. *Dilemmas of Democracy: Tocqueville and Modernization,* Pittsburgh: Univ. of Pittsburgh Press, 1968.

———. *Tocqueville and England.* Cambridge, Mass.: Harvard Univ. Press, 1964.

Eisenstadt, ed. *Reconsidering Tocqueville's Democracy in America.* New Brunswick and London: Rutgers Univ. Press, 1988.

Elster, John. *Psychologie politique.* Paris: Minuit, 1990.

Eschenburg, Theodor. "Tocquevilles Wirkung in Deutschland," pp. xvii–lxvii in Alexis de Tocqueville, *Über die Demokratie in Amerika,* ed. J. P. Mayer, Th. Eschenburg, H. Zbinden. Stuttgart: Deutsche Verlags-Anstalt, 1959.

Fabian, Bernhardt. *Alexis de Tocquevilles Amerikabild, genetische Untersuchungen über Zusammenhänge mit der Zeitgenössischen, insbesondere der englischen AmerikaInterpretation.* Heidelberg: C. Winter Universitätsverlag, 1957.

Freund, Dorritt. *Alexis de Tocqueville und die politische Kultur der Demokratie.* Bern and Stuttgart: Verlag Paul Haupt, 1974.

Furet, François. *Penser la Révolution française.* Paris: Gallimard, 1979. Trans. as *Interpreting the French Revolution.* New York: Cambridge Univ. Press, 1981.

———. "Le système conceptuel de *De la démocratie en Amérique,*" in *L'atelier de l'histoire.* Paris: Flammarion, 1982. Trans. by Jonathan Mandelbaum as *In the Workshop of History.* Chicago: Univ. of Chicago Press, 1984.

———. "Tocqueville," *Dictionnaire critique de la Révolution française.* Flammarion, 1988.

Gargan, E. T. *The Critical Years, 1848–1851.* Washington, D.C.: Catholic Univ. of America Press, 1955.

Goldstein, Doris. *Trial of Faith: Religion and Politics in Tocqueville's Thought.* New York: Elsevier, 1975.

Herr, Richard. *Tocqueville and the Old Regime.* Princeton: Princeton Univ. Press, 1962.

Jardin, André. *Alexis de Tocqueville, 1805–1859.* Paris: Hachette, 1984. Trans. as *Tocqueville, a Biography.* New York: Farrar Straus Giroux, 1988.

King, Preston. *Fear of Power: An Analysis of Antistatism in Three French Writers.* London, 1967.

Kirk, Russell. *The Conservative Mind from Burke to Eliot.* 7th ed. Chicago: Regnery Books, 1986.

Lamberti, Jean-Claude. *La notion d'individualisme chez Tocqueville.* Paris: PUF, 1970.

———. *Tocqueville et les deux démocraties.* Paris: PUF, 1983.

Lawlor, Mary. *Alexis de Tocqueville in the Chamber of Deputies: His views on Foreign and Colonial Policy.* Washington, D.C.: Catholic Univ. of America Press, 1959.

Leca, Antoine. *Lecture critique d'Alexis de Tocqueville.* Presses universitaires d'Aix-Marseille, 1988.

Lefort, Claude. *Ecrire à l'épreuve du politique.* Paris: Calmann-Lévy, 1992.

Lerner, Max. *Tocqueville and American Civilization.* New York: Harper, 1969.

Leroy, Maxime. *Histoire des idées sociales en France,* vol. 2, from Babeuf to Tocqueville. Paris, 1950. New ed., 1962. 3:49–53, 511–22.

Lively, Jack. *The Social and Political Thought of Alexis de Tocqueville.* Oxford: Clarendon Press, 1962.

Manent, Pierre. *Tocqueville et la nature de la démocratie.* Paris: Commentaire Julliard, 1982. New ed., Fayard, 1993. Trans. as *Tocqueville and the nature of democracy.* Lanham, Md.: Rowman & Littlefield, 1996.

Matteucci, Nicola. *Alexis de Tocqueville, tre esercizi di lettura.* Bologna: Il Mulino, 1988.

Mayer, Jacob-Peter. *Prophet of the Mass Age: A Study of Alexis de Tocqueville.* London: J. M. Dent and Sons, 1939]. Fr. trans. Paris: Gallimard, 1948. Trans. as *Alexis de Tocqueville: A Biographical Study in Political Science.* 1940; new ed., 1960; rept. Gloucester, Mass.: P. Smith, 1966.

Meyers, Marvin. *The Jacksonian Persuasion.* Stanford Univ. Press, 1957, 1964, chap 3.

Pierson, George. W. *Tocqueville and Beaumont in America.* New York: Oxford Univ. Press, 1938. Rept. Baltimore: Johns Hopkins Univ. Press, 1996.

Poggi, Gianfranco. *Images of Society: Essays on the Sociological Theories of Tocqueville, Marx, and Durkheim.* London: Oxford Univ. Press, 1972.

Salomon, Albert. *In Praise of Enlightenment.* New York: Meridian Books, World Publishing Company, 1963.

Schleifer, James. *The Making of Tocqueville's Democracy.* Chapel Hill: Univ. of North Carolina Press, 1980.

Shiner, L. E. *The Secret Mirror: Literary Form and History in Tocqueville's Recollections.* Ithaca and London: Cornell Univ. Press, 1988.

3. Articles

Amann, Peter. "Taine, Tocqueville, and the Paradox of the Ancien Regime," *Romantic Review* 52 (1961): 183–95.

Aron, Raymond. "La définition libérale de la liberté: Alexis de Tocqueville et Karl Marx," *Archives européennes de sociologie* 5 (1964): 159–89.

———. "Tocqueville retrouvé," *Tocqueville Review,* Fall 1979, 8–23.

Benson, Lee. "Group Cohesion and Social and Ideological Conflict: A Critique of Some Marxian and Tocquevillian Theories," *American Behavorial Scientist* 16:5 (May–June 1973): 741–67.

Berl, Emmanuel. Preface to *L'Ancien Régime et la Révolution,* pp. i–xiii. Club français du livre, 1964.

Biddis, Michael. "Prophecy and Pragmatism: Gobineau's Confrontation with Tocqueville," *Historical Journal* 13:4 (1970): 611–33.

Bourricaud, François. "Contradiction et traditions chez Tocqueville," *Tocqueville Review* 2:1 (1980): 25–39.

Braudel, Fernand. Preface to *Souvenirs.* Paris: Gallimard, 1978.

Bressolette, Michel. "Tocqueville et le paupérisme: L'influence de Rousseau," *Annales de la faculté des lettres et sciences humaines de Toulouse* 16 (June 1970).

Cafagna, Luciano. Introduction to *l'Antico regime e la rivoluzione,* pp. vii–xlv. Turin: Guilio Einaudi, 1989.

Diestelmeier, Friedrich. "Tocqueville lu par un magnat russe: Une *Zapiska* de S. I. Mal'-cov de 1858," *Cahiers du monde russe et soviétique* 19:3 (1978): 305.

Dion, Stéphane. "Tocqueville, le Canada français, et la question nationale," *Revue française de science politique* 40:4 (Aug. 1990): 501–19.

Drescher, Seymour. "Tocqueville's Two Democracies," *Journal of the History of Ideas* 25 (Apr.–June 1964): 201–16.

———, in collaboration with L. Marshall. "American Historians and Tocqueville," *Journal of American History* 55:3 (1968): 512–32.

Fabian, Bernhard. "Alexis de Tocqueville Souvenirs," *Archiv für Kulturgeschichte* 39 (1957): 103–11.

Feuer, Kathryn B. "Tocqueville and the Genesis of War and Peace," *California Slavic Studies* 4 (1967): 92–118.

Freund, Dorrit. "Aktuelle Gedanken zur Demokratie bei Alexis de Tocqueville und Max Weber," *Schweizer Monatshefte* (Zurich), 53 (Mar. 1974): 857–62.

Gauchet, Marcel. "Tocqueville, l'Amérique, et nous," *Libre* 7 (1980): 43–120.

Geiss, Imanuel. "Tocqueville und Karl Marx: Eine vergleichende Analyse," *Die neue Gesellschaft* 3 (1959): 237–40.

Gibert, Pierre. "Incroyance nouvelle et religion à venir," *Etudes,* Dec. 1966, 611–27.

Guiccardi, Jean-Pierre. "Tocqueville et les lumières," *Studies on Voltaire and the XVIIIth Century* (Geneva), 163 (1976): 203.

Guiral, Pierre. "Principes, vicissitudes, et persistance de la droite libérale en France," *Rassegna storica toscana* 7 (1966): 279–94.

Hoeges, Dirk. "Guizot und Tocqueville," *Historische Zeitschrift* 218 (1974): 338–53.

Jaume, Lucien, "Tocqueville et le problème du pouvoir exécutif en 1848," *Revue française de science politique* 41:6 (Dec. 1991).

Kelly, G. A. "Parnassian Liberalism in Nineteenth-Century France: Tocqueville, Renan, Flaubert," *History of Political Thought* 8 (1987): 479–86.

Lebacqz, Albert. "De Tocqueville à Valery Giscard d'Estaing," *RDM,* Jan.–Mar. 1982, 350–55.

Leroy, Maxime. "Alexis de Tocqueville," *Politica* 1:4 (Aug. 1935): 392–424.

Lukacs, John, "The Last Days of A. de Tocqueville d'après les archives de la congréga-tion de Notre-Dame du Bon secours à Troyes," *Catholic Historical Review* 50:2 (July 1964): 155–70.

Märker, Johannes. "Alexis de Tocqueville und Deutschland," *Die Deutsche Rundschau* 77:2 (1951): 887–93.

Mayer, J.-P. "Alexis de Tocqueville und K. Marx: Affinitäten und Gegensätze," *Zeitschrift für Politik* 13 (1966): 1–13.

Mitchell, Harvey. "Alexis de Tocqueville and the Legacy of the French Revolution," *So-cial Research* 56:1 (Spring 1989).

Nef, John. "Truth, Belief, and Civilization: Tocqueville and Gobineau," *Review of Poli-tics* (Notre Dame, IN), 25:4 (Oct. 1963): 460–82.

Nisbet, Robert. "Many Tocquevilles," *American Scholar,* Winter 1976–1977.

Onno, Joseph. "Renan et Tocqueville," *Information historique* 36 (1974): 107–18.

Ortega y Gasset, José. "Tocqueville y su tiempo," *Meditacion de Europa* (Madrid), 1960, 127–33.

Pappe, H.-O. "Mill and Tocqueville," *Journal of the History of Ideas* 25 (Apr.–June 1964): 217–34.

Pessen, E. "Tocqueville's Misreading of America, America's Misreading of Tocqueville," *Tocqueville Review* 4:1 (Spring–Summer 1982): 5–22.

Qualter, T. H. "John Stuart Mill, Disciple of de Tocqueville," *Western Political Quarterly* 13 (1960): 880–89.

Richter, Melvin. "Comparative Political Analysis in Montesquieu and Tocqueville," *Comparative Politics* 1 (Jan. 1969): 129–60.

———. "Debate on Race: Tocqueville-Gobineau Correspondence," *Commentary* 25 (Feb. 1958): 151–60.

Riesman, David. "Tocqueville as Ethnographer," *American Scholar* 30 (1961): 174–87.

Seidel, Karl-Joseph. "Tocquevilles Forschungsaufenhalt in Bonn 1854," *Rheinische vierteljahrs-Blätter* 41 (1977): 283–97.

Sennett, Richard. "What Tocqueville Feared," *Partisan Review* 46 (1979): 406–18.

Stackelberg, Jürgen von. "Bemerkungen zur Sekundärliteratur über Alexis de Tocque-ville," *Romanistisches Jahrbuch* 6 (1956): 183–90.

Thurston, C. J. "Alexis de Tocqueville in Russia," *Journal of the History of Ideas* 37 (Apr.–June 1976): 289–306.

Index

Index

Barante, Prosper de, 10, 113

Barba, Gustave, 229 n.52

Barbey d'Aurevilly, Jules-Amédée, 94, 99, 101, 123, 189, 237 n.60

Barrot, Odilon, 49, 81, 135

Bartholdi, Frédéric-Auguste, 159

Barthou, Jean-Louis, 186

Bastiat, Frédéric, 167

Baudrillart, Henri, 105, 135, 232 n.99

Baunard, Louis, 167, 168

Beard, Charles, 192

Beaumont, Antonin de, 174–75

Beaumont, Gustave de: and *Democracy*, 67–68; and *Old Regime*, 96, 98; *Penitentiary System*, 20, 29; prison study of, 16, 26, 34, 51; with Tocqueville, viii, x, 15, 258 n.17; Tocqueville edited by, 121–22, 124; *Vie*, 122

Béchard, 50

Bell, Daniel, 195, 199–200, 258 n.18

Bénichou, Paul, 222 n.106

Benoist, Charles, 254 n.104

Bergson, Henri-Louis, 195

Berl, Emmanuel, 183

Bert, Paul, 167

Bertall (caricaturist), 82

Bertauld, Alfred, 133, 244 n.62

Bicameralism, 24, 41, 51–52, 155, 217 n.44, 225 n.154

Bicentennial celebration, 203

Bismarck, 111

Blanc, Louis, 33, 68, 88, 104, 245 n.80

Boiteau, 104

Bonald, Louis-Gabriel-Ambroise de, 76

Bonaparte. *See* Louis-Napoléon Bonaparte; Napoléon Bonaparte

Bonapartists, 39, 49, 53, 99, 105–7, 147

Le Bon Sens, 33, 38

Bossuet, Jacques-Bénigne, 114

Bouchitté, Louis, 19, 26

Bouglé, Celestin, 185–86, 195, 200, 256 n.127, 256 n.128

Boulanger, Georges-Ernest-Jean-Marie, 166–67

Boulanger crisis, 54, 166, 171

Boulay de La Meurthe, 163

Bourgeois, Léon, 182

Bourgeoisie, 60, 104, 119, 136

Bourget, Paul, 76

Bourricaud, François, 199, 202

Boutmy, Emile, 57, 73, 151, 163, 170

Boyer, Adolphe, 39

Braudel, F., 4, 103

Broca, Paul, 167

Broglie, Albert de, 98, 117–18, 139, 151, 152, 156, 242 n.15

Broglie, Victor de, 154

Brunetière, Ferdinand, 75, 172–73, 178, 253 n.94

Bryce, James, 108, 170

Buchanan, Pat, vii

Buchez, Philippe, 33, 44, 45, 47

Bureaucratic immunity, 139–40

Burke, Edmund, 90, 91, 193

Cabet, Etienne, 34, 39, 68

Caesarism: from absolutism, 88, 204–5; fear of, 54, 136, 152; forces against, 158; Laboulaye and, 142; public support for, 137

Calippe, Charles, 178–79

Calmann-Lévy (publisher), 97, 174–75

Capitalism, 134–35

Caricatures, 82

Carlier, Auguste, 250–51 n.44

Carlo Republicans, 49

Carné, Louis de, 44

Catherine the Great, 109

Catholicism: and absolutism, 11, 233 n.116; consubstantial authority principle, 211; and democracy, 116–18, 167–69; *Democracy* on, 121; indifference to, 65; and Jacobinism, 224 n.127; *Old Regime* on, 121; Tocqueville and, 45–47, 78–80, 115–18, 232 n.105, 254 n.96

Centennial celebration, 203

Centralization, 146–48, 246 n.96

Cerisé, L., 33, 44

Cessac (at Académie Française), 85

Cestre, Charles, 257 n.136

Chalandon, Albin, 257 n.2

Chambord, comte de, 152

Channing, William Ellery, 233 n.122, 253 n.92

Charbonel (priest), 178

Charles VI, king of France, 102

Charton, Edouard, 243 n.55

Chassériau, F., 83, 234 n.123

Index

De la démocratie en France (Guizot), 221 n.87
De la démocratie nouvelle (Alletz), 30, 34
De la puissance américaine (Poussin), 30, 229 n.53
De l'humanité (Leroux), 68
Democracy: American model of, 1–2, 18–19, 22, 57, 85, 138–39, 159; and Catholicism, 116–18, 167–69; in England, 57, 70–71; and equality, 71–72, 90–91; Guizot on, 221 n.88; and liberty, 105; organization of, 251 n.49; origins of, 93; as party platform, 135–37; probability theory of, 58–59; public opinion on, 136–37; Puritan origins of, 88, 257 n.136; and religion, 115–18, 249 n.17; revolution under, 60; Tocqueville's conversion to, 17–20; on trial, 179–81
Democracy in America (Tocqueville): aging of, 149–51, 165; audience of, 25–36; on Catholicism, 121; and Chateaubriand, 36; on communal life, 49; on constitutional government, 40–43; discrediting of, 167–68, 170; as electoral platform, 32; endurance of, 209–10; European perspectives on, 110–11; in France, 4, 123–24; French history decentered by, 47–49; and Guizot, 119; historical perspective of, 2; hundredth anniversary of, 188; and Jannet, 159; and Laboulaye, 142; and Lacordaire, 118; and Lamennais, 117; *Old Regime* compared to, 84–85, 88, 90; 150th anniversary of, vii; plagiarism of, 30; political criticism of, 36–40; as political manifesto, 134, 135; publication history of, 18, 26–28, 66–67, 122, 191, 257–58 n.10; reception of, 29–30, 67–70; reexamination of, 191, 199–202; religious critique of, 46–48; second volume of, 55–56, 65, 67–70; on social power, 62; as sociology, 40; and Stendhal, 35; style of, 20–21; success of, 30–31, 81; as textbook, 133; translations of, 28
Democratic culture, 199–202
Democratic pluralism, against totalitarianism, 197–98, 202
Democratic universalism, 73, 199
Demolins, Edmond, 73
Deschamps, Gaston, 75
Des communes et de l'aristocratie (Barante), 10

Despois, Eugène, 98
Despotism, 64, 89, 137, 145, 198
"Des révolutions dans les sociétés nouvelles" (Tocqueville), 66
Destutt de Tracy, Antoine-Louis-Claude, 35
Dictionnaire politique (1842), 68
Doctrinaires: as conservatives, 34; Guizot as, 22, 120, 156, 158; against neo-Kantians, 156; on propertied-class rule, 45; and Providence, 37; Tocqueville and, 7–12, 13–14; Tocqueville's distancing from, 59–60
Dreyfus affair, 54, 177, 179
Droz, Joseph, 167
Duden, G., 29–30
Dufaure, Armand, 51, 151, 153
Duguit, Léon, 183
Dumas, Alexandre, 31
Dumont, Louis, 186, 199–200, 202
Dupanloup, Félix-Antoine-Philibert, 151
Dupont-White, Edouard, 144, 145, 246–47 n.101, 247 n.102, 247 n.105
Durkheim, Emile, 163, 182, 185, 200
Duvergier de Hauranne, Ernest, 134, 163

L'Echo Français, 68
Ecole Libre des Sciences Politiques, 151, 162–64, 169, 184–85, 187
Ecole Nationale d'Administration, 142
Economists, 219 n.70, 228 n.56
Education, 80, 151, 162–64
Egalitarian imagination, 196, 199
Egalitarian societies, 200
L'église et la liberté catholique aux Etats-Unis (Meaux), 177
Eichtal, Eugene d', 57, 163, 182, 238 n.76
Emancipation, 220 n.76
Engels, Friedrich, 57
England: democracy in, 57, 70–71; historical sketch of, 91; imperialism of, 202; as inegalitarian society, 200; prefiguring French history, 105–6; Tocqueville viewed by, 169
Enlightened self-interest, 63–64, 77
Enlightenment, 11, 22, 125, 168, 199, 204
Equality: and democracy, 71–72, 90–91; and liberty, 195; and materialism, 58; political consequences of, 60; Tocqueville on, 39, 70–72

Index